FAITH HOPE & ♥

JACOB HOLDT'S AMERICA

foreword

Faith, Hope and Love - Jacob Holdt's America is an ongoing drama of humanity and society. It consists of pictures from the past 40 years of Holdt's life - images of big city people in the rough ghettos, drug addicts on the streets, the poor in their apathetic loneliness, the well-heeled in their despondency, the sick with no money for health care, the white, the black and the hungry. But love, hope and faith in the future are depicted too - the heart is the watermark in Holdt's photographic project. This is about the Americans, but it is also about you and me. About people, about being human and about looking at the other and being with the others.

The social impulse makes Holdt's work an important human suite even before it is given a political address. Holdt is a photographer and storyteller - far more in tune with literary realism and the documentary gaze than with the more formal experiments of the history of photography. For him the images are nothing without the narrative, without the human beings at whose lives we, the viewers, are looking.

In this catalogue we have gathered together three authors, each of whom has been struck by Jacob Holdt's multi-faceted American pictures. The three essays take different routes into the core of the oeuvre. The artist Erik Steffensen, who gave the Louisiana the idea for the exhibition and, with his enthusiastic veneration for the pictures, has been its midwife along the way, brings home to us the things that are particularly true of Holdt's work, viewed as art; the prizewinning English novelist and photography expert Geoff Dyer turns the spotlight on Holdt's pictures as photographs both like and unlike the work of other photographers, and situates the Danish photographer in a prominent place in the history of photography; while the American law professor Sandra Ruffin, who as a young student at Harvard met Holdt on a tour of the USA, talks about how the oeuvre has played and continues to play a role as a socially and politically motivating factor for black Americans.

Holdt's pictures do not have the smooth appeal of the advertising aesthetic - perhaps even barely live up to today's standards of technical perfection. If the pictures are nevertheless outstanding photographs - crucial testimony with social and thus political power, which for a while can transport the viewer into the space of reflection that is called art - this is because of a specific praxis, which for Jacob Holdt is unlikely to have begun as a photographic praxis, but which in reality became one. On his first tour of the USA at the beginning of the 1970s the young minister's son from Ribe set out not only to get within shooting range *of* his subjects, but also to be in there with his subjects. In the early years, in every place where Holdt was invited in as activist-errant and curious conquistador, he came to his hosts and their world - and thus to the subjects of the photographic saga on which he soon embarked - as a friend of the family, someone who looked sympathetically and as an insider, so to speak, at people and conditions.

As will be evident from the long interview Holdt has given for this book, the distinctive objective vulnerability to be found in his pictures arose as a result of cultural and social differences so obvious that the best will in the world could not deactivate them. In other words, the differences generate awareness. Emotionally, they are no obstacle but a bridge for Holdt.

The viewer is free to step on to this bridge – and yet not quite free, perhaps. For is it not the case that these very pictures by Holdt affect us in a special way? They are hard to look away from, you almost feel obliged to look at them – even though, given Holdt's strong desire to show human, personal life in all its forms and nuances, they sometimes show us things we decidedly do not like to look at. On this issue the late American writer Susan Sontag wrote so aptly in the book *Regarding the Pain of Others* that we have considered it essential to draw attention to the essay once more by reprinting an extract.

Holdt is able to convey via the camera all the circumstances that crowd in on the lives we see with a low-key, sensitive rendering of empathy. It is the ambition of the exhibition to guide the viewer into Jacob Holdt's universe – shaped as it is by an indignation, an empathy and a sure artistic eye for the good picture without which it would all lose itself in well-meaning triviality.

For the Louisiana an exhibition of Jacob Holdt's work is a logical step along the path exploring the surrounding world that is the overall aim of the museum's activities, culturally, aesthetically, socially, whether the medium is art, architecture, music or the living word. A museum of modern art must have an active metabolism, a permanent succession of exchanges not only with the disciplines of art (insofar as these exist at all in pure form) but also with the world around us. Jacob Holdt – whom we cordially thank for his commitment, his pictures and his will to place his (lifelong) American project in the hands of the Louisiana and thus the many people who visit the museum – is a very fine example of this.

Poul Erik Tøjner
Director

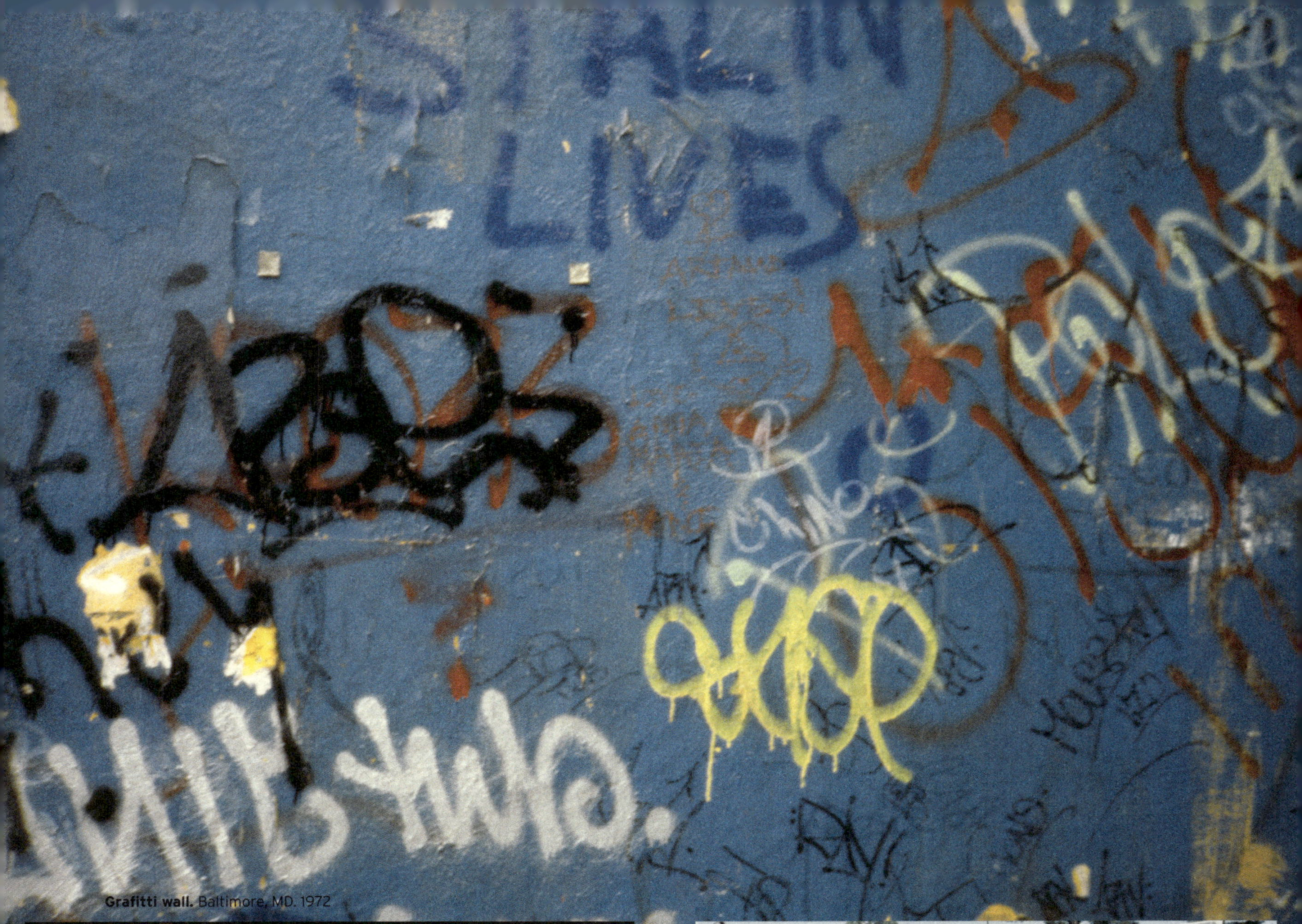

Grafitti wall. Baltimore, MD. 1972

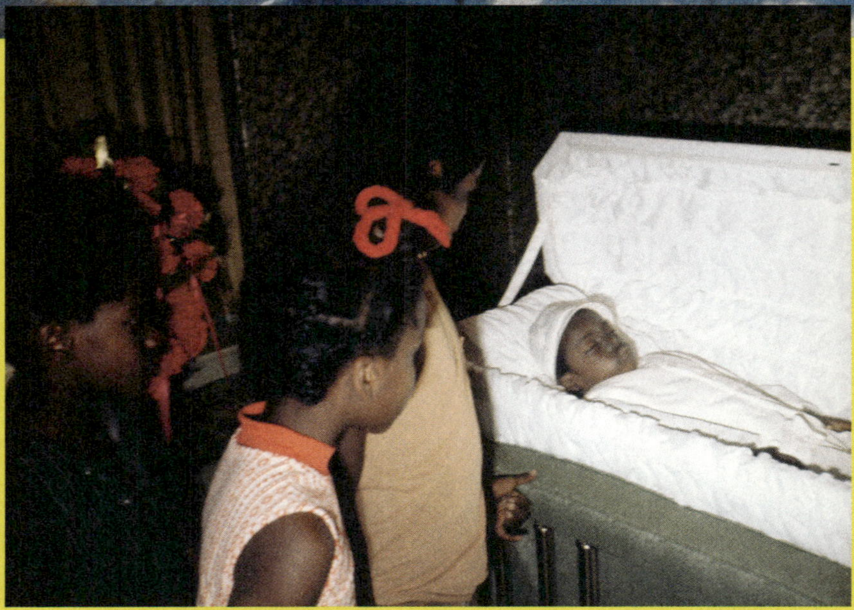

Child hit by stray bullets during a gang shoot-out. Harlem, NY. 1972

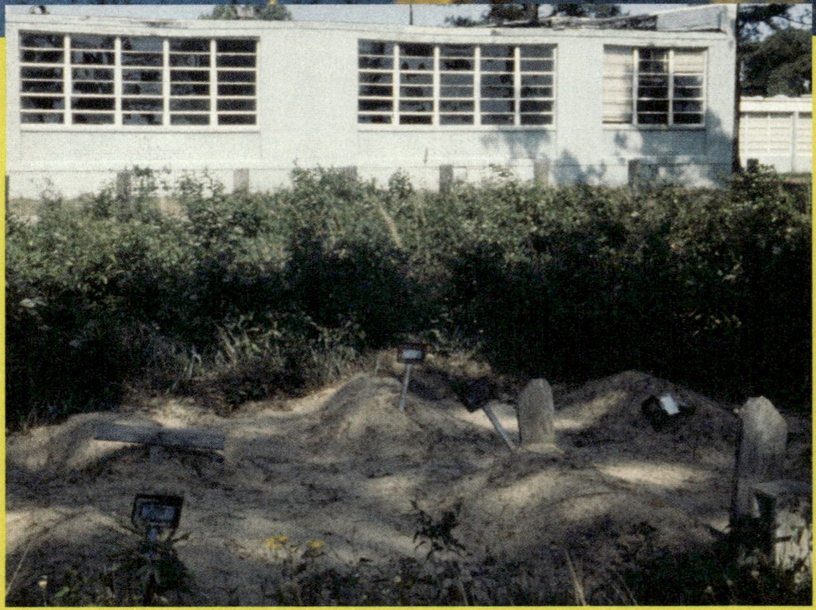

Children's graves. New Bern, NC. 1974

ERIK STEFFENSEN

where have all the flowers gone?

Flowers are non-existent in the world of Jacob Holdt's pictures. At least, there is a conspicuous lack of floral subjects in the artist's photographic production, which spans half a century and numbers thousands of images. American Pictures – A Personal Journey Through the American Underclass, his breakthrough narrative, came out as a book and multimedia show in the 1970s. The hippie age and the flower-power movement apparently left no visible traces in the America Holdt encountered a few short years after Woodstock, or did Holdt consciously leave out a whole generation's image of itself?

A person's self-image is not necessarily the same as an entire. Holdt looks like a tall, skinny hippie with his shaggy hair and long, braided pigtail beard. But his pictures are of another world. The question is, whose? Are they pictures of black America? A nation's self-image – who paints that? The media, individuals? America is a big country with much diversity among its citizens. At the Museum of the American Indian in Washington, D.C., which opened in 2003 and represents the story of the indigenous peoples, a Native American speaker on a video screen says, "When you listen, trust only your heart." For who is telling the story? The story of the American Indian has been handed down by oral tradition, but the media image is the white man's – from the early photographs of a proud prairie people living in harmony with nature to more warlike and alcoholic representations in Hollywood westerns. Holdt is a white man dedicated to relating his sometimes painful journey through black America. Can we trust what we see? Can we have confidence in his fascinating low-budget photographs made from equal parts human-rights engagement, sense of justice and Biblical drive for brotherly love? It's up to the viewer to judge. Holdt's pictures judge no one. They lay things bare. They are open, blurry, wild, beautiful, mute, grim, dark, colored, vulnerable, vulgar and, above all, handheld – Dogma 95 photographs from a life that dares to go up against the lives of others without losing focus or integrity. Holdt takes pictures with his heart. He is a master of neutral observation, an esthete of spiritual life, a genuinely present person, an artist without filters. And his pictures leave the rest – the interpreting – to us, the viewers.

Flowers are non-existent in Holdt's pictures. Well, not entirely. Coffin sprays and bouquets are seen at a child's funeral, with the recently deceased. Flowers of sorrow. Flowers are included at a few other ceremonial events, too. Either way, wedding or funeral, the flowers are depressing. They hold no messages of joy or hope. They are like broken little lilies in a beer mug on a bar top. Green is both good for the eyes and the color of hope. Nonetheless, Holdt's world seems to steer clear of vivid hues in favor of browns, grays, muddy yellows and dusty blues. His photos have the colors and the aura of instamatic vacation shots. Even big-city graffiti on raw walls in eye-popping colors seems to be experienced through the sedated eye of a plastic lens. The blurriness, of course, is due to his camera's quality, or lack thereof. Still, the everyman sense of his shots lends the project its true potential. Holdt has said that he is "good at getting into homes no one else could get into, but where anyone could have taken a good picture." One might add that anyone plunging into this kind of intuitive documentarism probably wouldn't survive very long. The America this 'vagabond' ventures into has a lot of firearms. Holdt is unique in his field. His work is not made for the art institution or out of any political conviction. That Holdt's work has been interesting to both sides of the aisle over the years is not really so strange. He has been on the road for a long time. If you're looking for beauty, it's there. If you're looking for messages, the opportunities for that are likewise unlimited. Parallels can be drawn between Holdt's tireless work as a visual storyteller and the opportunities America sees after electing Barack Obama in a landslide as its first black president. The story of America is a keystone of society. Identity is myth. And the myth is alive in every American.

Moreover, parallels can be drawn between the universality of the photography in the artistic practice of Jacob Holdt and, for instance, Andy Warhol and Nobuyoshi Araki. In these three artists, presence and unfolding life is contained in the medium's stream of images. Warhol photographed celebrities. Like American Pictures, Warhol's 1985 book AMERICA is a collection of originals, one-of-a-kind human specimens, celebrities or people in the artist's surroundings, depicted with apparent neutrality on a par with other items from mass-culture's array of junk, foods and odd designs. The Statue of Liberty seems to be the unifying principle behind everything between heaven and earth – everything American, that is. A flower is a flower, but Mick Jagger is a flower, too – or a commodity, if you like. The Japanese artist Nobuyoshi Araki has a similar appetite for photography as a common denominator of the great, big all or nothing of the world around us. Araki's photographs look staged, but make no mistake: He lives out his staging among prostitutes, orchids, cats, snails and plastic dinosaurs on a gaudy backdrop of landscapes, signage and primordial or artificial nature. Like Holdt, Araki takes the whole world in through his lens in a chaotic, unstructured pile of snapshots that, appallingly enough, end up being excellent photographs every single one – meaningful, at any rate, and most often extremely beautiful. The German painter Gerhard Richter – whose book Atlas also tracks photography's gray flow – has said, echoing Karl Valentin: "Art is great, but it takes a lot of work. So, it doesn't matter whether we paint heaven or earth – the main thing is that they are well painted."

Warhol, Araki and Holdt use their cameras both in heaven and hell – as long as they are observable – on earth. Big series of decorative, opulent flowers are found in Warhol. In Holdt, practically none. For its part, Holdt's imagery includes a lot of trash. Not the appealing packaging of a soup can, as in Warhol, or neatly arranged, controlled nature in the form of a hogtied woman, as in Araki. As seen through Western eyes, bonsai, ikebana and bondage are expressions of an outré and decadent packaging culture, after all. Surfaces are what we observe. Holdt's focus is European, conscientious, moral, interior. He doesn't simply photograph the latest thing the world around him has to offer but includes the residue, all the crap littering the streets. All those things that have been opened and used. From human lives to food to car wrecks. Pictures of filthy rooms and filthy people who, however involuntarily, have ended up in the gutter. Photographs of great beauty and value. Heaven and hell are *well* photographed. Holdt has goodness in his heart, but his practice can seem neutral, to some even emotionally cold. "How could he even think of taking such a humiliating picture?" A characteristic of great artists precisely is that they express themselves very little. They stick to the subject, the work, the world outside themselves, which the viewer can be a part of without having any particular opinion stuffed down his throat. Holdt's photography evokes feelings, empathy, sorrow and joy, but in their starting points they are all fairly neutral.

The philosopher Roland Barthes once remarked, on a photo of a traditional French village house: "I want to live there….". The ordinary, the overlooked, often these are the things that awake our deepest longing for life change. Looking at Holdt's photos from Harlem tenements or derelict Southern cotton pickers' shacks doesn't stress us out. On the contrary, we are included in the bell jar of apathy that encloses the pictures. Then, so what? What's the use? Can I make a difference? We know we exist in the same world as the people depicted and their bleak surroundings, even if the photograph represents *another world*. President Obama has written about the political tradition that "it binds us together, it's bigger than the things that drive us apart." Looking at Holdt's pictures, we don't just see the differences and inequality in the world, we see the basic conditions on which we all exist. The planet's at-risk people exist. And photography reminds us that they are common property, like global warming, democracy and Nazism are. The world's problems may seem insurmountable. But an individual has no trouble sensing the meaningful community inherent in a better world. Very few people would say, "I want to live there," when they look at the peeling wallpaper, the paper-thin walls in poorly heated corrugated-iron shacks and the moldy coffee dregs in Holdt's photographs. But we can be sure that the people in the pictures live right there, that they even pay to do so.

These American pictures by a Lutheran minister's son are both physically and mentally demanding constructions. They are pleas for hope to individual human beings. If God exists, He is for everyone. Holdt's subject is simple and direct: our planet's at-risk people – from every stratum of society, that is. In that respect, he stands shoulder to shoulder with other great artists of that tradition, from Goya to Richter, from Picasso to Palle Nielsen, the Danish artist whose work has fixed *suffering* for use by eternity's eyes. Holdt philosophizes with his camera as his tool, without judging at-risk people. Compassion and empathy are his oeuvre's watermark. Holdt decodes reality's depths without abandoning his artistic integrity and esthetic freedom. It's a tough balance to strike. It takes guts and independence. Maybe that's his lot in life, and the ticket to his matchless, timeless pictures. Taking pictures is just something he *does*.

"Can you make that happen?" is a typically direct Holdt question. He only small talks a few minutes at a time, then he's back on the track of his life's work. In Holdt's use of language, there are millionaires and poor people. The distinction is sharply drawn and the chasm between the "classes" deep. But everyone, without prejudice, is described as a friend, almost as on Facebook. Holdt communicates his life's work and his life's work is communication. Photography is at the hub. Without it, there would be no narrative. Or, without it there would be no art. The esthetics, thus, drive the politics. Holdt's fight isn't between minorities and the majority or between blacks and whites, rich and poor. He chooses the side that chooses him. I guess that would be a vagabond photographer's mantra. Perhaps that's why there are no flowers in his pictures. He didn't leave them out. But he chose not to immortalize them:

Not I – not anyone else, can travel that road for you / You must travel it for yourself.

Walt Whitman

Erik Steffensen (b. 1961)
Has functioned as a consultant on the exhibition *Faith, Hope & Love – Jacob Holdt's America*. Steffensen works artistically as a visual artist, curator and author. He trained as a visual artist at the Royal Danish Academy of Fine Arts in 1986-92 and his works are represented at among other places Fotomuseum Winterthur in Switzerland and the Louisiana Museum of Modern Art. Steffensen was a professor at the Royal Danish Academy of Fine Arts in 1998-2007. Today he is chairman of the board of the Danish Arts Foundation from 2008-2010.

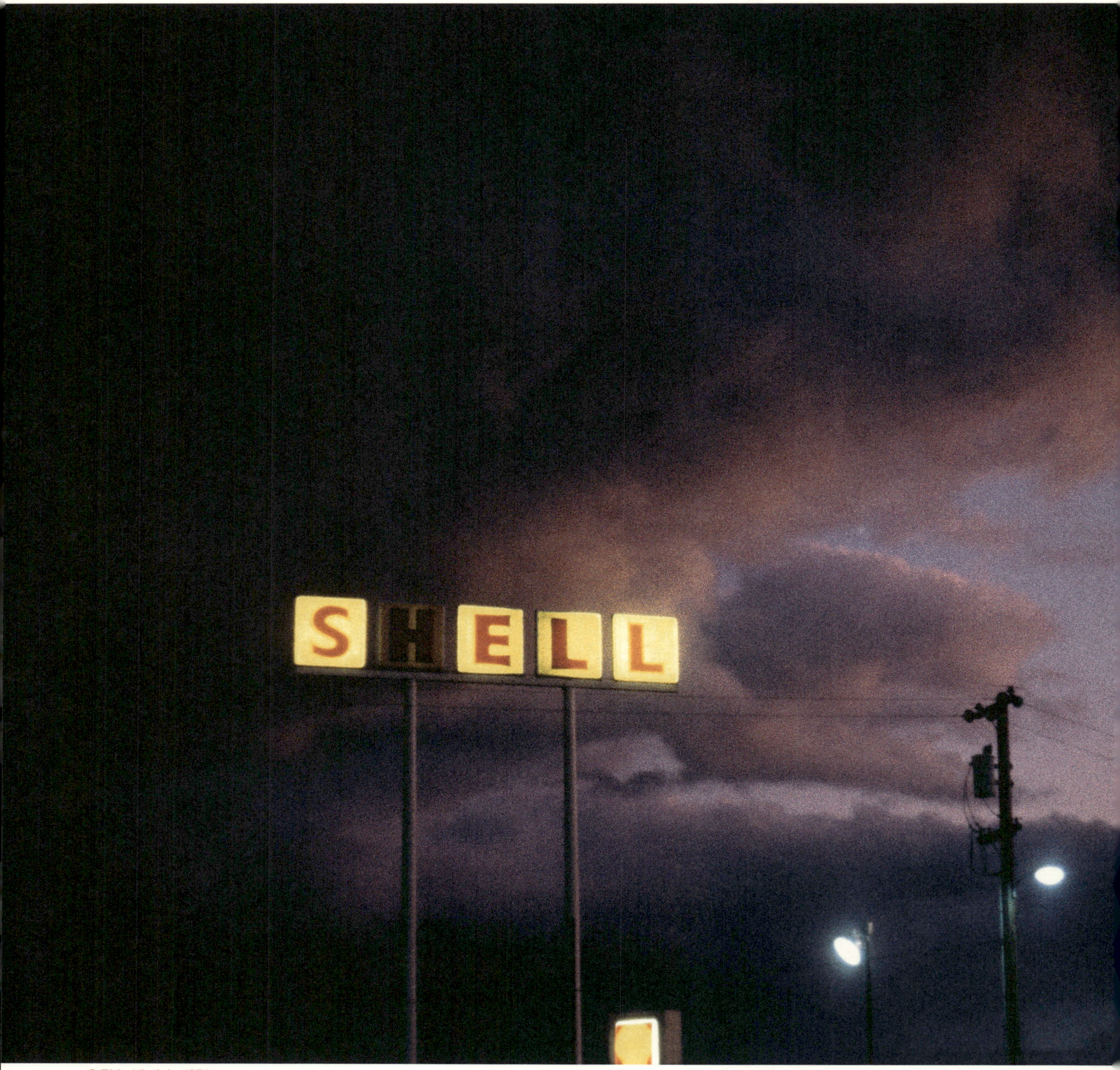

S ELL. Virginia. 1974

GEOFF DYER
vagabonding

Artists are part of a tradition even if they are oblivious to it - even if they do not consider themselves artists and are actively hostile to being regarded as such. Photography is a particularly broad and welcoming church in this respect. You don't disqualify yourself by claiming to be interested in the medium only as a lobbying tool, as part of a larger agenda of social activism. By making this plea for exemption, you're actually enlisting in a regiment with a particularly distinguished and proud photographic history. Commit yourself to the wider, non-ideological role of bearing witness and providing visual testimony, and you move still closer to the mainstream of that history. But what if you're a self-proclaimed vagabond, if you not only refuse to consider yourself an artist, but are adamant that you are 'not a photographer' either[1]? Then step inside, please, you will meet many kindred spirits and fellow refuseniks with whom you have much in common.

In 1975, in a bookstore in San Francisco, Jacob Holdt chanced upon - and stole - a copy of *How The Other Half Lives* by Jacob Riis. Holdt was otherwise unaware of - or, at the very least, indifferent to - the fact that he might be treading in the footsteps of earlier photographers, but for anyone with basic photo-forensic skills their prints are easy to find and follow. Temperamentally and technically, Holdt may have nothing in common with Robert Frank but - whether he cares about it or not - both are part of that mini-tradition of Europeans crossing the Atlantic and, to borrow the title of Richard Poirier's book of essays, "trying it out in America[2]."

Part of the fascination of what Holdt found and photographed in America lies in its unconscious relation to work that has gone before or that was being made at roughly the same time. A tacit dialogue insists on being - if there is a visual equivalent of overheard - over*seen*. The black-and-white sign above the gas pumps in Frank's The Americans urged us to S A V E; the one snapped by Holdt urges us, red-and-yellowly, to S ELL.

Holdt did not share Frank's devotion or debt to Walker Evans but elements of the America catalogued by Evans form an unavoidable backdrop to Holdt's project. In terms of what they sought to accomplish and how they wished their work to be viewed the two men could not have been more different. Evans wanted his photographs to be seen without any ideological filtering. 'NO POLITICS whatever'[3], he insisted, though of course this disavowal of political intent did not mean there was no political content. There may have been something a bit disingenuous about Evans's claim (he was even more vehemently opposed to the "screaming aesthete" Stieglitz) but the description of how he 'kept his white gloves on' while photographing slums has the ring of critical as well as anecdotal truth[4].

However starkly and unsentimentally Evans recorded the poor sharecroppers of Alabama, his pictures have, over time, acquired a stone-washed glamour of their own. Free of the vulgar trappings of modern poverty, those 1930s shacks now look quaint and clean. Like some high-intensity detergent, black-and-white smartens a place up, gets rid of dirt in a gradual flash. Concerned that his pictures might be doing something similar, Holdt was adamant that his experience of the shacks of the rural African-American poor "was far, far worse than they appear in photographs. In such pictures you can't see the wind which whistles through the many cracks making it impossible to keep warm in winter. You can't see the sagging rotten floors with cracks wide enough for snakes and various vermin to crawl right into the living room[5]."

This may be true, but few photographers have made the day-to-day poverty of an affluent society - plenty of TVs; a huge fridge, filthy, and crammed with nothing that looks safe to eat - look more *impoverished*. So much so that his photographs of people and their homes look like they were made not in the 1970s but seventy years ago, as if they were a recently exhumed part of the stash of colour pictures taken under the auspices of the Farm Security Administration, FSA - minus the bright, uplifting imperatives encouraged by the organisation's director, Roy Stryker, who planed the photographic documentation of the countryside of America. Like many petitioning photographs, Holdt's depend on an initial reluctance to accept what they show, to reject what they seek to prove: surely people could not be living like that in the 1970s, in America. By then, by the 1970s, Evans's pictures had acquired a texture and glow that brought about a retrospective improvement to the lives he had recorded. Roughly the same amount of time has already passed since Holdt made many of his best-known pictures and it seems unlikely that they will ever undergo a similar kind of upgrade. It looks like it might be quite nice to sit on the stoop of one of Evans's shacks and suck down a cold one with Floyd Burroughs, but you'd never want to sit on one of the sofas in Holdt's places, let alone sleep in one of the beds. But that's being too solemn and snooty. Put it this way: If Holdt was showing us these images as holiday snaps (which, in a sense, they are) we'd have to say, "Man, you stayed in some shit holes!"

There is a qualitative technical difference too between Holdt and Evans. Made by a man assured of his vocation, Evans's work aimed at deep permanence. His prints are luminously beautiful.

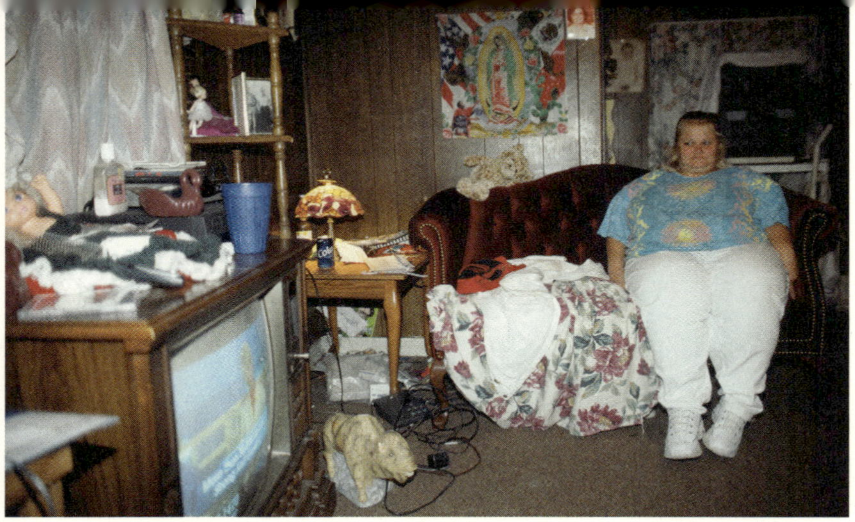

Nancy, first wife of KKK leader's four wives with whom he shares the shack together with her Mexican lover. Lexington, NC. 2005

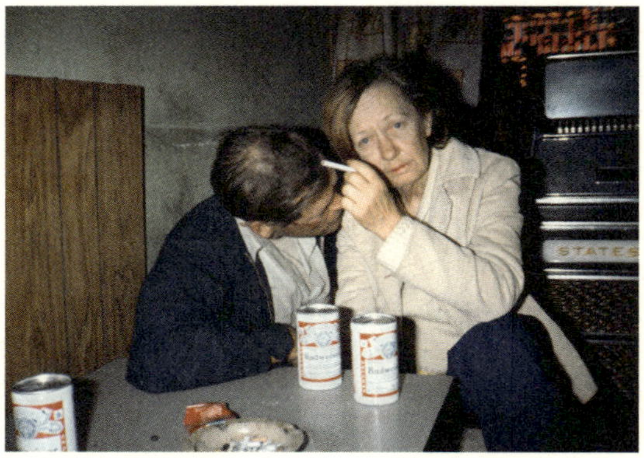

Poor white couple who entertained me (JH) while my black landlady committed murder. Jacksonville, FL. 1974

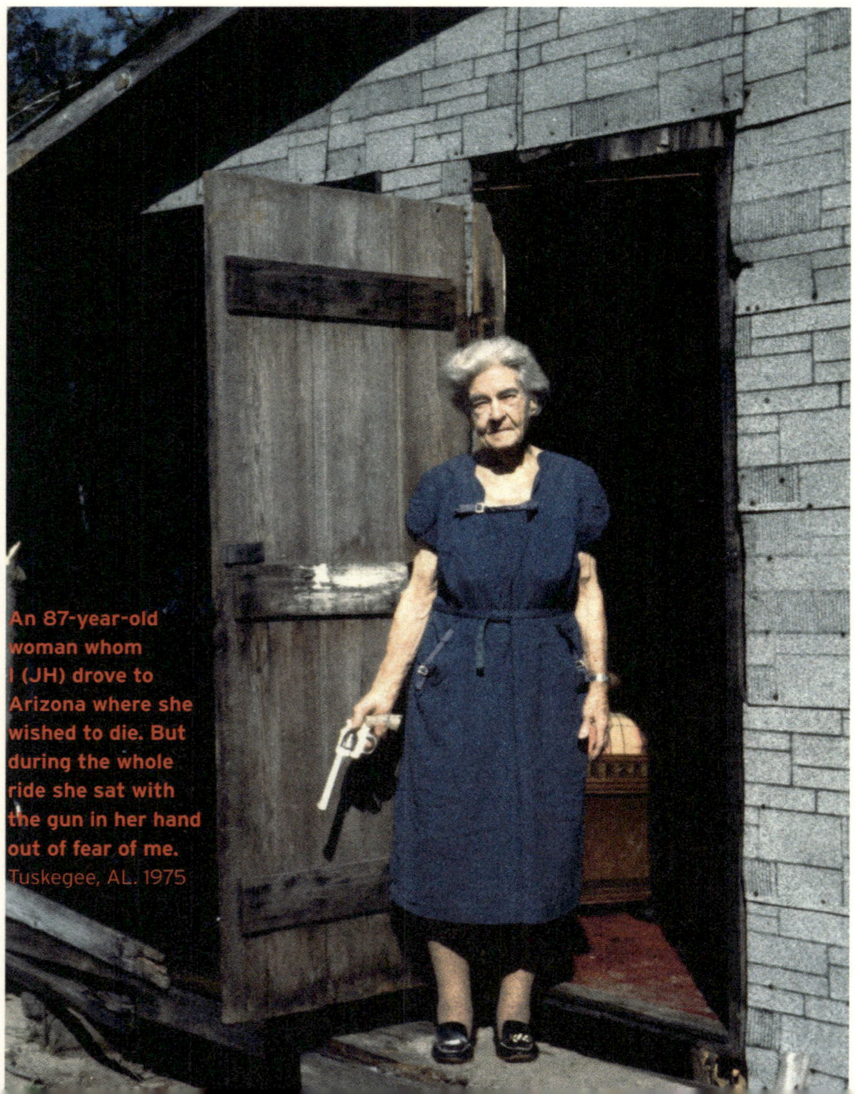

An 87-year-old woman whom I (JH) drove to Arizona where she wished to die. But during the whole ride she sat with the gun in her hand out of fear of me. Tuskegee, AL. 1975

Shot with cheap film, Holdt's photographs were notes made in passing, 'a kind of diary' or visual journal of a man who abjured all sense of vocation and purpose other than hitching a ride or finding a place to sleep. There's minimal disjuncture between what he was photographing and the means with which he recorded it.

As with homes and furnishing, so with people. FSA-style photography, especially in the magisterial images by Dorothea Lange, meant that even when stripped of everything else the Okies retained their dignity. So much so that the Depression became a form of visual attrition, stripping people down to their essential dignity. There are occasional traces of this in Holdt's work. The woman that he finds in Florida - haven't we seen that deeply lined, dried-out, life-ravaged face before? We have, of course; it is the stoically defiant face of the Great Depression, but whereas Lange's Migrant Mother cradled her children, this woman nurses a cigarette over cans of Budweiser in a bar; and it's not her helpless children, it's a husband or boyfriend who is sidling drunkenly up to her. His neck might be red but the face of the guy Holdt meets in a bar in Mississippi has the battered charisma of a Johnny Cash song - and his shirt's nice too. Around the younger women photographed by Holdt there sometimes lingers the possibility, not just of a place to stay but the dangerous allure of cross-racial romance.

The deprivation witnessed by Holdt often robbed people of everything, including their dignity - with the coming of junk food, poverty tended to bloat, physically, rather than erode - but this is balanced by the way his pictures lack the single-minded pride that Evans, Lange and others took in their medium and in their own status within the pantheon of its greatest practi-tioners. The disconnect between what is recorded and the way in which it is recorded is at its starkest and most blatant in Richard Avedon's photograph, *William Caseby, Born a Slave, 1963*. It's a great picture, an unflinching depiction not just of a man's face but of the very thing that obsessed Holdt: the psychological and historical residue of slavery, of internalised powerlessness. Unlike Caseby, the picture of him is absolutely confident of its power, of its self-evident right to rub shoulders with works by any of the masters of portraiture from the entire history of art. While Avedon called the shots, as it were, Holdt addressed his subjects - like Charles Smith, *a former slave* - more modestly, on their own terms and in their own homes. As vagabond and photographer he depends upon and graciously accepts people's hospitality. That's the advantage of the vagabond-artist method: Everyone - black, white, rich, poor, racists, junkies, hookers, pimps, Klansmen, gun nuts, rednecks - extend their kindness and trust to Holdt and, as a result, are seen at their best, at their most *American*.

Unobtrusively, almost incidentally impressive, Holdt's photographs have - as we have seen - ended up in a museum in spite of their maker's declared intentions. It was only recently, after a quarter-century wait, that they took their place alongside the work of his contemporaries and successors. As soon as they did, certain resemblances were so striking, the feeling of kinship so strong, that it was as if a prodigal had finally agreed to show up for a long-postponed get-together. The 87-year-old woman Holdt drove all the way from Alabama to Arizona, the one brandishing the gun in the doorway of her shack, meets up with the old guy sitting on a bed with *his* gun (photographed by William Eggleston) in Morton, Mississippi. Actually, once you make adjustments for some variation in palette, there is evidence of a whole generation of interbreeding between Holdt and Eggleston, especially if we bear in mind the latter's declared intention to photograph 'democratically'.

'Eggleston' has become a kind of shorthand or metonym for colour photography generally and, in Holdt, there are glimpses of the kind of stuff that fascinated another renegade colourist, Stephen Shore in American Surfaces. What Luc Sante said of Nan Goldin – that she was able to 'take the most squalid corner of the worst dump and find colours and textures in it no one else saw' – almost holds true for Holdt[6]. Whereas she finds 'oceanic' blues and 'crepuscular' oranges, Holdt sees the same, unexceptional colours as the rest of us but – like Helen Levitt in her colour work – coaxes an understated harmony from the muted maroons, pale greens and (in one of his best pictures, of a girl on a bed, watching telly) dullish purples, grey-mauves. What he shares with Goldin is an absolute lack of distance or inhibition between photographer and subjects. In Goldin's The Ballad of Sexual Dependency (which, like Holdt's American Pictures, enjoyed it's first incarnation as a slide show) we get an hermetic account of a community with a fairly fixed cast of characters within a city at a particular historical moment. The same is true of the grey rush of Larry Clark's Tulsa (1971). With Goldin it's transgressives, bohemians, and druggies on the Lower East Side; with Clark it's teenage speed freaks shooting up in Oklahoma. Holdt's project is inherently less circumscribed. His readiness to go along with whatever happens and to get along with whoever he happens to run into makes for a sprawling odyssey of serial intimacies and random proximity. Along the way he occasionally gets to watch a bit of TV (there *are* a lot of them about) or to watch people watching it (or, on one occasion, to watch them stealing it). In the image of Baggie feeding her baby while Nixon is beamed into the room, the political irony is implied silently. In others there is the sense, observed by Lee Friedlander (in photographs) and later verbally corroborated by Jean Baudrillard, that a television might be broadcasting from 'another planet' or showing 'a video of another world'[7]. In this world, meanwhile, Holdt accidentally witnesses the scenes of violent death sought out by the Mexican Enrique Metinides, another photographer only recently promoted to gallery status.

That Holdt's pictures did not go knocking on the doors of museums, as it were, did not plead for institutional recognition or art-critical approval is a prime reason why they deserve admission. As more and more people use cameras as a way of gaining acclaim not as photographers but as artists, so the status of this surrogate medium is in danger of becoming somewhat overblown. Literally. The question one asks repeatedly in gallery shows of 6 x 10 prints (feet, I mean, not inches!) is: Does this work earn its size? Would this photograph be able to make the grade as a work of art if it had not been pumped up with the growth hormones of the artist's huge aspirations and ambitions? The paradox is that some of the most artistically valuable contemporary photographs are content with being *photographs*, are not under the same compulsion to pass themselves off – or pimp themselves out – as art. The simple truth is that the best exponents of the art of contemporary photography continue to produce work that fits broadly within the tradition of what Evans termed 'documentary style'[8].

Holdt's movement from the photographic fringes to the walls of a museum – and the corresponding shift of emphasis in any assessment of his career, from activist to photographer – is not just deserved, it is historically inevitable. Records of moments in time, these photographs have outlived their time in a way that the words surrounding them in the book, American Pictures, have not. Perhaps this conforms to a more general truth about the relative longevity of words and images when paired together in this way, for the same thing happened to Let Us Now Praise Famous Men (1941) by Evans and James Agee. Gore Vidal wittily scorned the 'good-hearted, soft-headed admirers of the Saint James (Agee) version of poverty in America'[8] which, over time, has come to seem at odds with the enduring value of Evans's 'austere' photography. Holdt's engaging naiveté saves him from the kind of Scandinavian omniscience that becomes wearisome in Sven Lindqvist's later, polemical writing, but the text of American Pictures would not be reprintable today except as a historical document or exhibit, like one of those mammals found preserved in a glacier. The enduring vitality of the photographs, on the other hand, is evident in two, apparently contradictory, ways.

First, they wouldn't look out of place in Claude Brown's Manchild in the Promised Land (1965), a firsthand testament to the problems of addiction, poverty and deprivation that pre-dates Holdt's arrival in America. Second, they could readily be inserted into more recent accounts of the drug-ravaged American ghetto, such as Richard Price's novel Clockers (1992) or David Simon's and Ed Burns's masterpiece of 'stand-around-and-watch' reportage, The Corner (1997)[9]. Holdt photographed Ronald Reagan in 1972, 'long before he became president'[10]; Simon and Burns quote him years later, saying that "we fought a war against poverty and poverty won", a line that could serve as a caption for any number of pictures in this exhibition[11]. The so-called war on drugs, the authors insistently remind us, actually became a war against the poor. Holdt, in this sense, was a combat photographer, embedded in the frontline. His experience renders him more, not less sympathetic to those caught up – or actively engaged – in the conflict, visually affirming Simon's and Burns's claim that "if faith and spirituality and mysticism are the hallmarks of any great church, then addiction is close to qualifying as a religion for the American underclass[12]." The issue, as always, is one of precision and detail which the pictures provide in deliberate and accidental abundance. (Strangely, the hair-styles and clothes

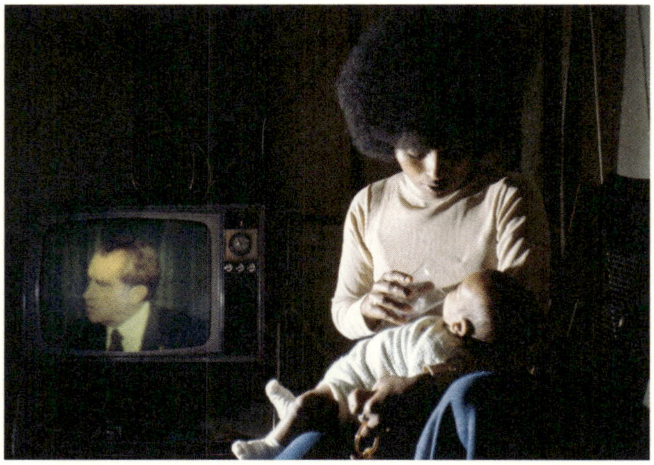

The Beauty and the Beast. Baggie feeding her baby while Nixon speaks on TV. Greensboro, NC. 1974

date the pictures in the sense of identifying them with a period – Jacob Holdt was working at the same time as Garry Winogrand, obviously without confining their relevance to that time.) There is a good deal of rhetoric in Holdt's writing, almost none in the pictures. This is partly because some of the pictures are not *about* anything; certain moments or events just happened to catch his eye. And partly it is because some are about so much more than what they are ostensibly about.

For a photographer whose interest is primarily documentary or polemical, Holdt's work is surprisingly rich, psychologically. The people in his pictures are never just representatives of the fallen condition in which they find themselves. The stories implied by the photographs are often more subtly individualised than the ones set out by the text of American Pictures. As with Eggleston – again – a tacit narrative seems poised to unfold *within* each frame. Some are tense with expectation, like a Jeff

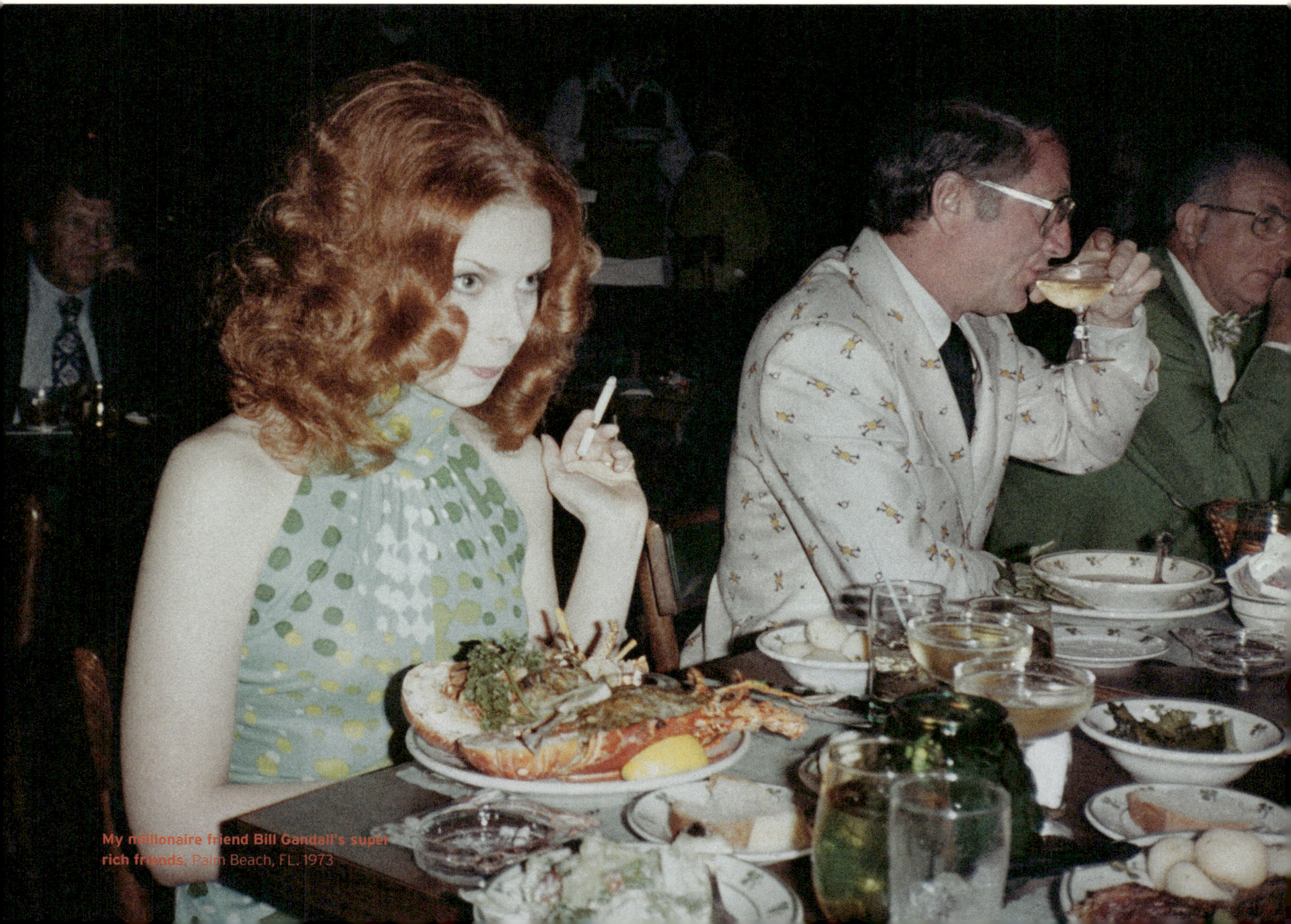

My millionaire friend Bill Gandall's super rich friends. Palm Beach, FL. 1973

Wall tableaux, almost, frozen in the act of time. But even off-the-cuff ones condense an unexpected amount of time into the split-second of the photograph's creation.

Take the picture of the woman in the green halter-neck dress, eating a lobster and smoking a cigarette at a lavish dinner in Palm Beach. The photograph is neither caustic nor judgemental - how could it be when the man seated between the woman in green and the fellow in the related green blazer, is wearing one of the funniest jackets ever seen? - but its overt message or social meaning has to do with the gluttony or vulgarity of someone eating and smoking at the same time (weirdly, the one thing she does not seem to be doing is *breathing*). The fact that these two activities - eating and smoking - normally occur successively rather than simultaneously suggests that the exposure has taken twenty minutes (i.e. the time it would take to tuck into the lobster and *then* smoke a cigarette) while the guy swigging momentarily from his champagne shows the real speed of time. Perhaps that's why there is a sense that she has slid out of the shared time of the table and into some kind of private trance (technically a result of Holdt's flash?) as if she might actually be one of the undead, the unbreathing, or an alien in human form, some kind of Stepford Wife who found that those two lines of coke before dinner had really put the kibosh on her appetite. When Deckard subjects Rachel to the Voight-Kampff test in Blade Runner it takes far longer than usual to establish that she is actually a Replicant - because she is under the illusion that she is a human being. Holdt here photographs, or suggests, someone during a moment when she gets an inkling that all the things that make her life humanly meaningful might actually be illusory, false. Or maybe we're being too solemn again: Could be she's *really* feeling that coke, so intent on appearing to listen to whatever the (unseen) guy across the table is blahing on about that she's not heard a goddamn word, even though it seems like he's been talking at her since the dawn of time and no punch line is yet in evidence. Either way, the condensation of time in the image means that this moment lasts for both a 100th of a second (shutter and flash, sip of champagne), twenty minutes (eating and smoking) and, extrapolating from there, a lifetime.

[1] **J.H., quoted in *Deutsche Borse Photography Prize 2008*, edited by Stefanie Braun, The Photographers Gallery, London, 2008, p. 72.**
[2] **Farrar, Straus, Giroux, New York, 1999.**
[3] ***Quoted in Walker Evans at Work*, London, Thames and Hudson, London, 1984, p. 112.**
[4] **Quoted in Belinda Rathbone: *Walker Evans: A Biography*, Thames and Hudson, London 1995, p. 114.**
[5] ***American Pictures*, American Pictures Foundation, Copenhagen, 1985, p. 64.**
[6] **"All Yesterday's Parties", in Nan Goldin, *I'll Be your Mirrror*, Whitney Museum of Art/Scalo, New York, 1996, p. 101.**
[7] ***America*, Verso, London, 1988, p. 50.**
[8] **quoted in *The Camera Viewed: Writings on Twentieth Century Photography,* Volume 1, edited by Peninah R. Petruck, , Dutton, New York, 1979, p. 127.**
[9] **Quoted in United States: Essays 1952-1992, André Deutsch, London, 1993, p. 632.**
[10] **new edition, Canongate, Edinburgh, 2009, p. 611.**
[11] ***United States 1970-1975* Steidl, Göttingen, 2007, p. 187.**
[12] ***The Corner*, p. 99.**
[13] ***The Corner*, p. 81.**

Geoff Dyer (b. 1958)
Is the author of many books including But Beautiful (winner of the Somerset Maugham prize), The Ongoing Moment (winner of an ICP Infinity Award for writing on photography) and, most recently, Jeff in Venice, Death in Varanasi, a novel.

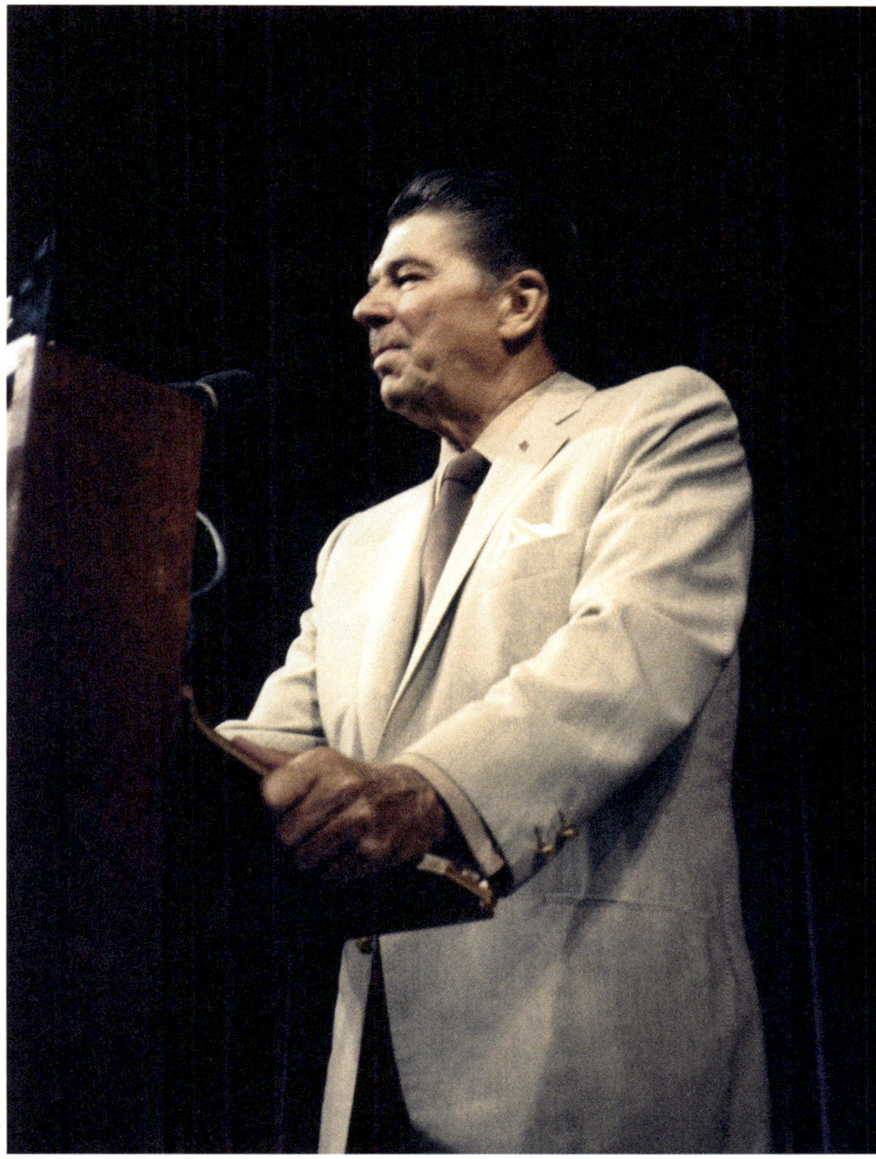

Ronald Reagan before he was elected president. Miami Beach, FL. 1972.

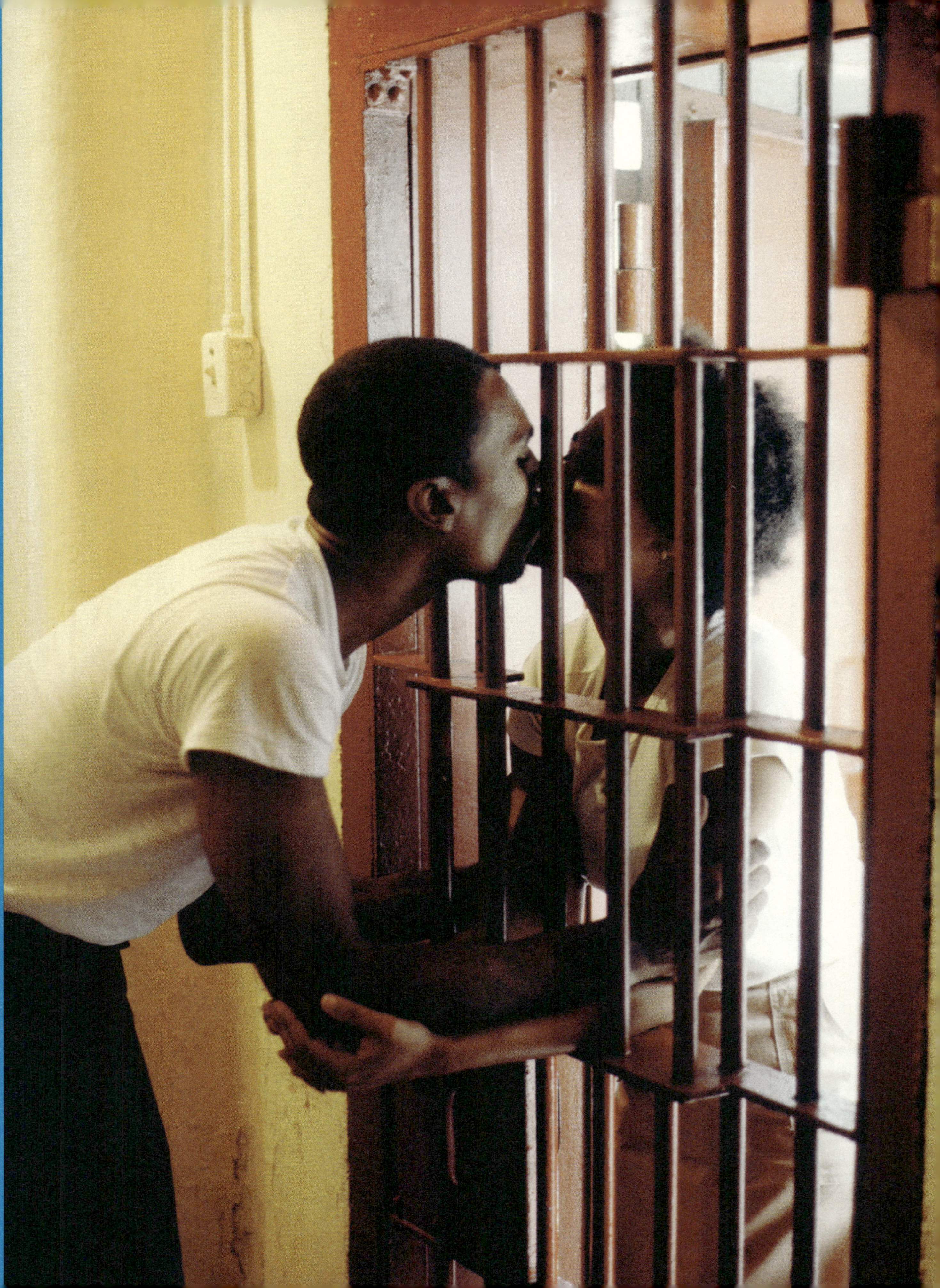

Henry's wife is visiting. Washington, GA, 1974

SANDRA RUFFIN

from advocacy to art

I AM. I am Woman. I am African-American. I am Mother/ Daughter/ Sister/ Friend. Although that is not the totality of ME; in this moment, I am looking through that lens and speaking from that heart. In this piece I reflect upon and comment on Jacob's presentation and use of Blackness, especially the Black Nude, in *American Pictures.* His body of work is broader and more expansive but, just as Jacob's life-walk was revealed to him through American Pictures, so is the whole of its purpose revealed in the soulful reflections of the "Least of Us" (and therefore the least within us) captured and re-presented in his images of Blackness in America.

TO BE OR NOT TO BE? This question is about power – the power TO BE. Right here and right now. It is not about be-coming, be-having, be-stowing. It is about Be-ing who and what you are, where you are, in every moment. America has never been very ALLOWING when it comes to the BEINGNESS of Black People – any Colored People for that matter, except White People. Mainstream whiteness was defined out of the cultural-color scheme; it was neutralized and presented as the standard to which all other color-cultures had to aspire. Make no mistake, in 1970's America, Blackness was its opposite.

The America of American Pictures was born out of the power movements of the 1960s. These movements were about seizing/ claiming power; they were about seeing and being seen, speaking up and being heard, loving and being loved. The Black Power Movement in particular was an integral part of, if not the impetus for, other and/or larger liberation movements within and without America. Traditional/historical power structures were dis-integrating and re-forming.

The timing of the shooting of American Pictures was fortuitous. Jacob came to Black and White America at a time when people-of-color, women and men, rich and poor began to abandon the ego-centered, individual-mind-identity, to rally around their common causes and to relish in the relative security of group-identity. The Group became a source of power and the power-of-the-group became an undeniable force in American social and political life. Solidarity was the buzzword and it was a force to be reckoned with. The various power movements built upon the successes and learned harsh lessons from the failures of any singular effort to expose exploitation, demand and command voice and/or to re-define identity. Mainstream whiteness as objective, neutral standard was privileged by invisibility. Whites who through their own multidimensional experience un-covered the reality of privilege and dis-covered its illusory character abandoned the entitlement and joined various grass-roots movements for change. There, in this new place, they re-covered the multidimensional Self.

I met Jacob in 1983 when he came to Harvard Law School to show/do American Pictures. I was a student and President of the Black Law Students Association. Just being me, I embodied in some peculiar way an intangible something that was interpreted as symbolic of the black/ female/ revolutionary. I did not intend this but was aware of it. As symbol, my choices had significance for the community of progressive students at the law school; therefore, in meeting Jacob and being introduced to American Pictures as workshop and slide show, I faced the interesting question of whether or not to support the show. Despite ruminations in academia of the unlocated, multidimensional Self that is the touchstone of the postmodern interpretation of self and the world; when I met Jacob, modernity reigned. People were firmly located and identified in and by groups. The dual/binary mind categorized and excluded. You were either part of the problem or part of the solution. What was American Pictures?

On the one hand, it graphically and effectively presented class issues in America. It showed the poverty, the hopelessness, the disempowerment, the intentional neglect, and the despair of America's underclass. It exposed the duplicity and complicity of American institutions in the continued exploitation and perpetuation of that underclass. It offered the opportunity to dis-play and dis-mantle the false god that America had become. VOTE YES.

On the other hand, because of a history of race-based slavery and the dominance of race-ism in American thought, the co-incidence of Blackness and Femaleness with Poverty and Sexual Exploitation was so pervasive that these diminished states of existence were encouraged to become identified with Black Womanhood. The co-incidence of Blackness and Maleness with Drug Addiction, Drunkenness and Incarceration was so pervasive that these diminished states of existence were encouraged to become identified with Black Manhood. Image is perception. Moreover, Jacob, a Slavic (white) Jesus-looking male was/is exploiting images of women generally and poor black women in particular for fame and fortune. Even if such exploitation was/is not the primary purpose of the work, it's hardly incidental. Subjugation of women, exotification of black women, perpetuation of anti-black stereotypes-classic Blaxploitation. VOTE NO.

Blaxploitation as theory and practice in its modern iteration emerged in the film industry in the early 1970's, the very time during which Jacob shot his 15,000 photos from which American Pictures was made. The word itself is a portmanteau of the words "black" and "exploitation." (Wikipedia 2009). Some of the power wrenched from the system by the power movements of the 60s found expression in the film industry where Blacks re-presented themselves as self-actualized agents in their own lives and the life of their communities. For the most part, Blacks were not the owners of the film or the final industry decision makers, but the genre sought to appeal to the black urban audience and as a result employed numerous black writers, composers, musicians, actors and directors. The dominant thematic formulas for successful American filmmaking in the 1970s were not very different from the current formulas – violence, action, sex and love. As a result, Blaxploitation films repeated the formulas – cops and robbers, pimps and whores, fast cars and fast lives. Stereotypes abounded – sexual prowess, female subjugation, and street life. To be sure, that was not the entire picture presented by the genre, but it was dominant enough to spark protest from empowered organizations within the Black community. In retrospect, what we learned from the debate over Blaxploitation is to ask: (1) What are we (Blacks) getting out of it? And (2) what is it costing us? These are the questions that had to be answered in determining whether or not to support American Pictures.

What is it costing us?

The concern and response of African-American women to the Black Nudes and the relational depictions included in the show do not arise out of some abstract notion of puritan decency but out of the particularized experience of African-American women in America. The legacy of slavery, the commodification of Blackness and its over-sexualization, are at the core of the African-American response to the use of Black Nudes in the show. The sex-on-demand status of slaves, poor women, and women generally is necessarily present in and part of the experience of the Black Nudes as protest and advocacy. Recall that American Pictures was originally presented and experienced as a workshop. American Pictures was process – participants were invited and expected to "un-cover," "re-cover" and "work through" their perceptions. As workshop, the role of the facilitator/narrator was functionally important if not absolutely necessary, and Jacob, as facilitator/narrator, raised additional concerns.

There were cultural and language differences which hindered effective verbal *and* non-verbal communication between Jacob and workshop participants. Given the sensitive issues associated with the Black Nudes in particular, effective, culturally-proficient communication was critical when presenting and commenting on these particular photographs. Jacob's compromised-ability to "pick-up" on the feedback from the participants and to strategically guide their gaze based on that feedback was a serious issue. The ability, both, to present and perceive the beauty and naturalness of the Black Nudes would invariably be compromised if the gaze was not effectively guided. Potential result—exotification, resentment, anger. Of course, exotification of the Black Woman is troubling for several reasons; definitional issues aside, the sexual exploitation and violation of Black Women was/is a global problem. The question of power, its potential mis-use and ab-use was unavoidably and conspicuously presented by the show despite the fact that we, as observers/participants, somehow knew that neither photographer nor subject was, in the specific relational moment, a conscious agent or victim of such abuse. Nonetheless, Jacob's status as white man and subject's status as black woman/man immediately bring this power relationship into play. African-American observers/participants are especially sensitive to this dynamic. Oftentimes, it is the apparent victimization of the subject that is the source of power in the image. Paradoxically, lack of power becomes source of power in this context.

Even in today's world, today's America, we must ask as we did in the era of blaxploitation, whether there is any transformative potential in the image and, if so, whether that potential outweighs the risk of reinforcing overt or ambivalent sexism, racism and/or classism. Of significant, if not equal importance and concern, is the response of the non-African-American community to the Black Nudes and the relational depictions included in the show. Regarding the white observer/participant, the transformative impact of the show may be enhanced by the potential racial/gender identification with Jacob, and the possible presumption of objectivity conferred by his status as "foreigner." However, as beneficiaries of the power and privilege flowing from the *status quo ante*, whites are likely to shift only incrementally if at all.

So, what do we get out of it?

Despite the fact that it has taken 35 years for Jacob's photographs to grace the walls of Louisiana, from the moment I first saw the photographs, it was the Art that silenced the criticism. There is nothing more beautiful, more artful than Life itself, and few are present enough to capture and preserve it in any medium. Any authentic slice of life is a hologram of the whole of life, and Jacob gives us many holographic images. While journeying through America, Jacob practiced the art of present-moment-awareness. Just recently, we laughed as he credited Attention Deficit Disorder for this unwitting capacity. During significant periods of his visits, there was no interpretation-of-the-moment based on past experiences or future predictions. What was, was. Perhaps he could not have achieved this state without traveling great distances from his home, being unmoored from mundane responsibilities, and landing in strange environments. While in America, his willingness to live without bonds or boundaries moved him from Mind to Moment. Mind uses time to judge/compare what is; without time (past or future) judgment of what is disappears, and one simply responds creatively to the moment in the moment. It was through this practice that Jacob was able to BE with his subjects without noticeably impacting their BEING. (T)here but not (t)here. And in those photographs where the subjects are also practicing present-moment-awareness, the most profound Art is produced:

In the SCREEN DOOR, the young boy does not simply look out onto the world; he looks in upon himself; he looks out and into the observer. His Beingness and Beauty are undeniable. We SEE him; we LOVE him; we ARE him.

THE RETURN HOME, one of the most beautiful and profound nudes in the show, pushes the observer outside herself by pulling the observer in. The longer the gaze the more YOU are drawn out and in. So close until the image is YOU. This kind of intimacy is not the intimacy between photographer and subject or even between the subjects of the photography. It reveals the intimacy between the Self that you authentically ARE and the self that you ALLOW in that moment.

THE KISS. Through it we glimpse Divine Longing - the spark of Creation. It occurs between bars, as if the Creator is reaching out across the VOID declaring that there BE light and there IS light, embedded, yet embraced, even in the most impoverished social conditions. THE KISS is the container of all our reality and potentiality.

In May of 2007, I journeyed to Copenhagen to join family, friends, and compatriots in the celebration of Jacob Holdt's sixtieth birthday. It was a spiritual re-union. I saw, felt, touched some who I had experienced only through Jacob's photographs, reconnected with others who I had met only once or twice over the last 25 years and joined in celebration some who I had never experienced in any way before. Yet, we were united in the joy of celebration and in our common experience of Jacob. As part of the celebration, Jacob mounted an ambitious exhibit entitled, "The Ghetto in our Hearts." The exhibit re-presented the spiritual, human, and social costs of subjugation, domination and alienation. At the time I wondered about the title of the exhibit thought that it might have been a bit weak, soft even, given the magnitude of the problem generally and the particular issues facing Denmark. In retrospect, I think the title expressed as succinctly as possible the very depth and magnitude that was the source of my original concern. After all, there can be no ghetto in the world unless there is a ghetto in the collective heart of the world. As co-creators, collectively, we are the source of ALL that we see around us. The outer reflects the inner, has its source and its beginning in the inner; it reflects that which exists invisibly in our vibration, our collective thought. So, I am gently reminded of why, over 25 years ago, I said YES to American Pictures and YES to the charism of Jacob Holdt.

Jacob, just being Jacob, personifies the archetype of the empty vessel. The empty vessel simply allows. It goes with the flow; it does not resist. In its nonresistance is its Power. The empty vessel needs no narration; its BEINGNESS tells its own story. None of us is empty all the time, but so few of us are empty any of the time. The story of American Pictures is also the story of the Empty Vessel.

As protest and advocacy, American Pictures functions in the world and one might debate its effectiveness. As Art, American Pictures moves in the Spirit and ain't no debatin' that.

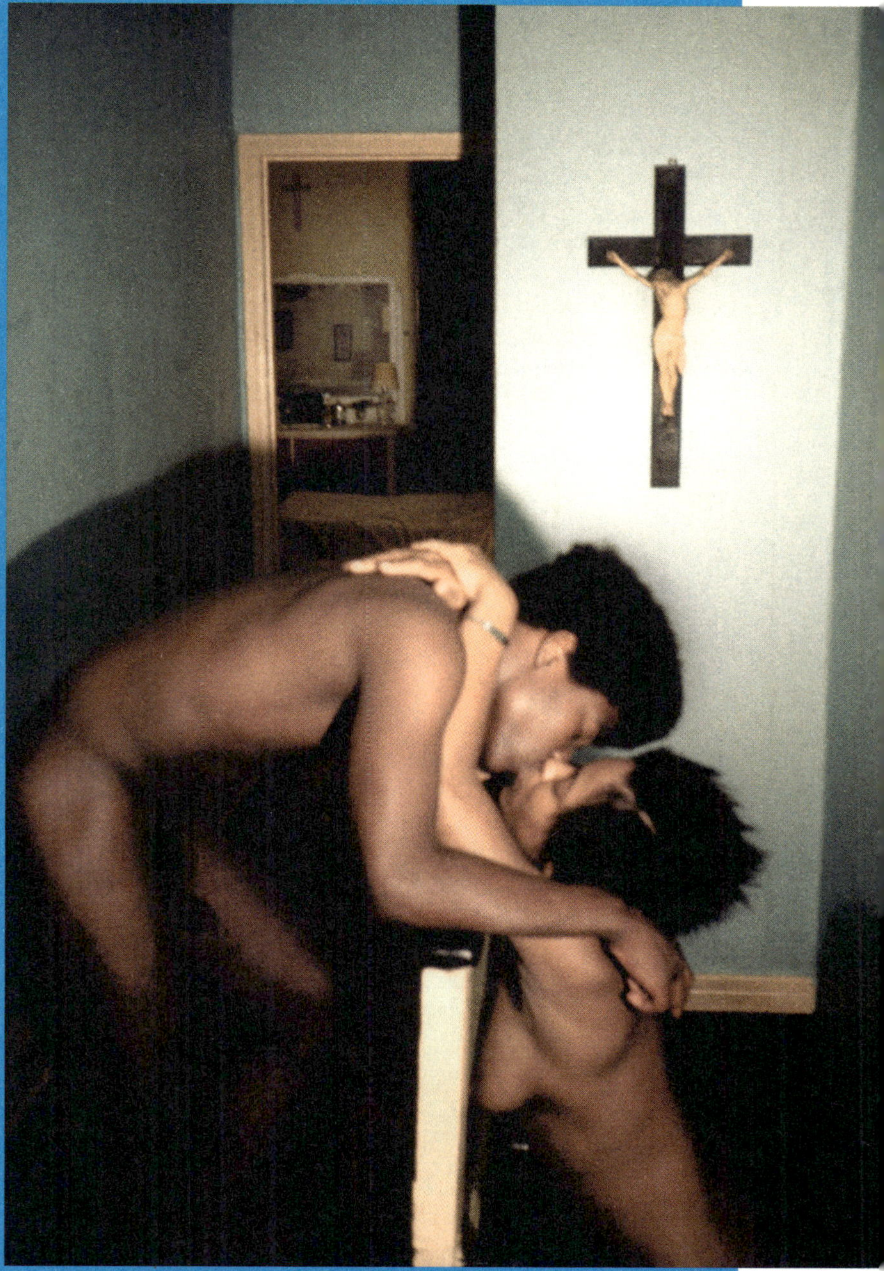

Young couple in the ghetto of Philadelphia.
Philadelphia, PA. 1974

Sandra Ruffin
Sandra Ruffin is an Associate Professor of Law at Lincoln Memorial University, Duncan School of Law in Knoxville, Tennessee. Professor Ruffin has a B.A. from the University of Maryland and a J.D. from Harvard. She was born and raised in the Washington, D.C. metropolitan area and is a seasoned community organizer and activist. Professor Ruffin views documentary photography as central to the global struggle for social justice and greatly admires Jacob Holdt's contribution to this effort.

guns

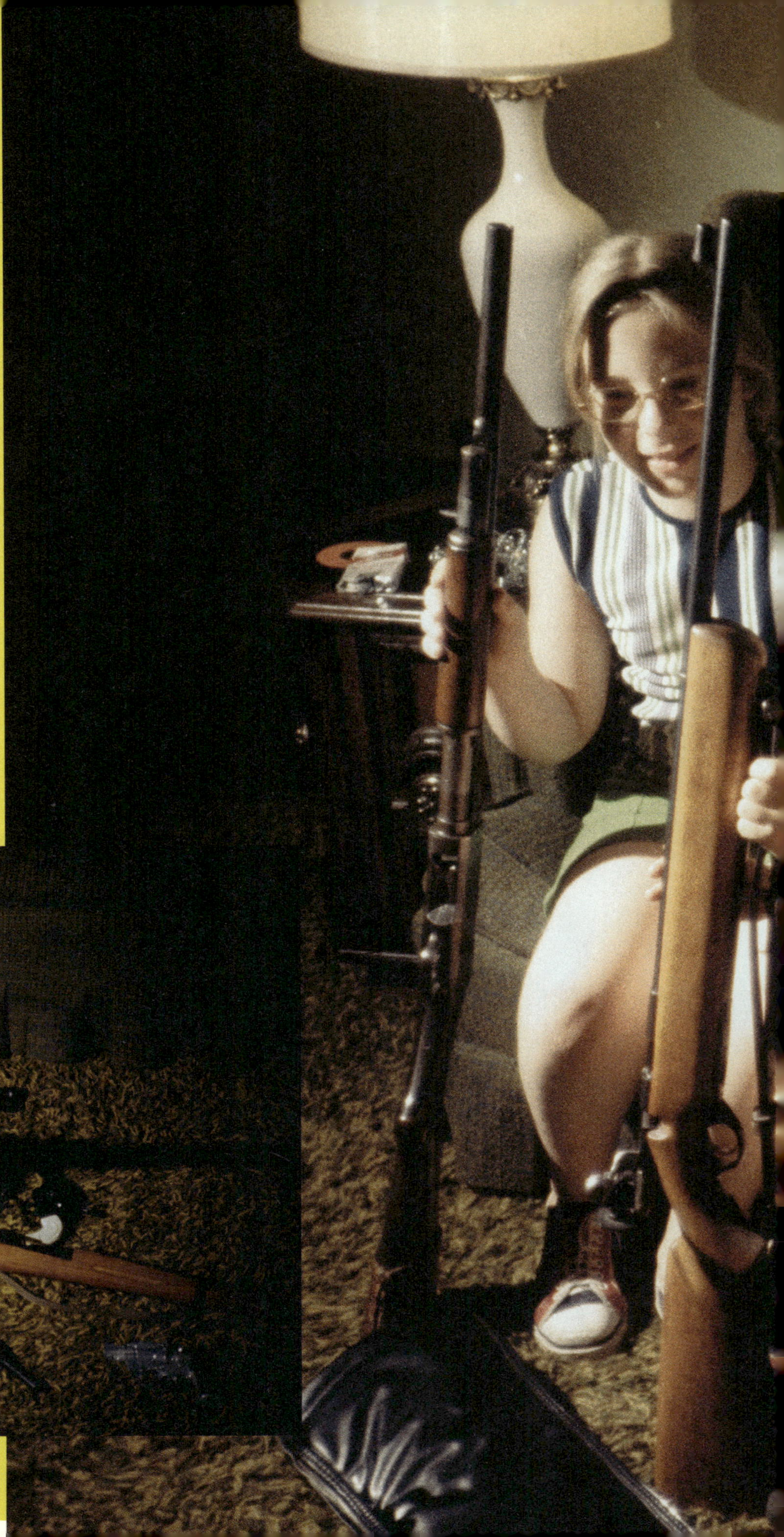

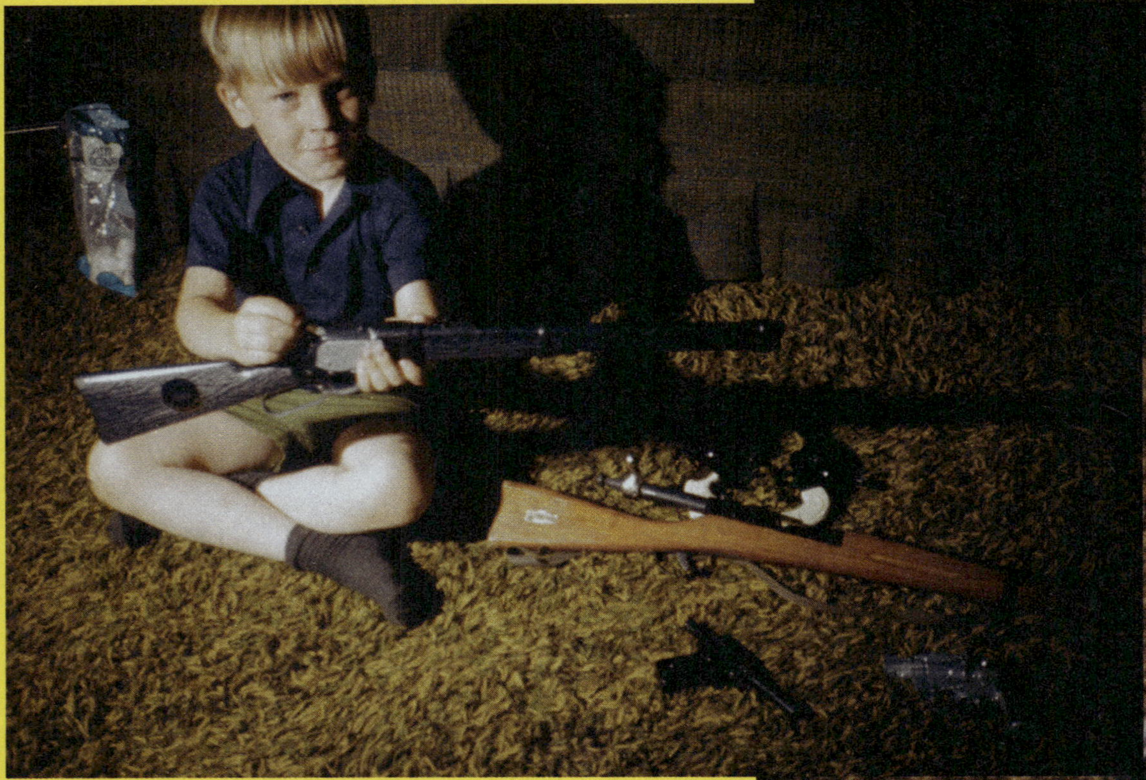

My girlfriend Vicky's little brother. Jackson, MI. 1972

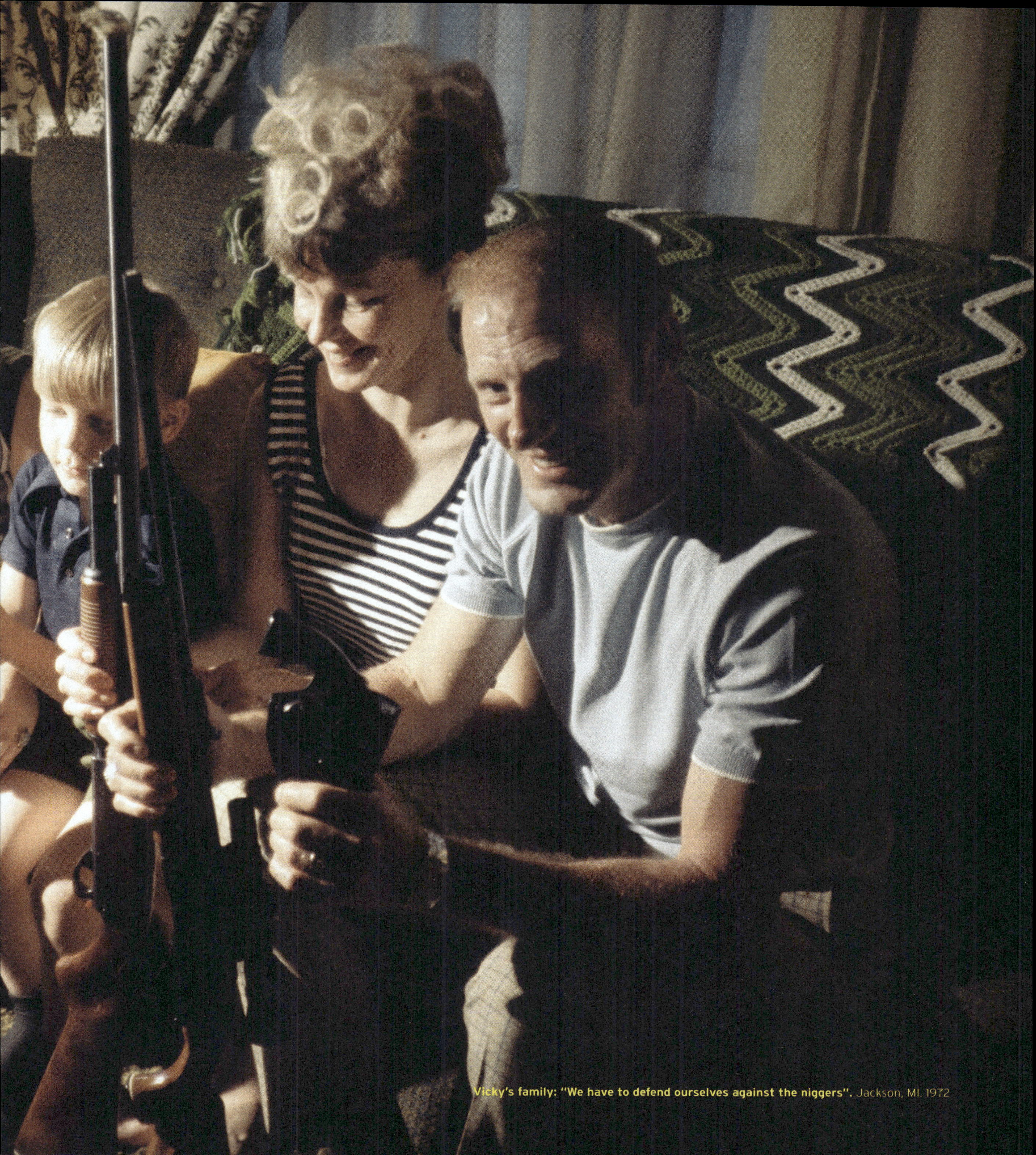

Vicky's family: "We have to defend ourselves against the niggers". Jackson, MI. 1972

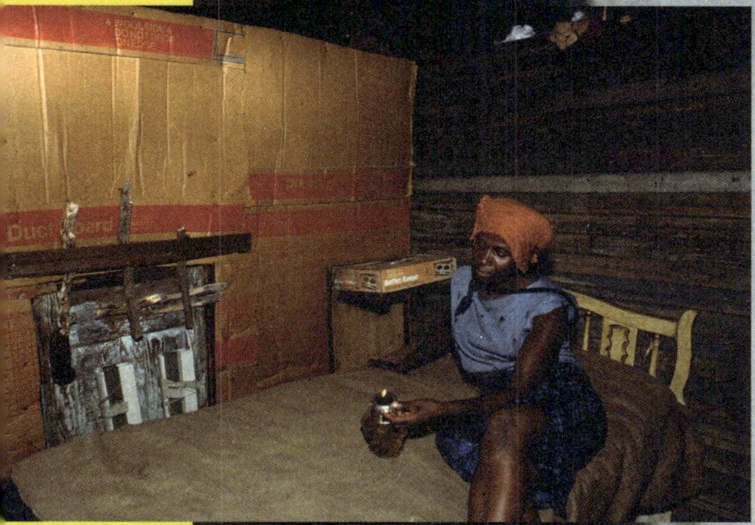

Wilma in her old one-room shack without running water and electricity. Cecil, AL. 1990

Status updates on Jacob Holdt's Facebook profile, 2009

Jacob Holdt:
Falling asleep from U.S. jetlag in my car during my show at Viborg Seminarium. As in a nightmare, the school was locked and my audience gone, when I woke up. Will be awake, though, during today's confirmation for my niece and Facebook friend Marie Holm....since family is more important than work (my family keeps telling me)!
May 21, 10:26 a.m.

Jacob Holdt:
Looking forward to be "kicking off" the New York Photo Festival as their opening "historical figure" ... I sure will show them that I am still alive and kicking! But especially to tonight's VIP party and later opening parties. Please come all New York friends!
May 13, 9:09 p.m.

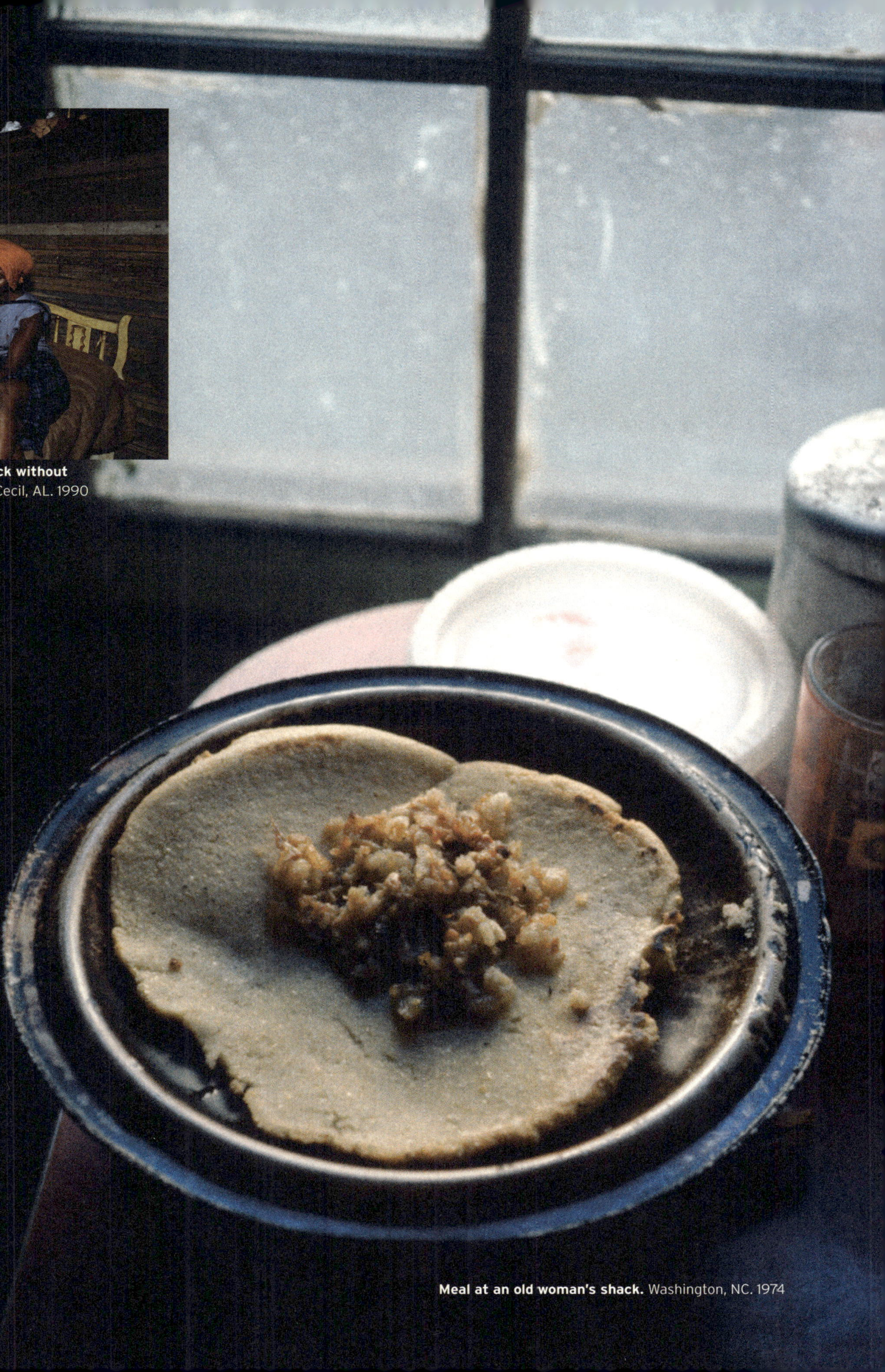

Meal at an old woman's shack. Washington, NC. 1974

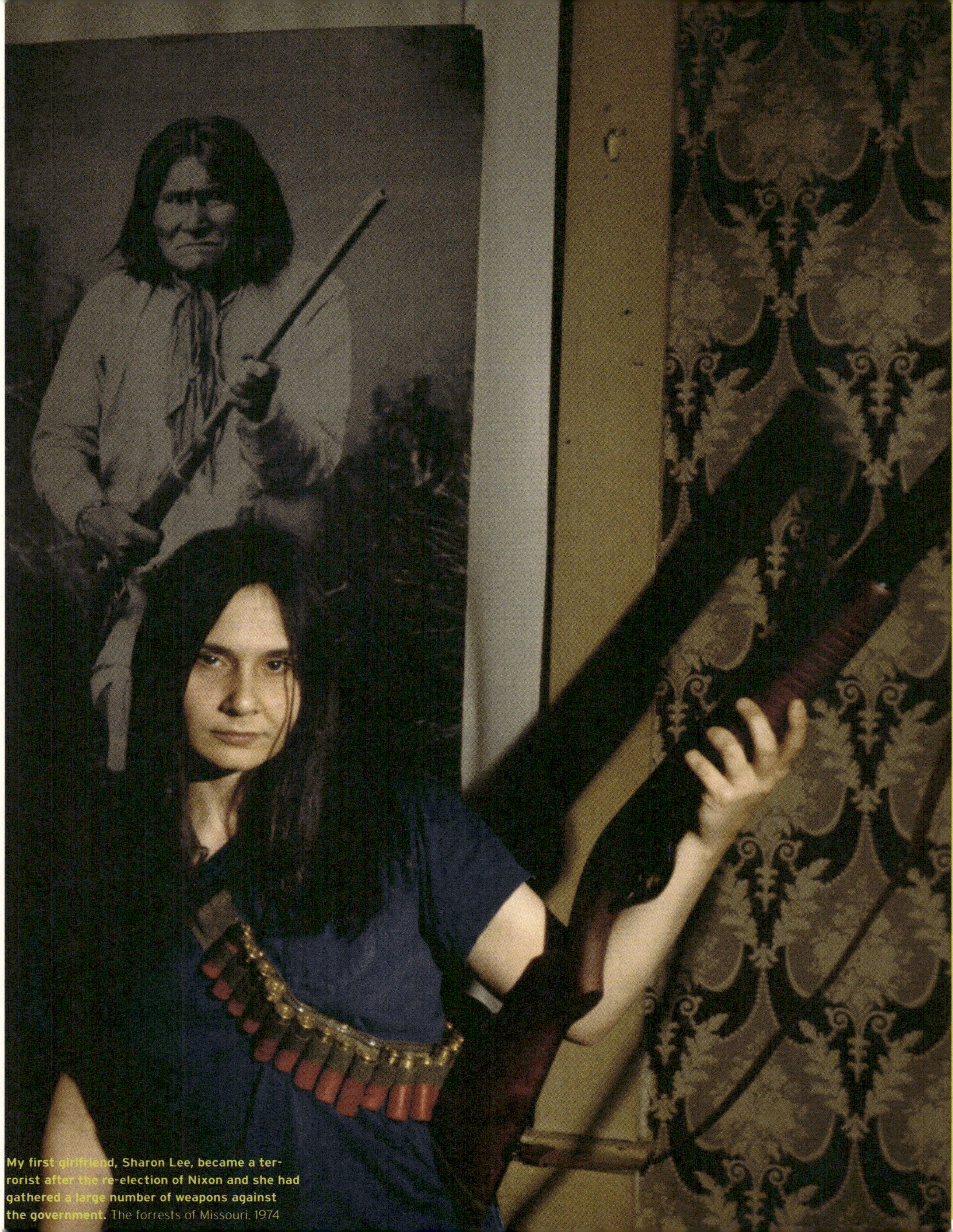

My first girlfriend, Sharon Lee, became a terrorist after the re-election of Nixon and she had gathered a large number of weapons against the government. The forrests of Missouri. 1974

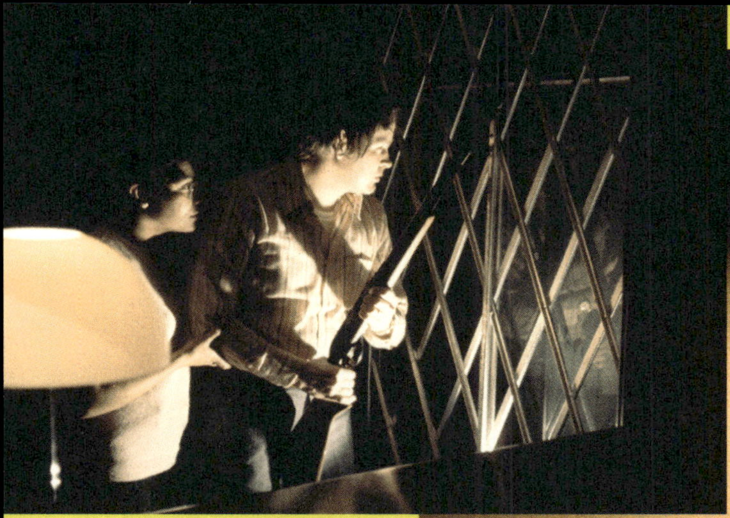

John was married to the sister of my Haitian girlfriend, but was afraid of blacks. Brooklyn, NY. 1973

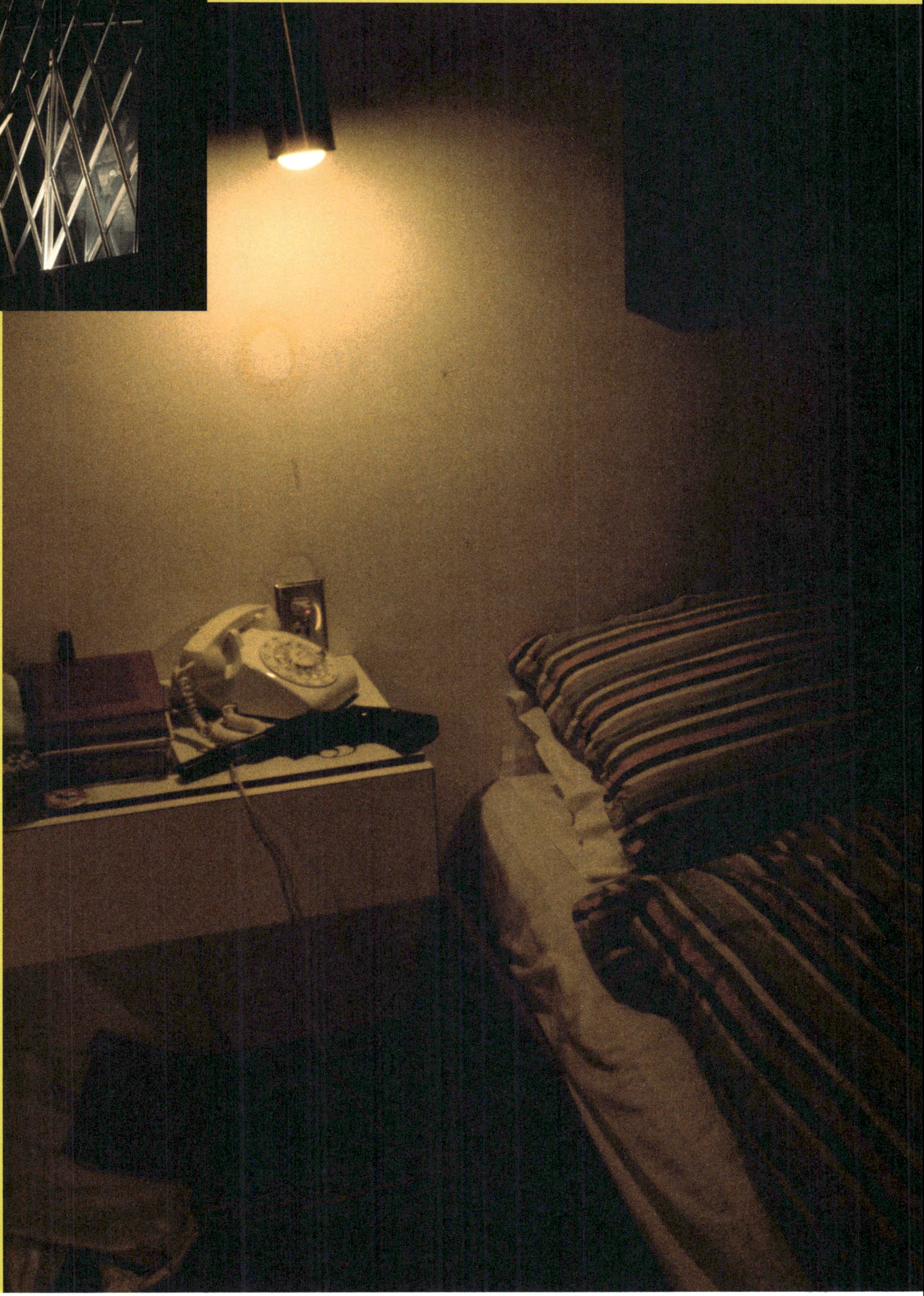

When I affectionately put my arm under Gene from the black middle class, it touched the gun under her pillow. Atlanta, GA. 1978

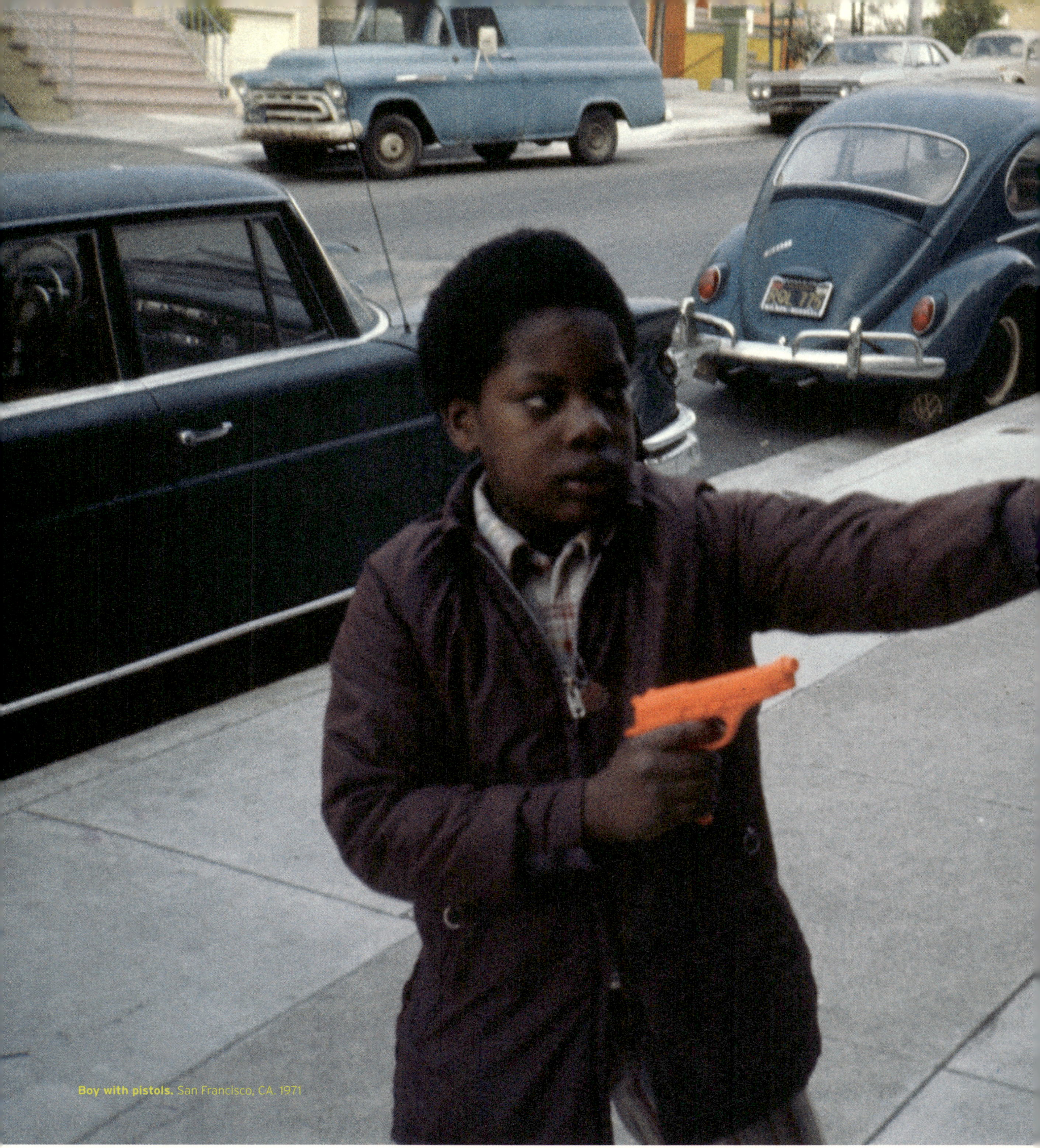

Boy with pistols. San Francisco, CA. 1971

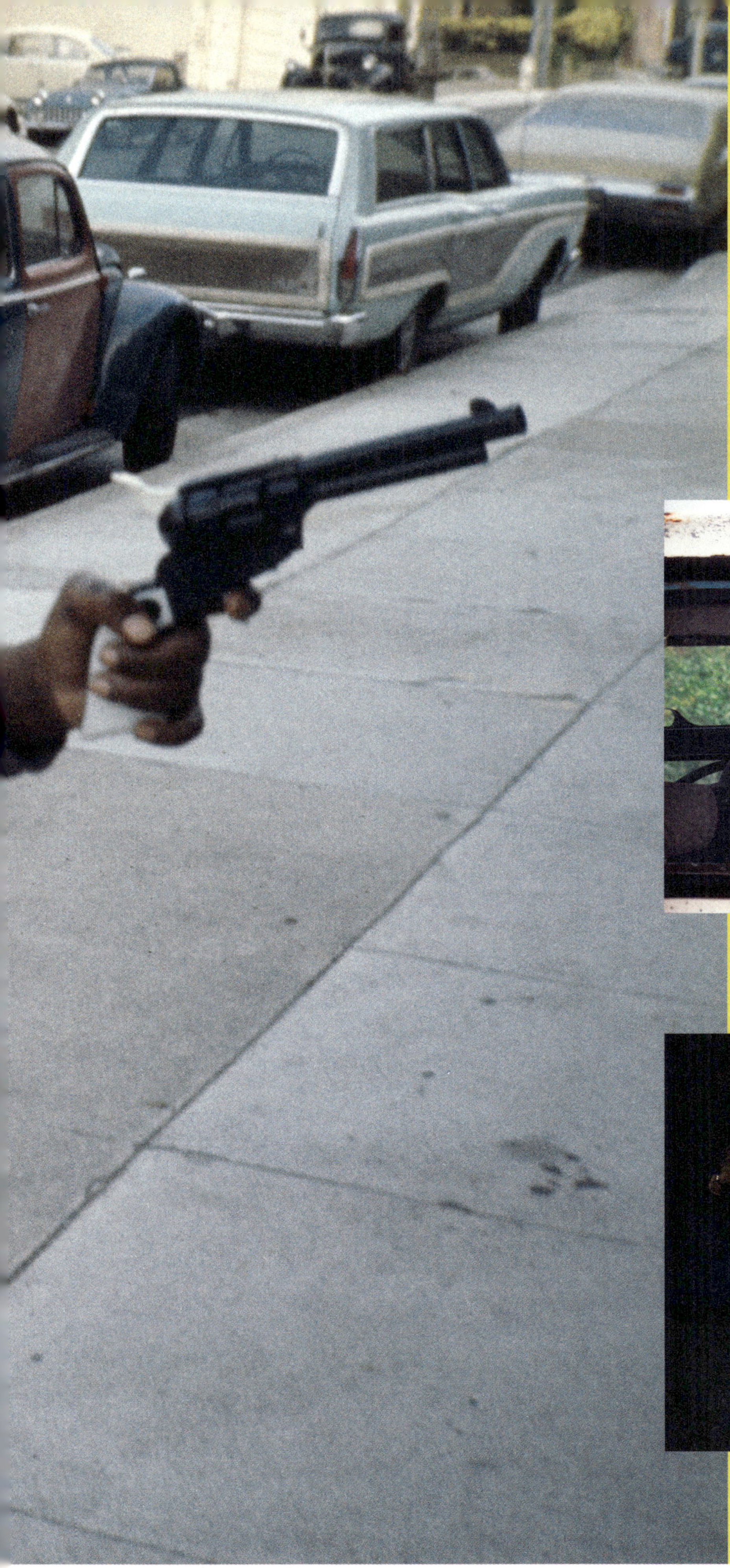

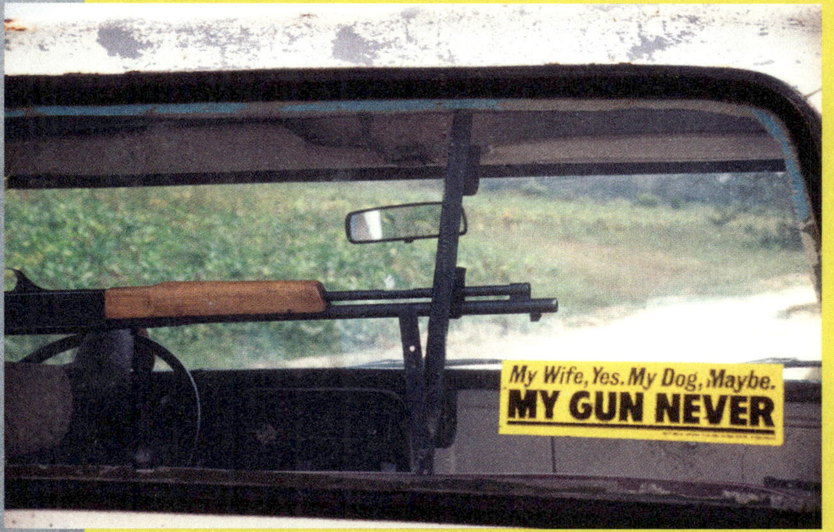

A truck giving my 2-year-old son and me a ride. I hitched 16,000 miles with my son to give him a positive counterbalance to the fear-based racism which paralyses other children before the age of 3-4 years.
Amarillo, TX. 1982

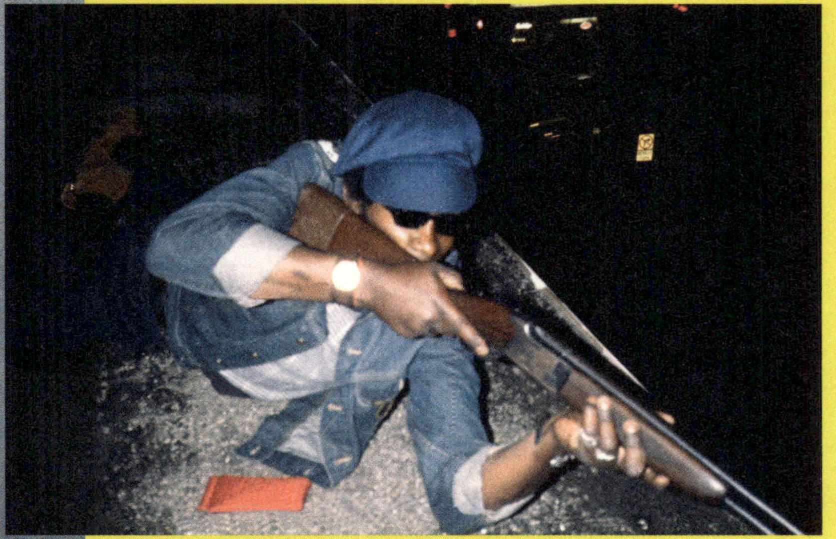

My criminal friend Burt, with whom I stayed in the "Tenderloin" ghetto.
San Francisco, CA. 1975

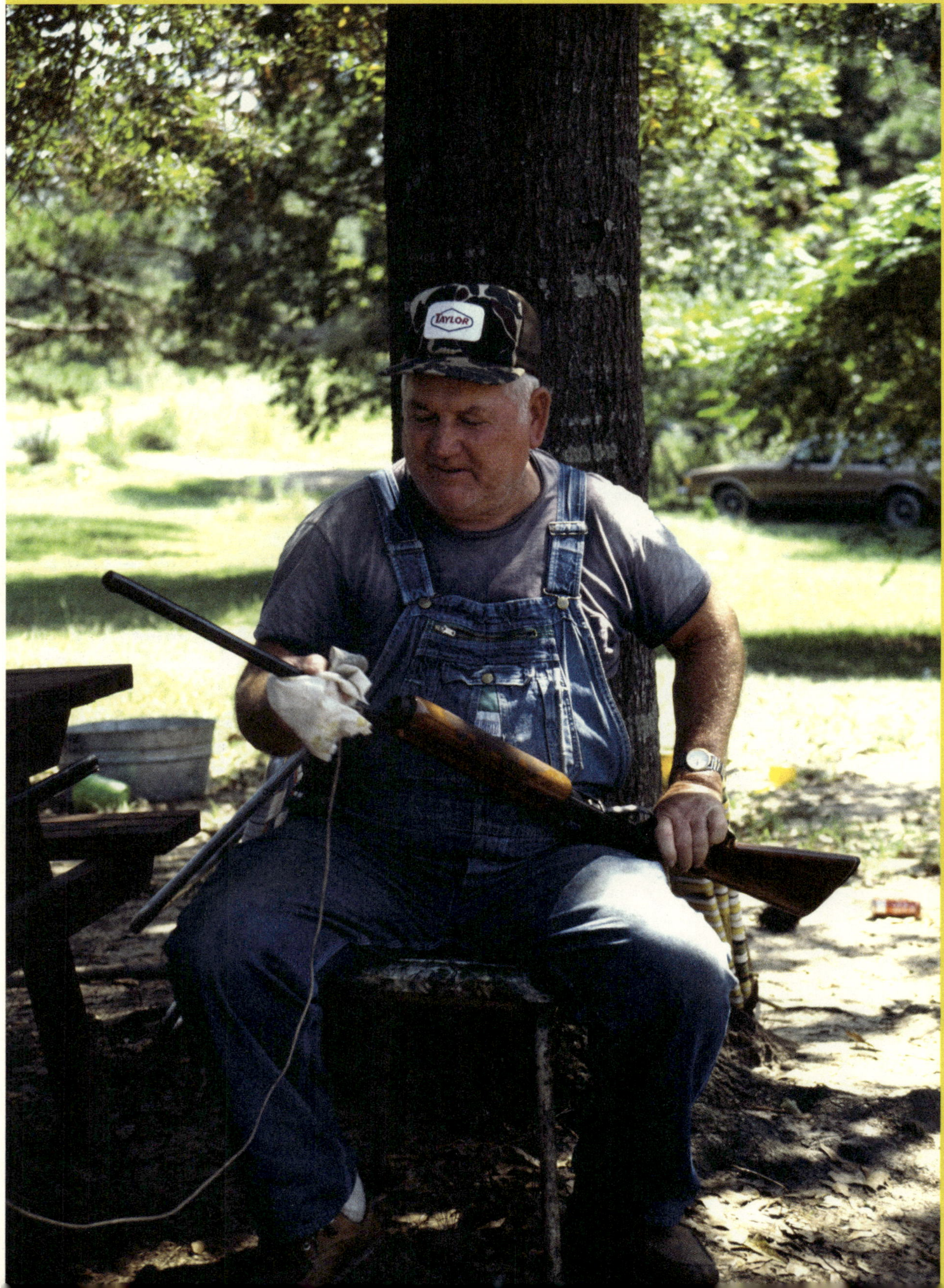

A man in my ex-wife's hometown where the KKK ravaged in the '60's.
Philadelphia, MS. 2003

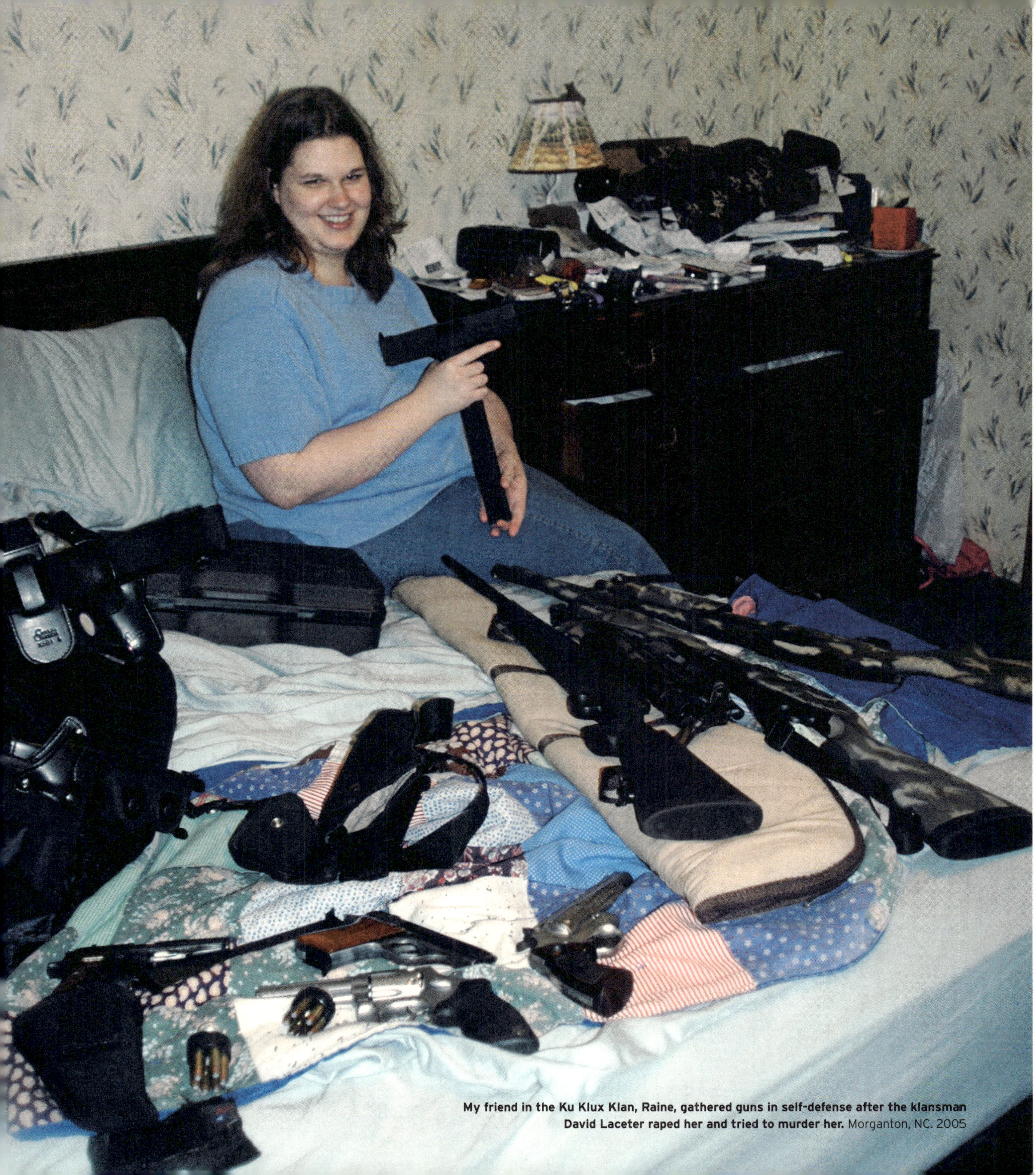

My friend in the Ku Klux Klan, Raine, gathered guns in self-defense after the klansman David Laceter raped her and tried to murder her. Morganton, NC. 2005

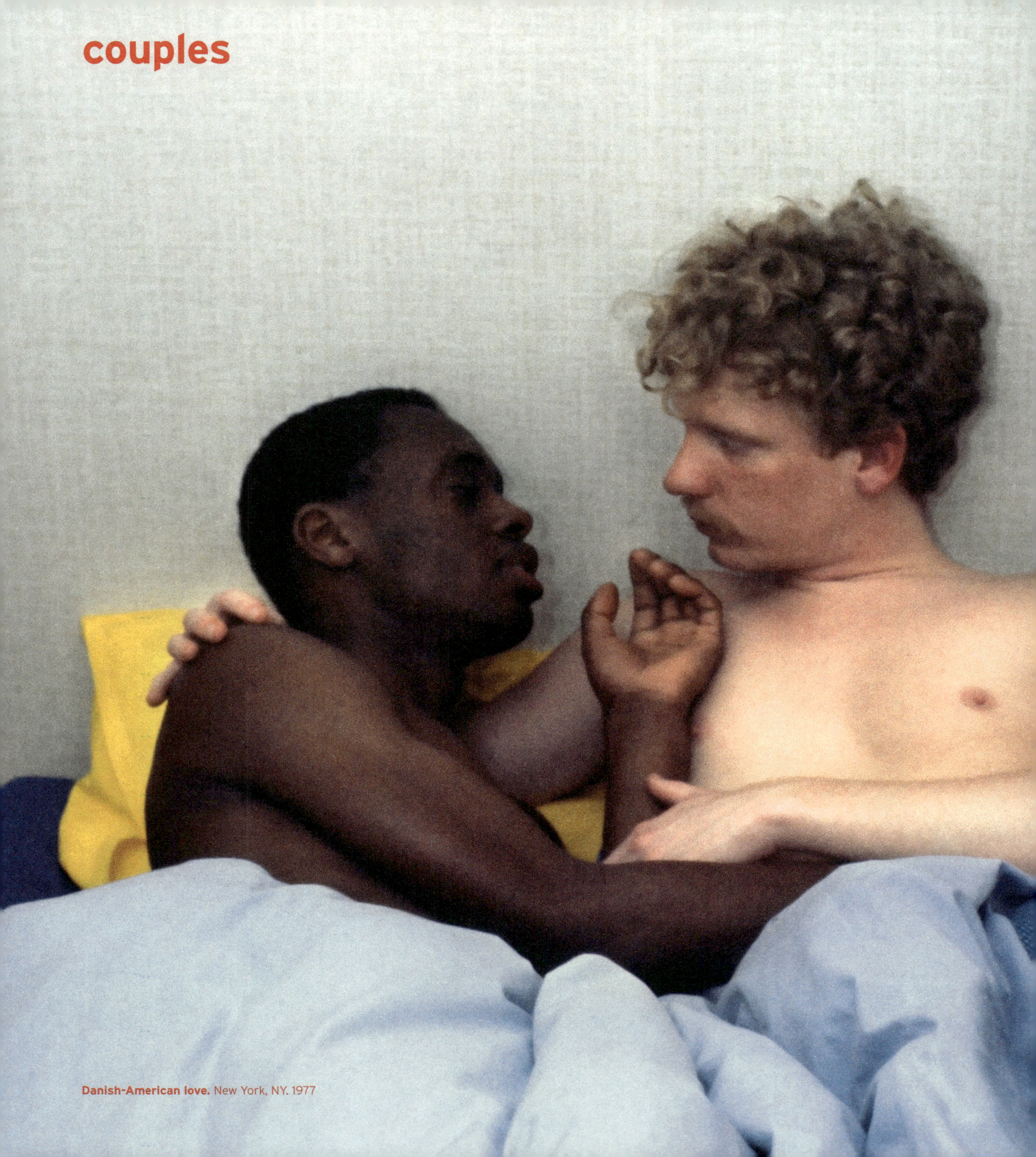

Danish-American love. New York, NY. 1977

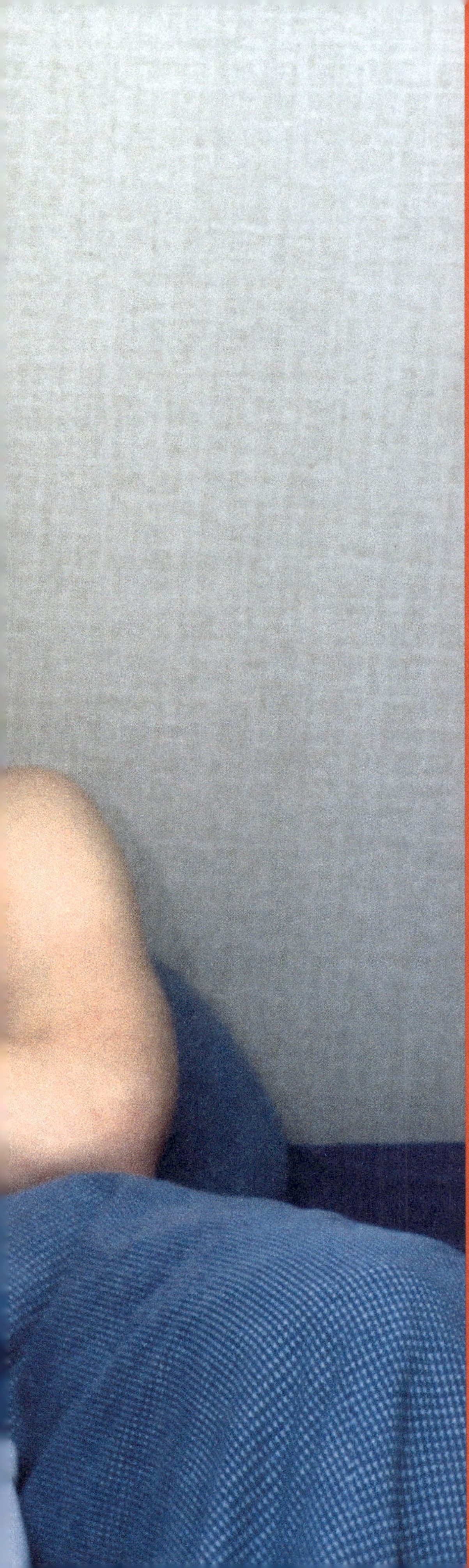

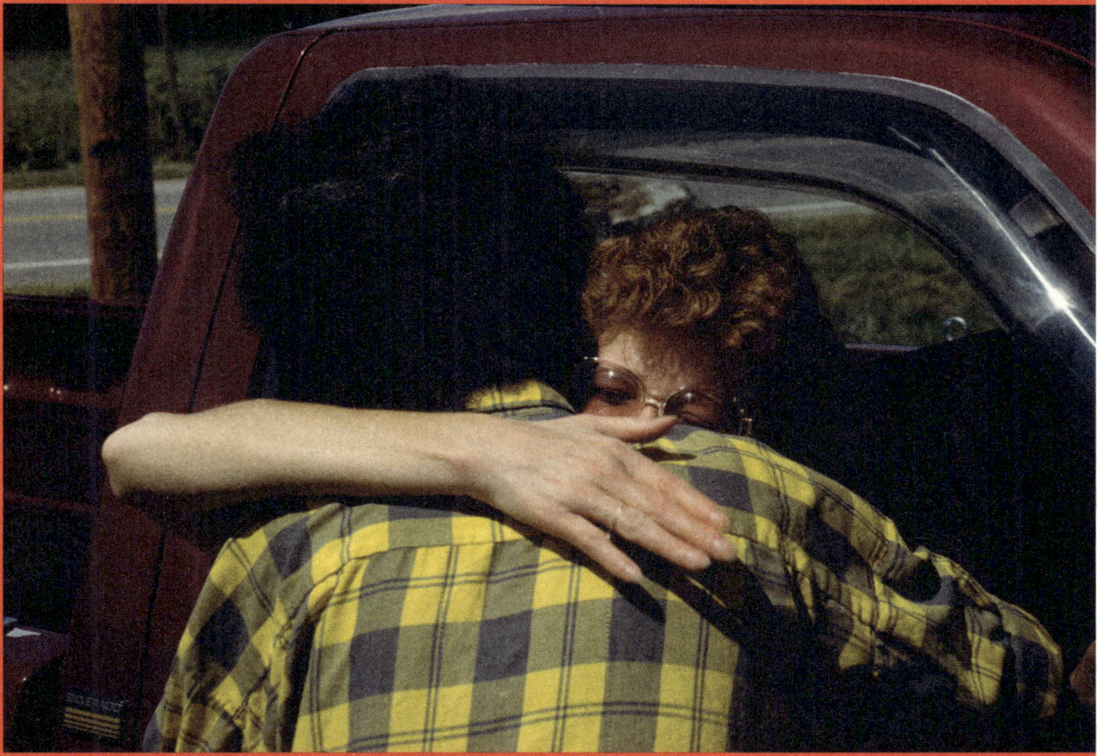

Red-haired "redneck" with her black girlfriend. Union Springs AL. 1998

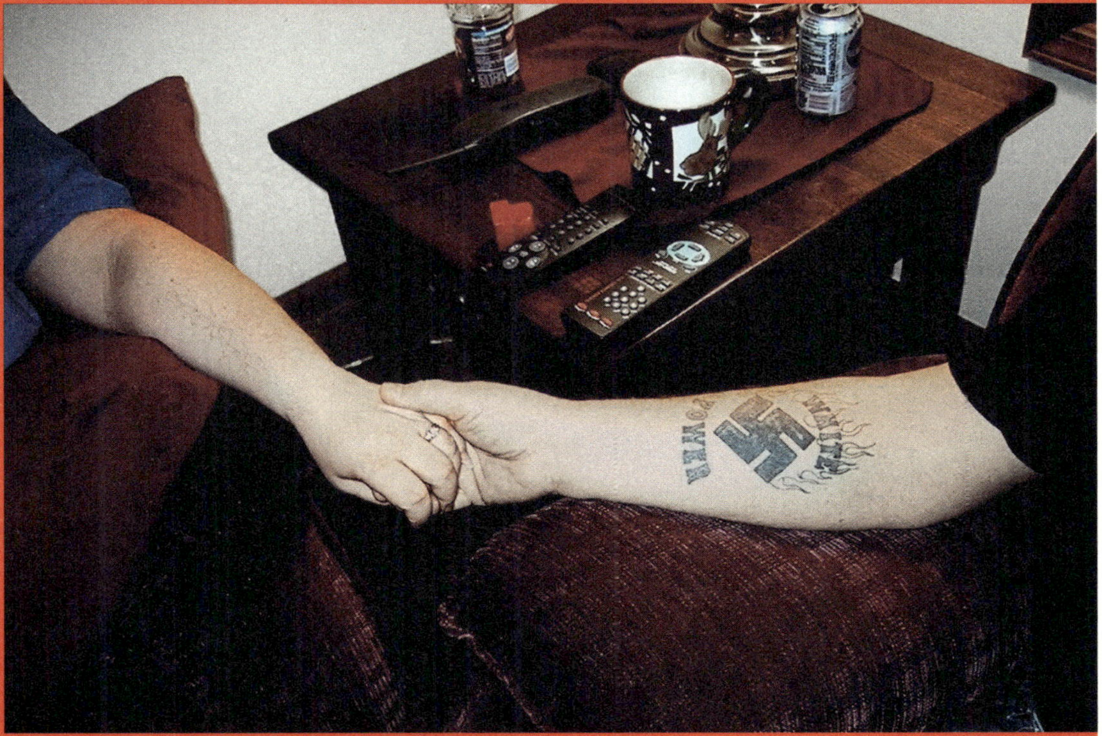

Love between a KKK member and a Nazi. Butler, IN. 2002

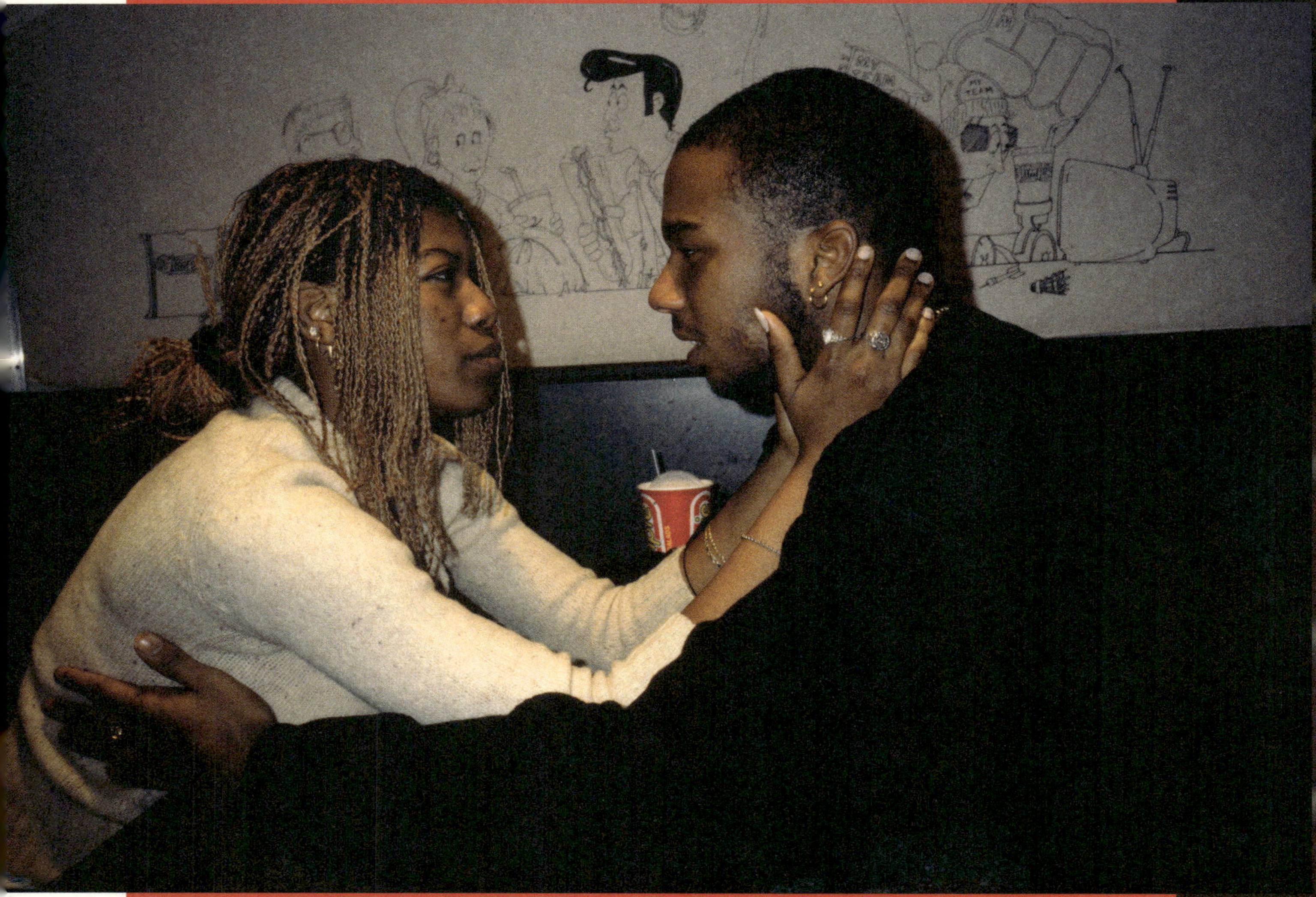

Young couple in a restaurant. New York, NY. 2005

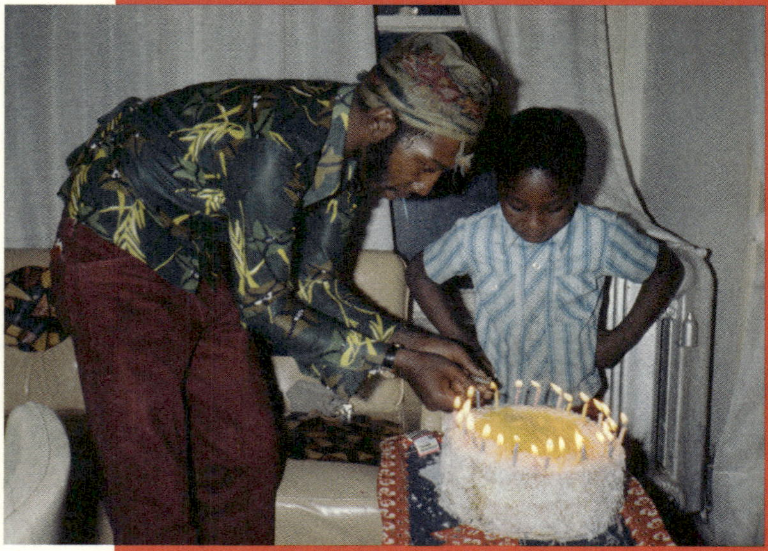

Birthday for my transvestite friend, Tania, her boyfriend and her boyfriend's son. San Francisco, CA. 1975

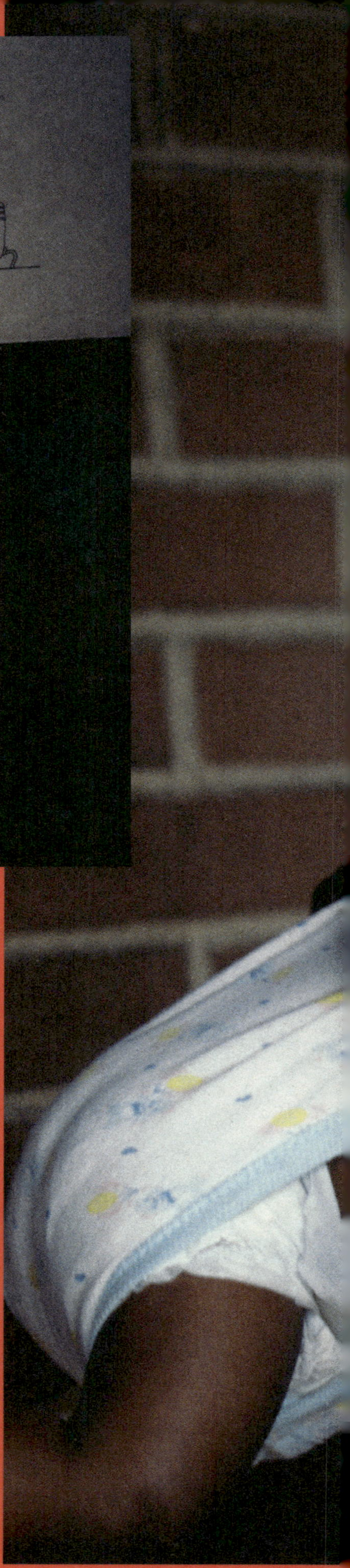

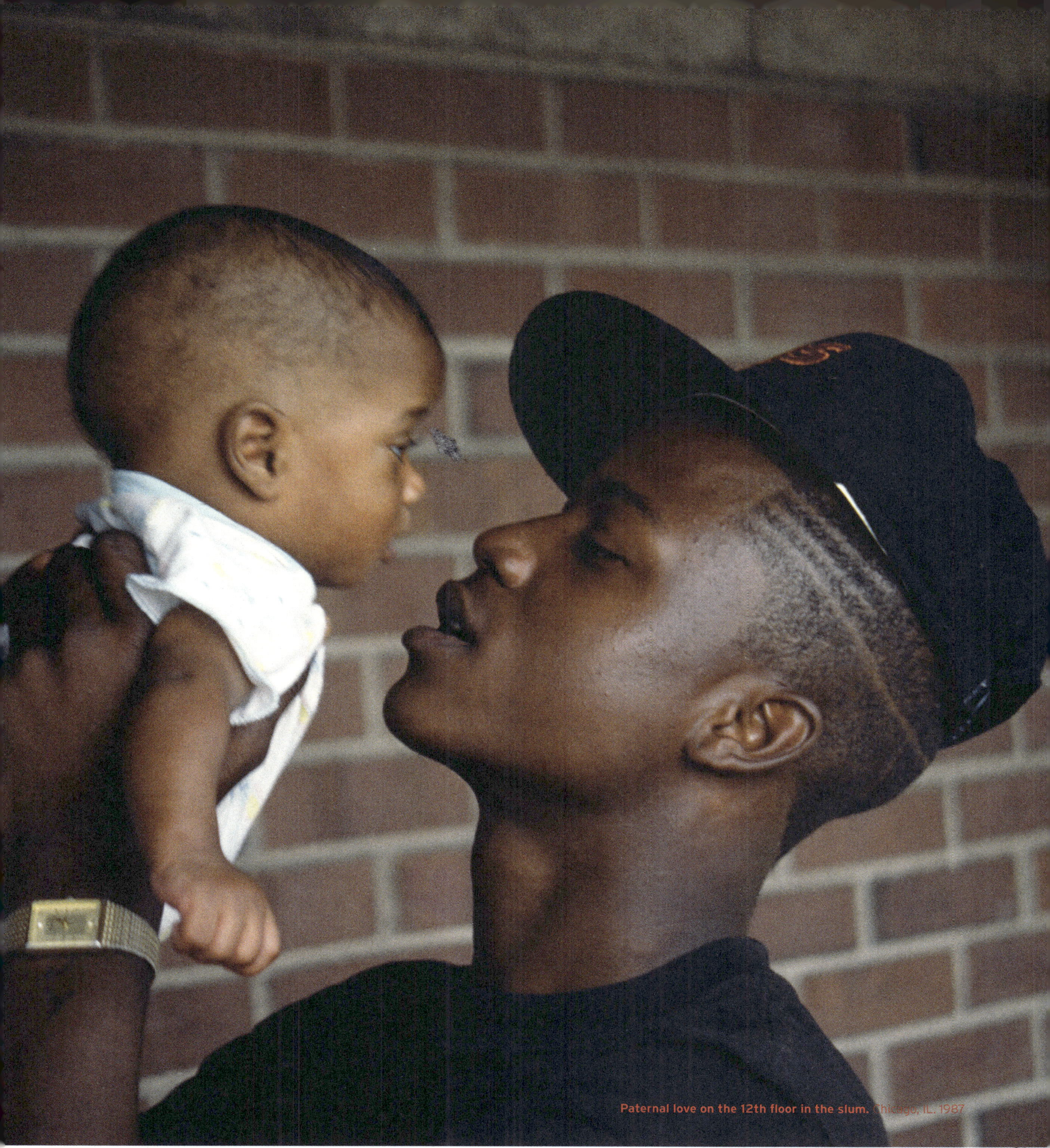

Paternal love on the 12th floor in the slum. Chicago, IL. 1987

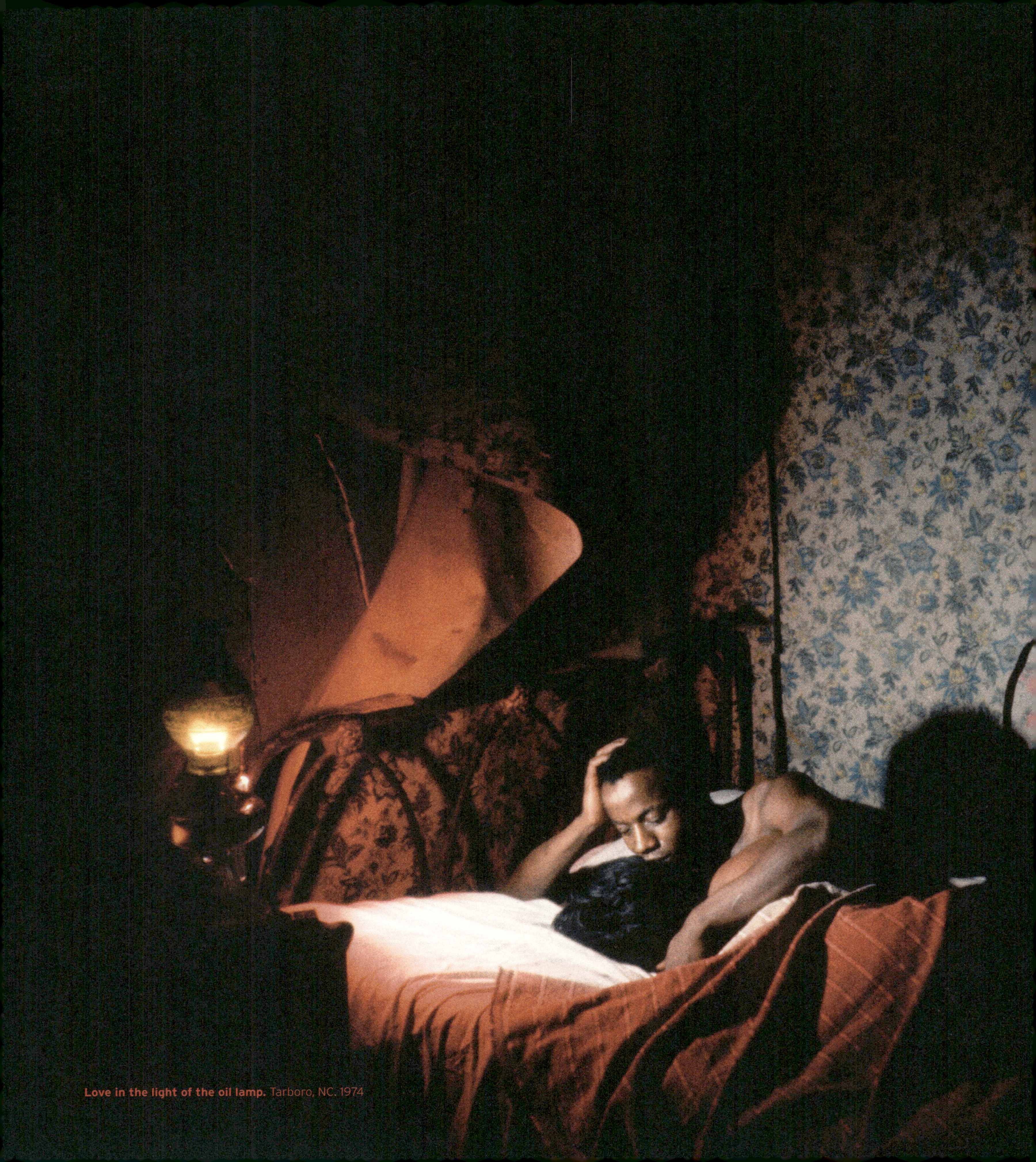

Love in the light of the oil lamp. Tarboro, NC. 1974

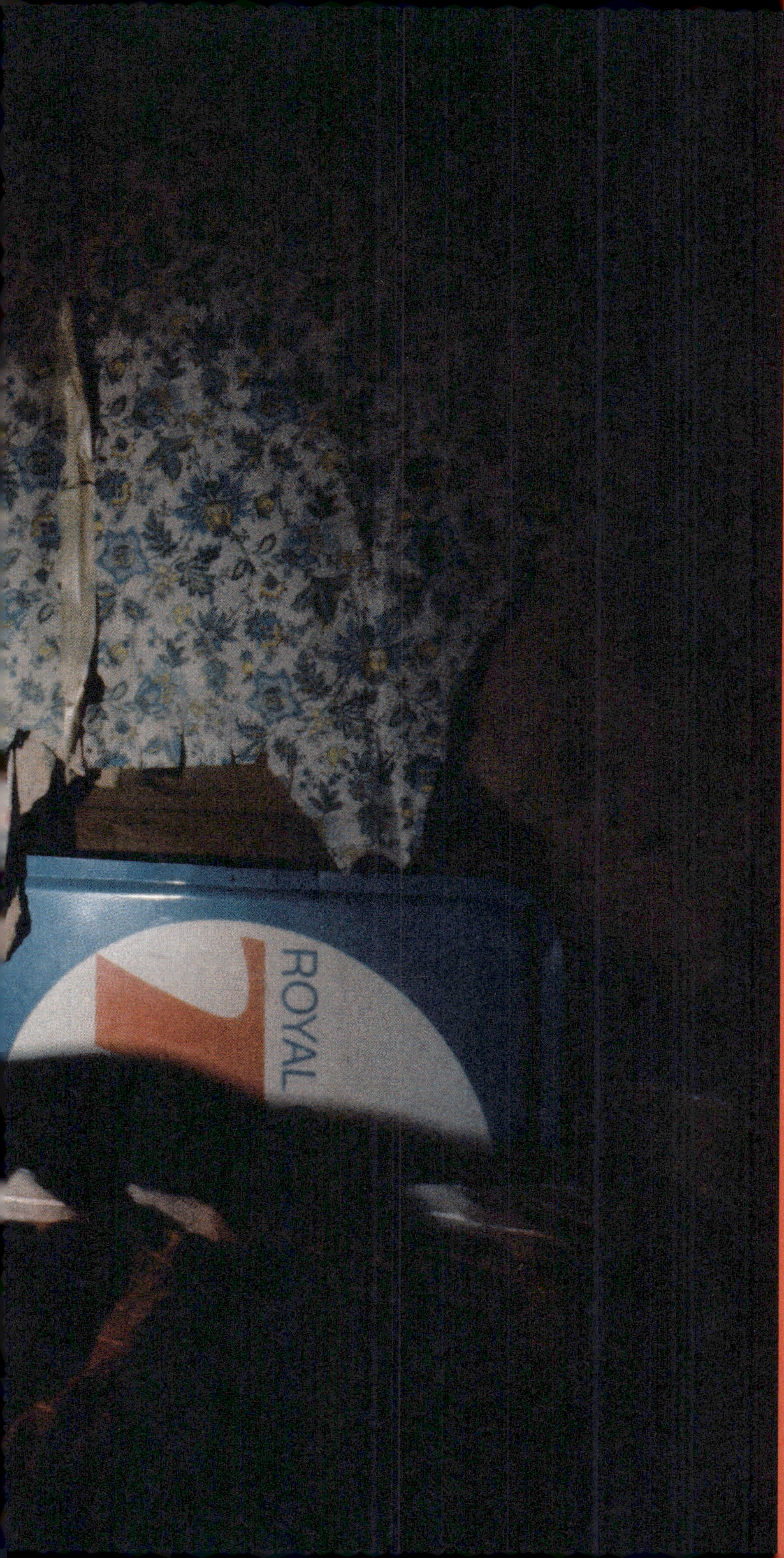
ROYAL

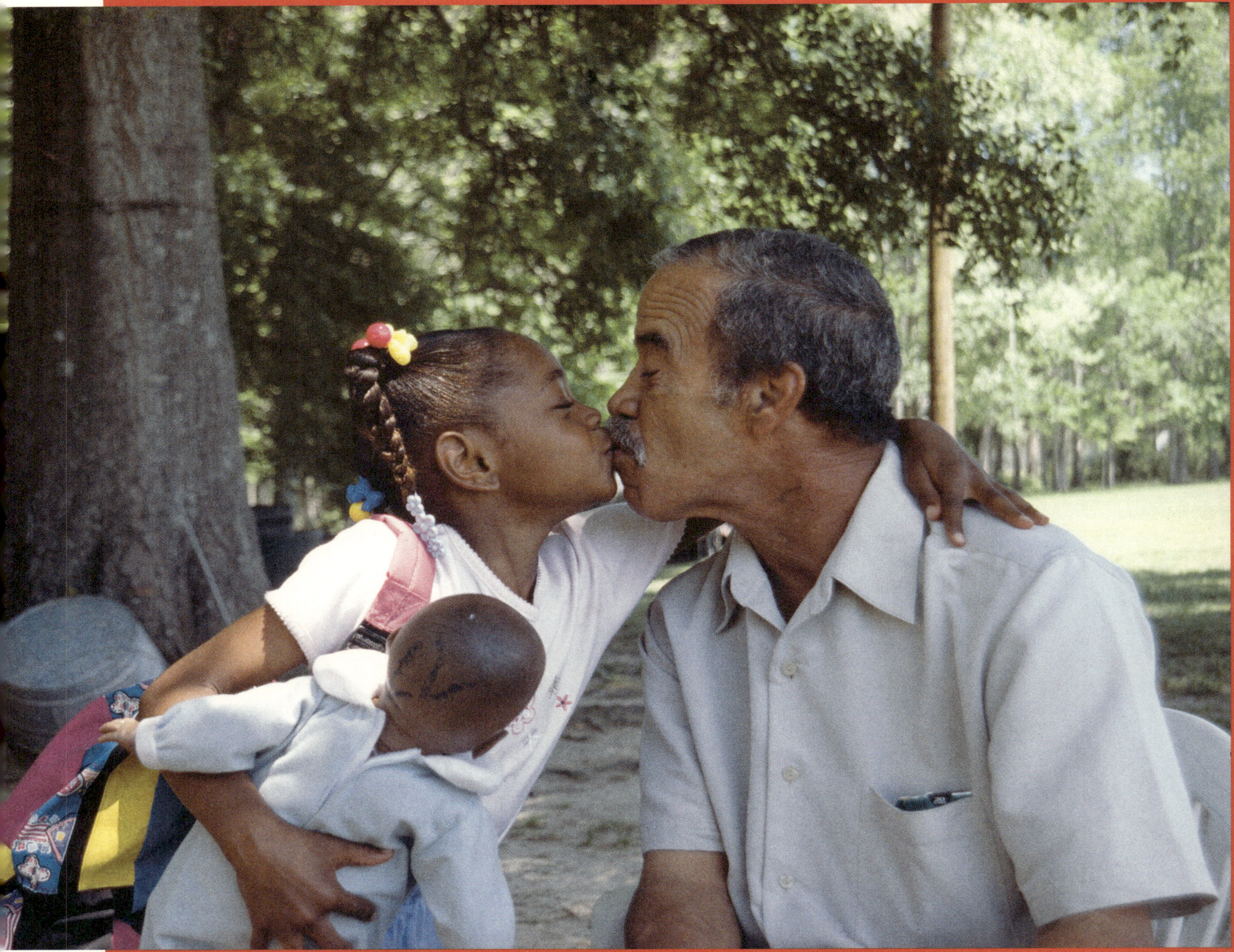

Prison guard with his step-grandchild. Tunica, LA. 2003

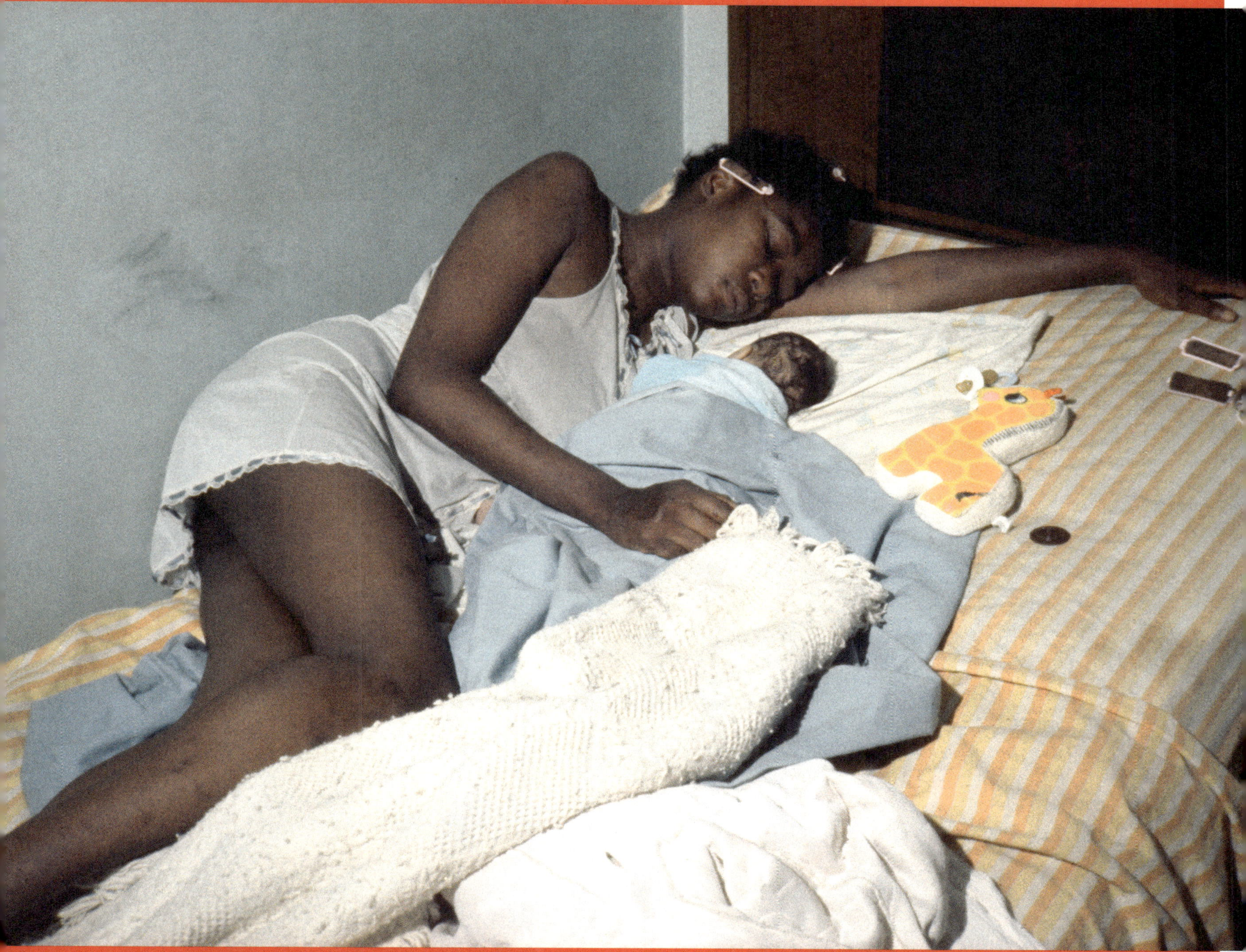

Evelyn Hall with her baby the day after its birth. Jersey City, N.J. 1974

police

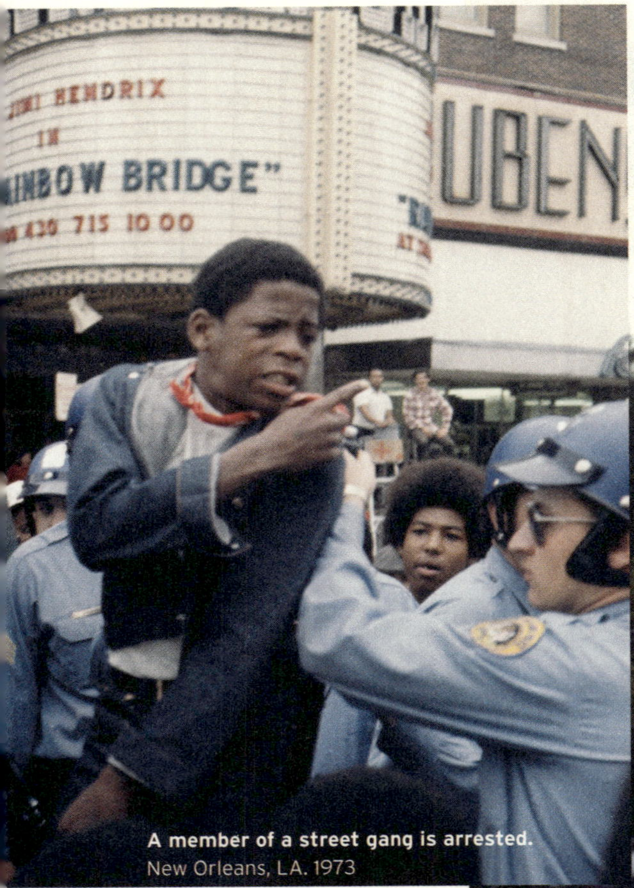

A member of a street gang is arrested. New Orleans, L.A. 1973

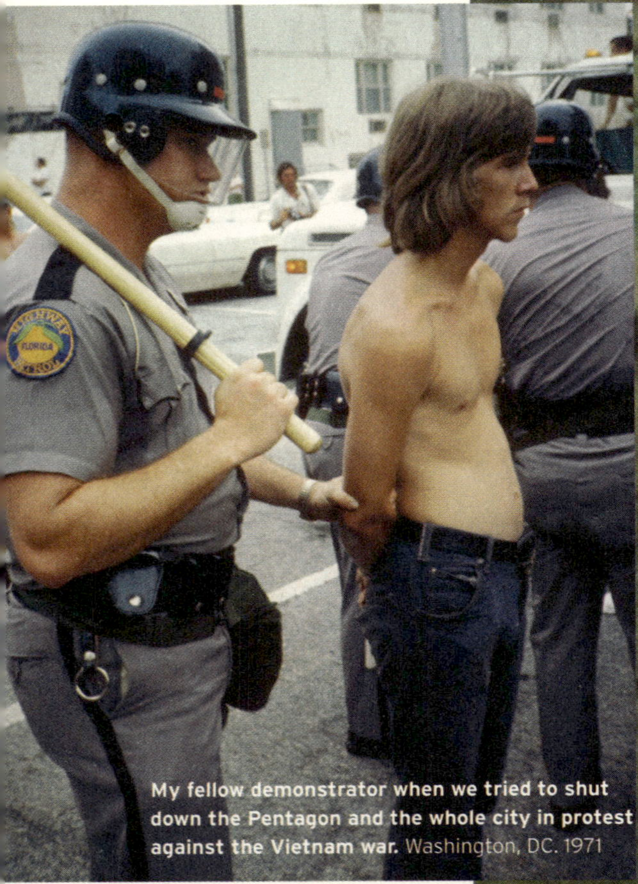

My fellow demonstrator when we tried to shut down the Pentagon and the whole city in protest against the Vietnam war. Washington, DC. 1971

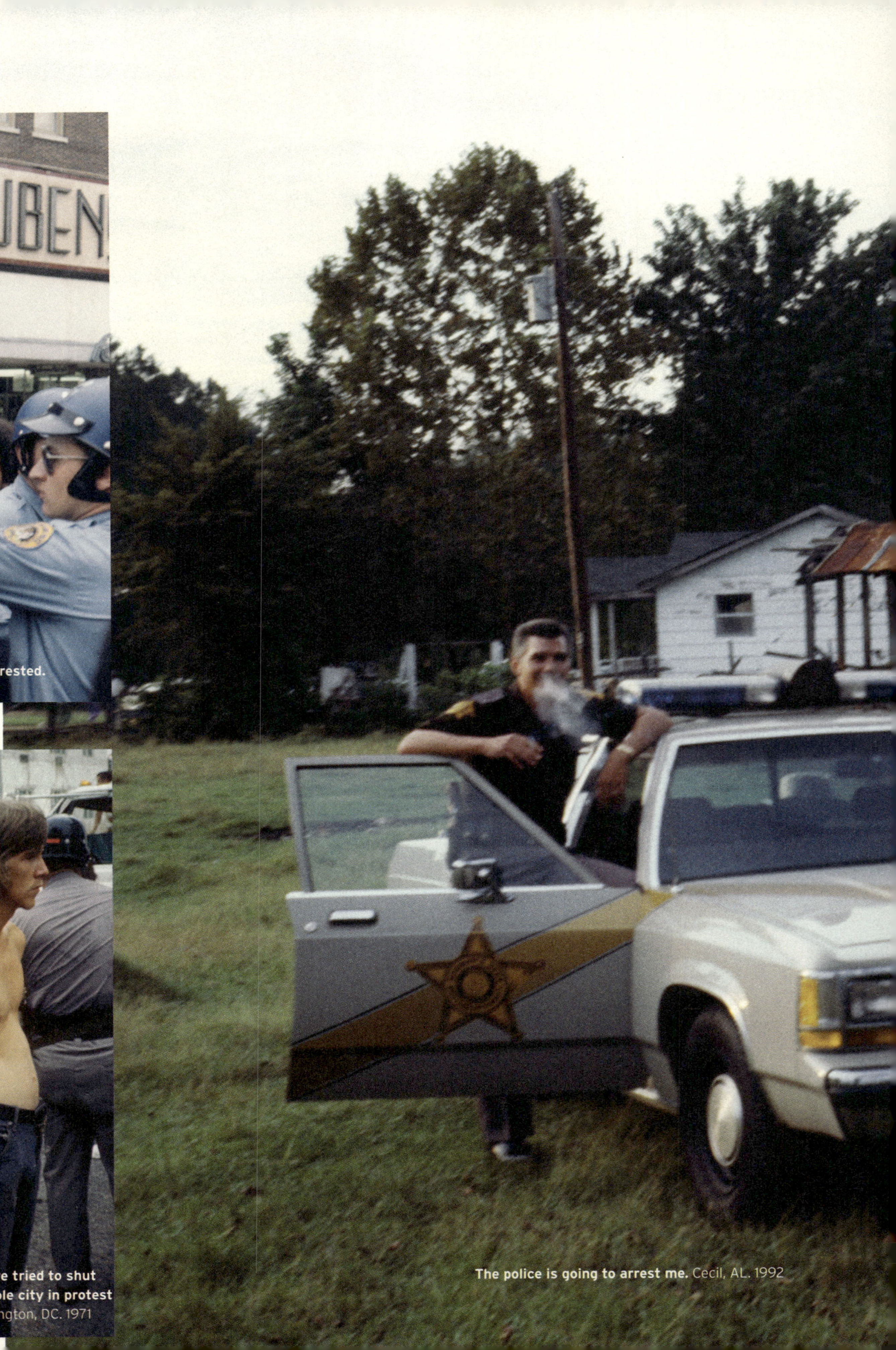

The police is going to arrest me. Cecil, AL. 1992

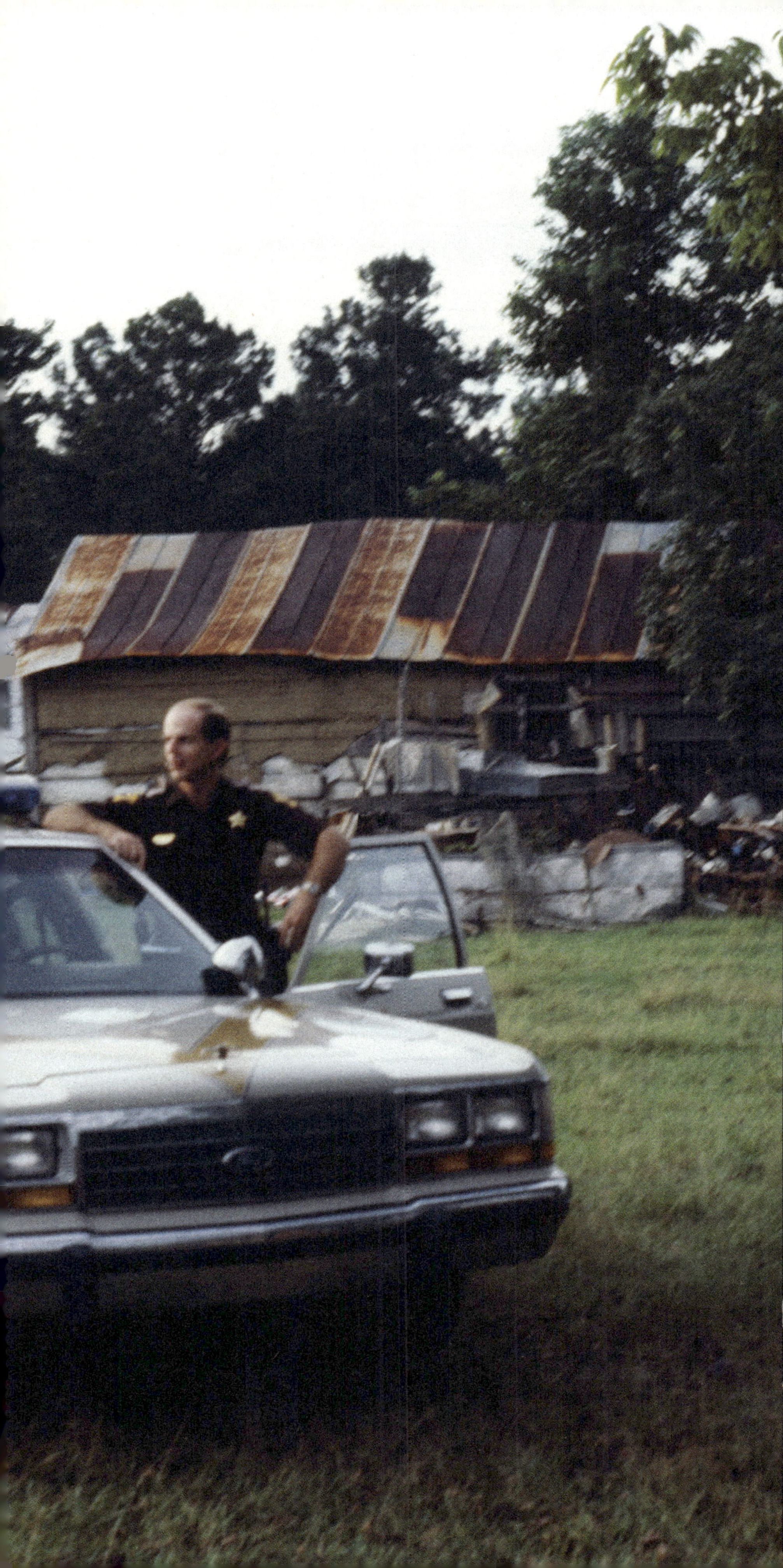

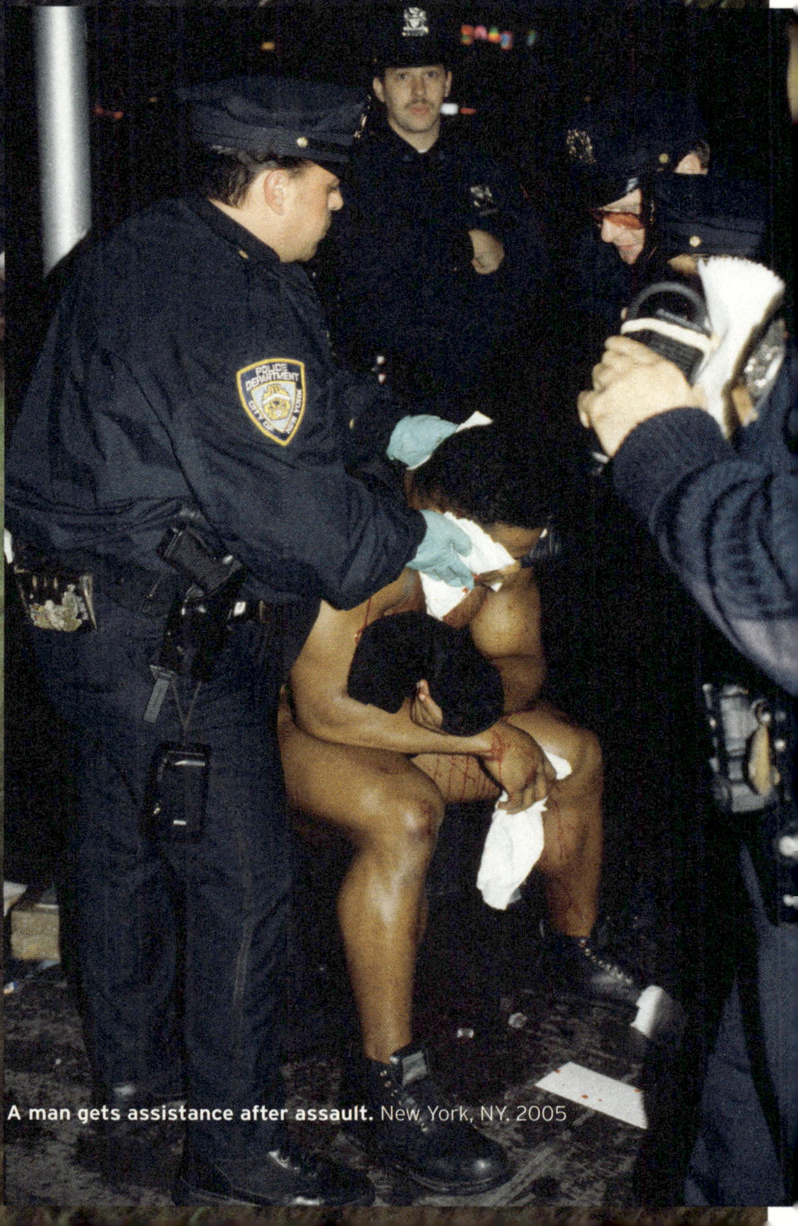

A man gets assistance after assault. New York, NY. 2005

Martha

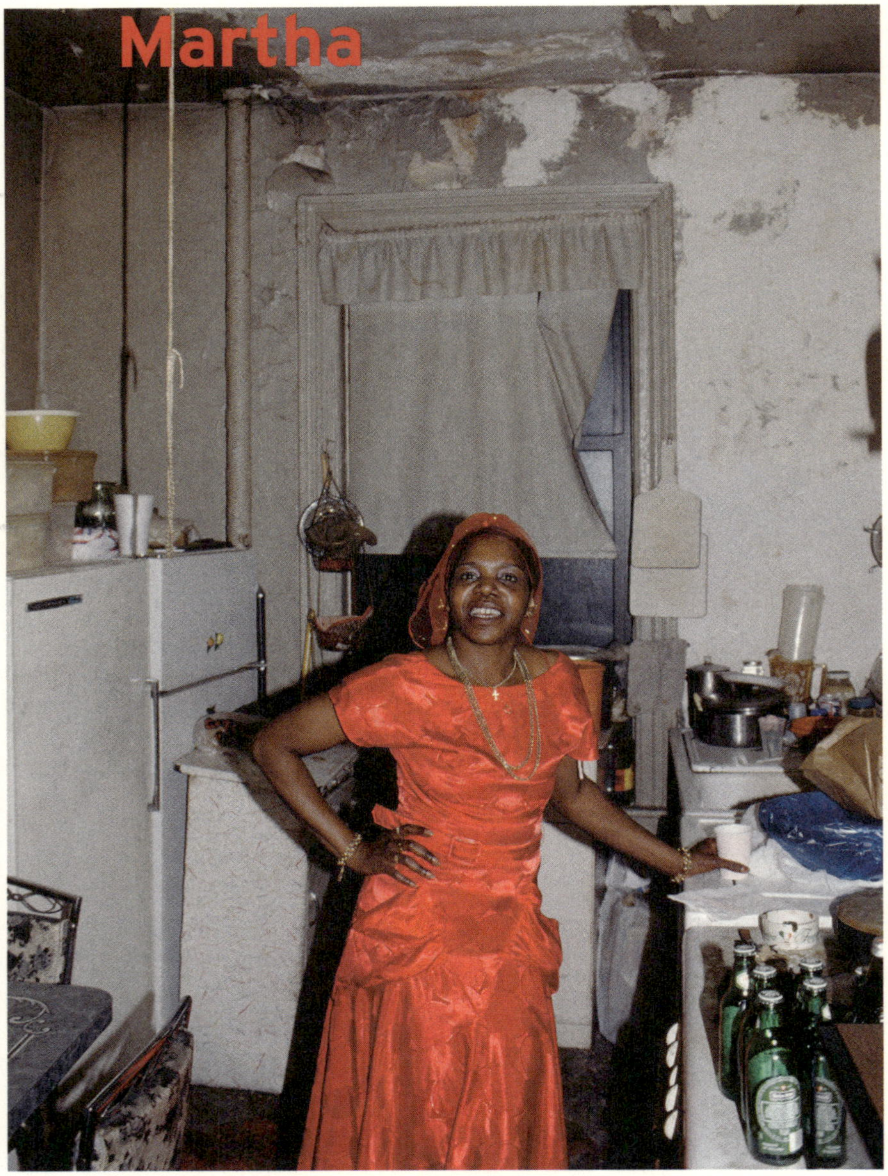

Martha, a 'woman about town', when I stayed with her the first time. Harlem, NY. 1987

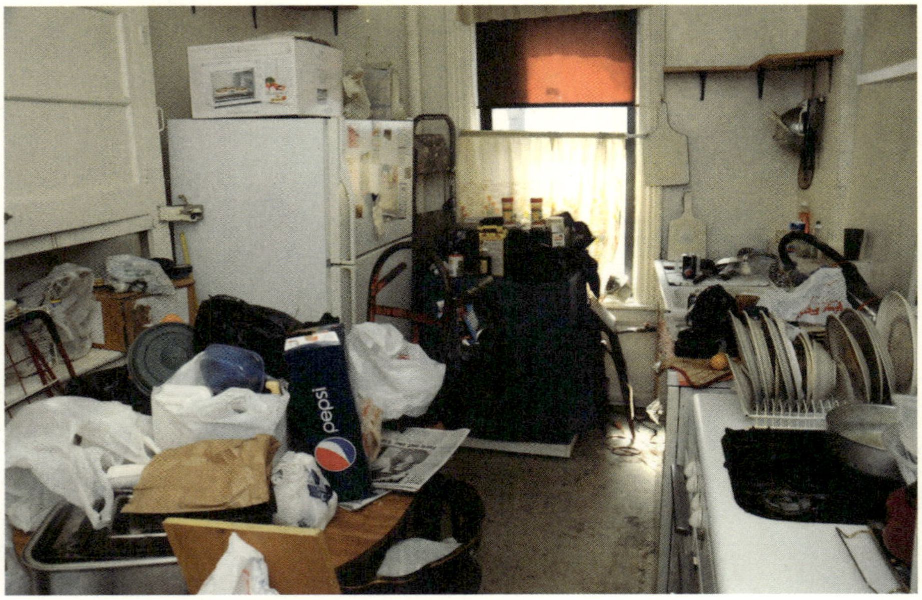

Martha's kitchen. Harlem, NY. 2009

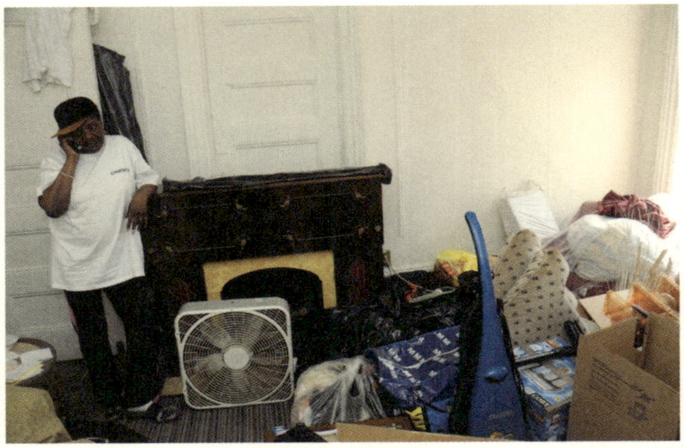

Martha in the living room where I normally sleep. Harlem, NY. 2009

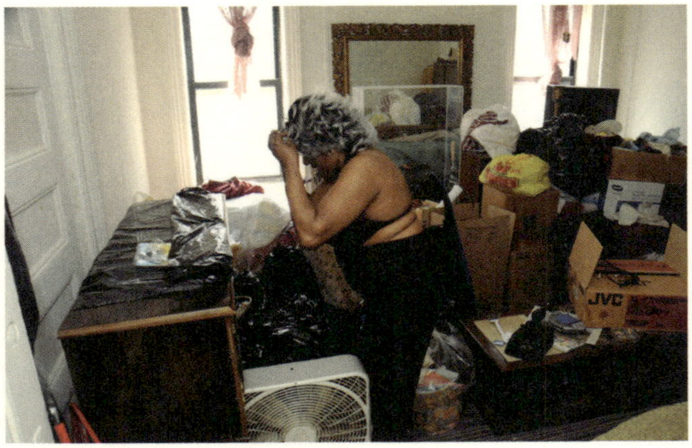

Martha changes wig. Harlem, NY. 2009

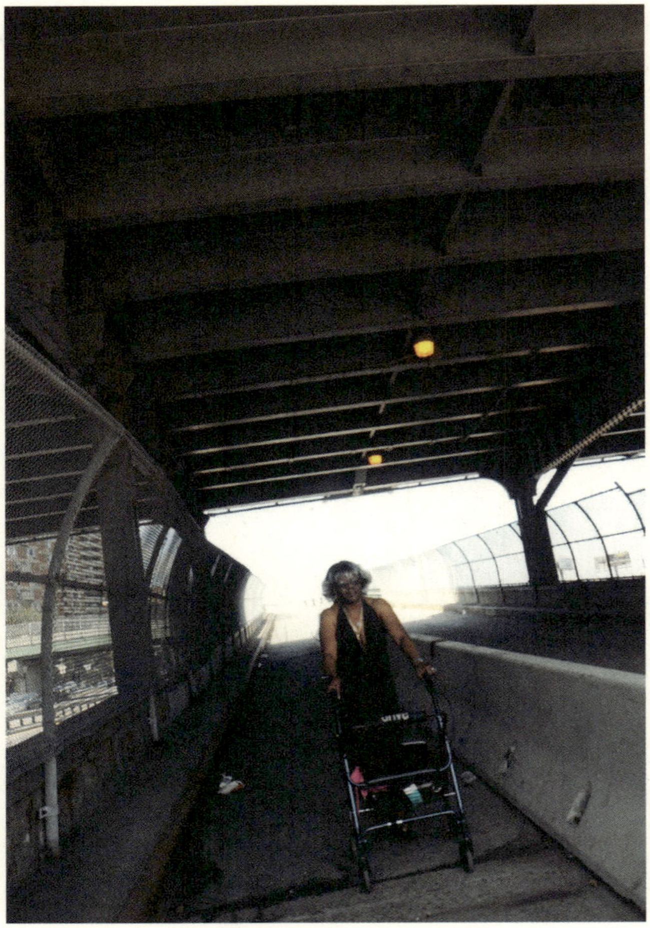

Martha on her way to the park. Harlem, NY. 2009

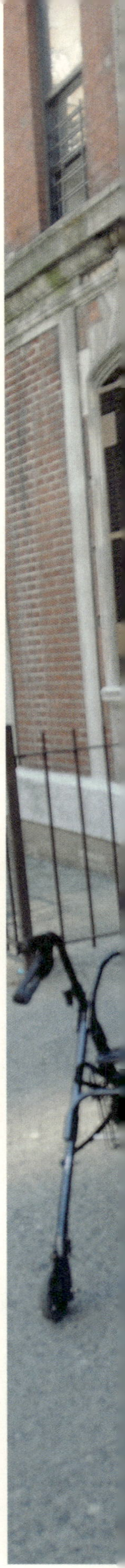

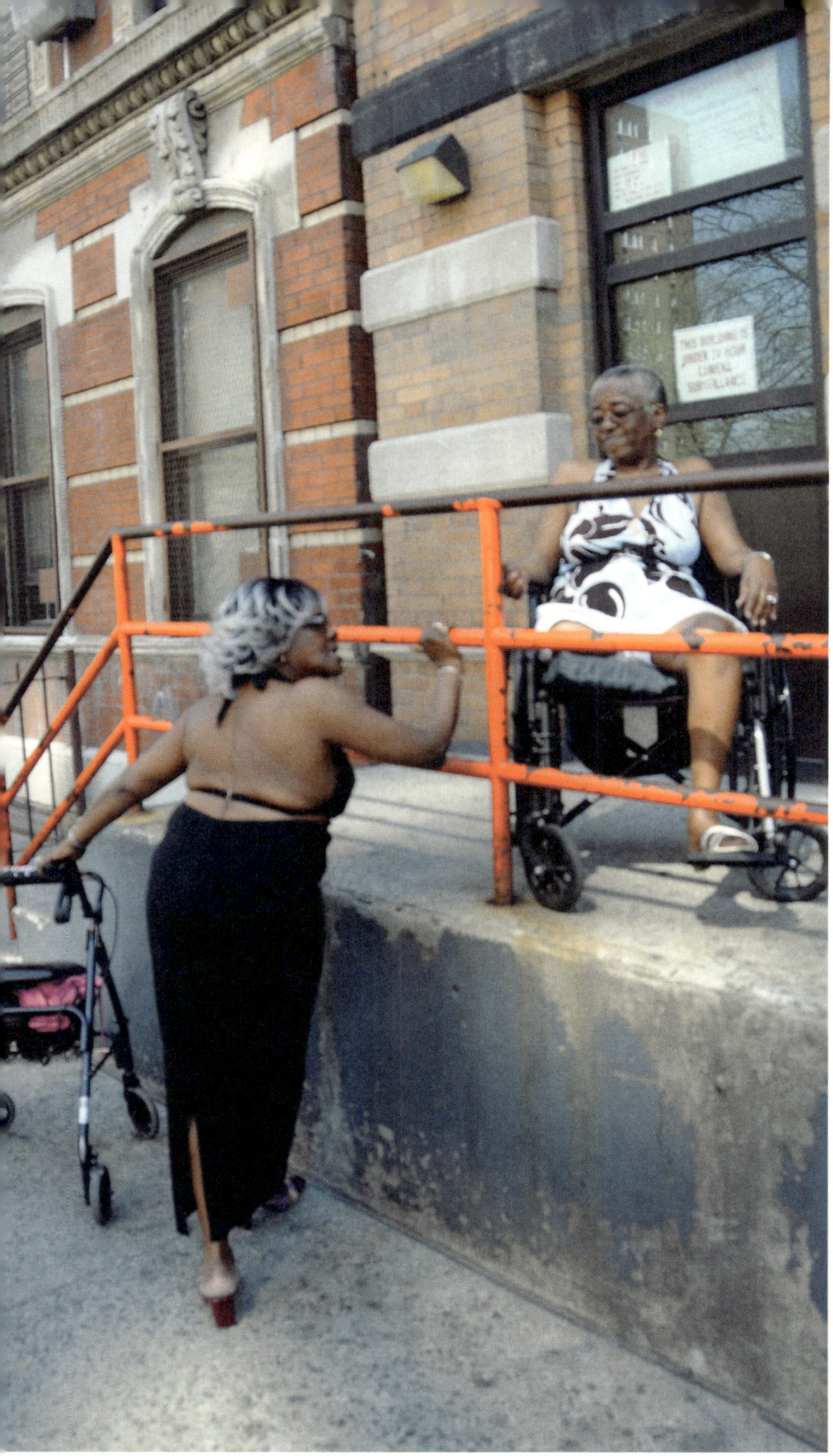

Martha seeing friends. Harlem, NY. 2009

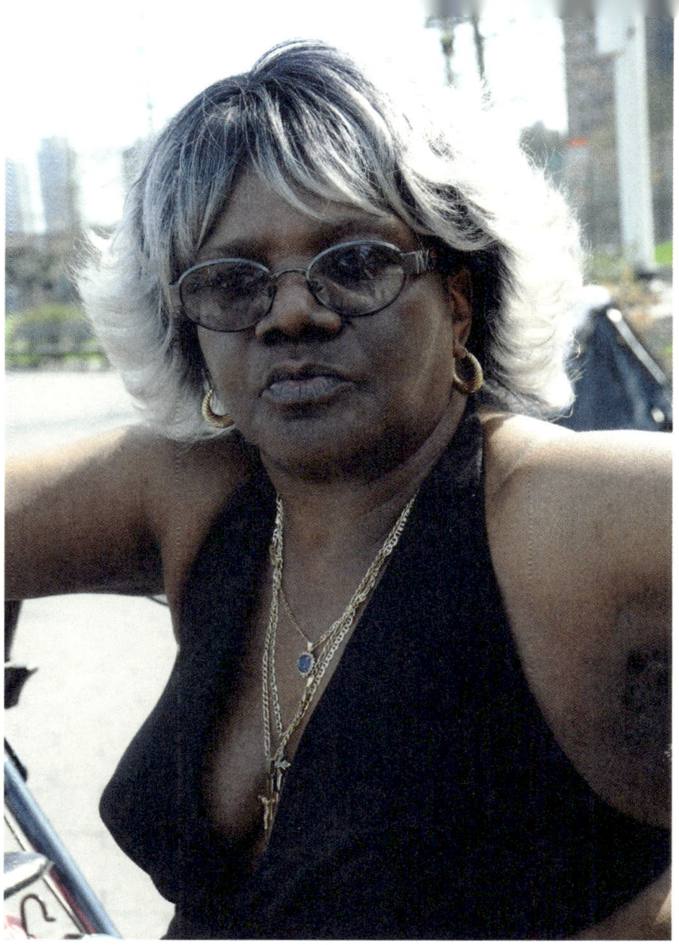

Martha by the river. Harlem, NY. 2009

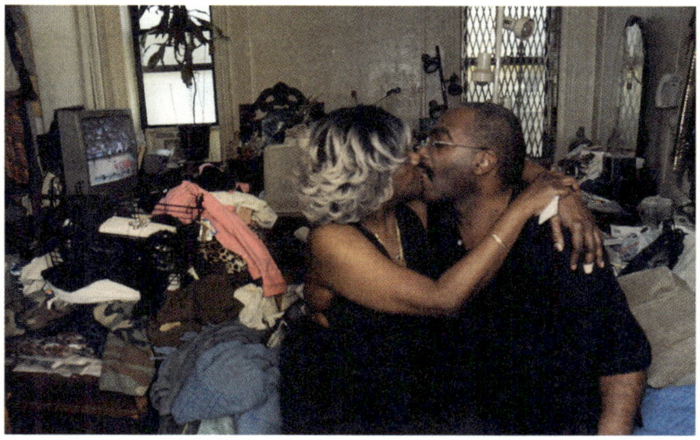

Martha with a client / lover. Harlem, NY. 2009

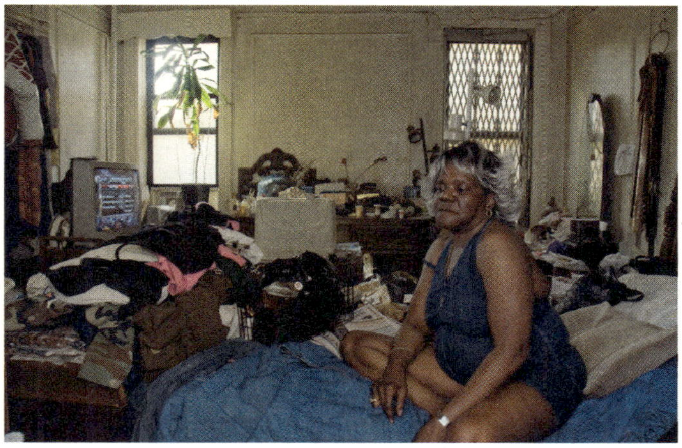

Martha in her bedroom. Harlem, NY. 2009

prisons

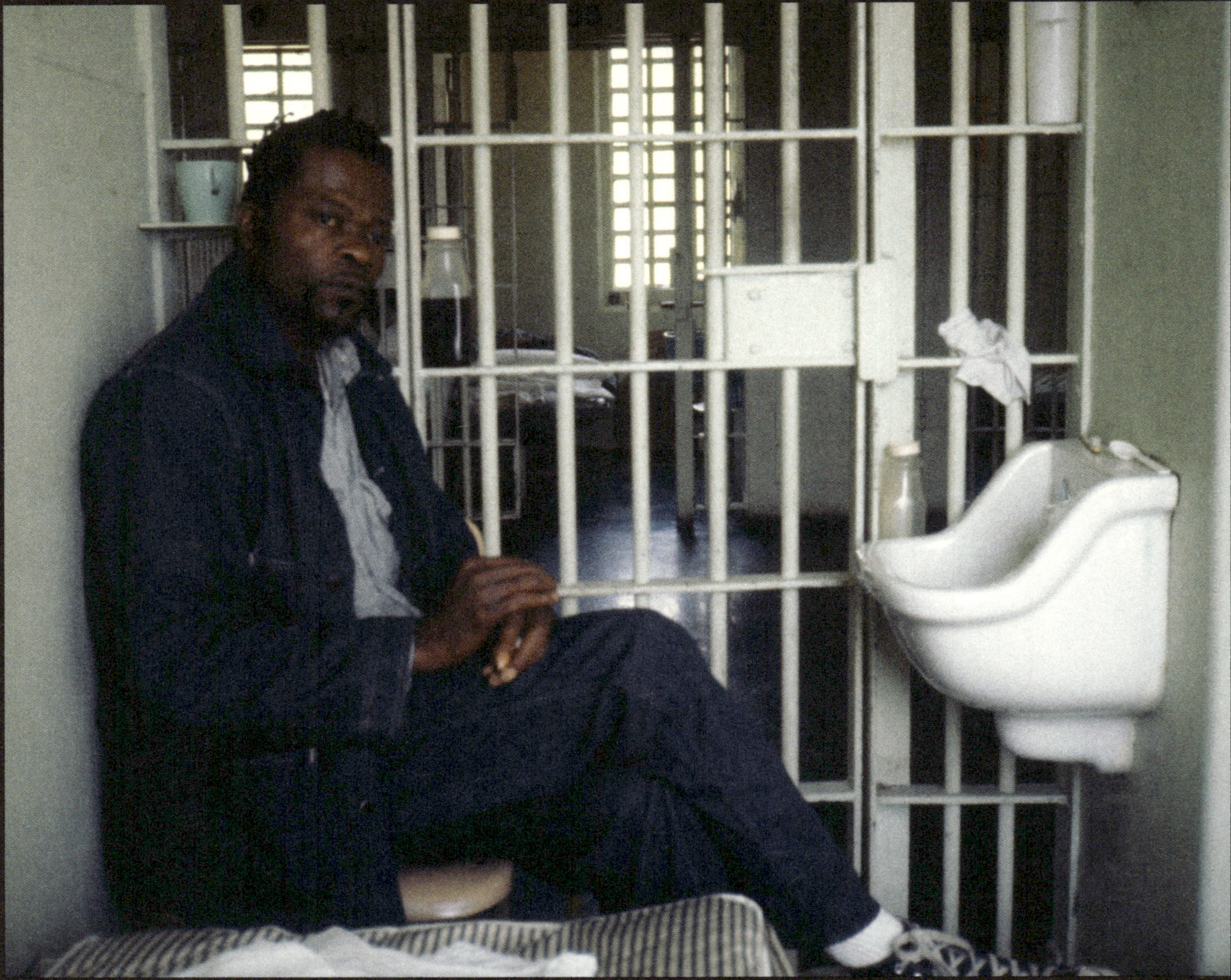

Popeye a week before he is murdered. San Francisco, CA. 1975

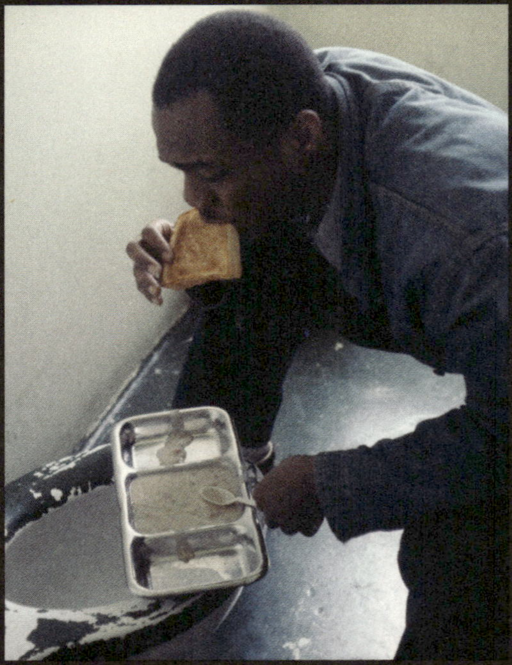

Prisoner eats his dinner. San Bruno. CA. 1975

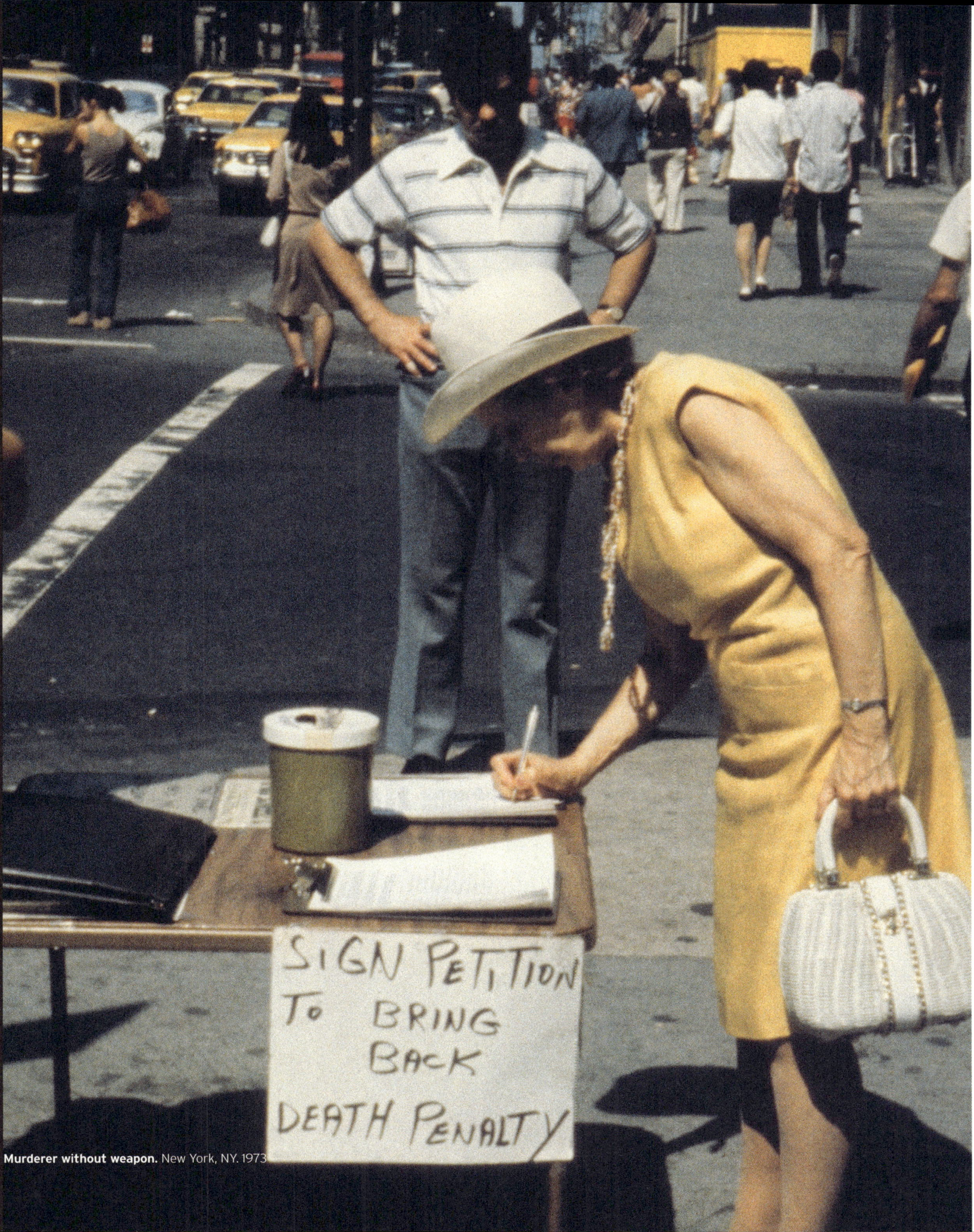

Murderer without weapon. New York, NY. 1973

highways

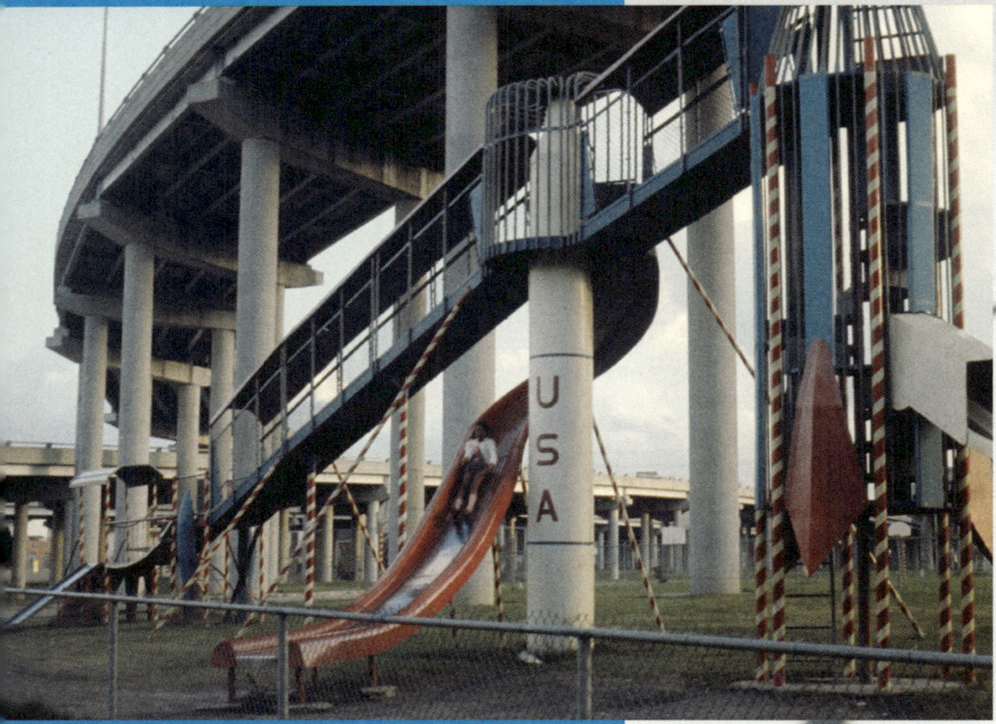

Playground. Baton Rouge, LA. 1973

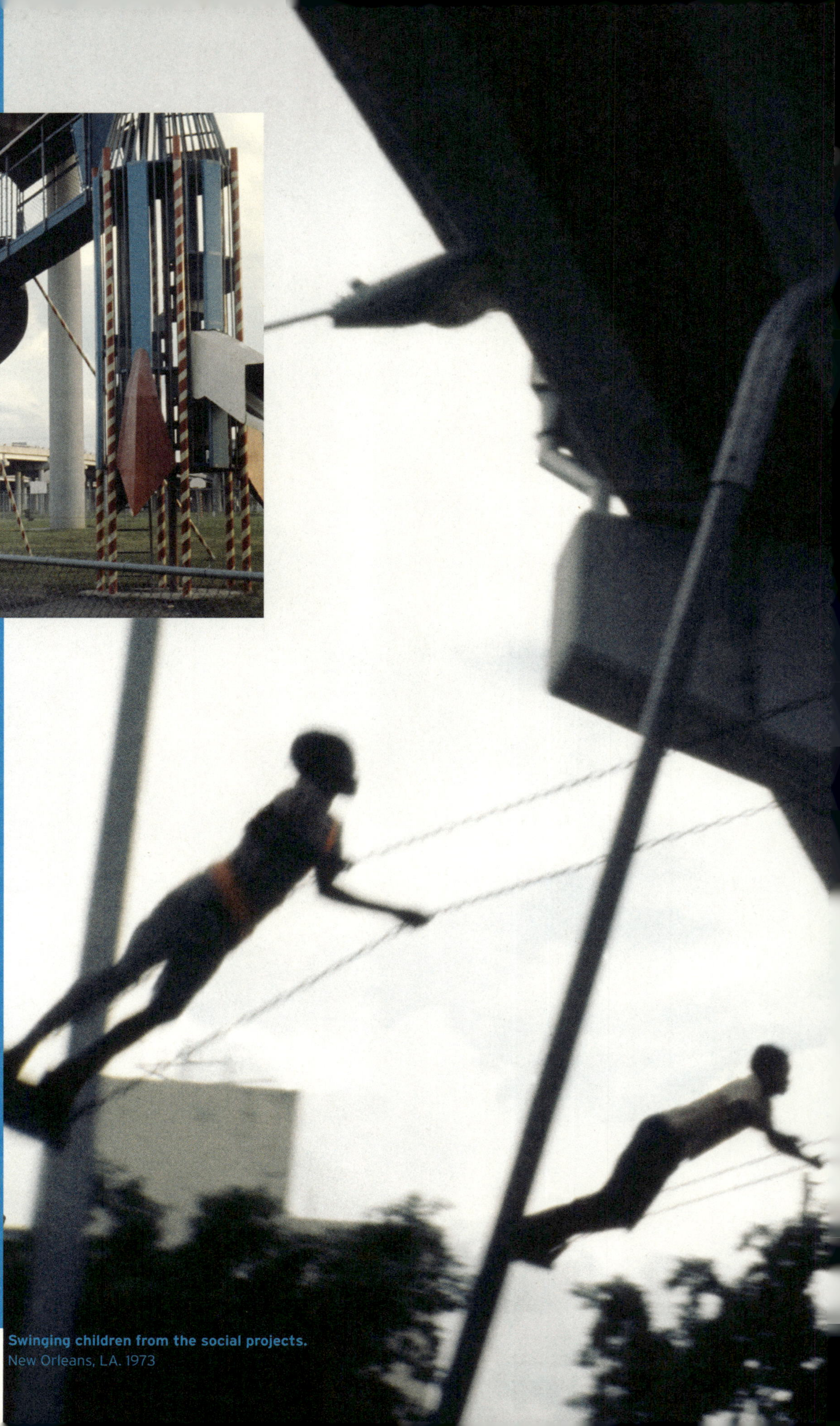

Swinging children from the social projects.
New Orleans, LA. 1973

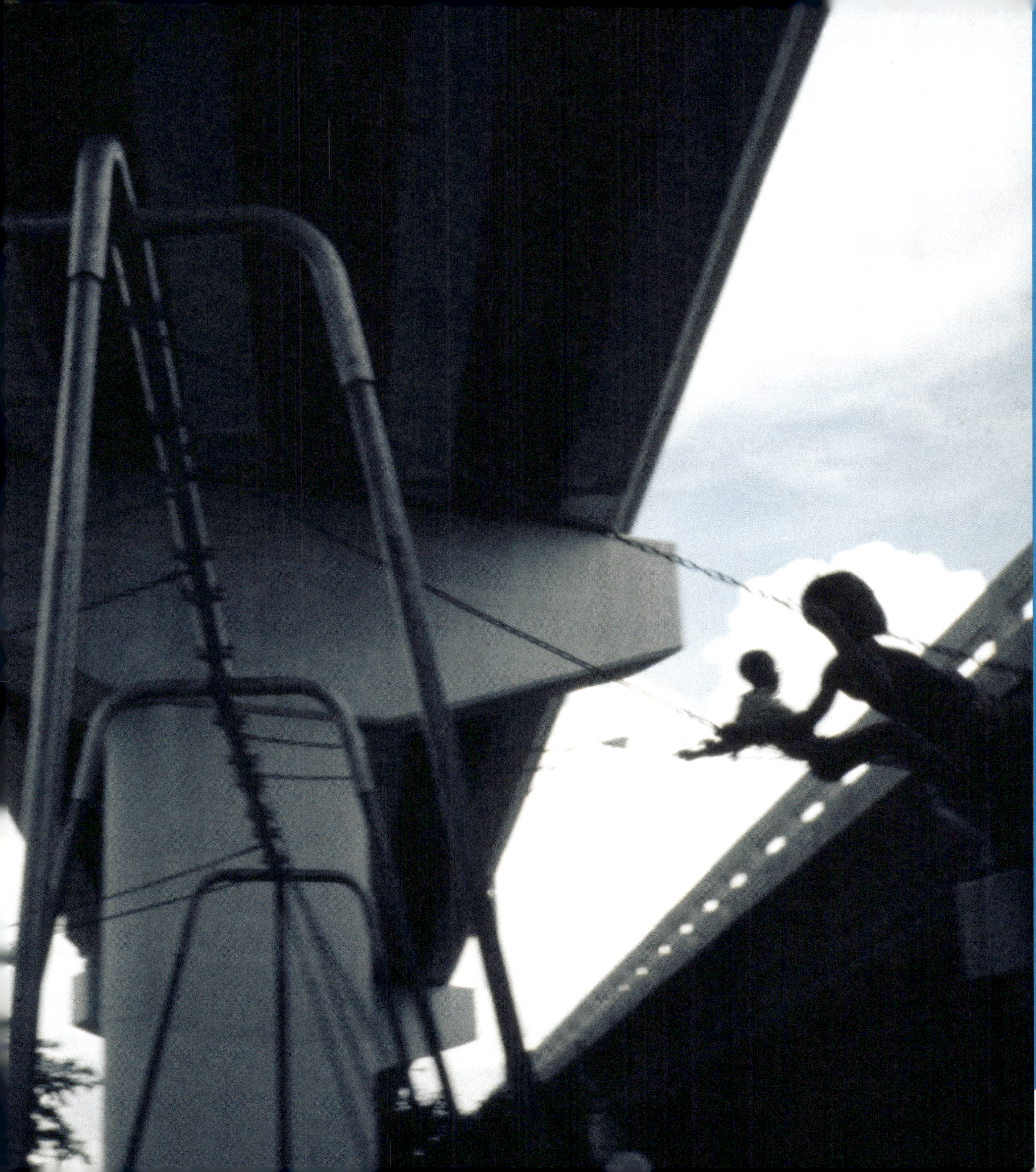

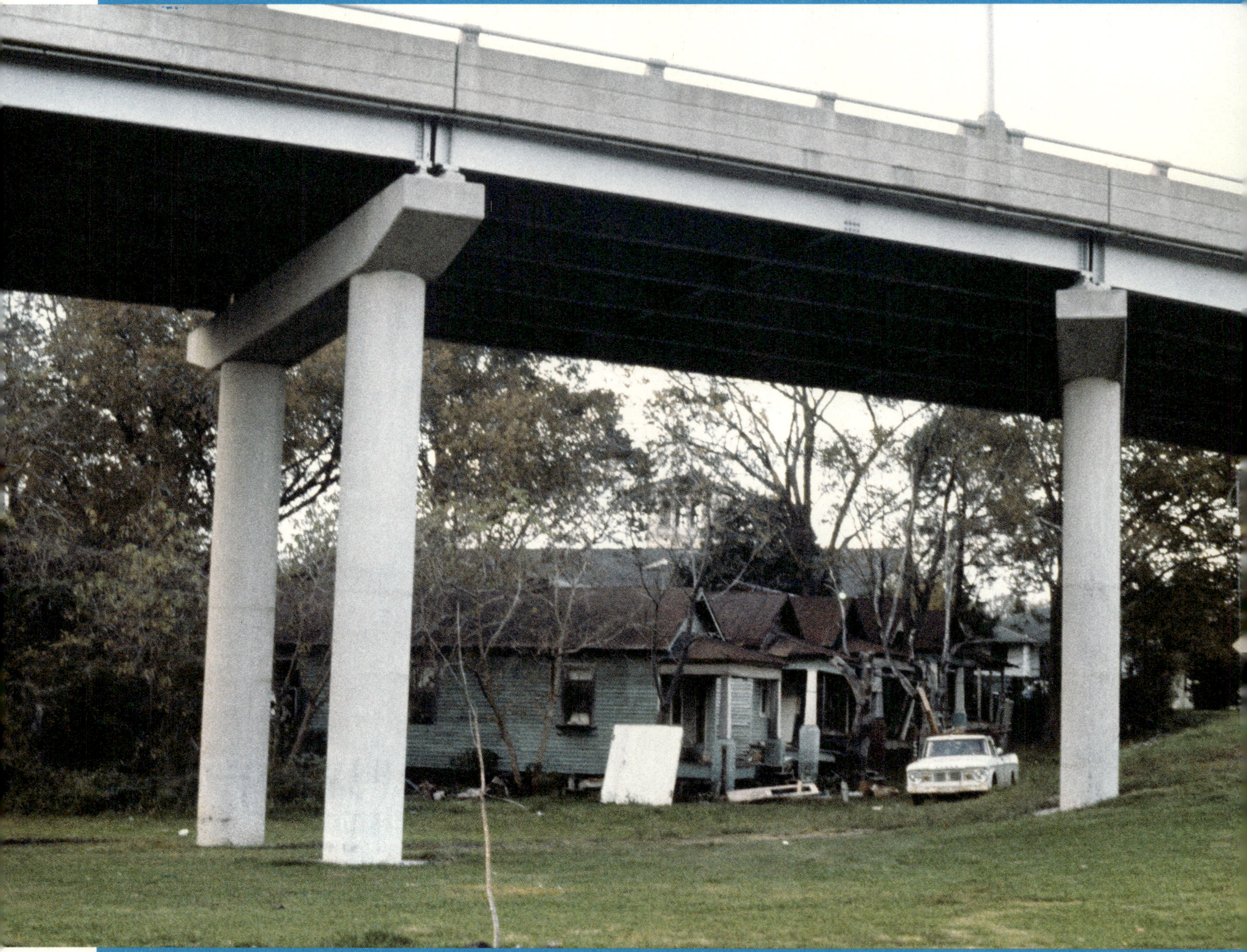

Many of the same people still live there. Baton Rouge, LA. 1973

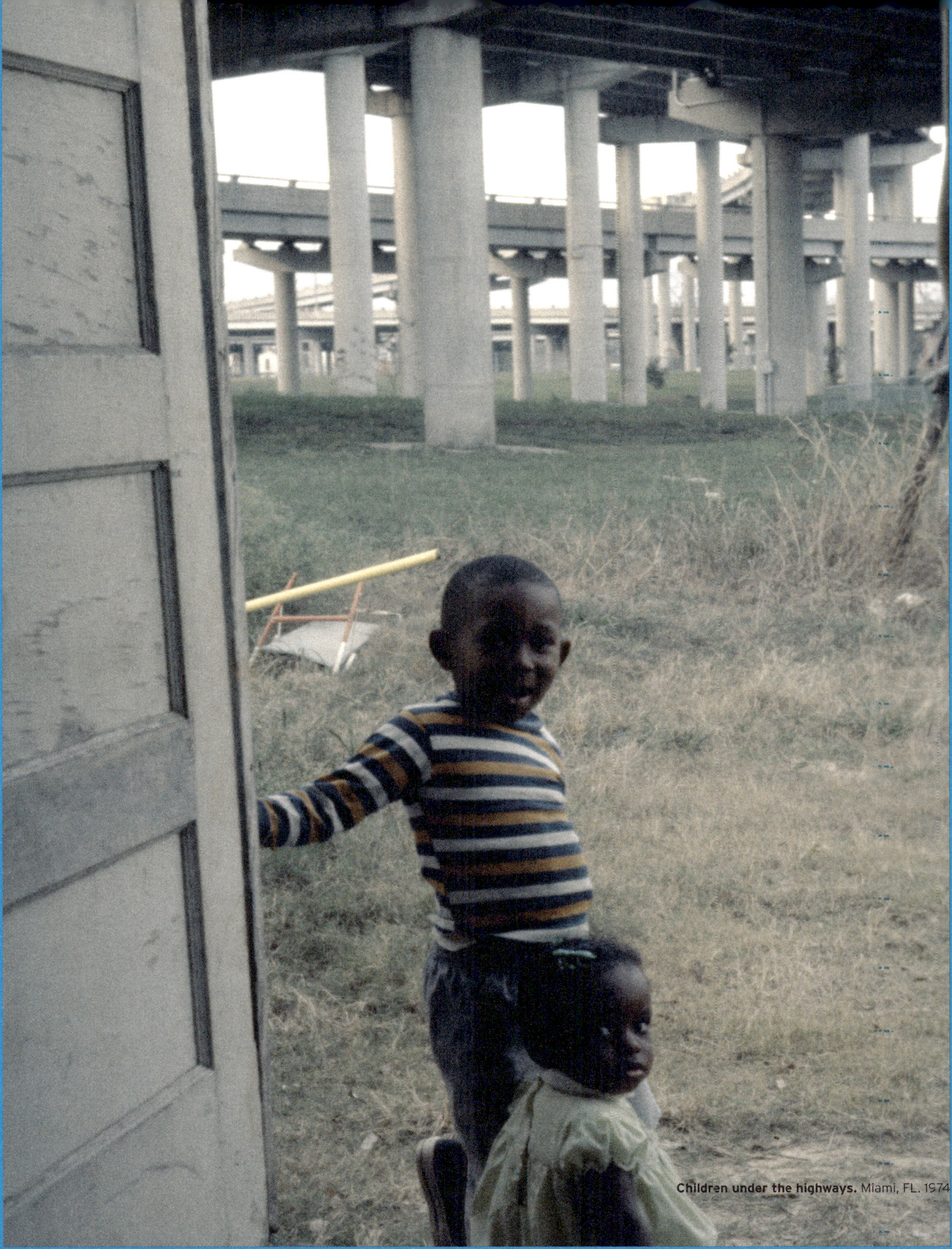

Children under the highways. Miami, FL. 1974

death

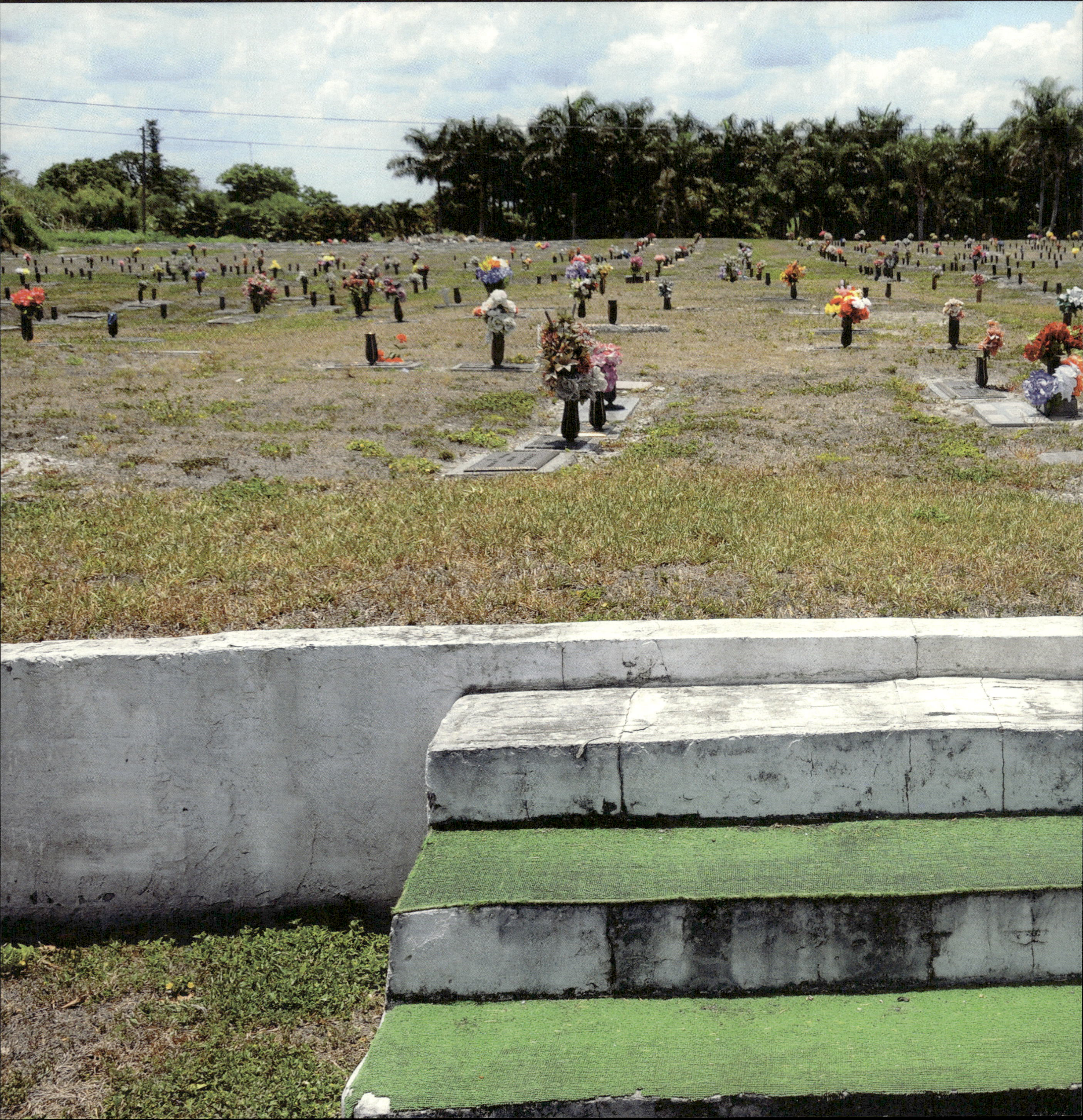

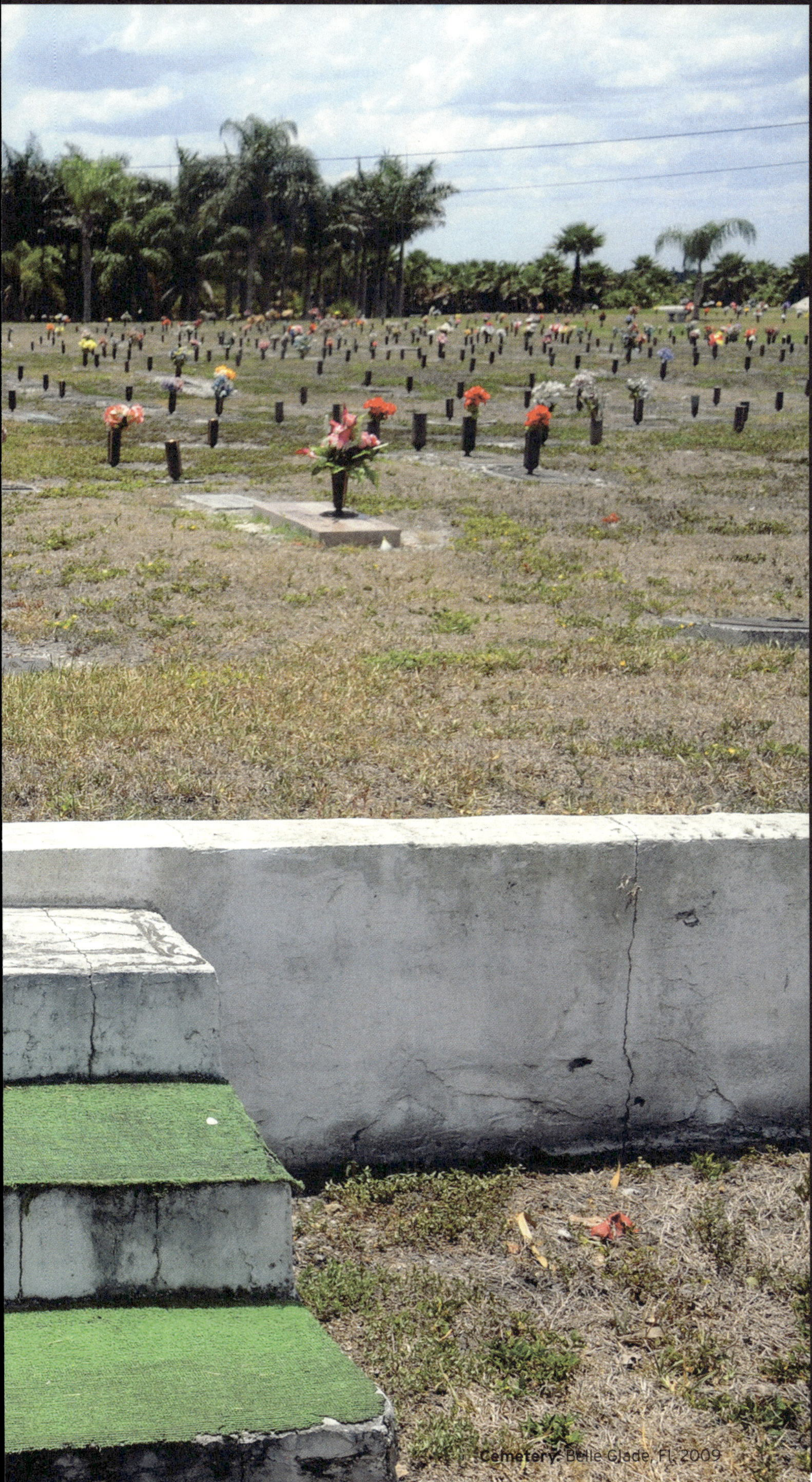

Cemetery. Belle Glade, FL 2009

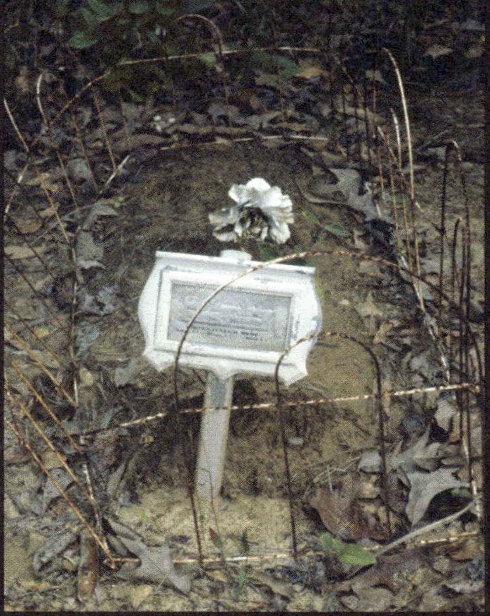

A child grave. Lisbon, NC. 1974

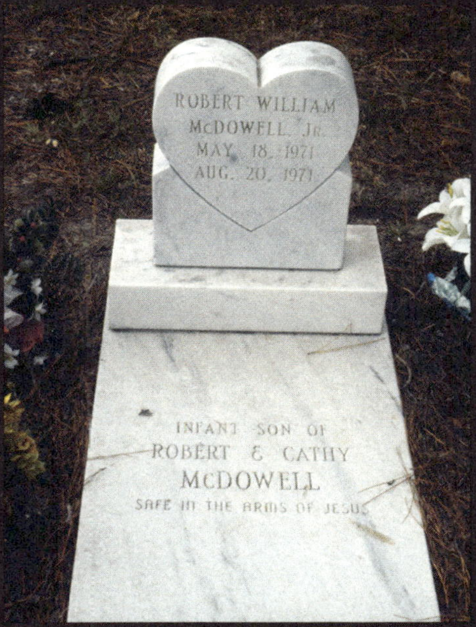

A white child's grave. Wilmington, NC. 1974

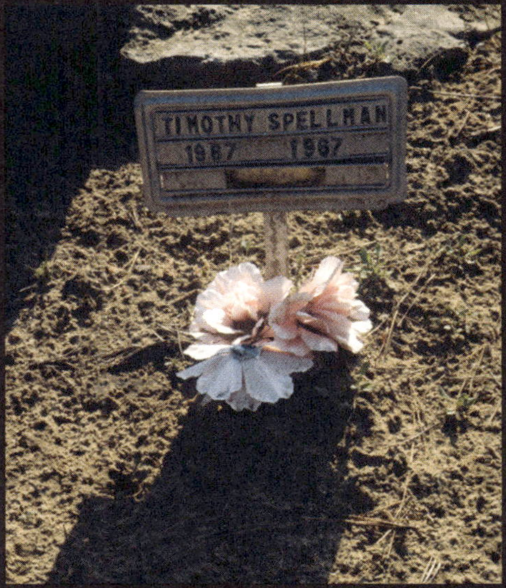

A child grave. Washington, NC. 1974

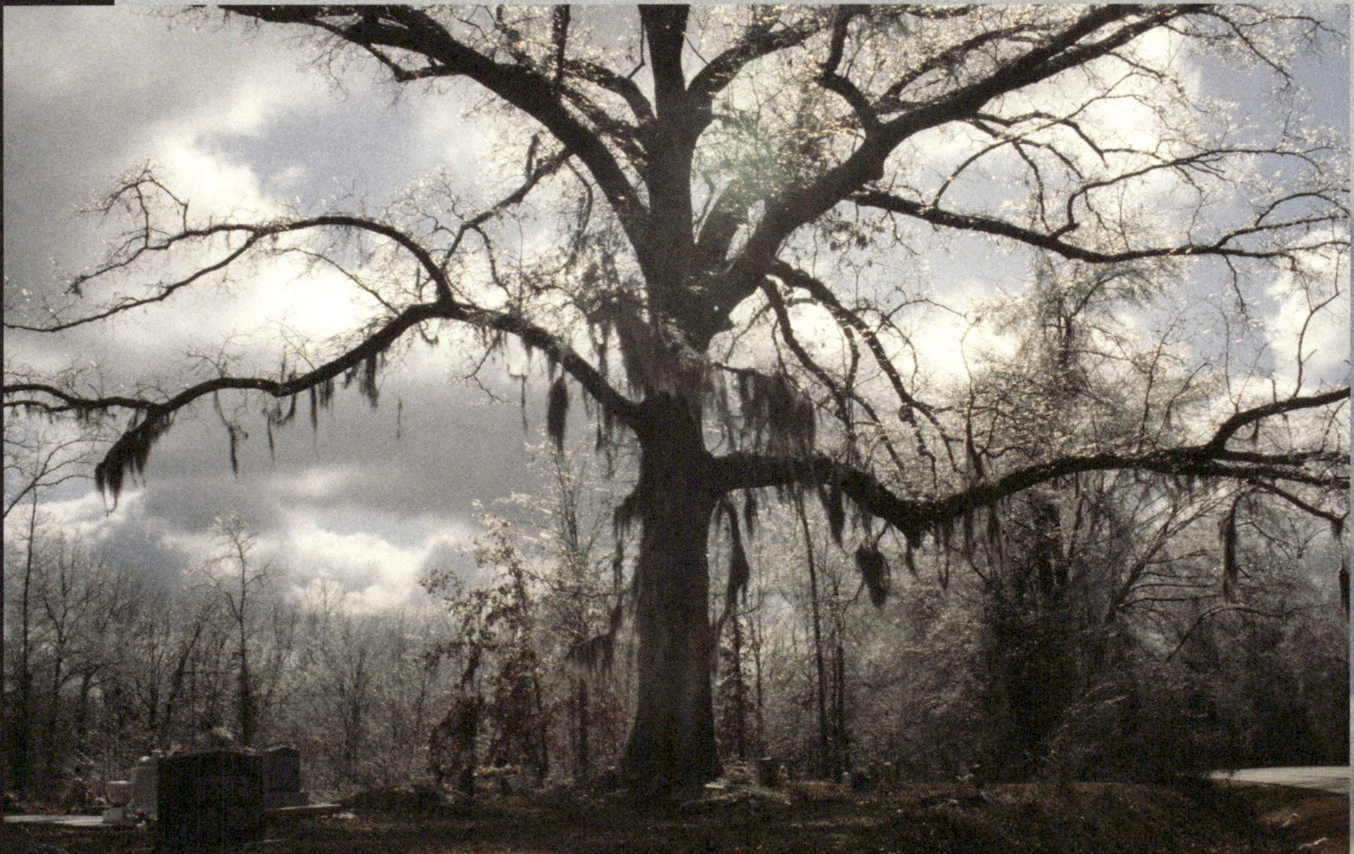

Cemetery for blacks - after an ice storm. Natchez, MS. 1996

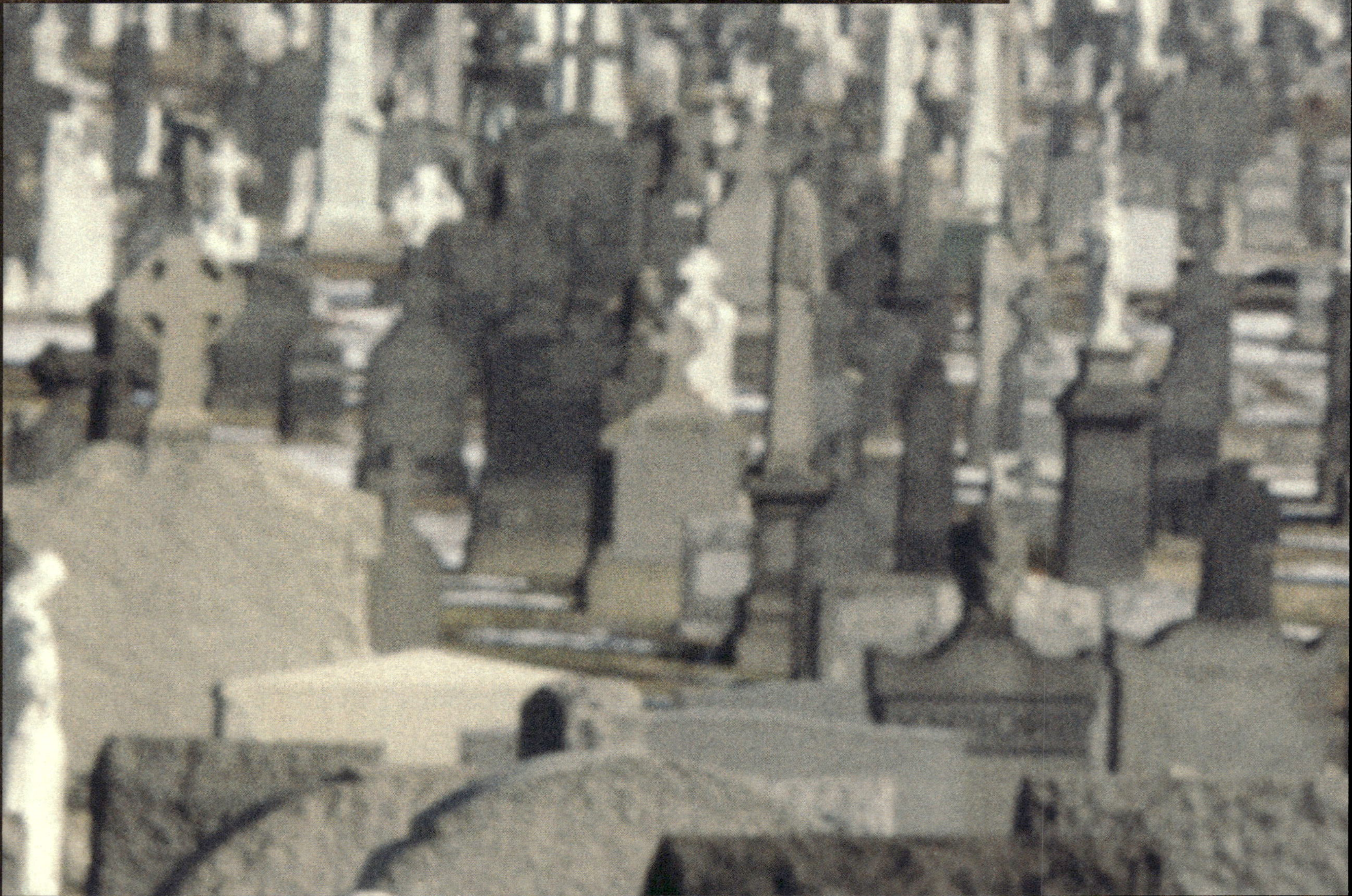

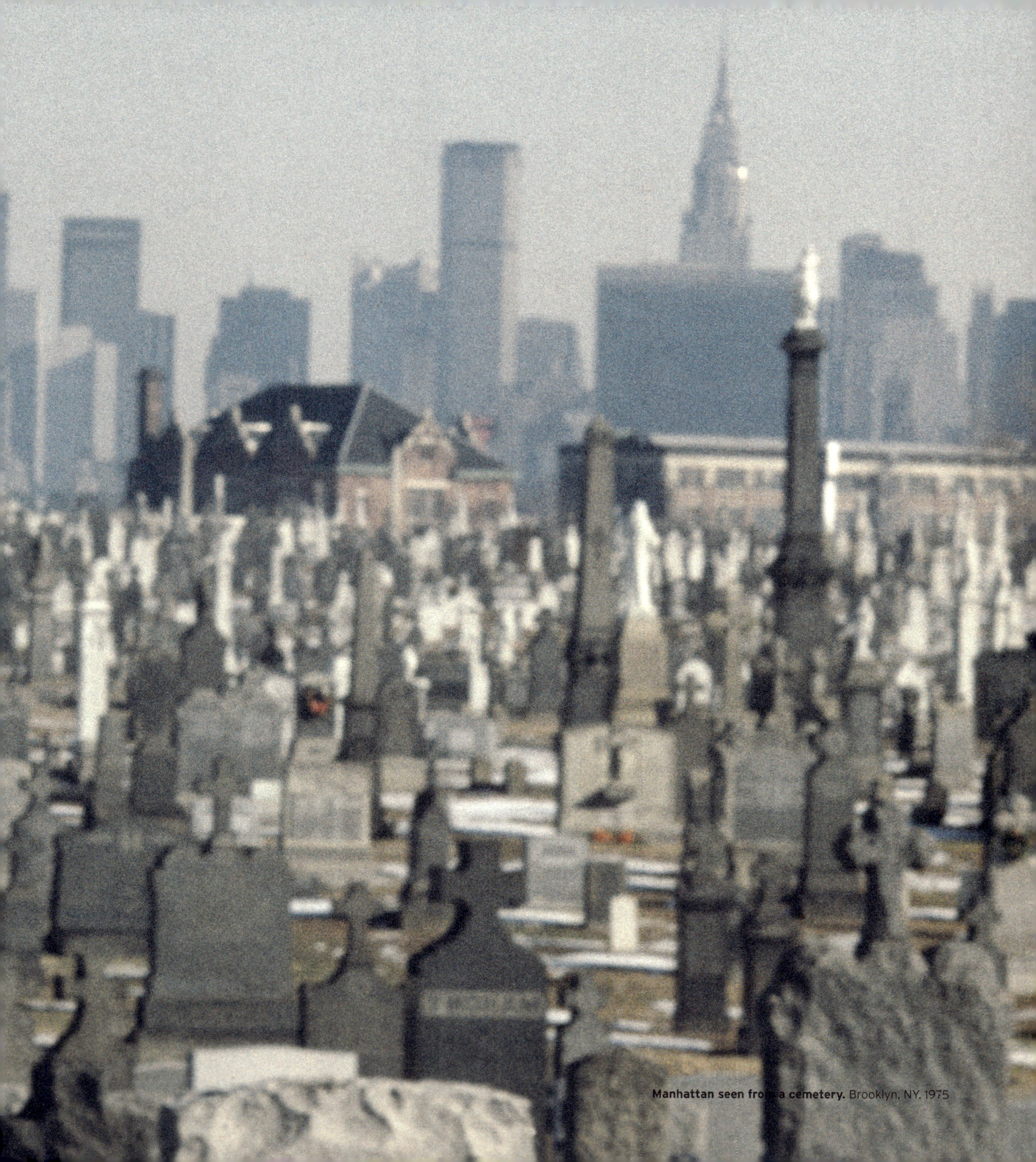

Manhattan seen from a cemetery. Brooklyn, NY. 1975

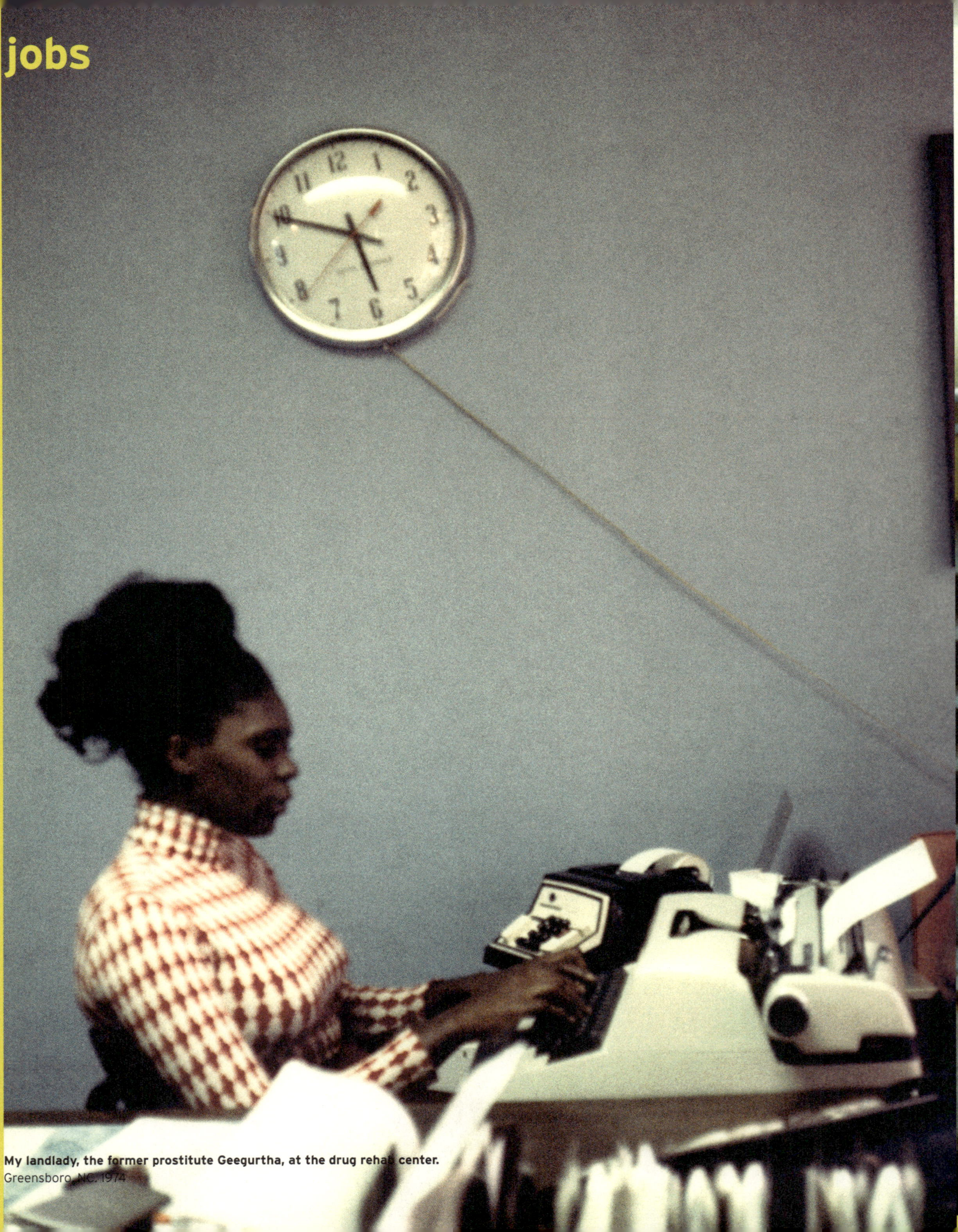

My landlady, the former prostitute Geegurtha, at the drug rehab center.
Greensboro, NC. 1974

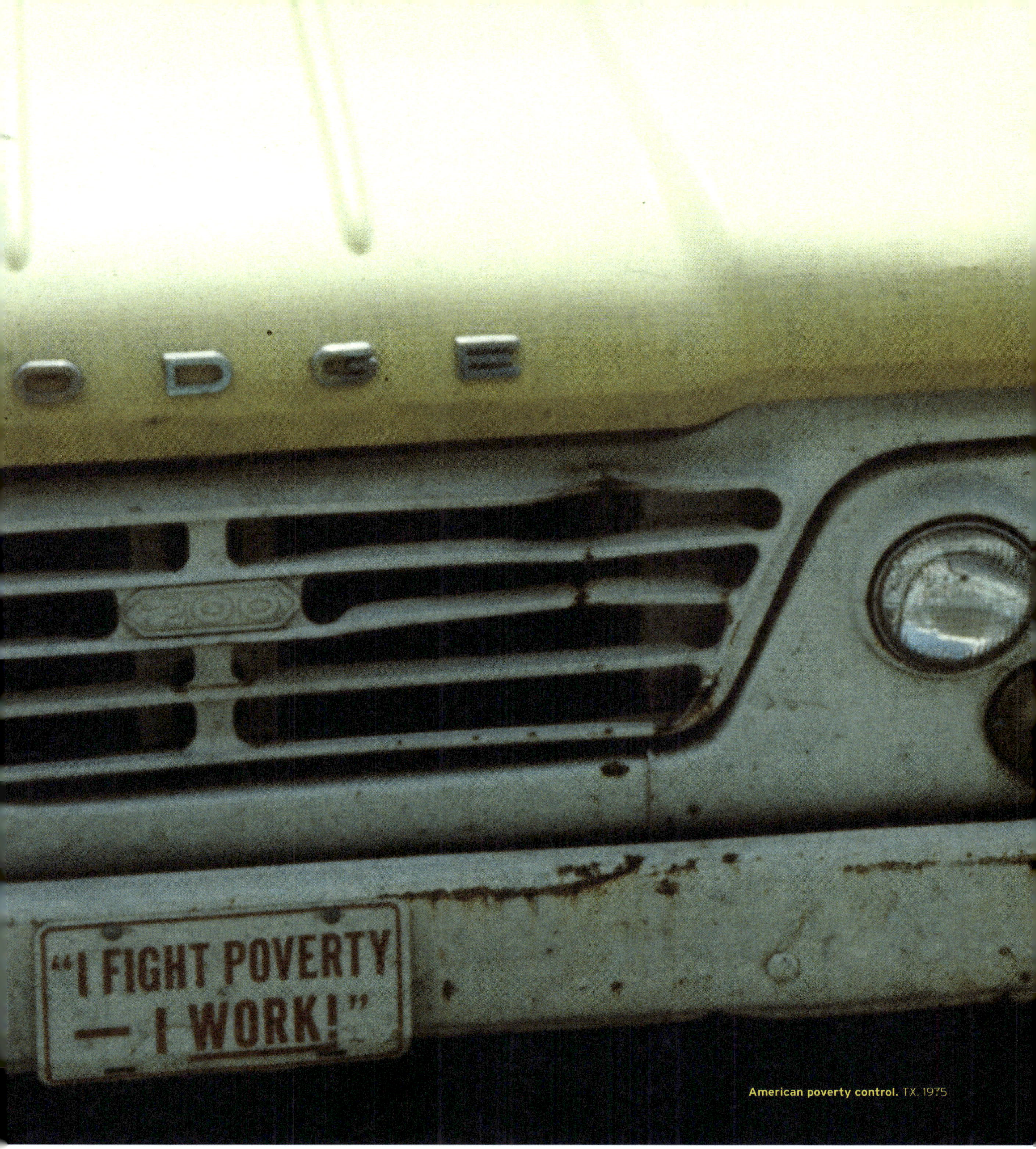

American poverty control. TX. 1975

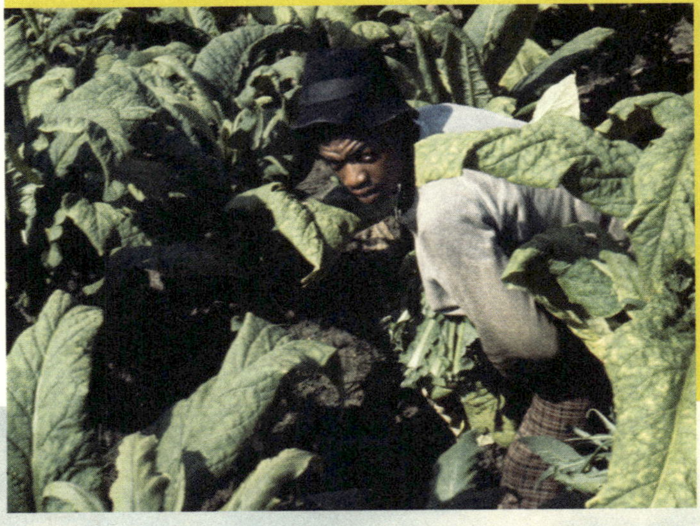

Tobacco picker.
Tarboro, NC. 1974

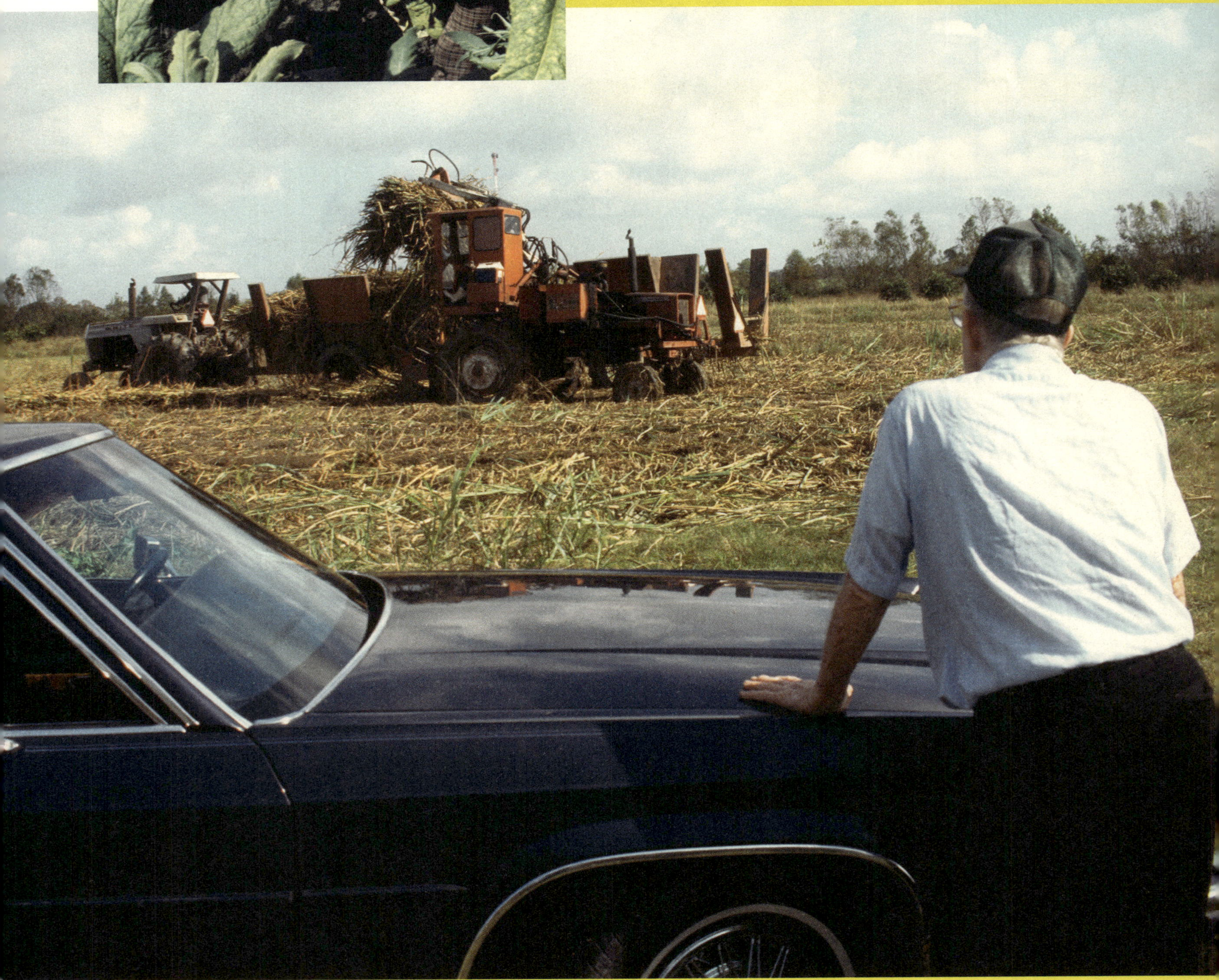

Planter watching his sugar cane workers. Houma, LA. 1996

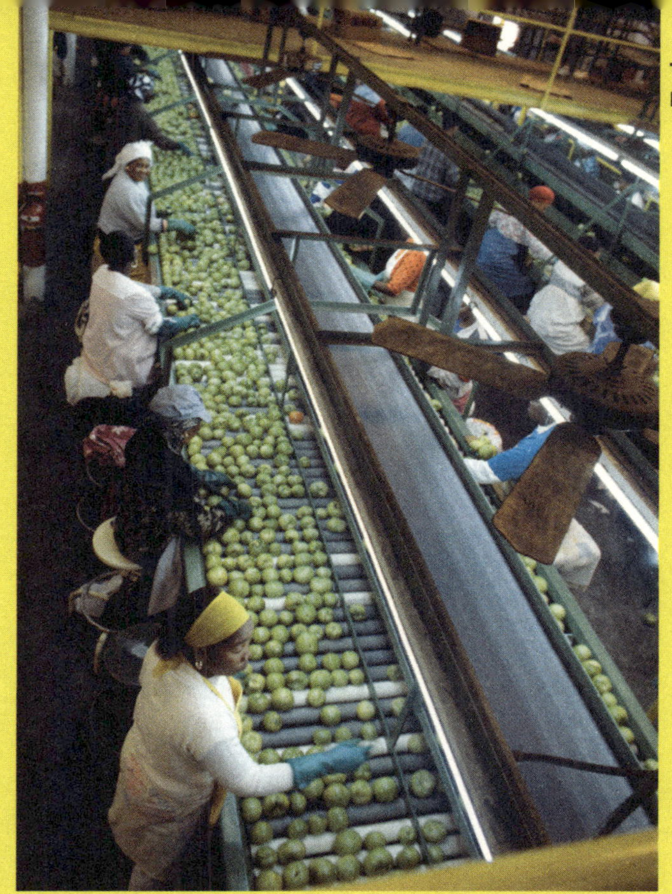

Tomato workers.
Immokalee, FL. 1996

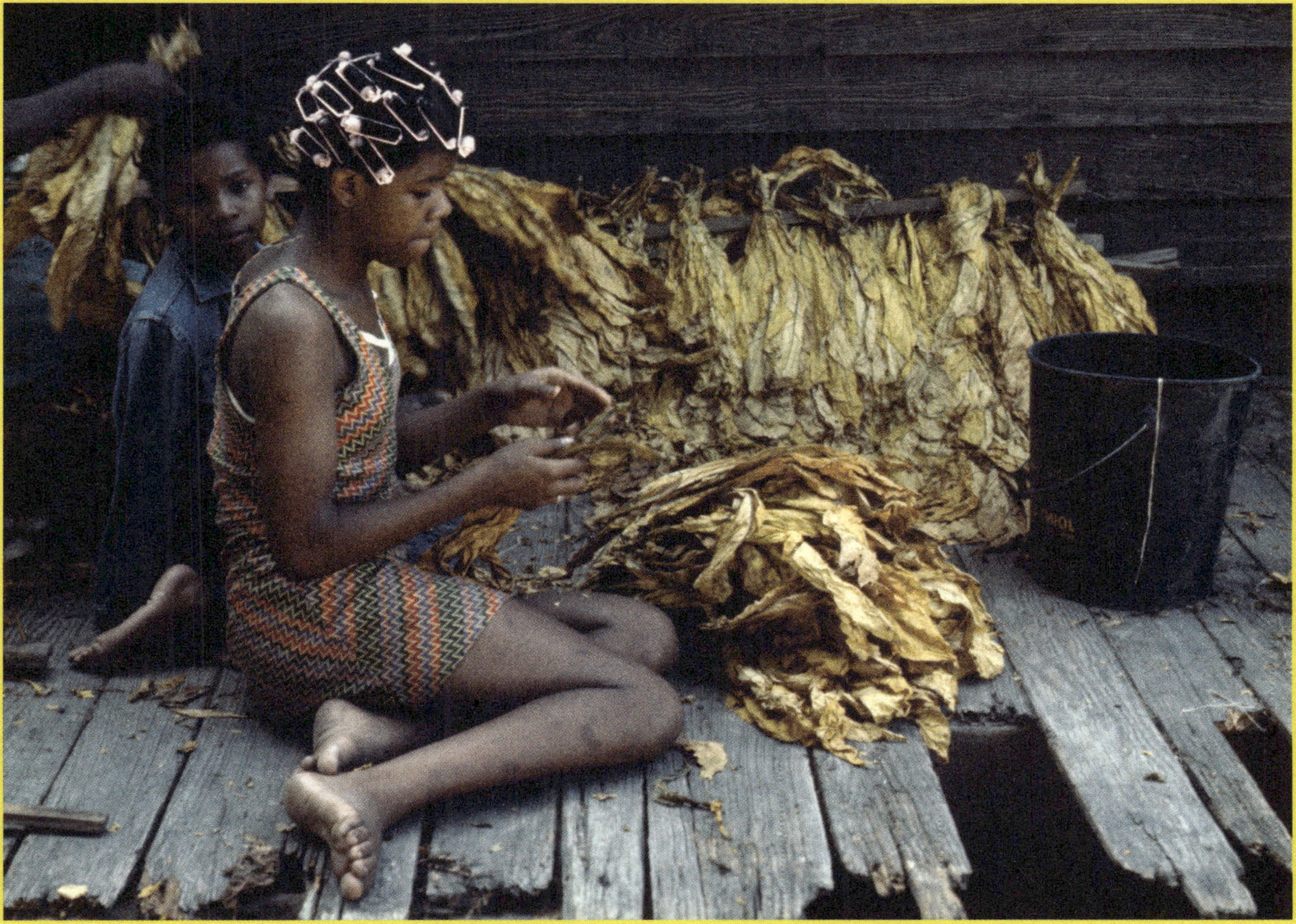

Children grading the tobacco harvest. Zebulon. NC. 1974

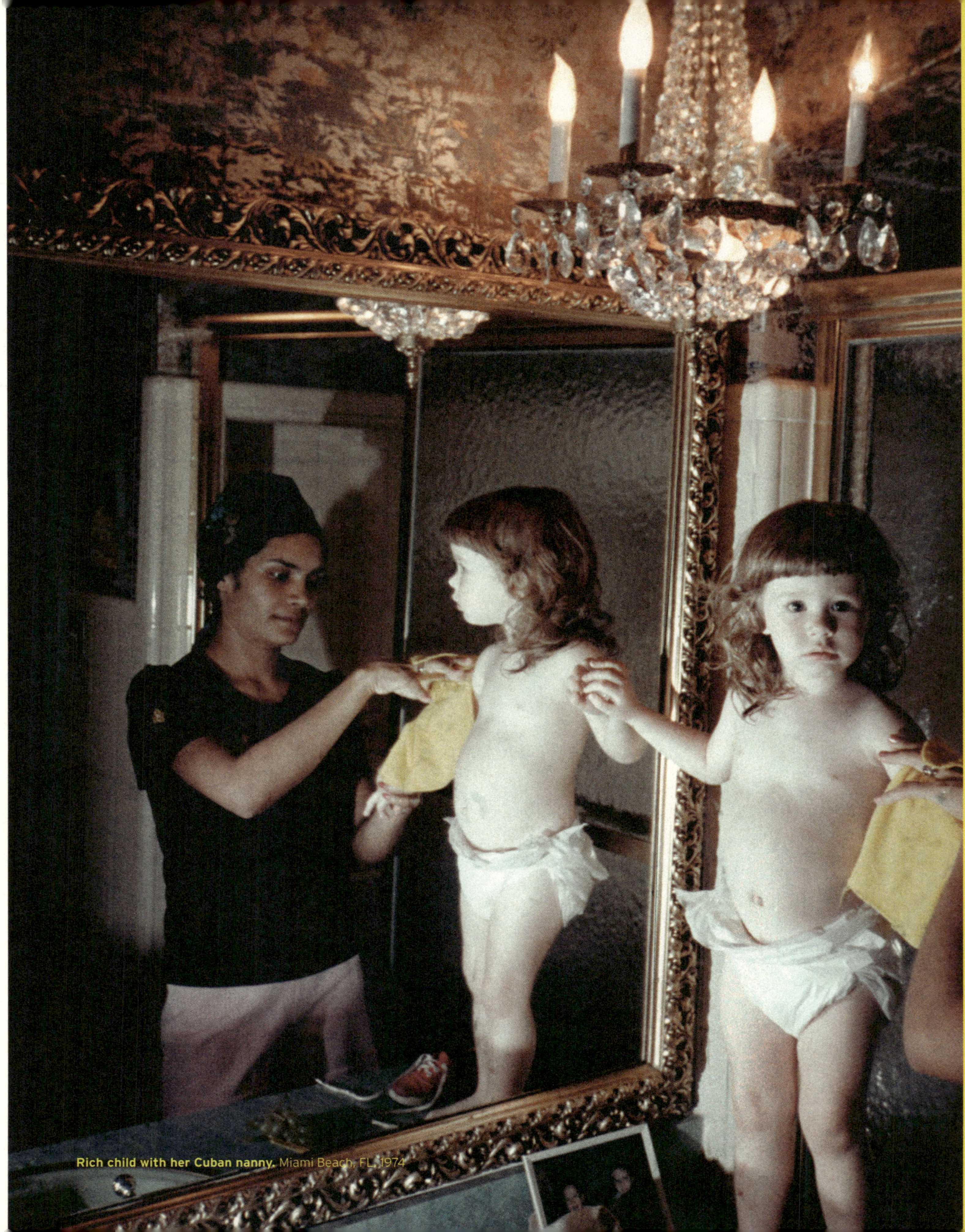

Rich child with her Cuban nanny. Miami Beach, FL, 1974

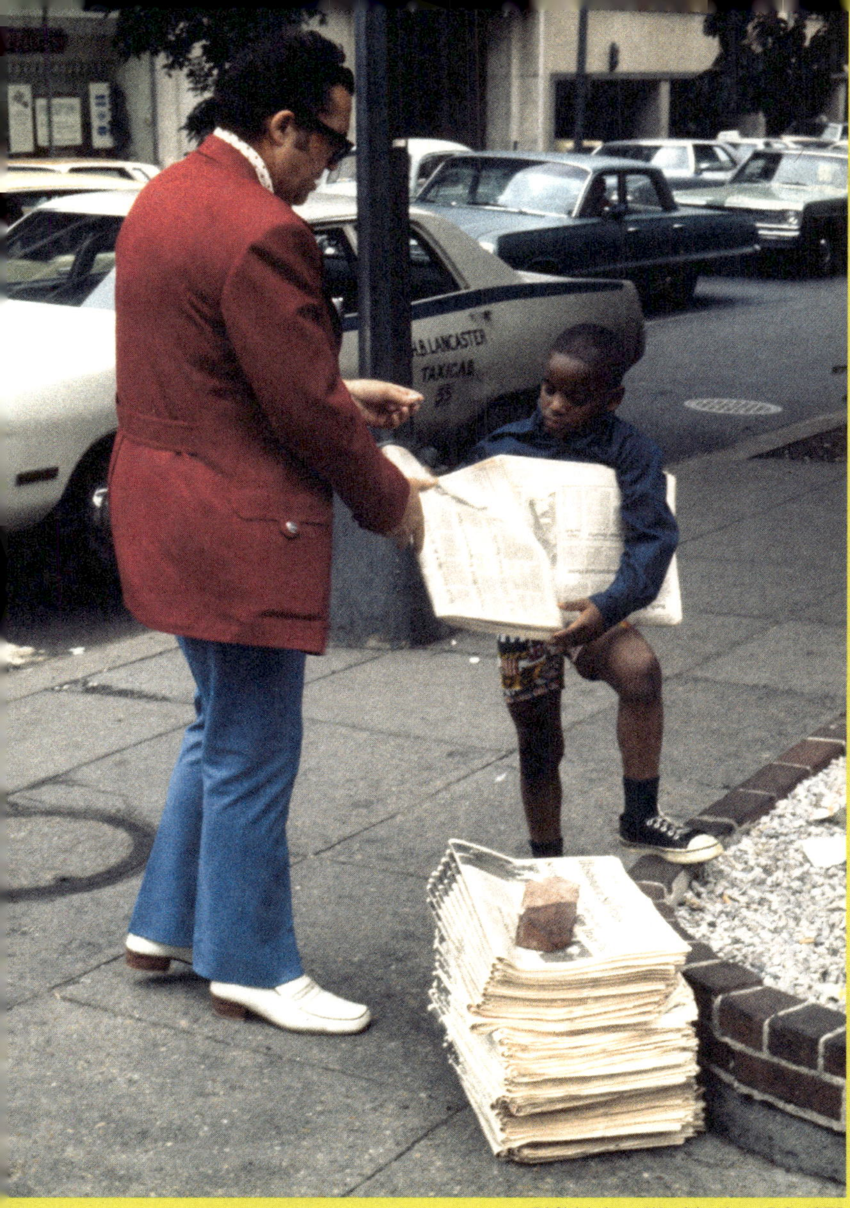

Child labor. Washington, DC. 1972

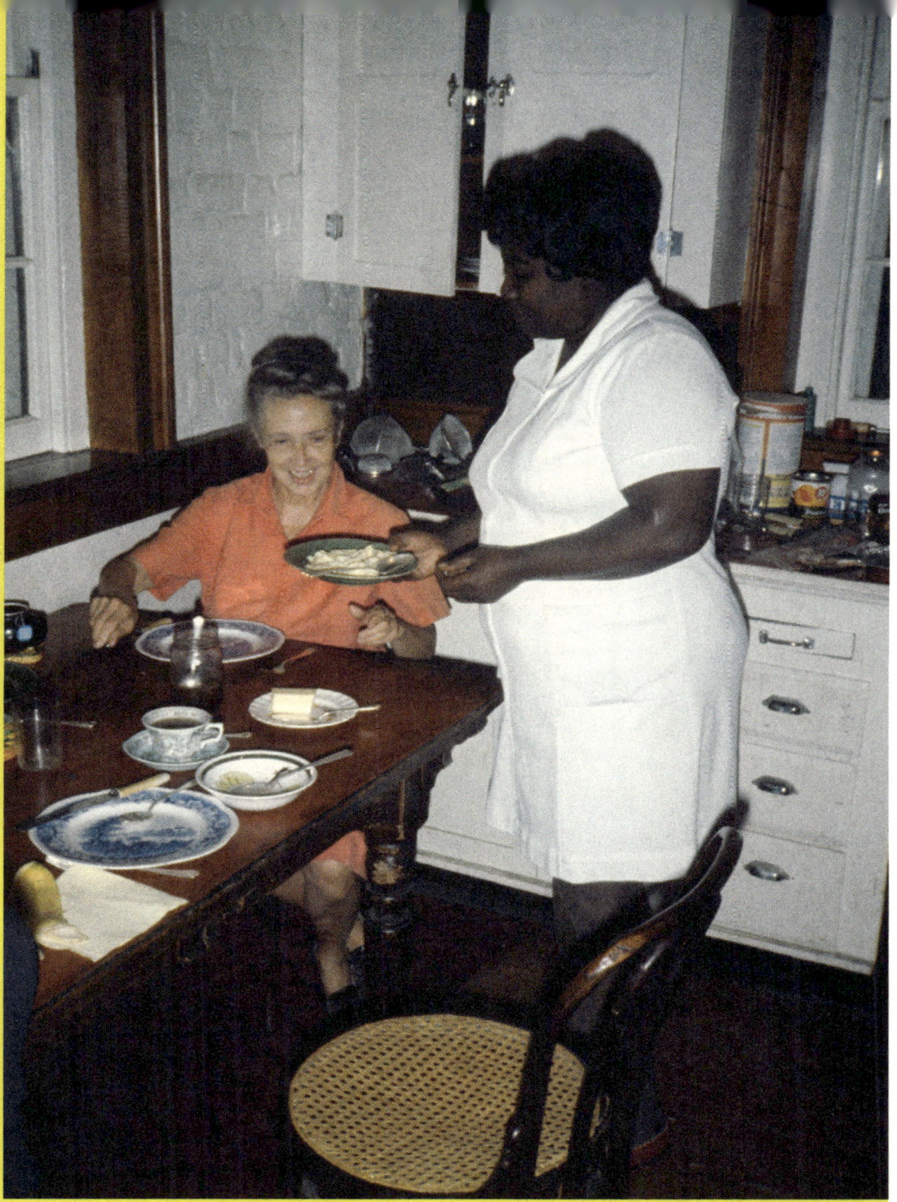

Serving Mrs. Barnett in her "Gone with the Wind" plantation home. Washington, GA. 1974

ku klux klan

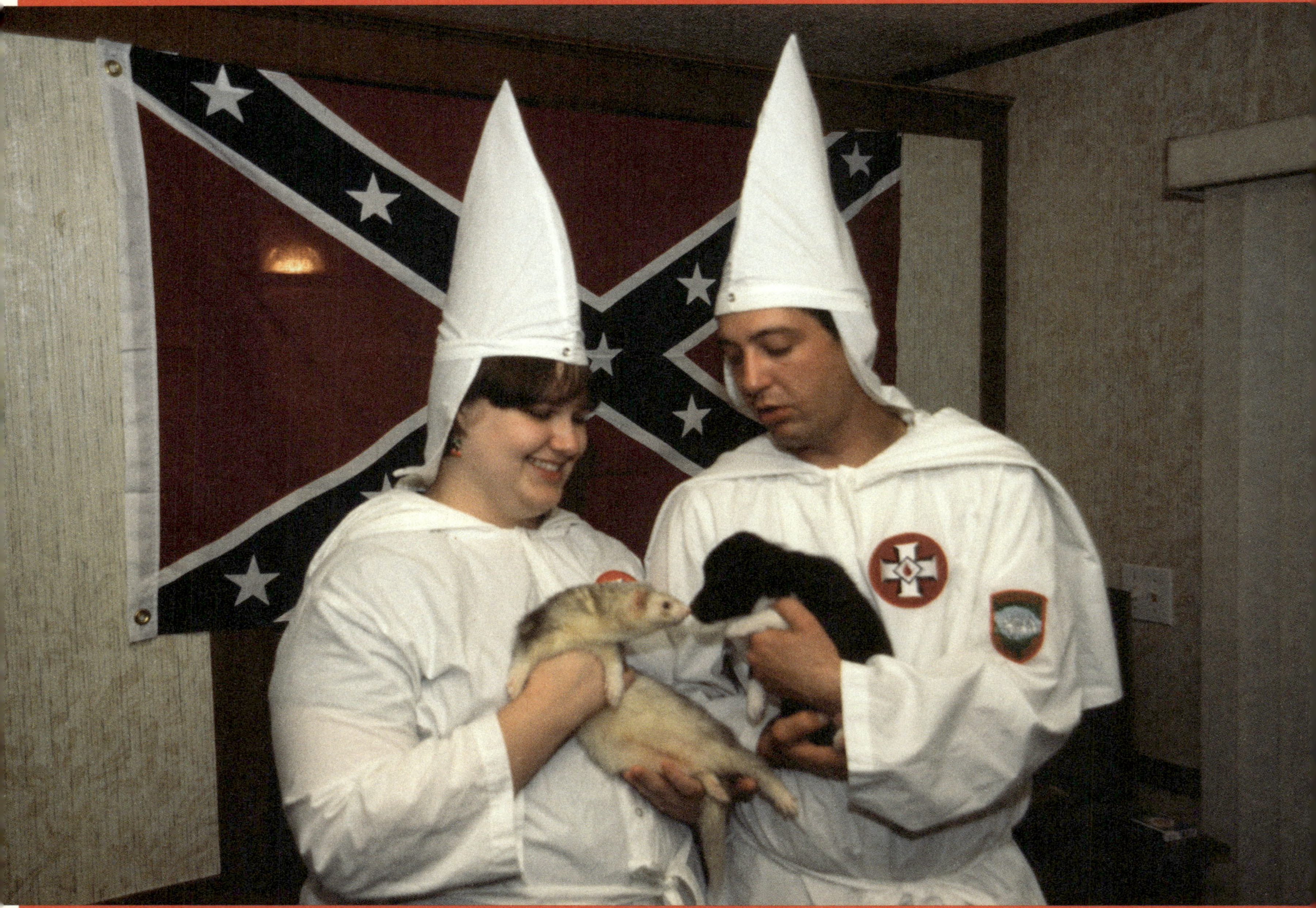

Raine and Bob shortly before the attempt on her life. Morgantown, NC. 2003

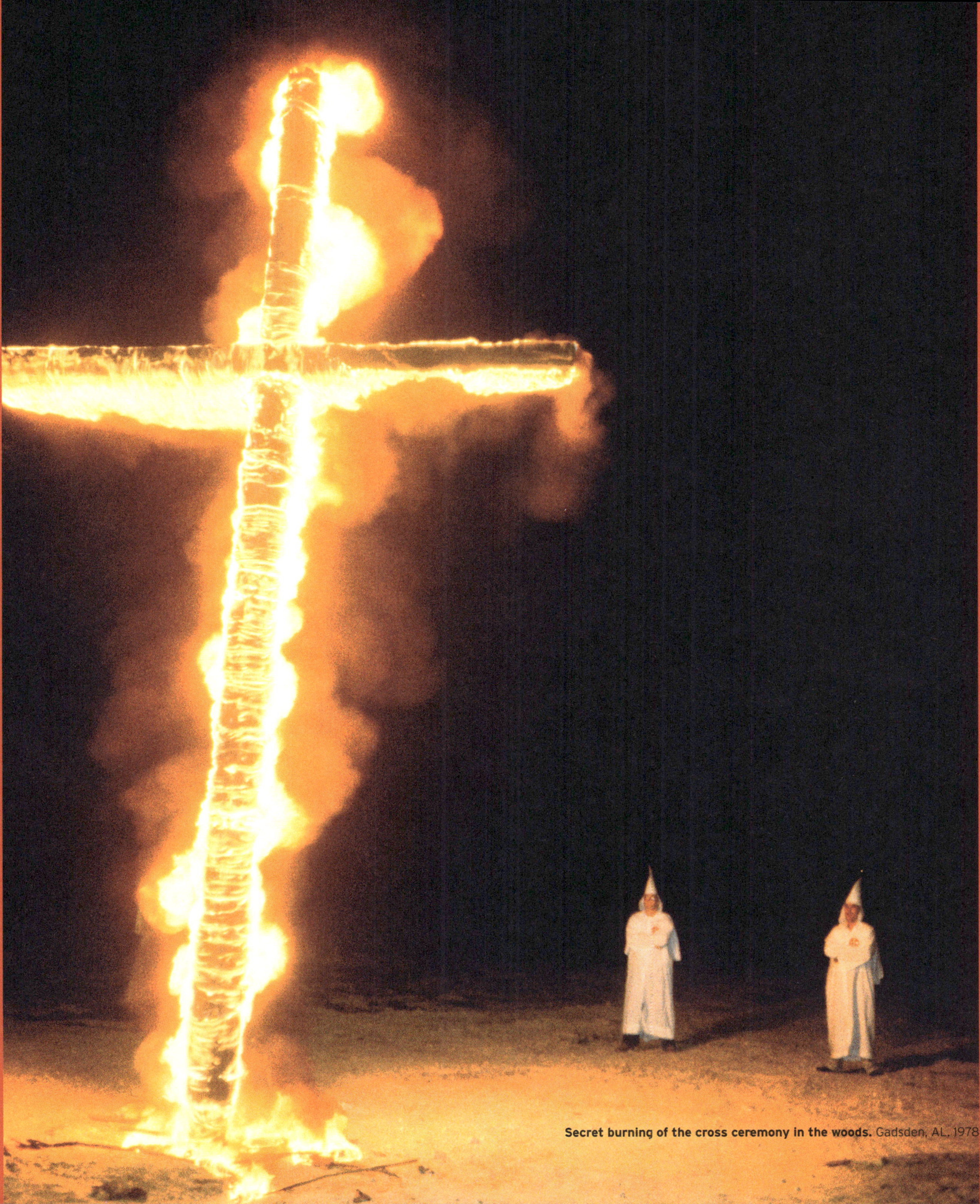

Secret burning of the cross ceremony in the woods. Gadsden, AL, 1978

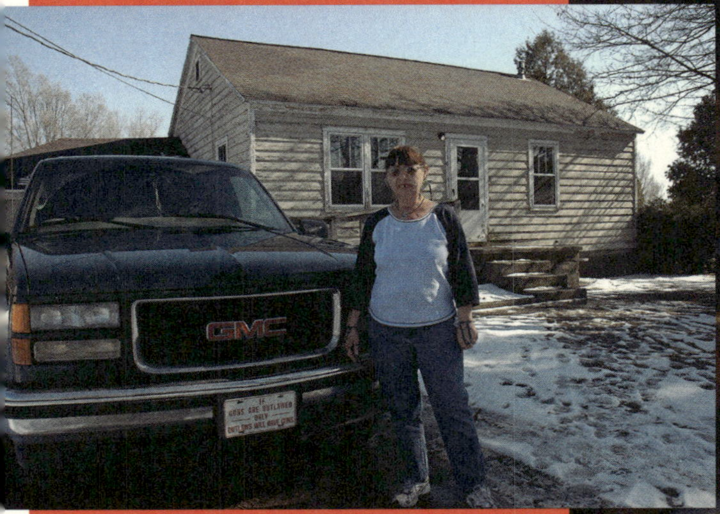

Woman Grand Dragon outside her home. Goshen, IN. 2004

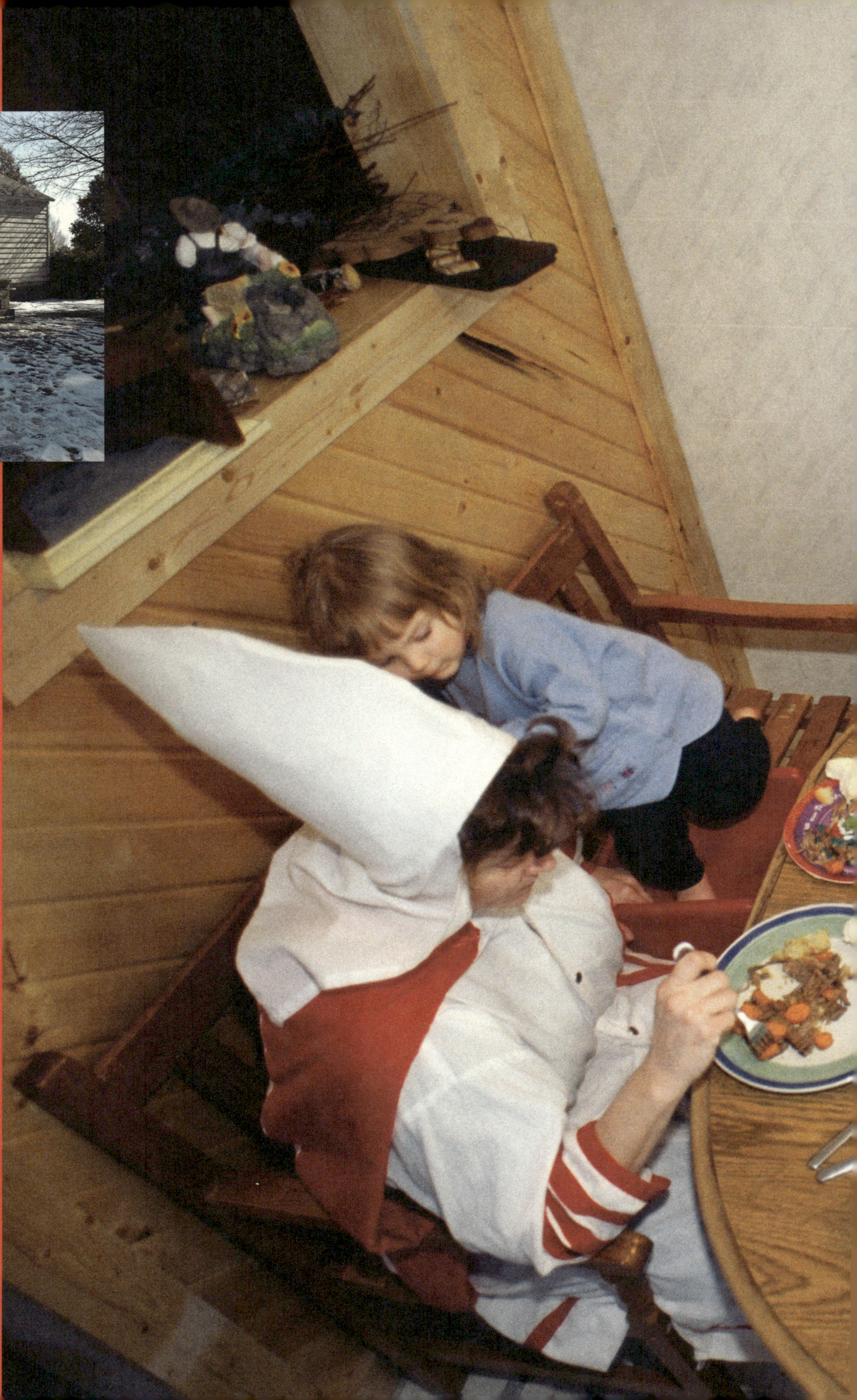

The Klan leader's Sunday meeting with the Grand Dragon of Illinois. Butler, IN. 2002

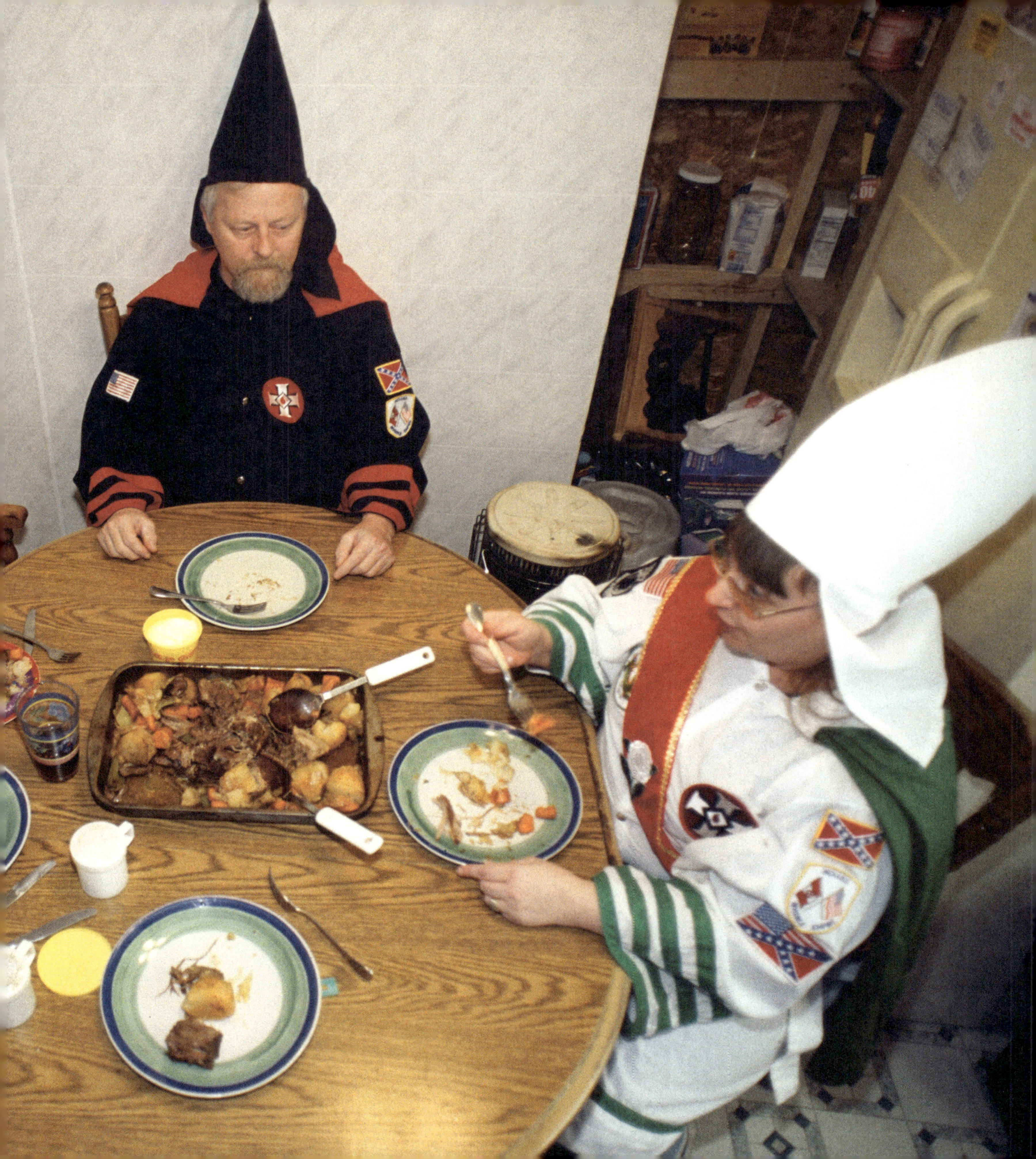

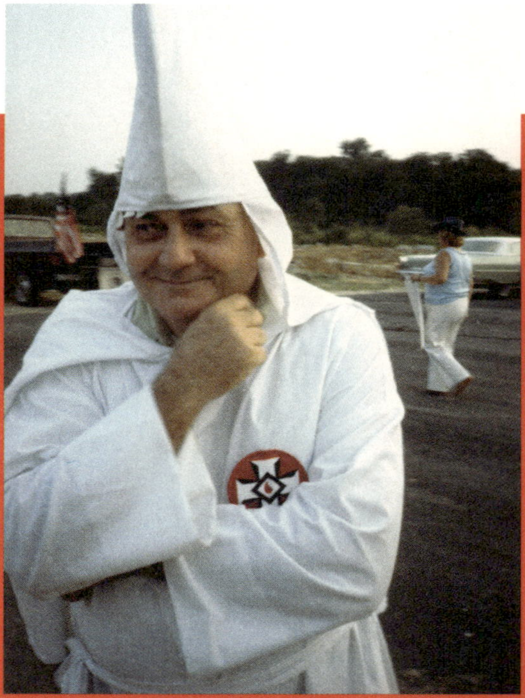

A Klansman. Gadsden, AL. 1978

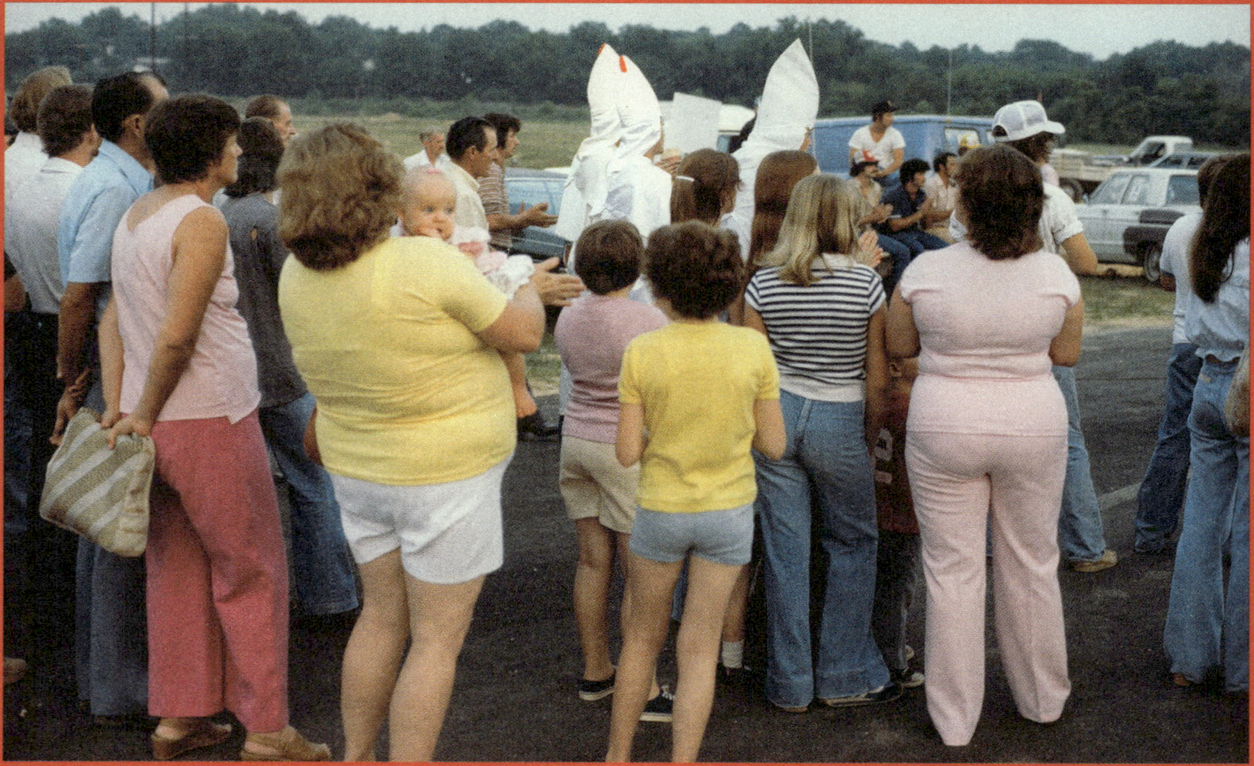

Poor white audience at a klan rally. Gadsden, AL. 1978

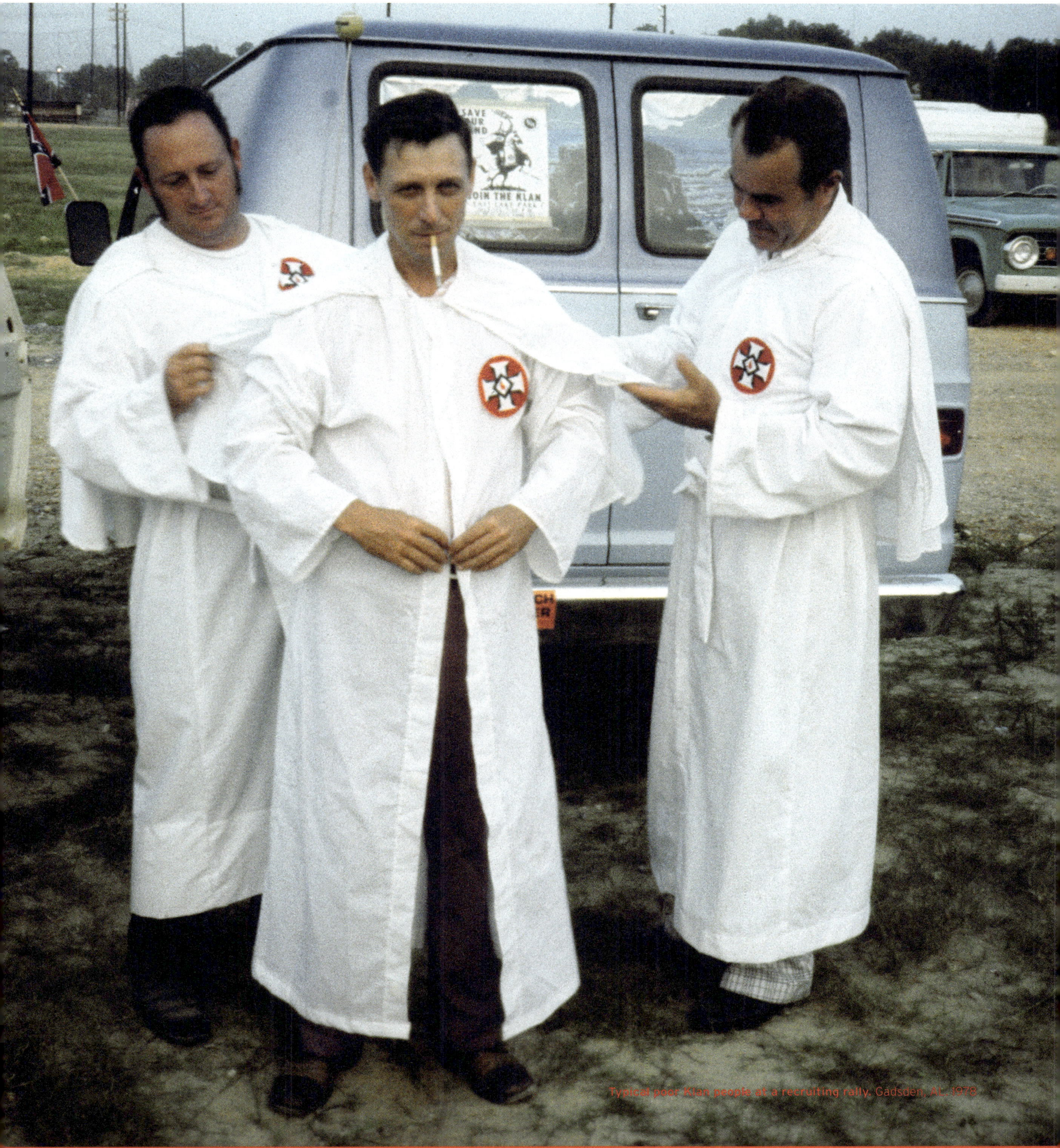

Typical poor Klan people at a recruiting rally. Gadsden, AL. 1978

Mary

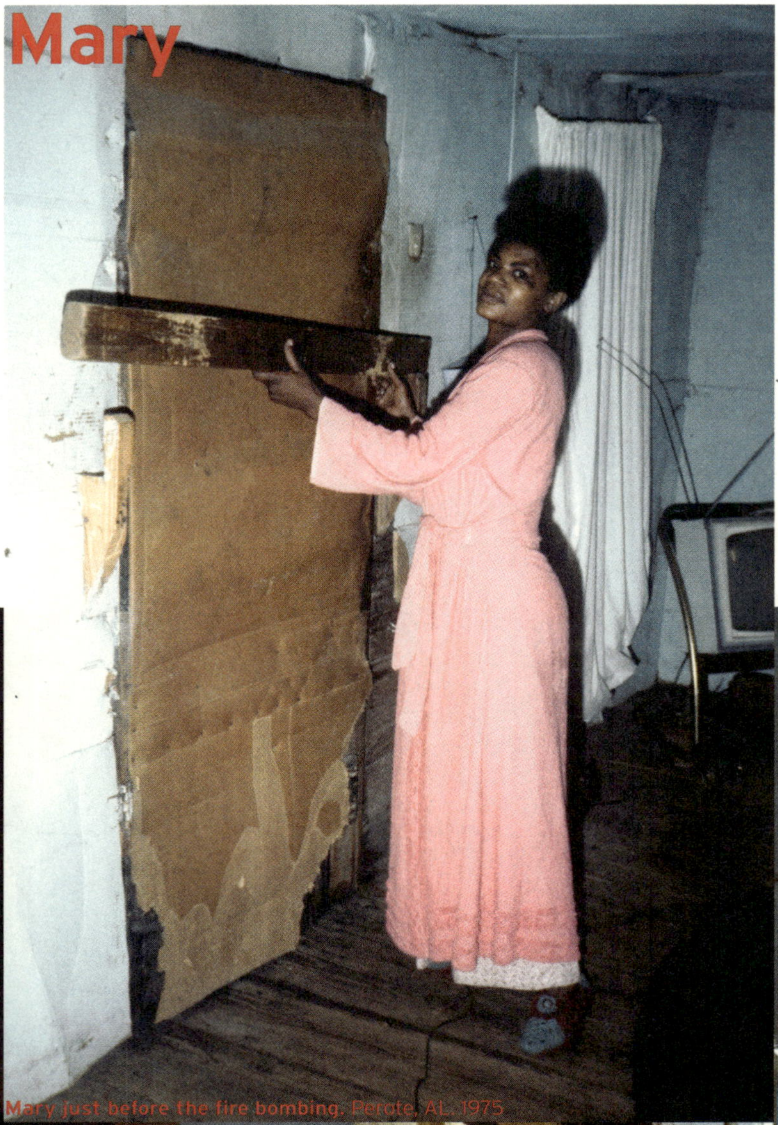

Mary just before the fire bombing. Perote, AL. 1975

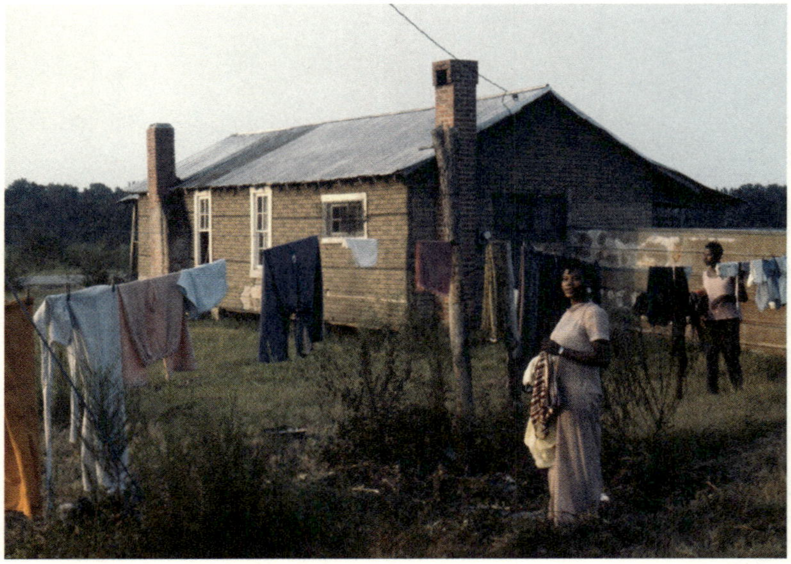

The only picture of her brother who died in a fire. Perote, AL. 1975

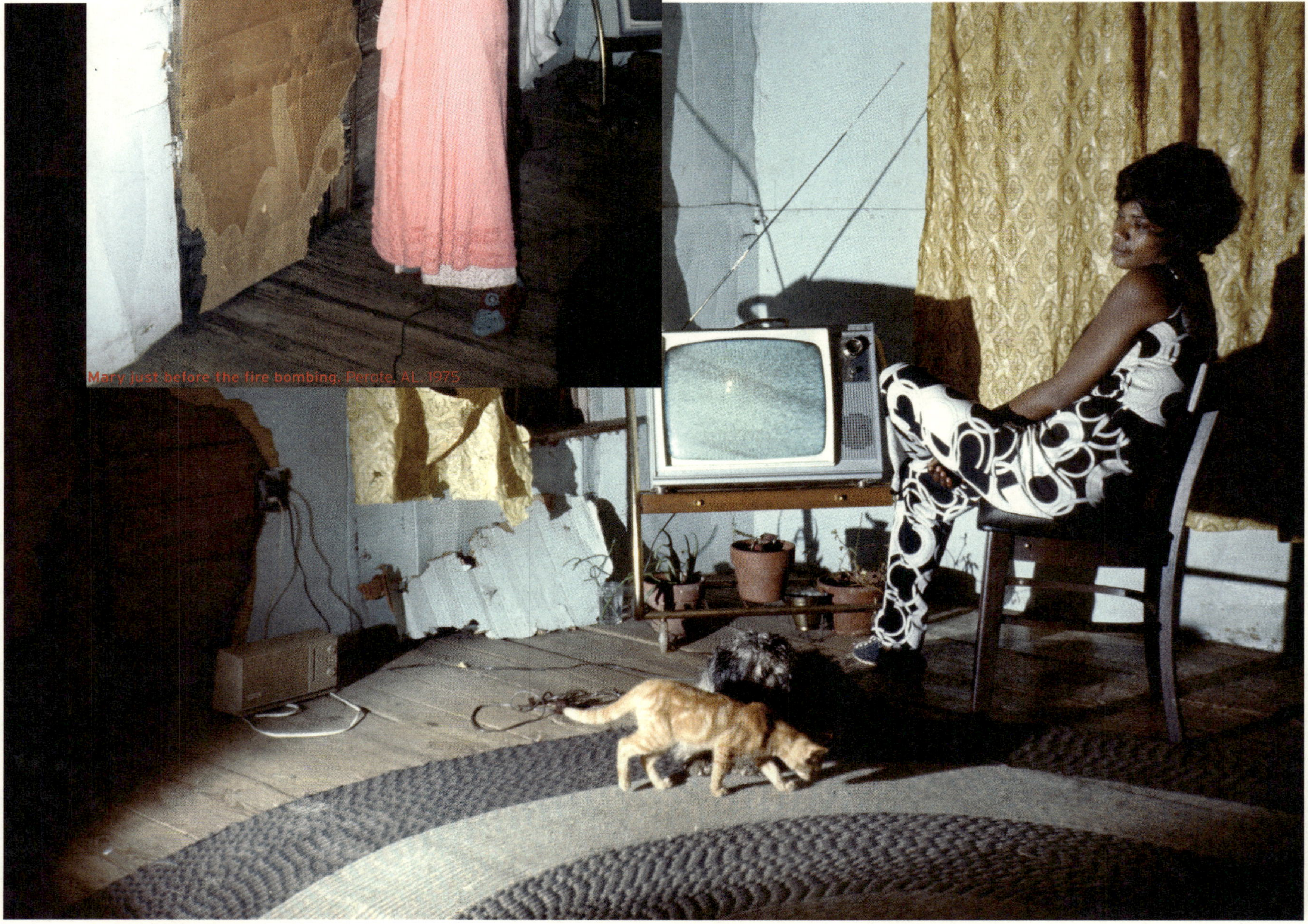

Mary all dressed up in her old shack. Perote, AL. 1975

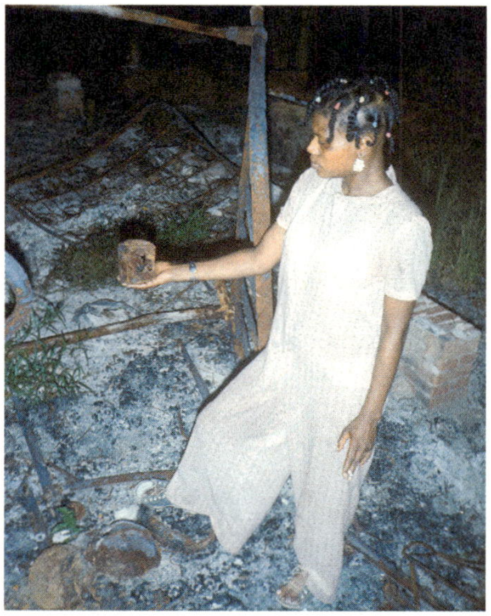

Mary at the bombed out house after the fire. Perote, AL. 1975

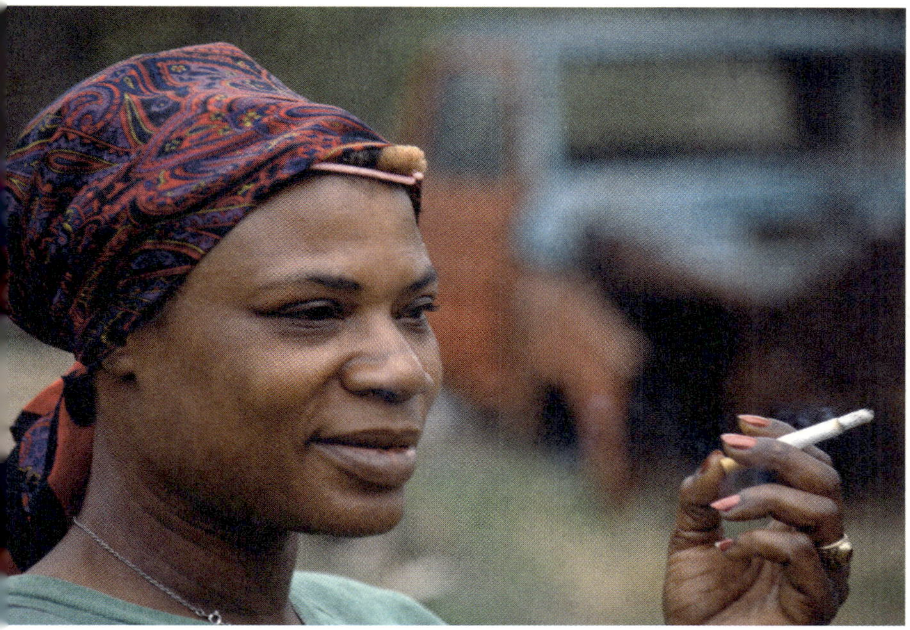

Mary outside Ida Ford's shack. Perote, AL. 1986

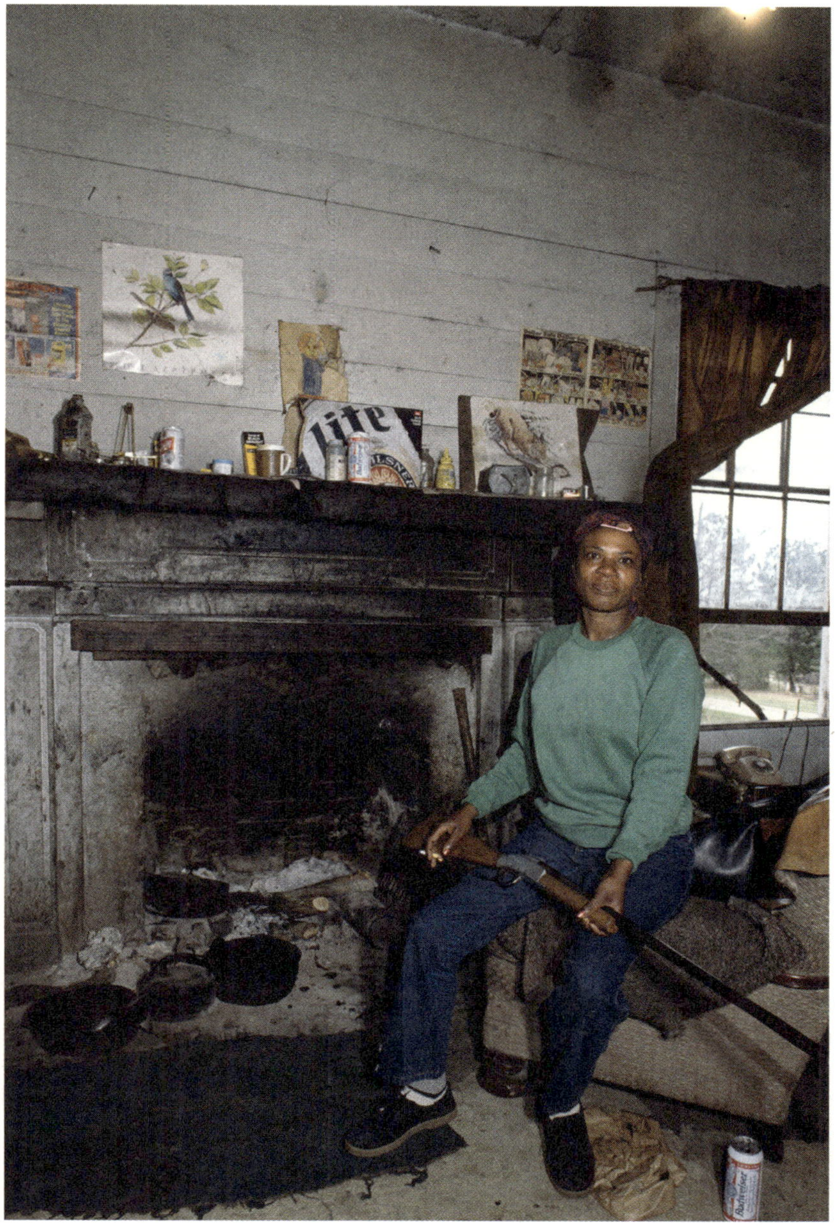

Mary visiting Ida Ford. Perote, AL. 1986

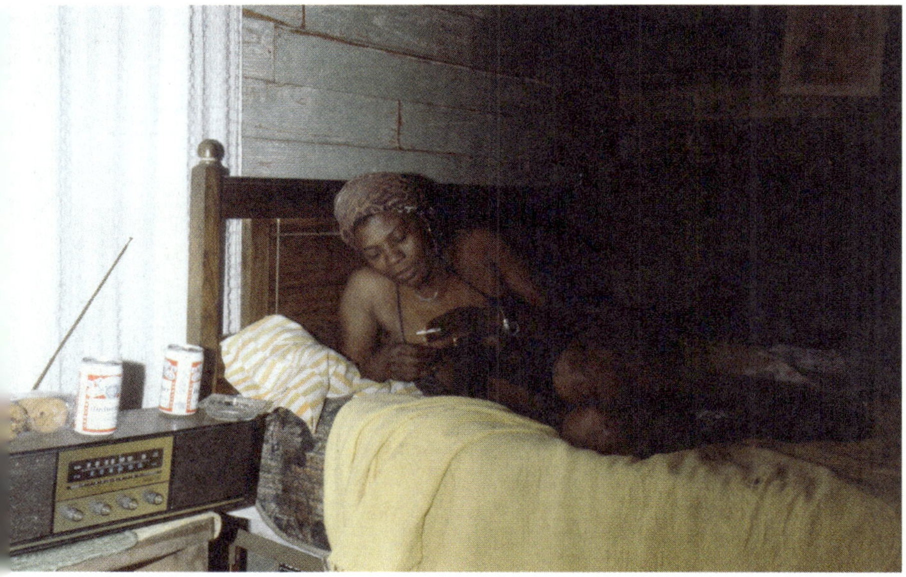

Mary in her new shack. Perote, AL. 1989

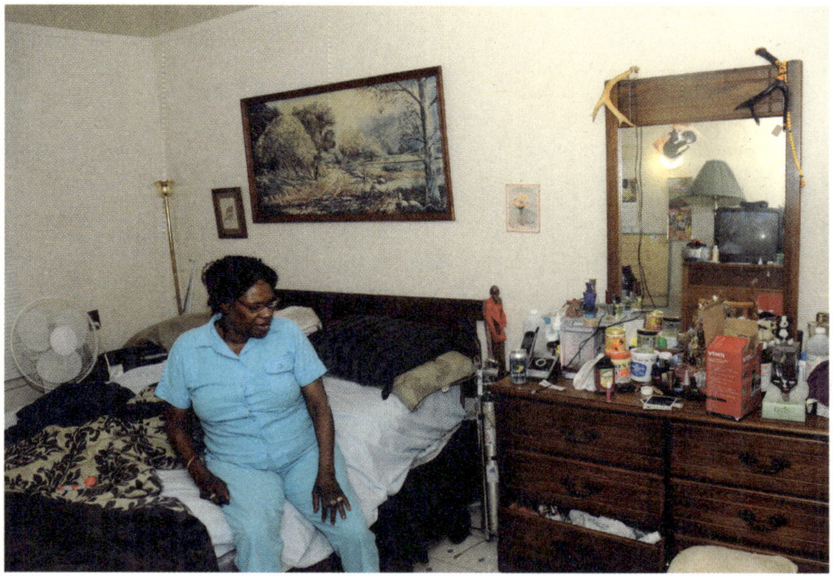

Mary, very sick from cancer. Union Spring, AL. 2009

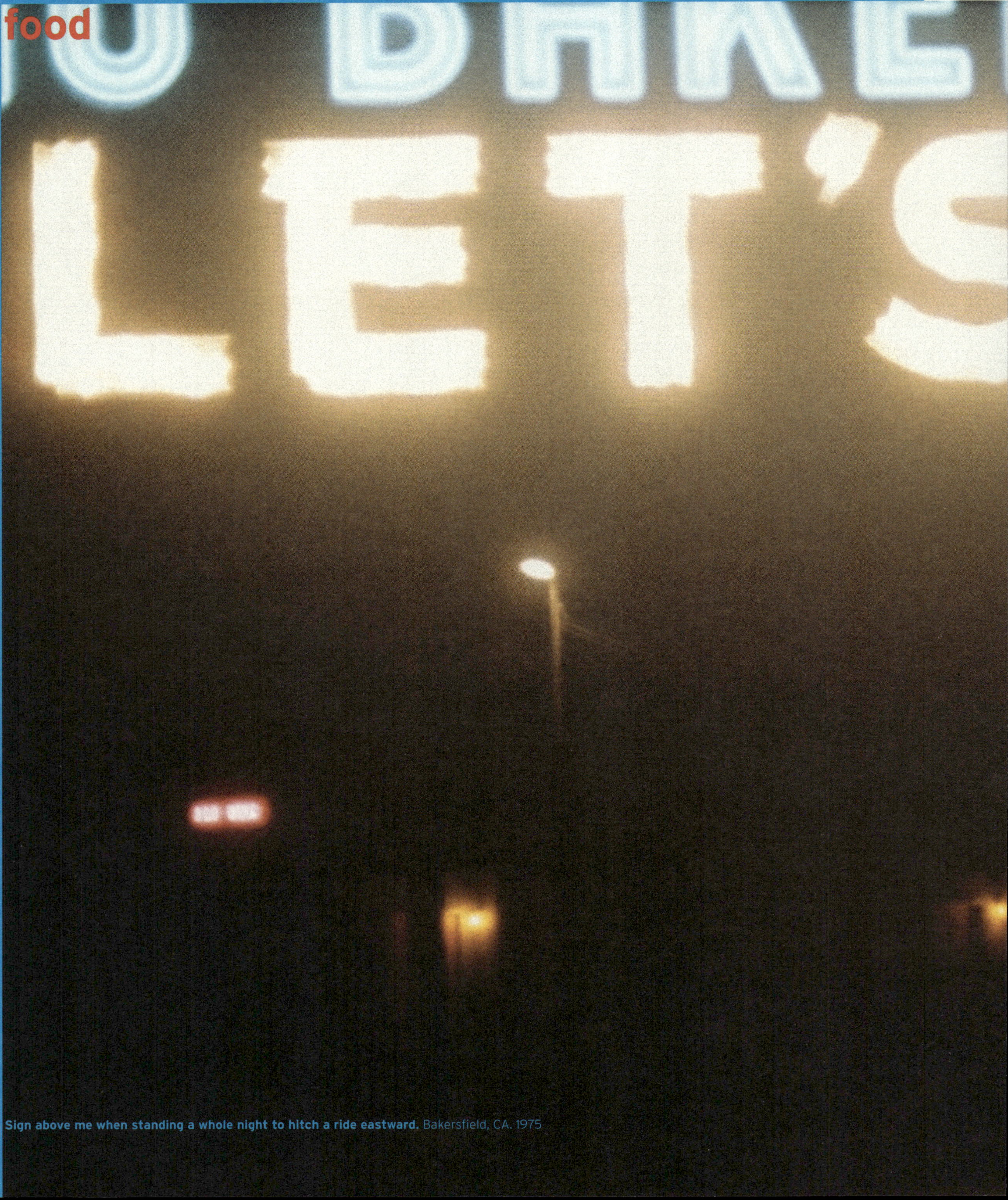

Sign above me when standing a whole night to hitch a ride eastward. Bakersfield, CA. 1975

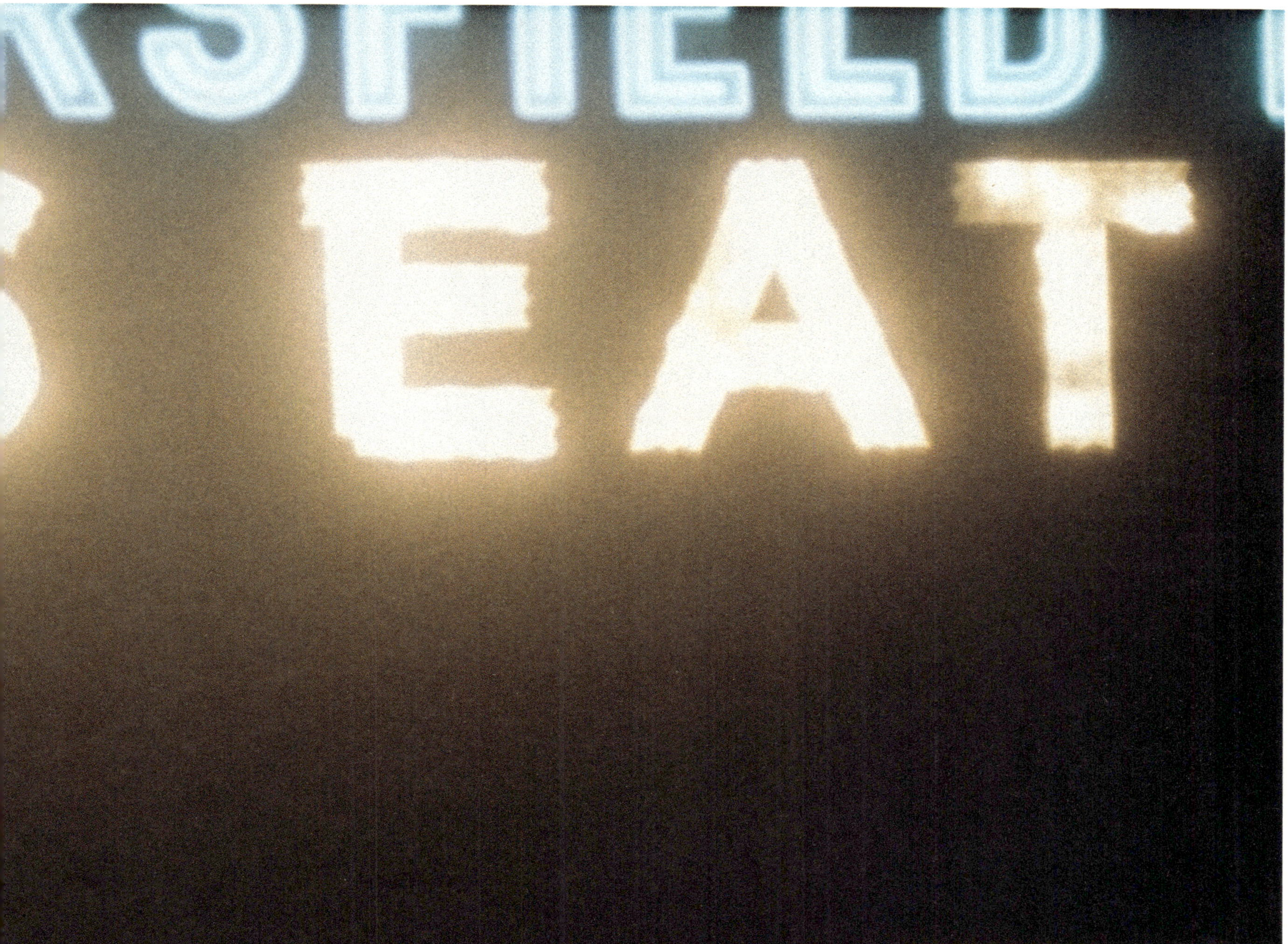

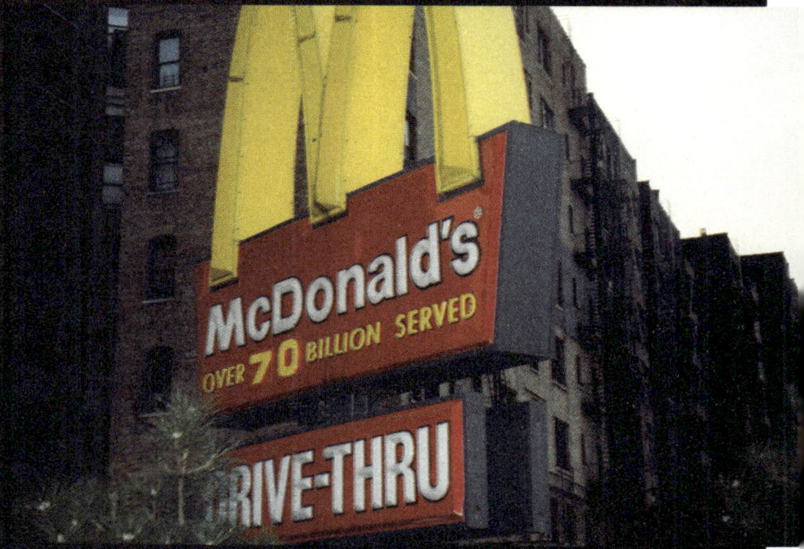

Sign at the station on 125th street. Harlem, NY. 1972

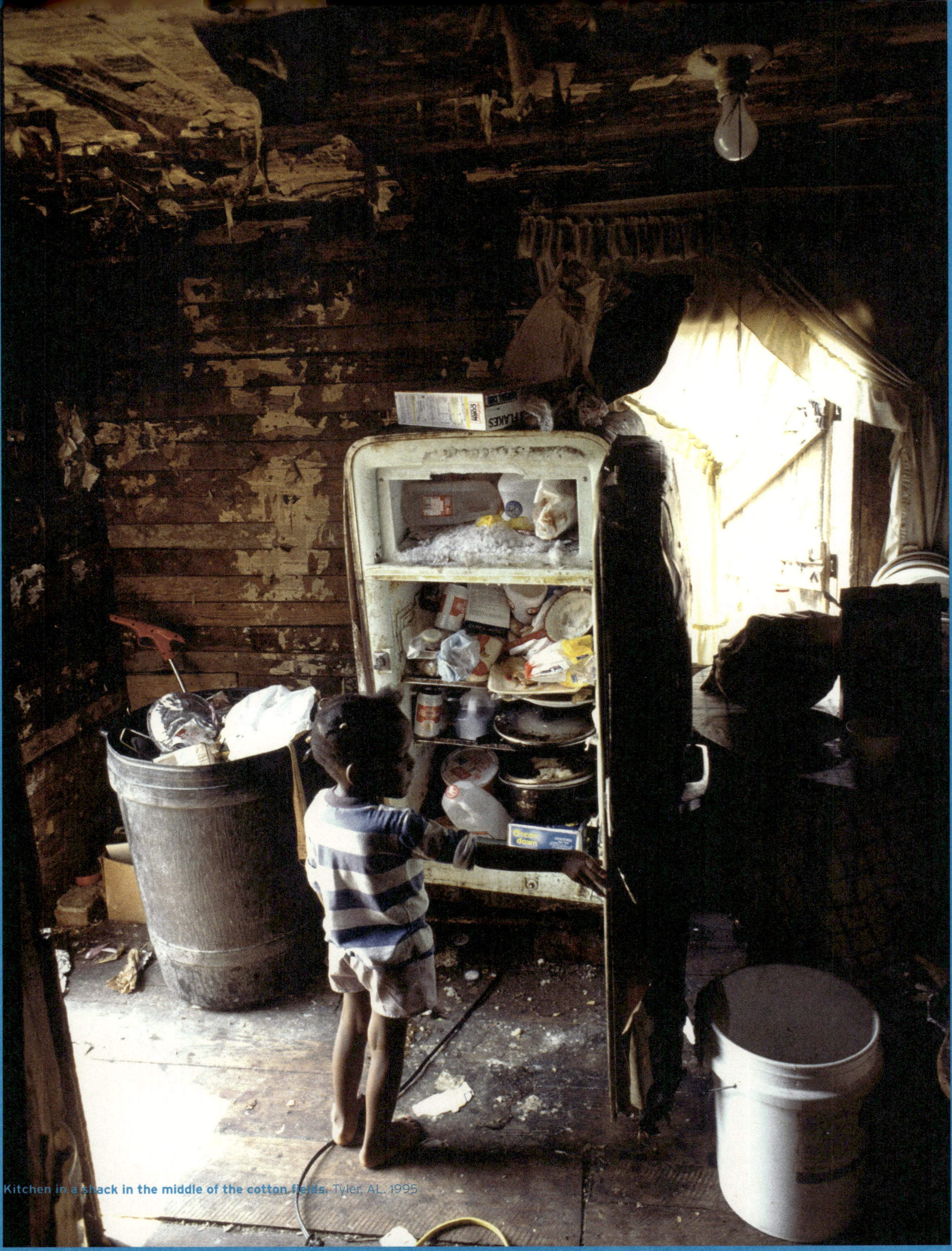

Kitchen in a shack in the middle of the cotton fields. Tyler, AL, 1995

I served food to a homeless in the Glide Church. San Francisco, CA. 1975

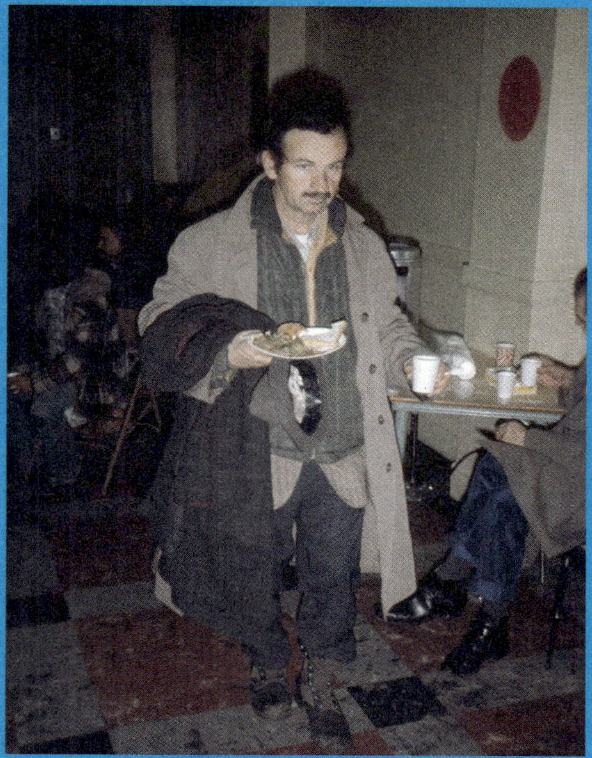

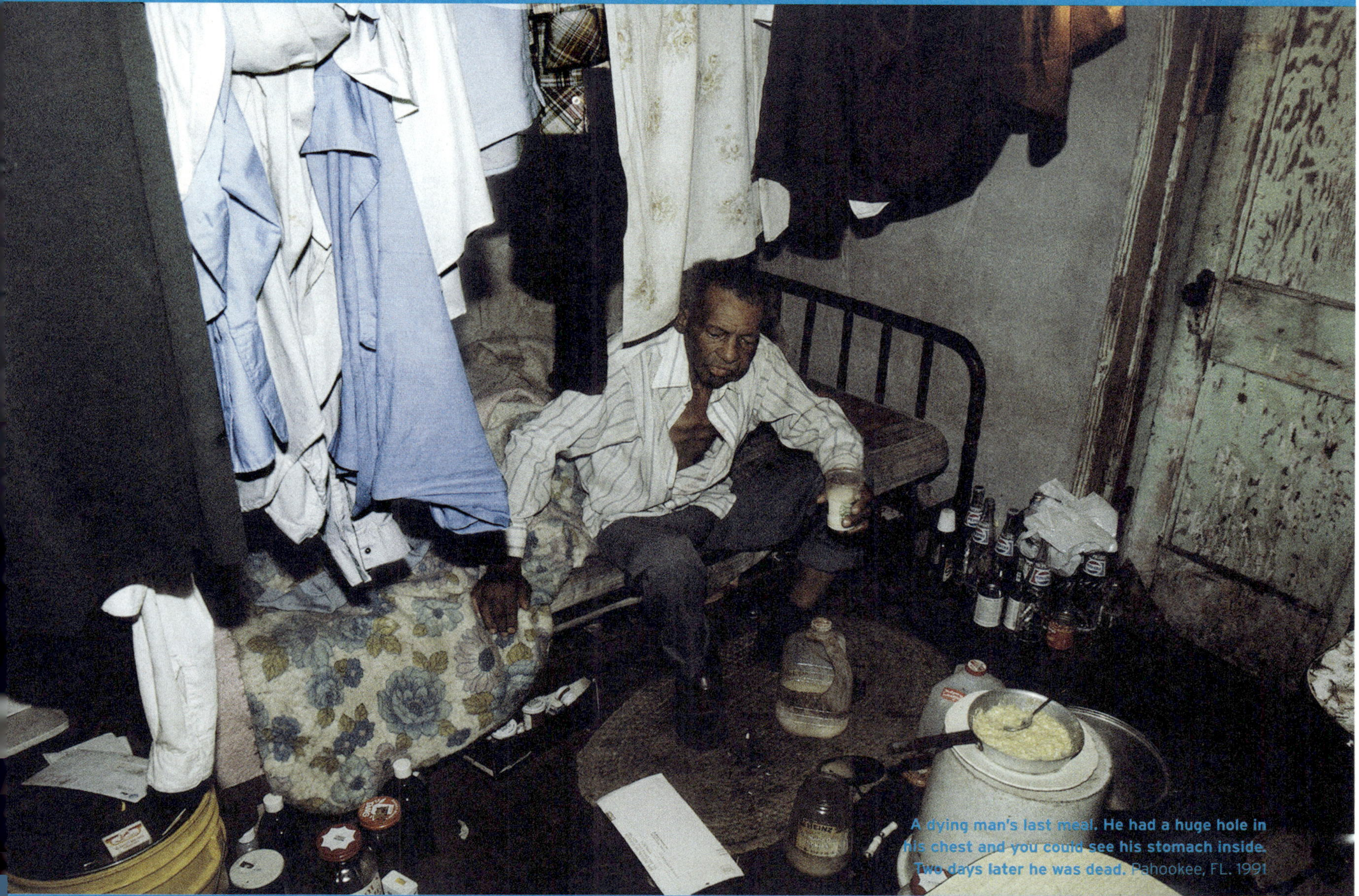

A dying man's last meal. He had a huge hole in his chest and you could see his stomach inside. Two days later he was dead. Pahookee, FL. 1991

landscapes

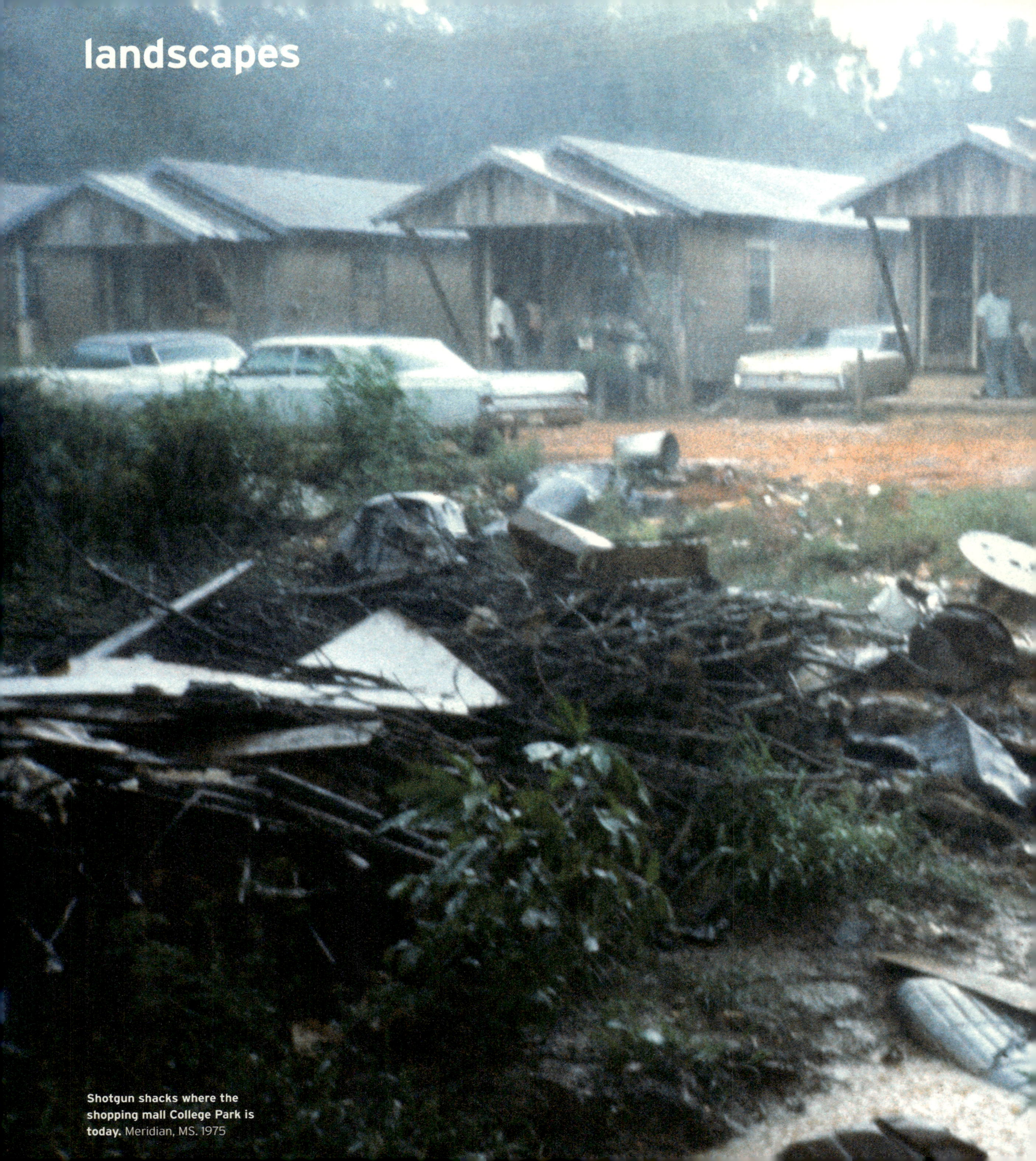

Shotgun shacks where the shopping mall College Park is today. Meridian, MS. 1975

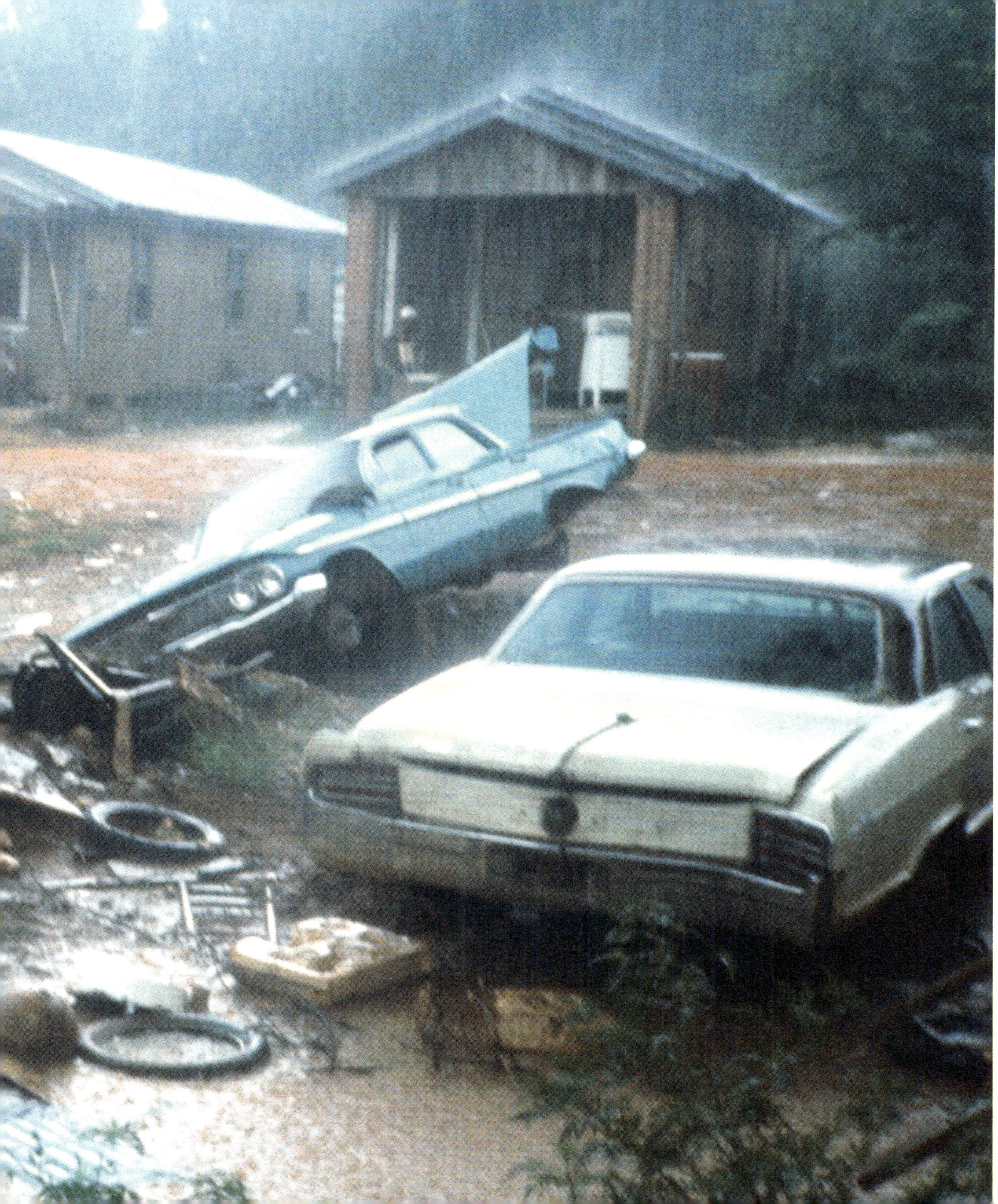

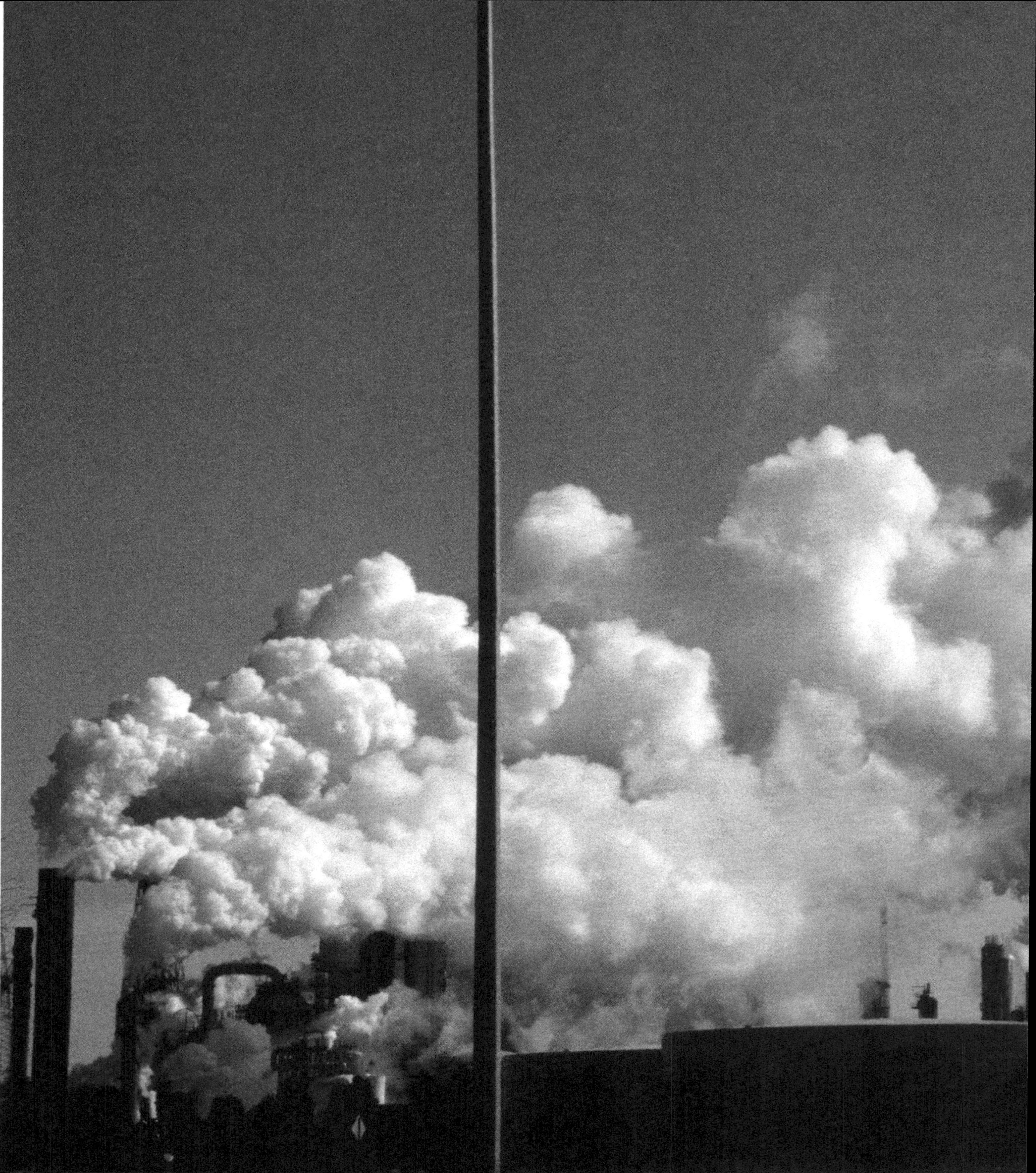

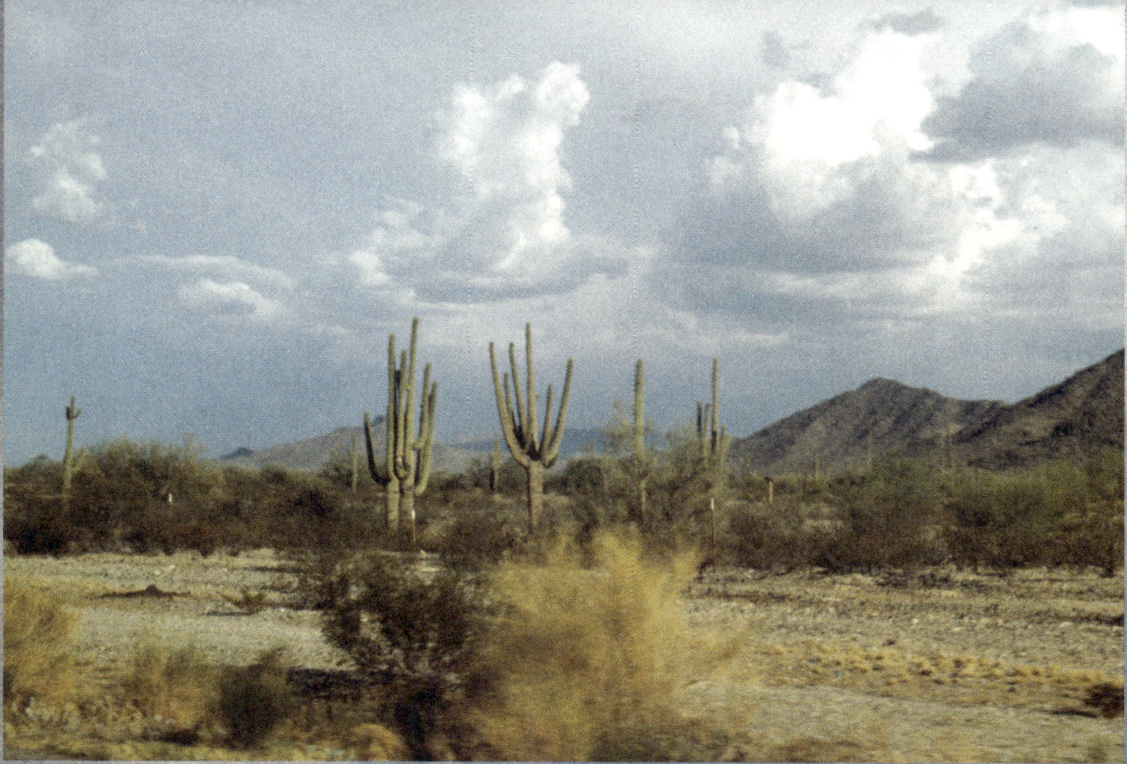

Hitchhiking through the desert. Arizona. 1975

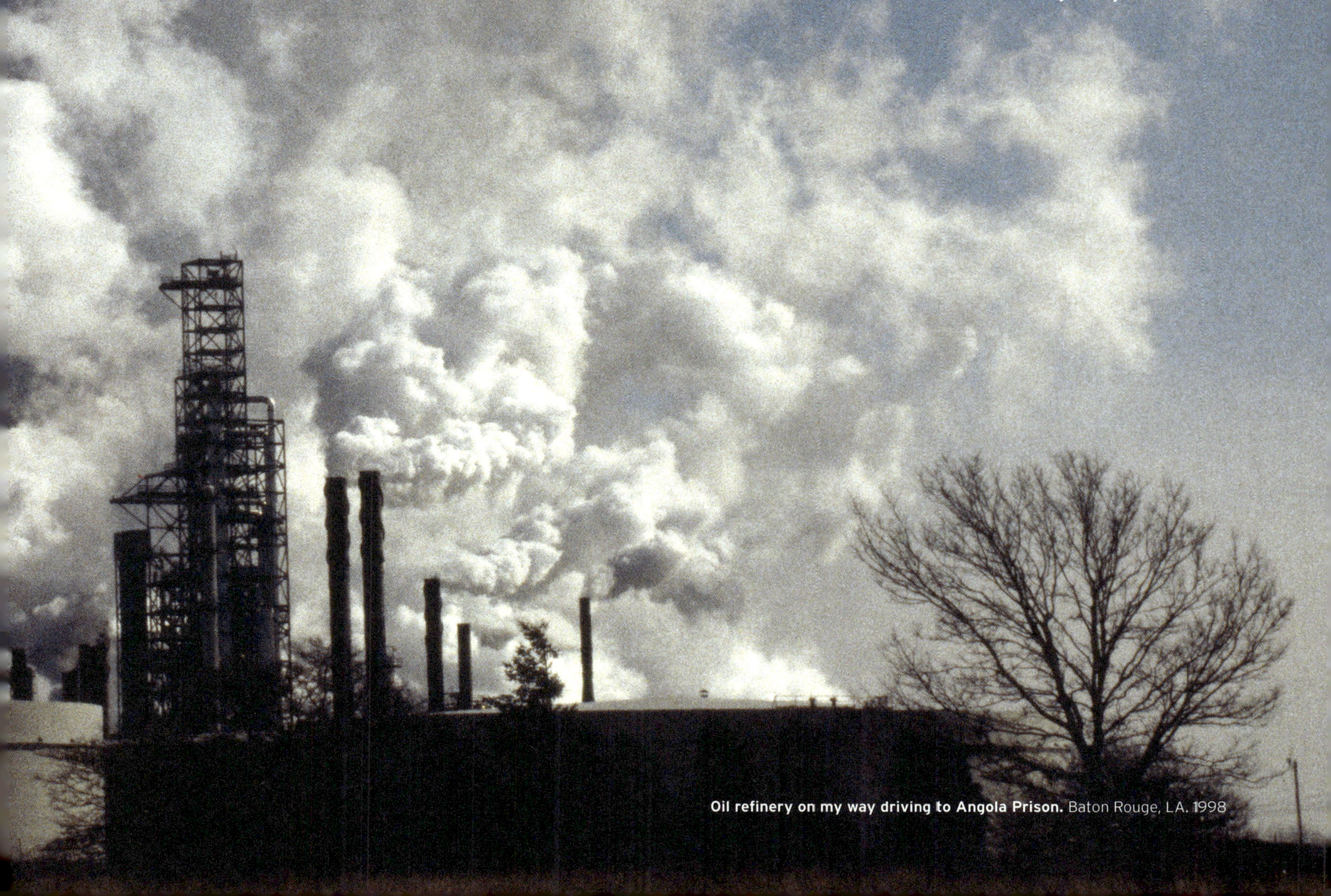

Oil refinery on my way driving to Angola Prison. Baton Rouge, LA. 1998

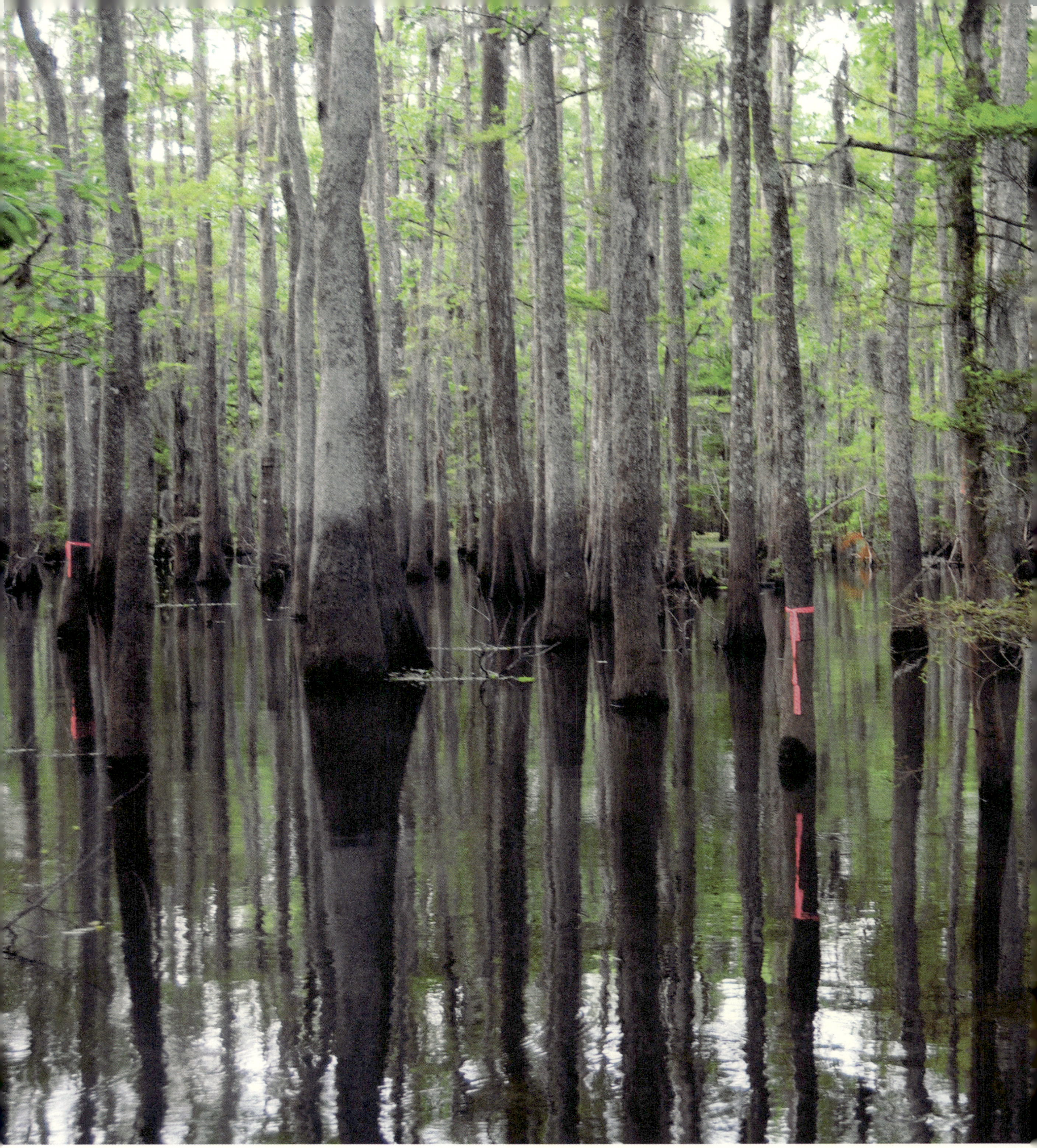

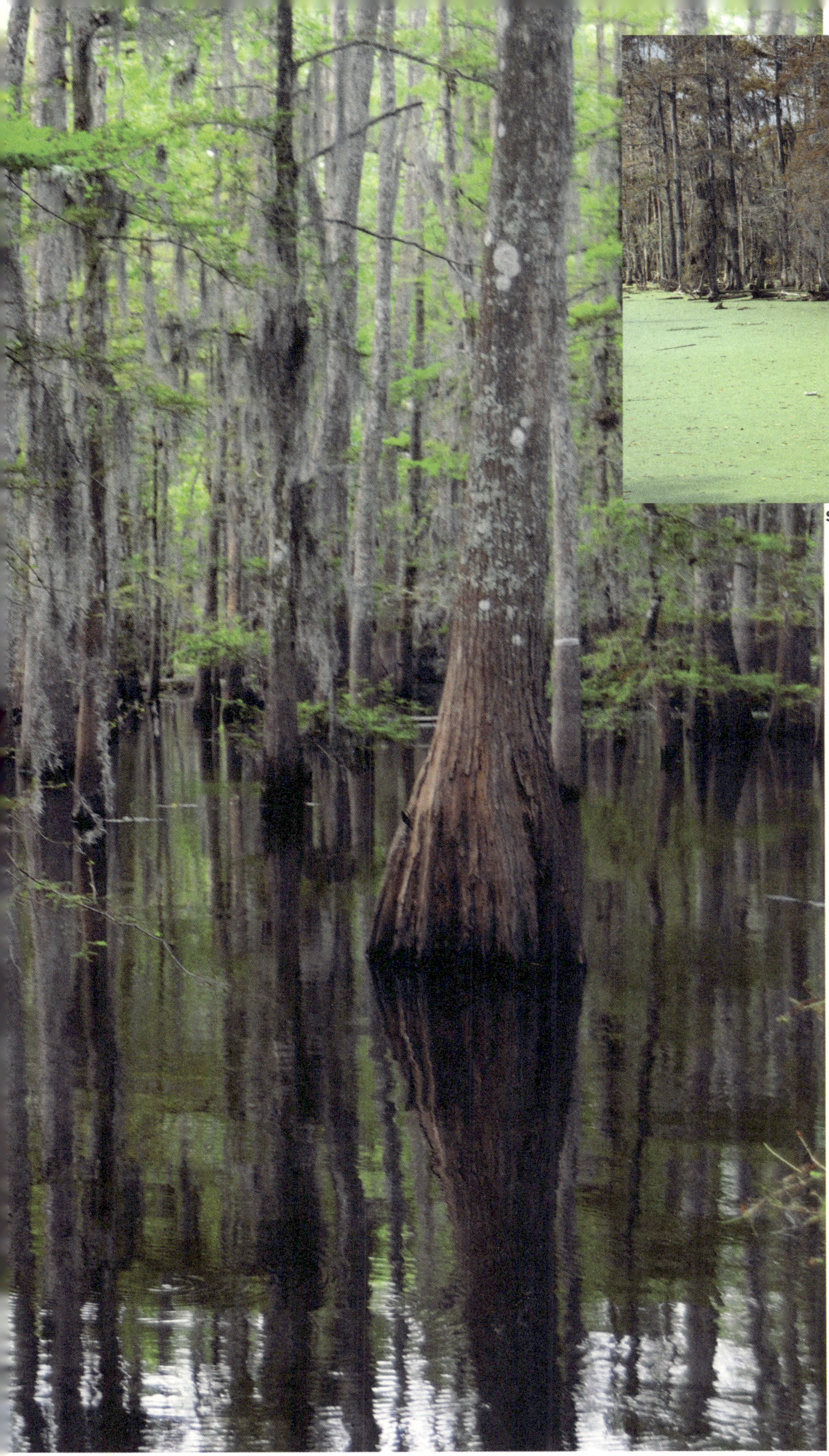

Swamps. Louisiana. 2009

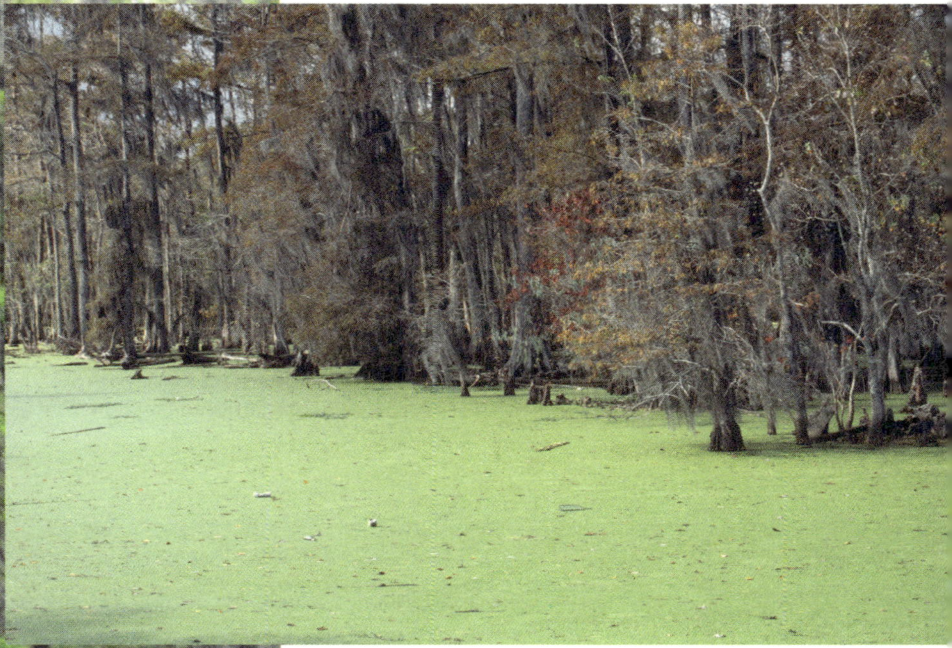

Swamps. Gibson, LA. 1996

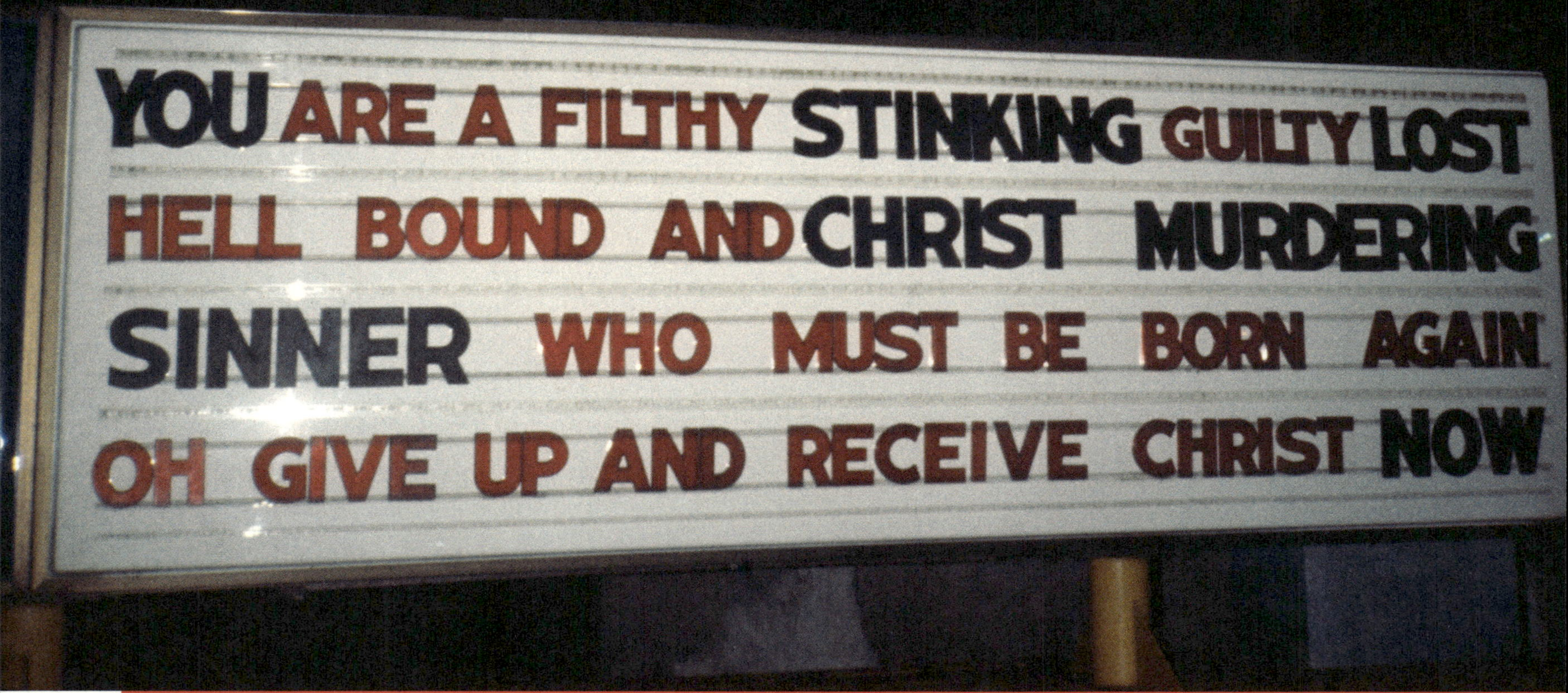

Signboard. Augusta, GA. 1975

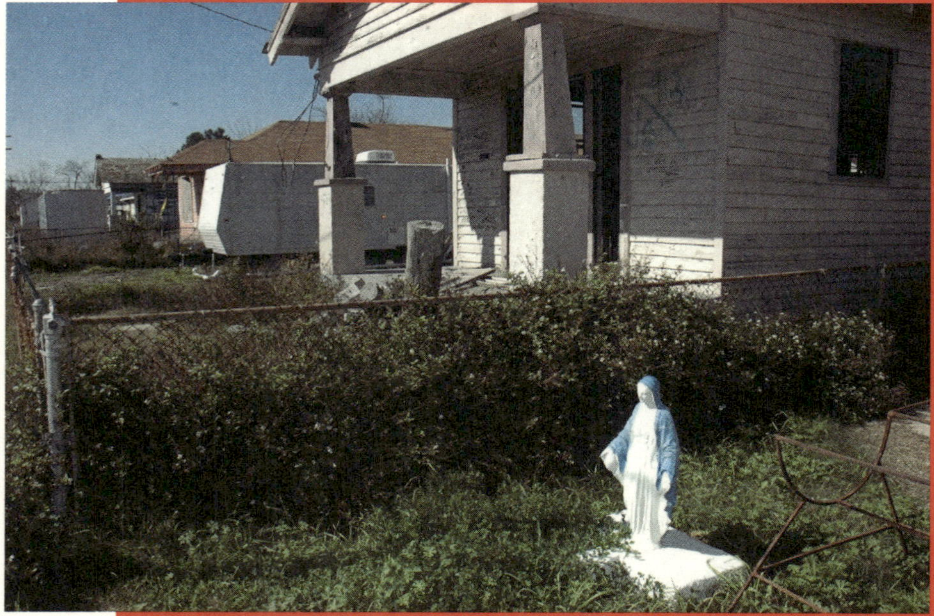

Abandonned houses in New Orleans after the hurricane Katrina. LA. 2007. 2008

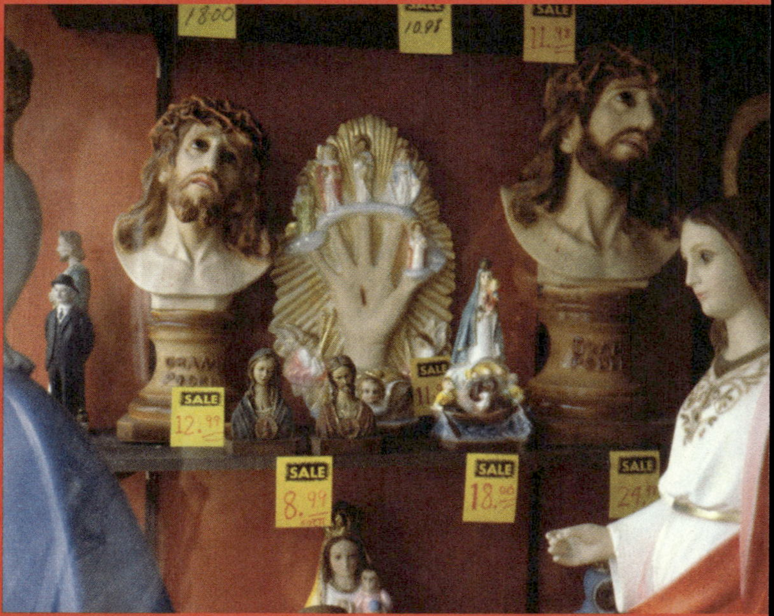

Shop in Latino area. Jamaica, NY. 2008

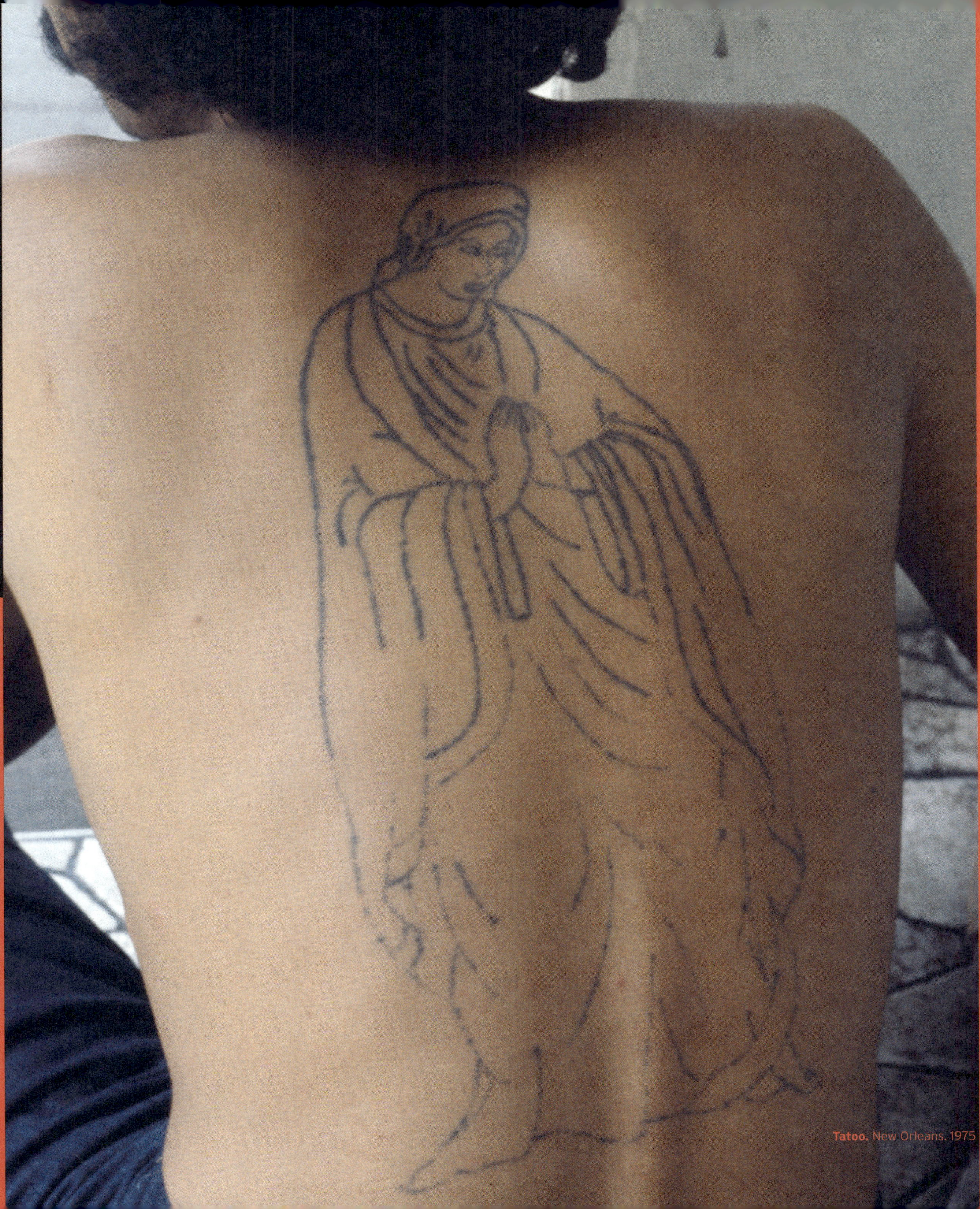

Tatoo. New Orleans, 1975

Evening prayers with my landlady Baggie's children – a few days before she robbed a bank.
Greensboro, NC. 1974

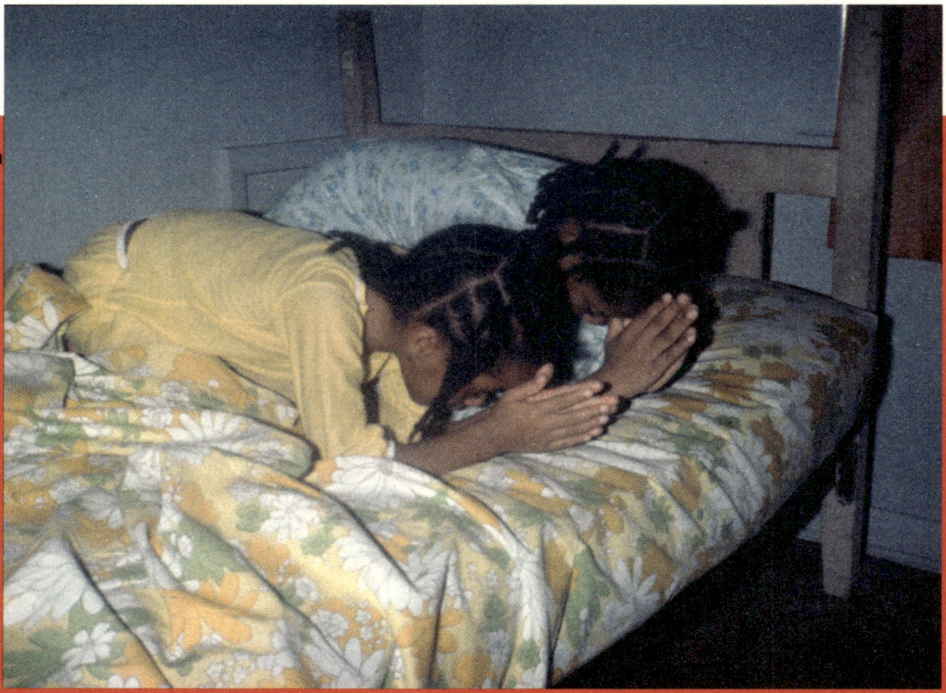

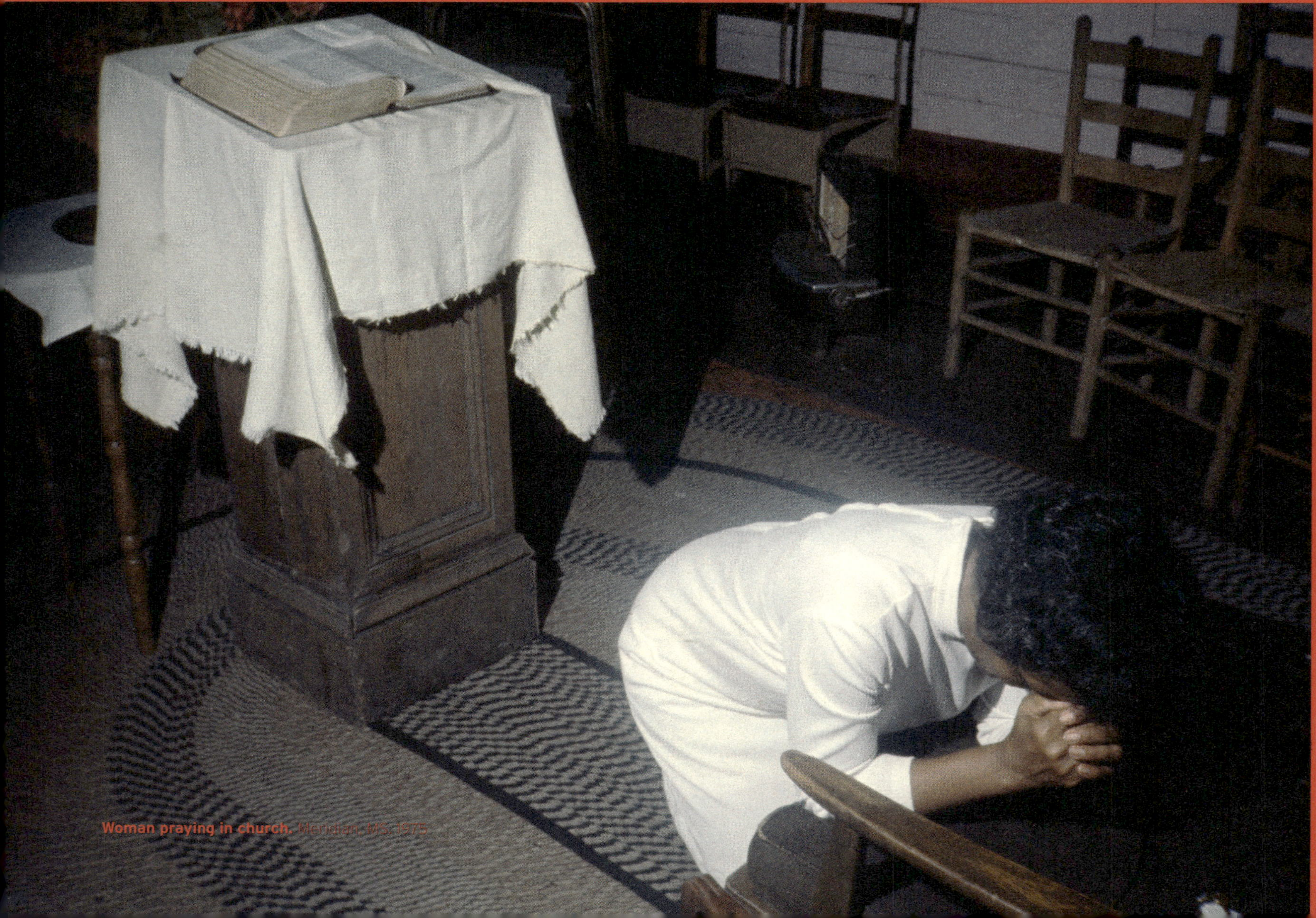

Woman praying in church. Meridian, MS. 1975

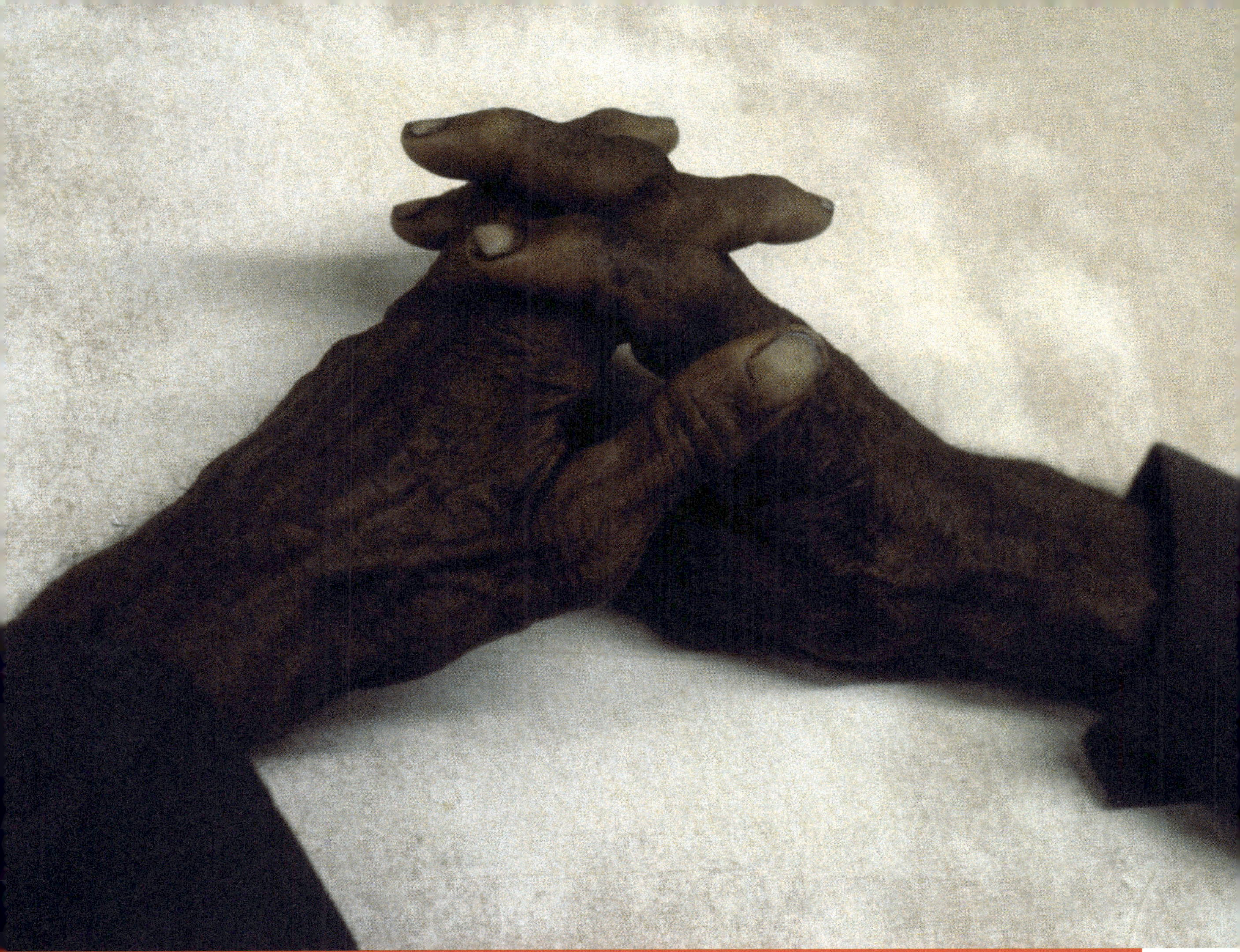

My father-in-law, Pastor Rush, is saying grace. Philadelphia, MS. 1975

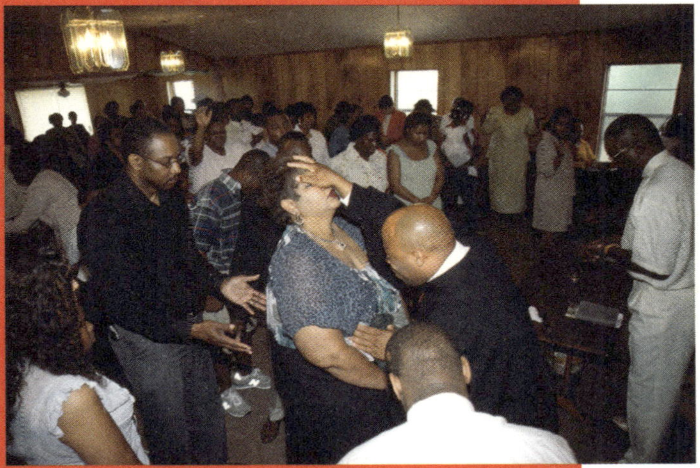

Laying on of hands on my friend Beverly in the church of my father-in-law on Easter Morning.
Philadelphia, MS. 2003

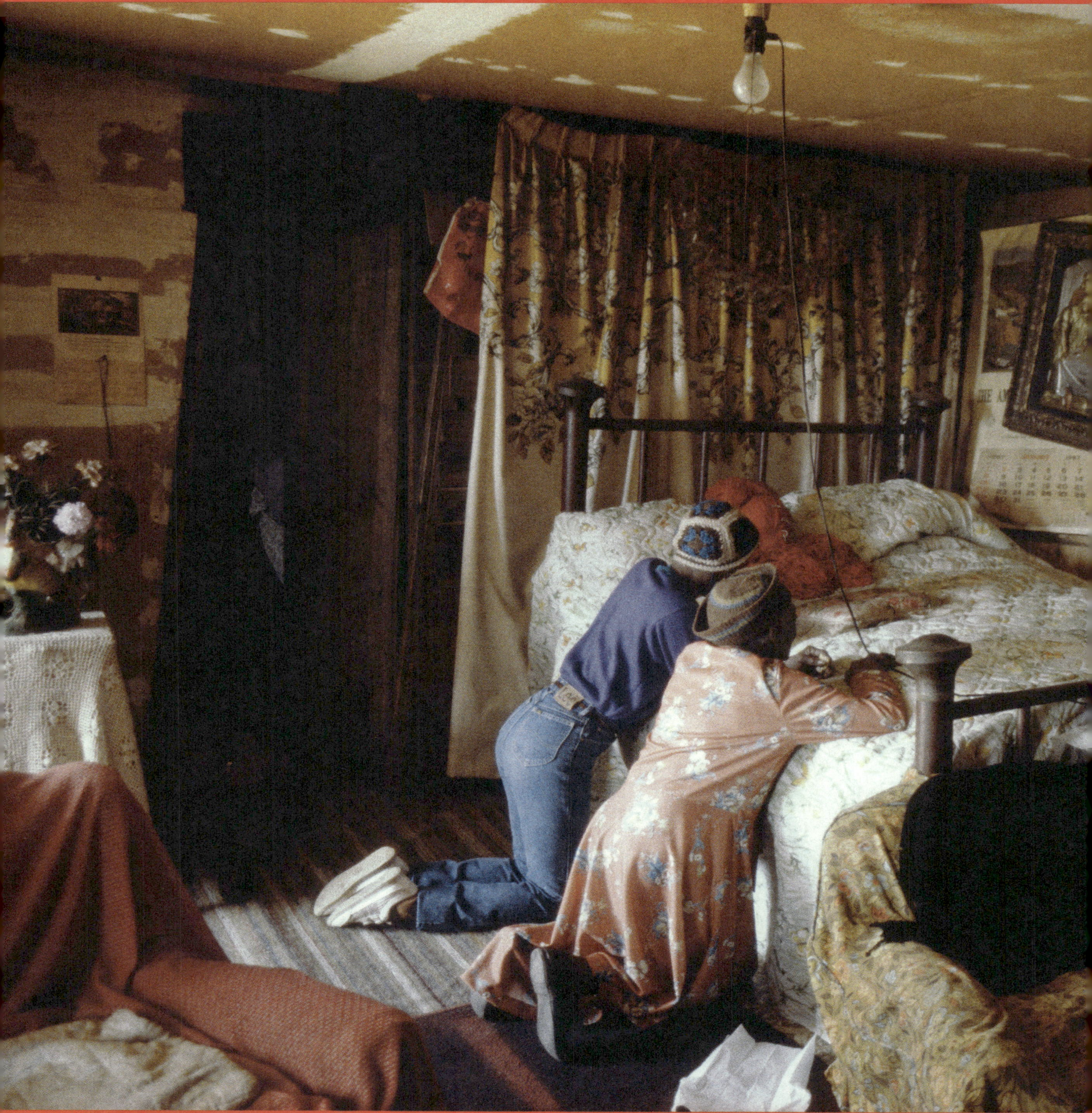

Mary praying with her 92-year-old aunt. Perote, AL. 1991

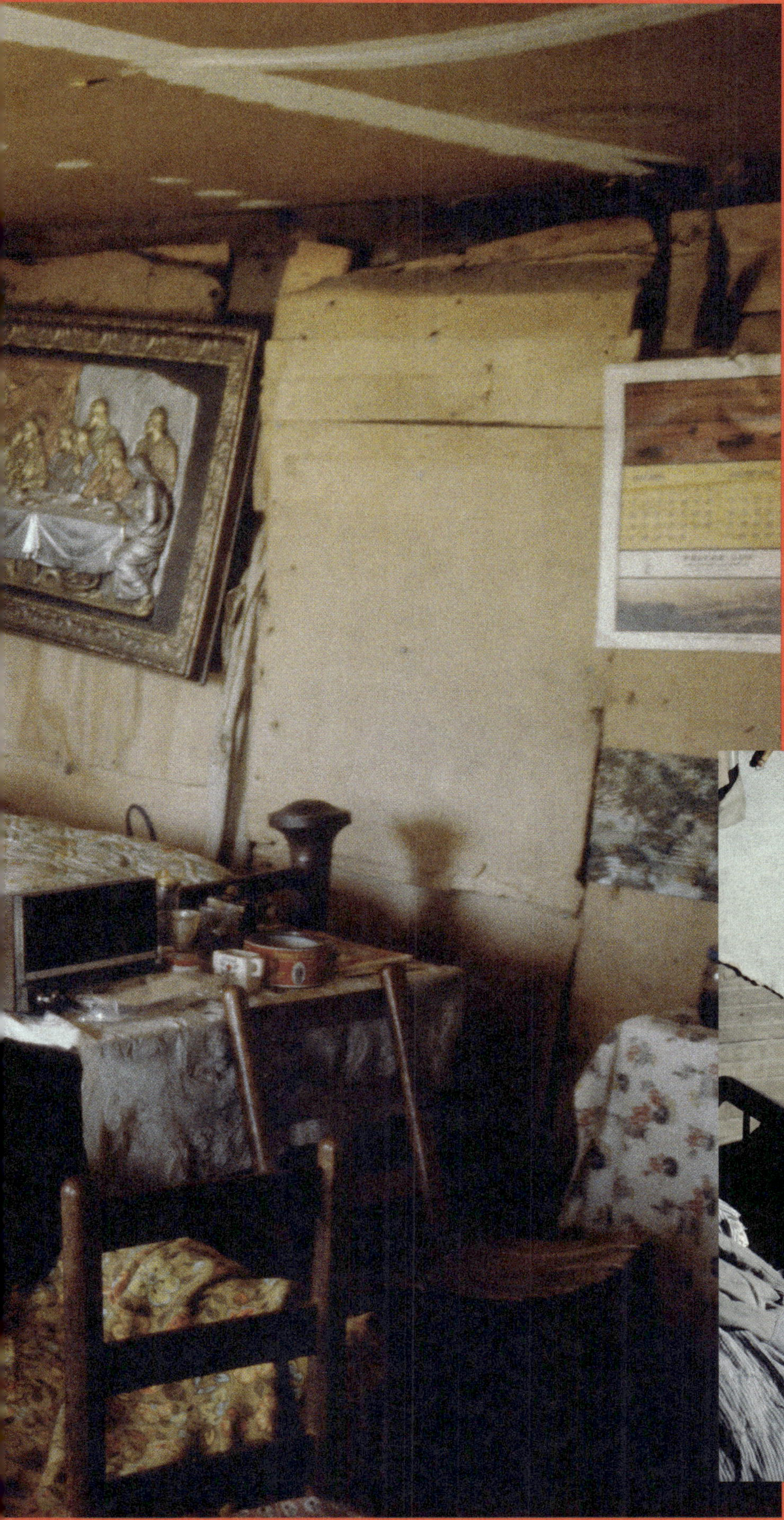

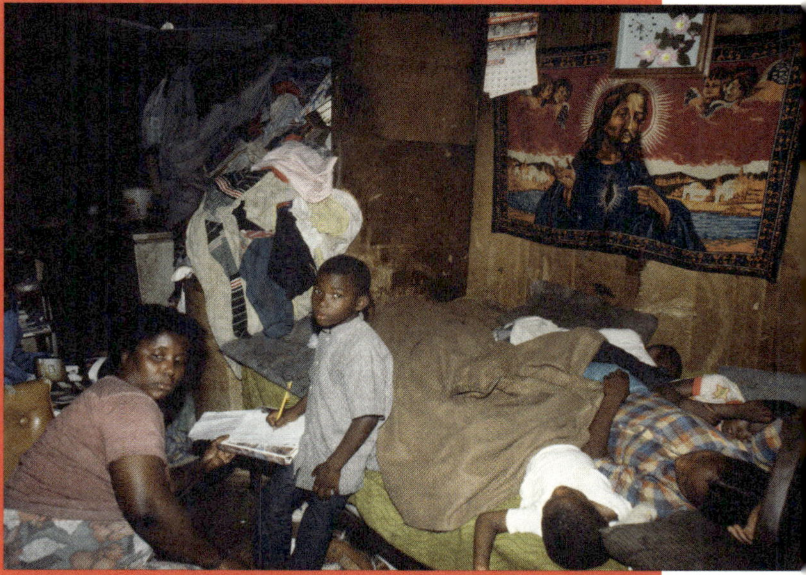

Jean is helping her grandchild with his homework in a shack housing 24 women and children.
Sardis, GA. 1989

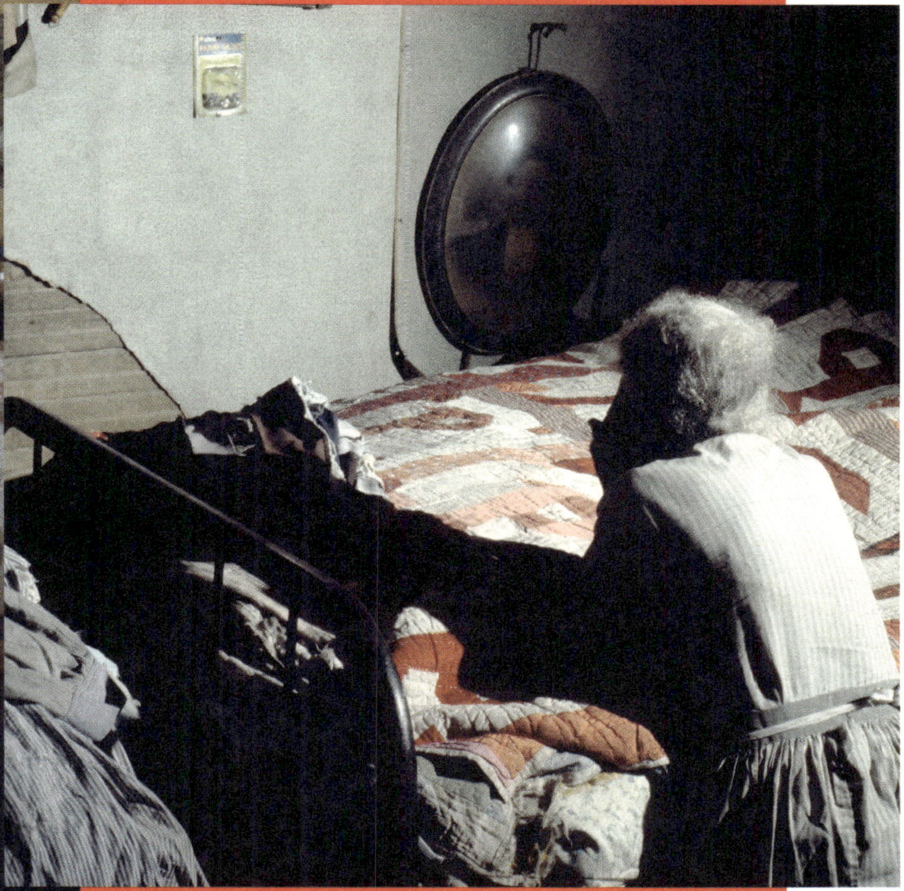

Gloria praying in her shack.
Waynesboro, GA. 1978

John

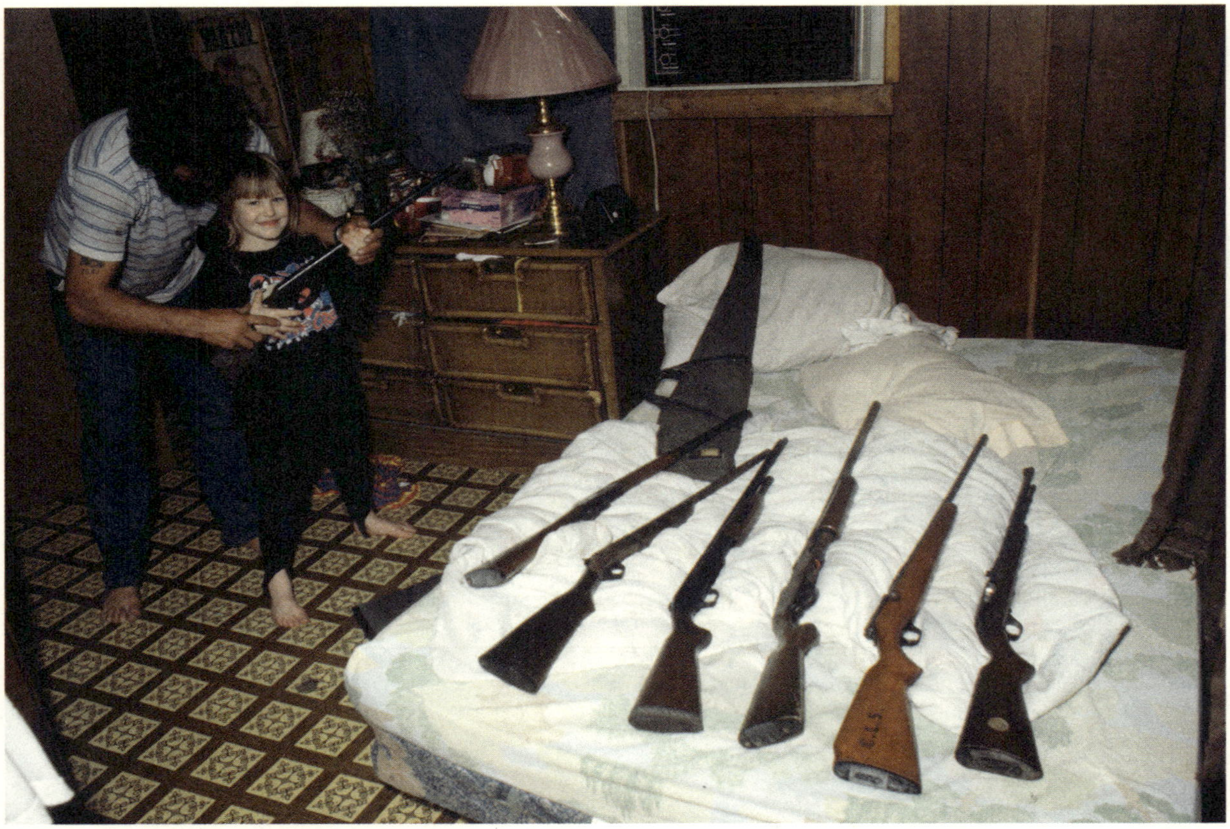

Murderer teaches his daughter the use of guns. Mississippi. 1996

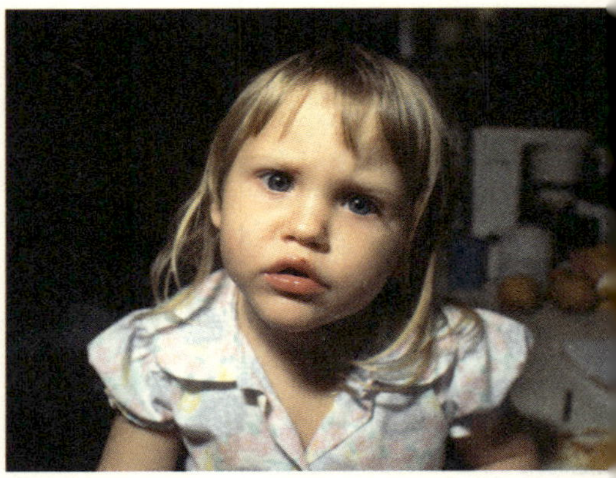

Two-year-old Gene, who is now in jail. Mississippi. 19

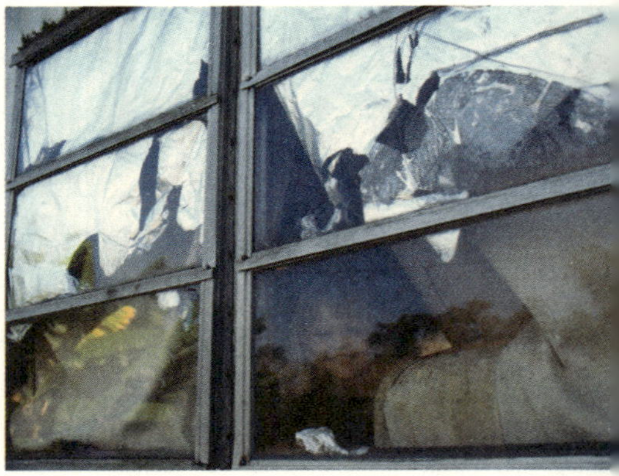

Samantha looking at the swamp from the trailor. Mississippi. 1996

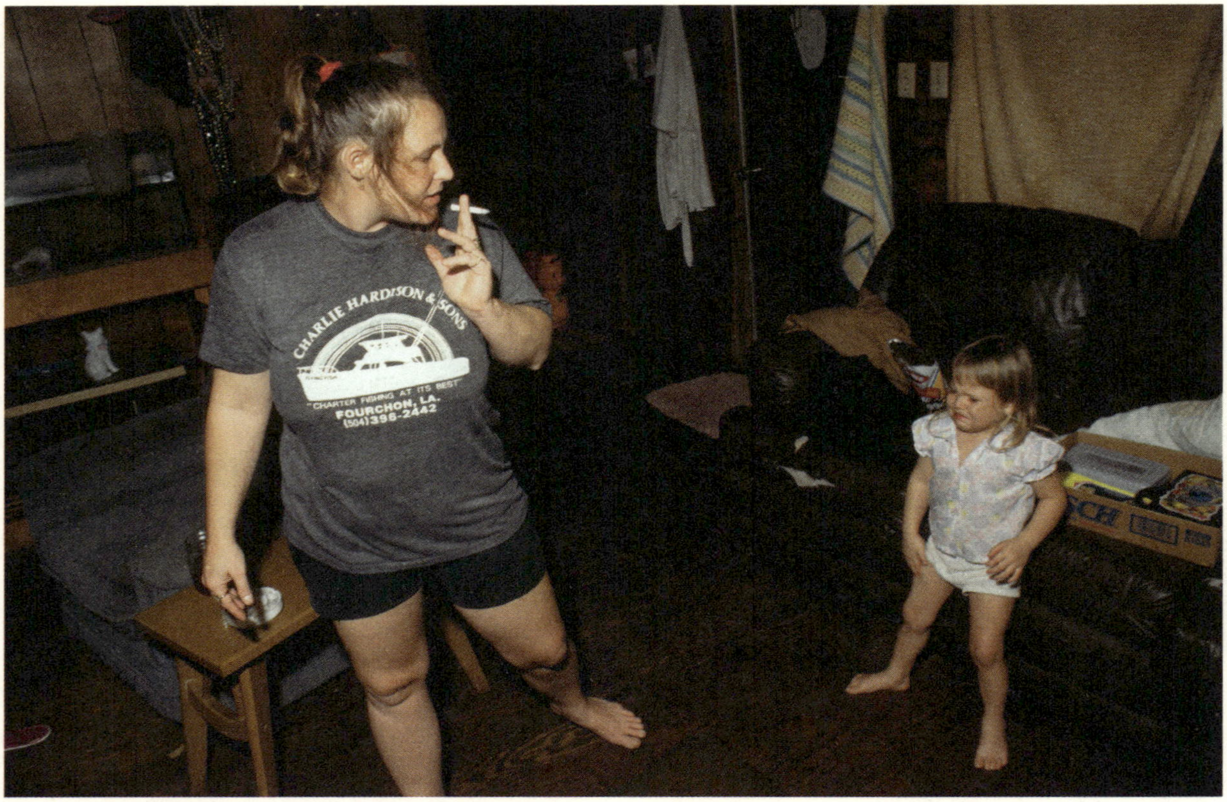

The mother Tina during one of the frequent abuses of Gene. Mississippi. 1996

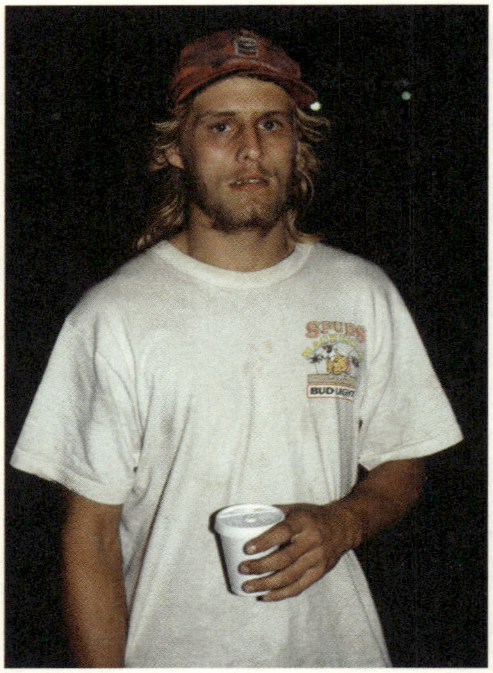

The hitchhiker Woody tells me about his killings of blacks. Mississippi. 1996

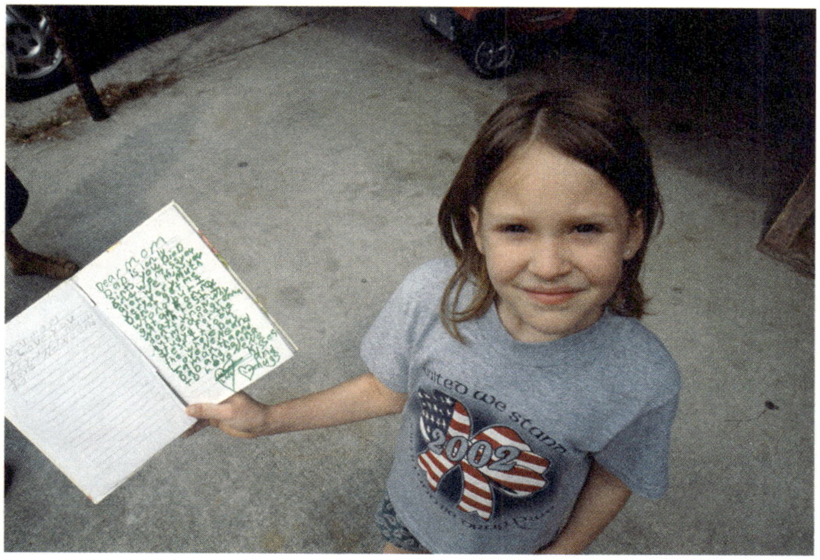

Gene tells about her mother's death. Mississippi. 2003

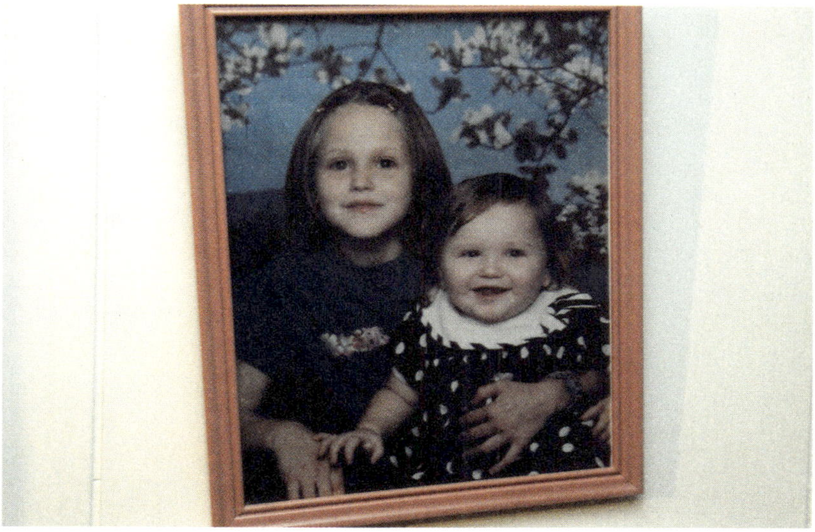

Gene with her little sister. Mississippi. 2003

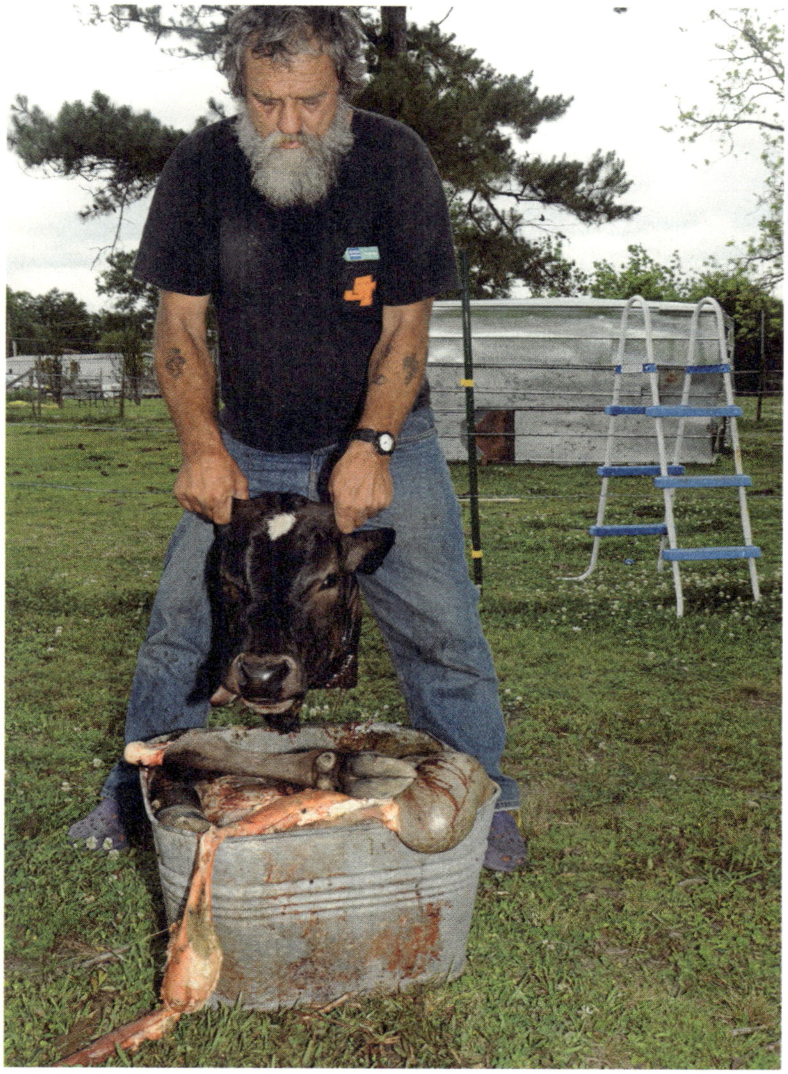

John is showing us the head of the cow that he shot when drunk the previous night. Mississippi. 2009

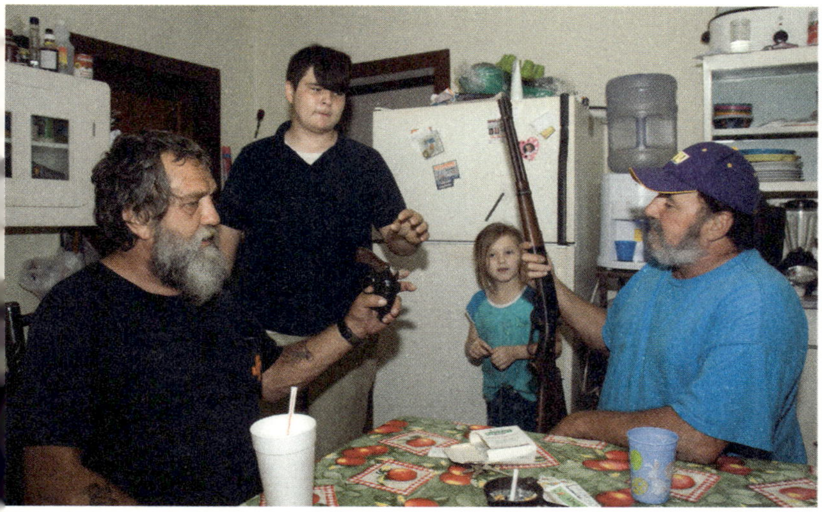

John is demonstrating how he killed his cow when he was drunk the previous night. Mississippi. 2009

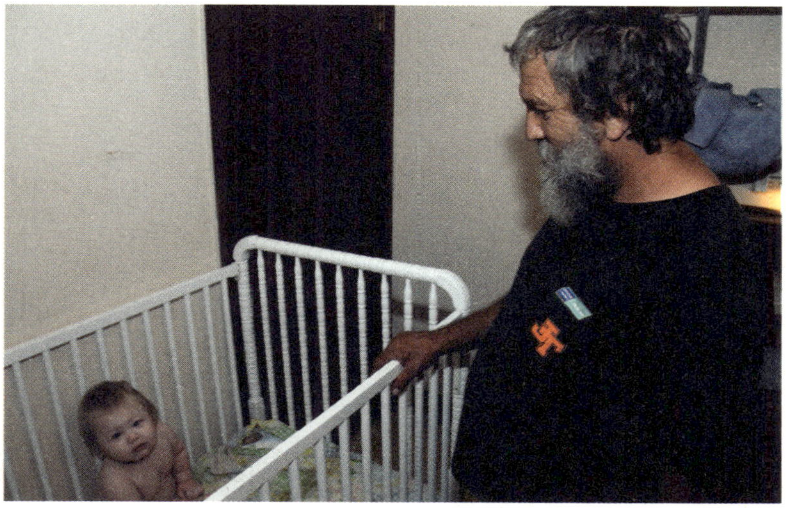

John is taking care of the child of the missing Samantha. Mississippi. 2009

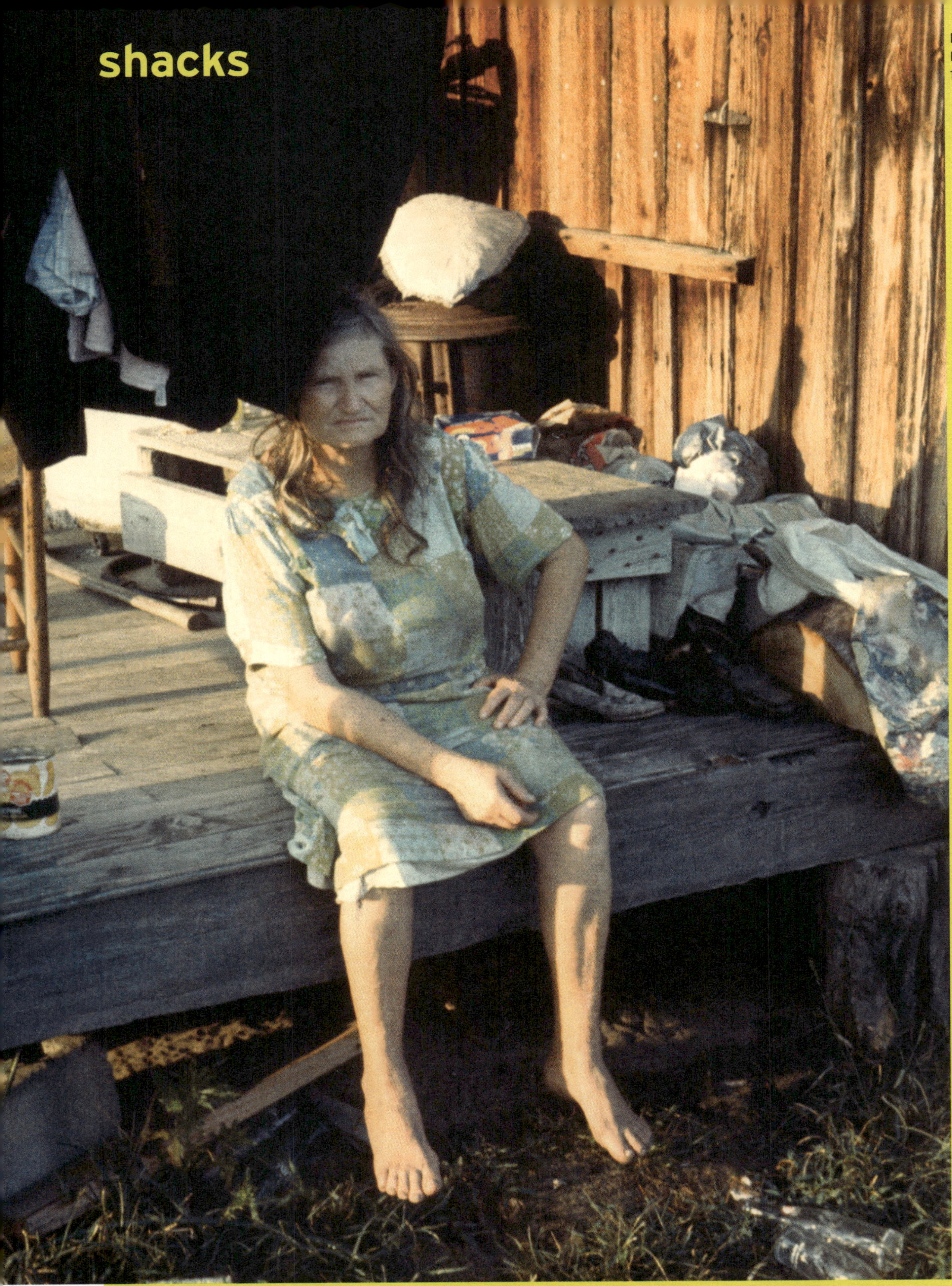

Poor white woman.
Elizabethtown, NC.
1974

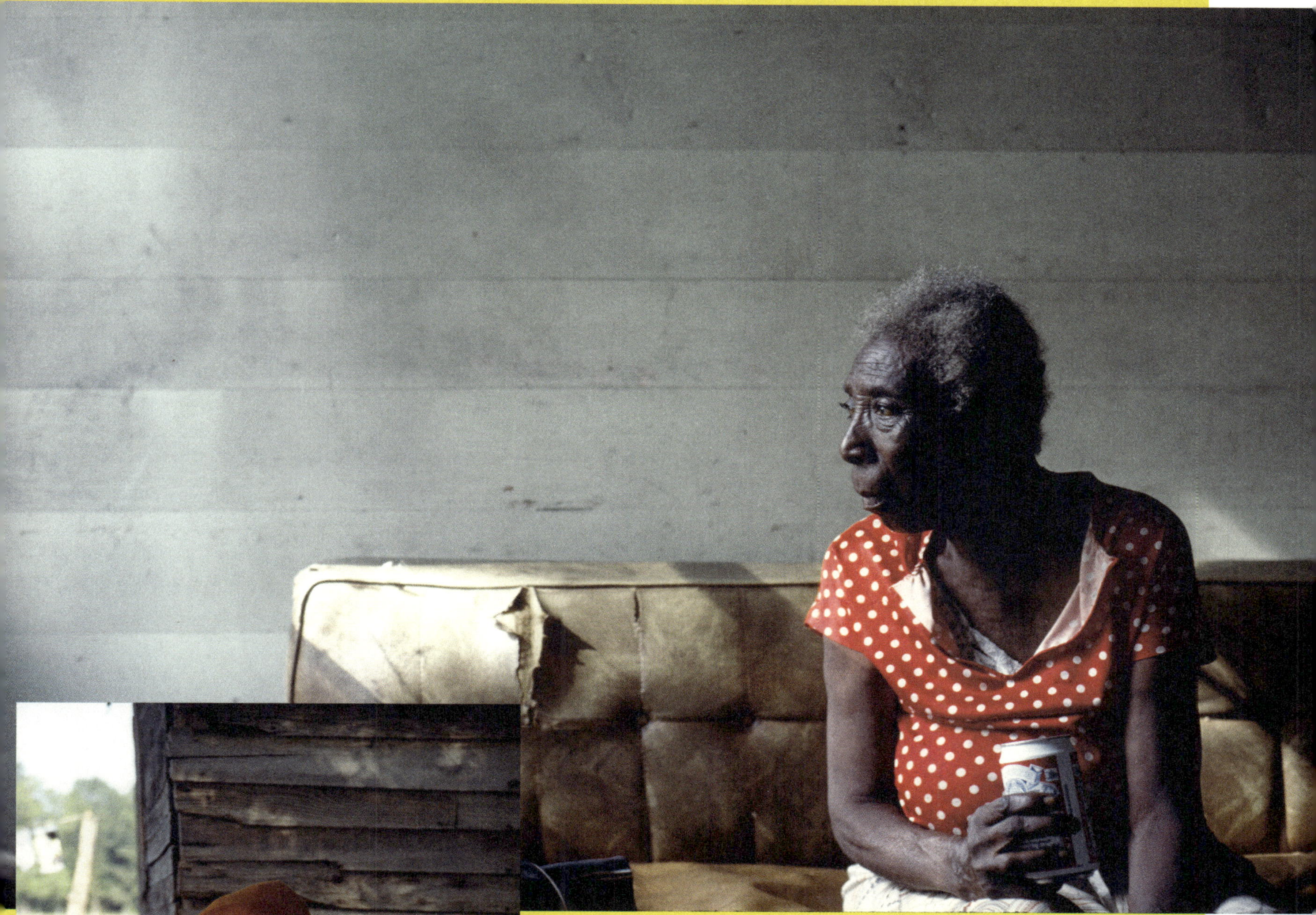

Ida Ford in her new shack. Perote, AL. 1994

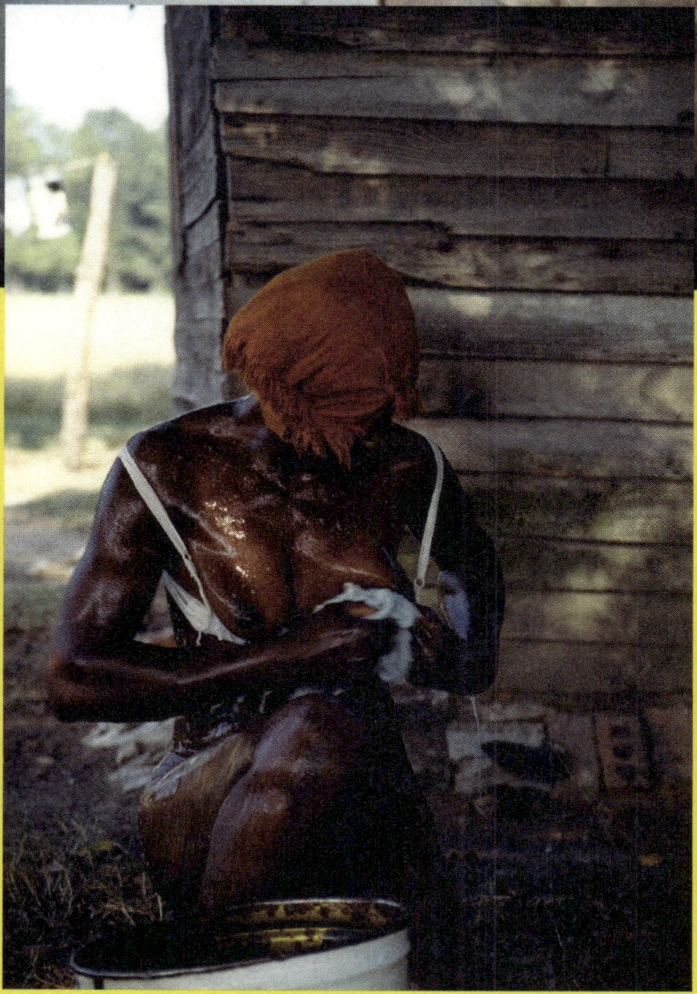

Wilma washing herself outside her shack. Cecil, AL. 1990

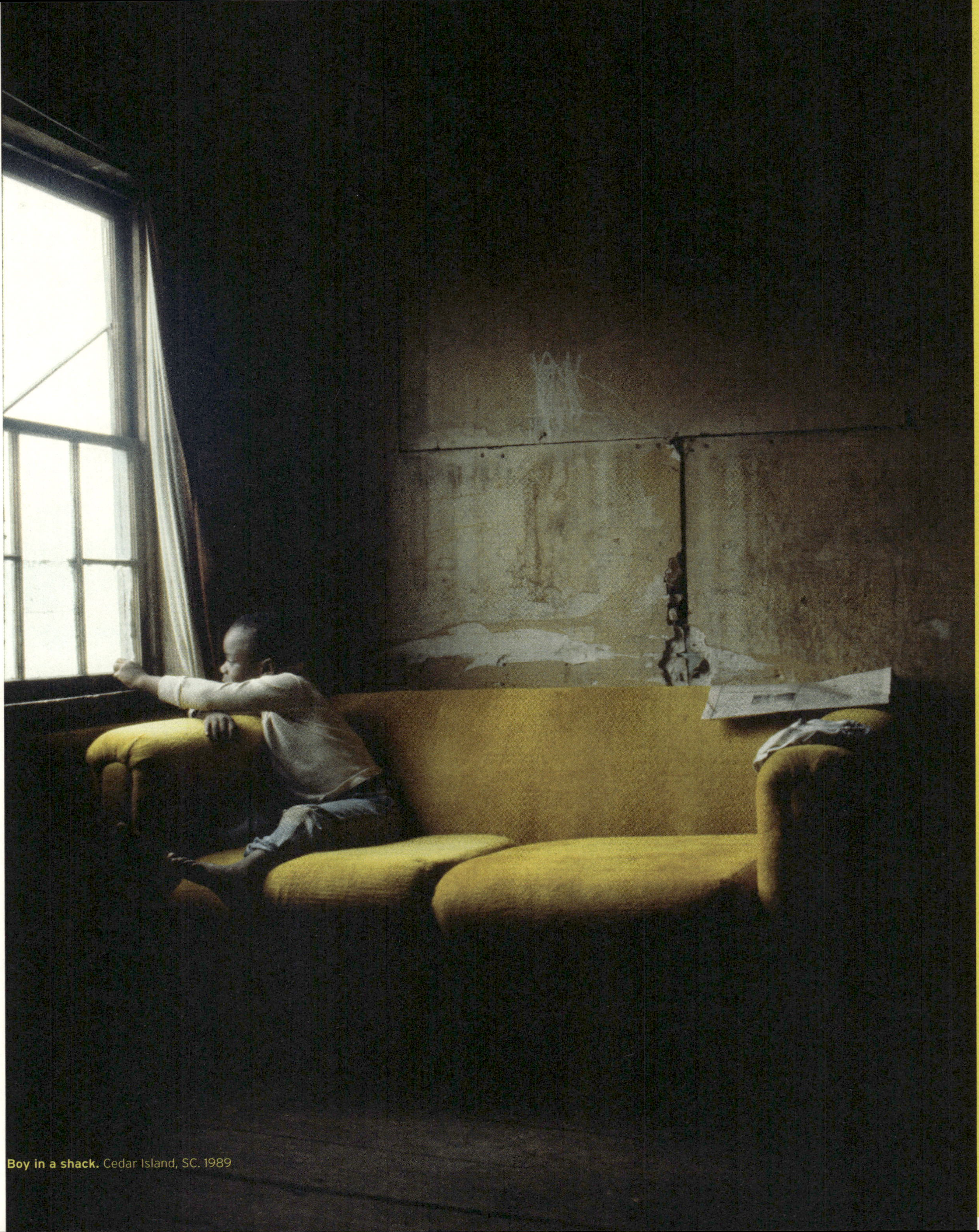

Boy in a shack. Cedar Island, SC. 1989

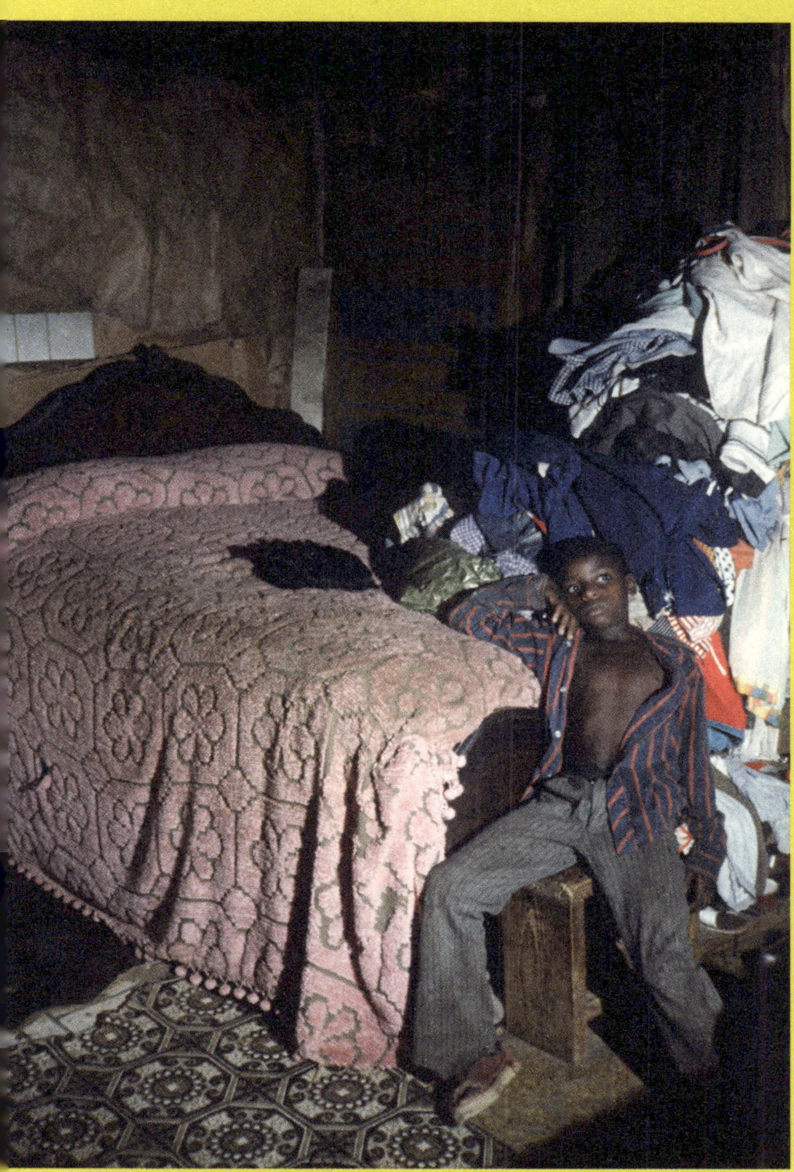

My first picture of 34 years of photographing the life of Carl Overstreet. Philadelphia, MS. 1975

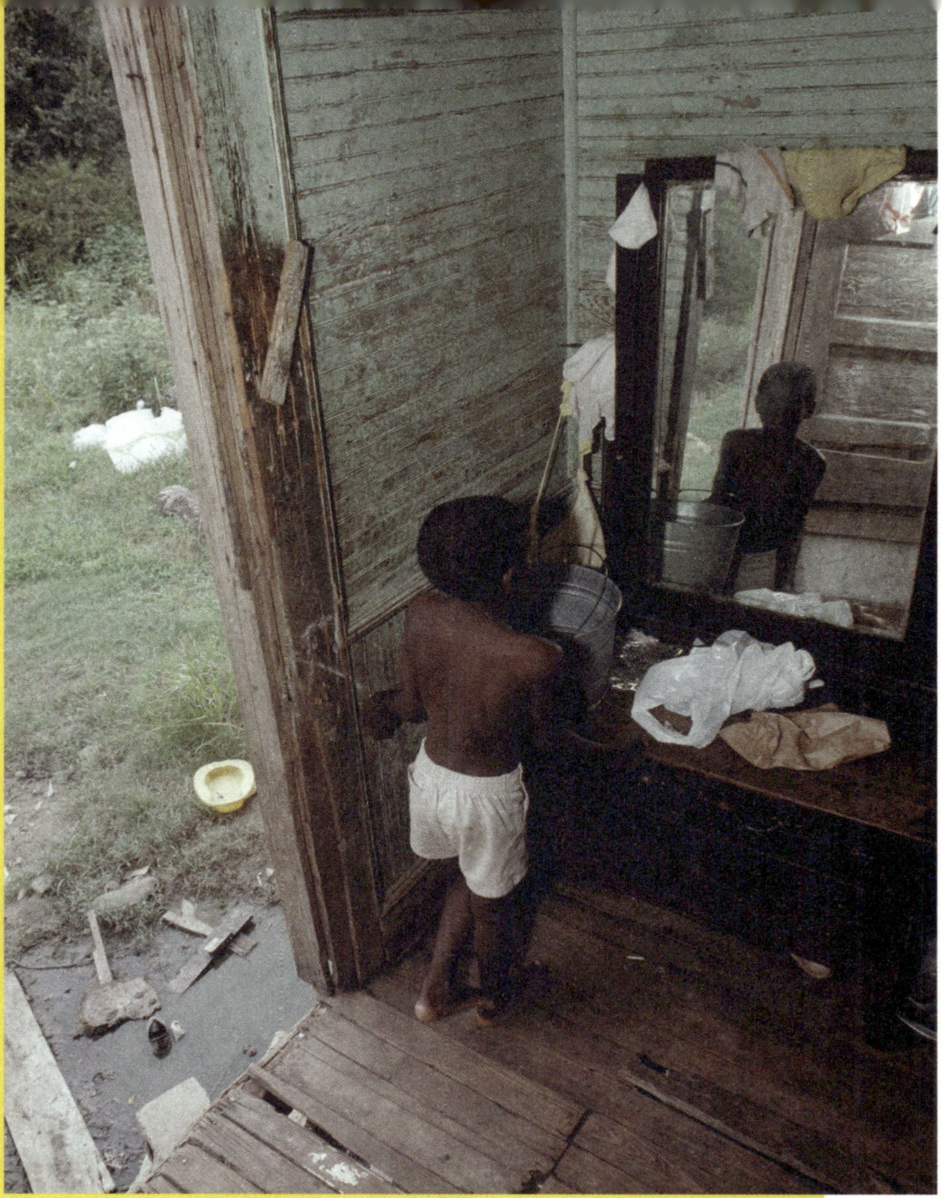

Boy in a shack. Thompson, AL. 1989

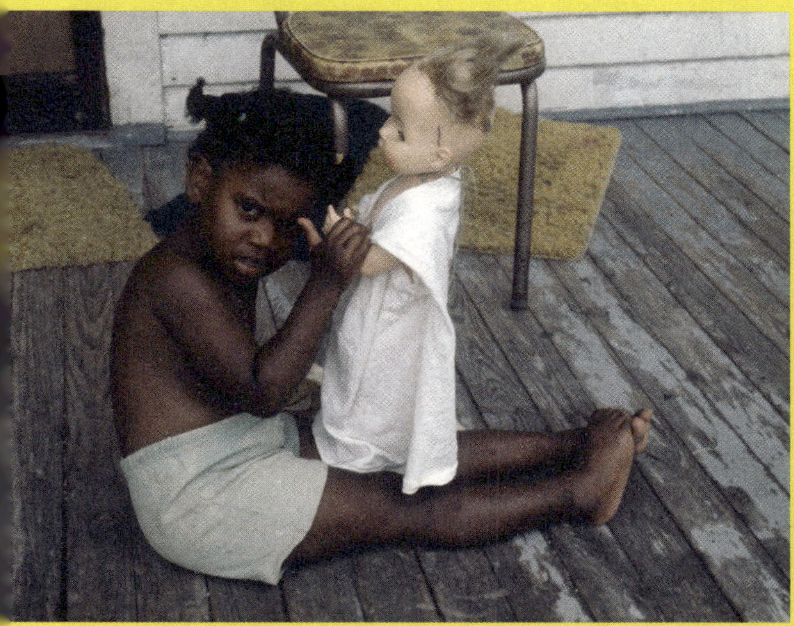

Girl with white doll. Detroit, MI. 1972

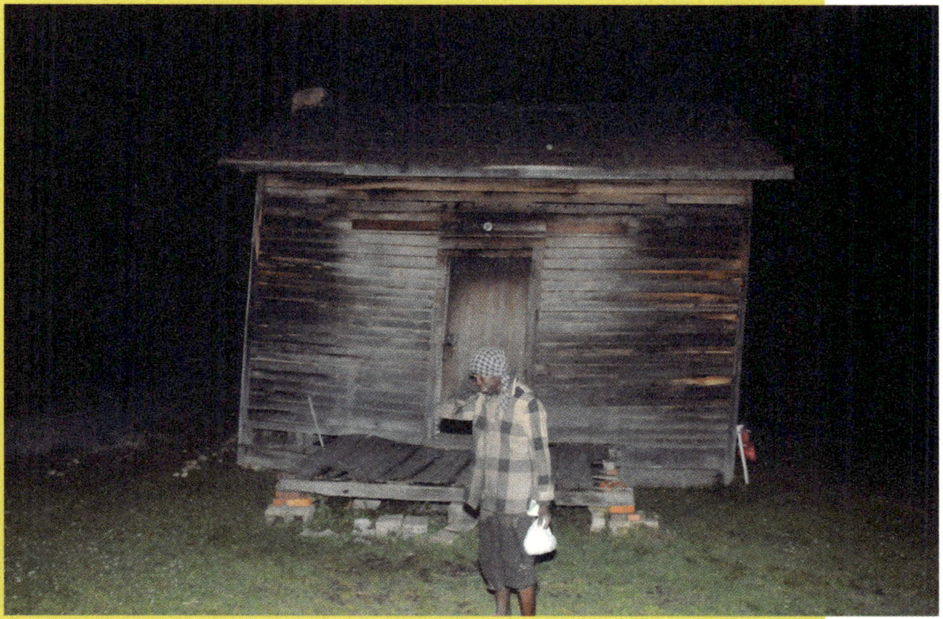

Wilma outside her new one-room shack without running water and electricity. Cecil, AL. 2009

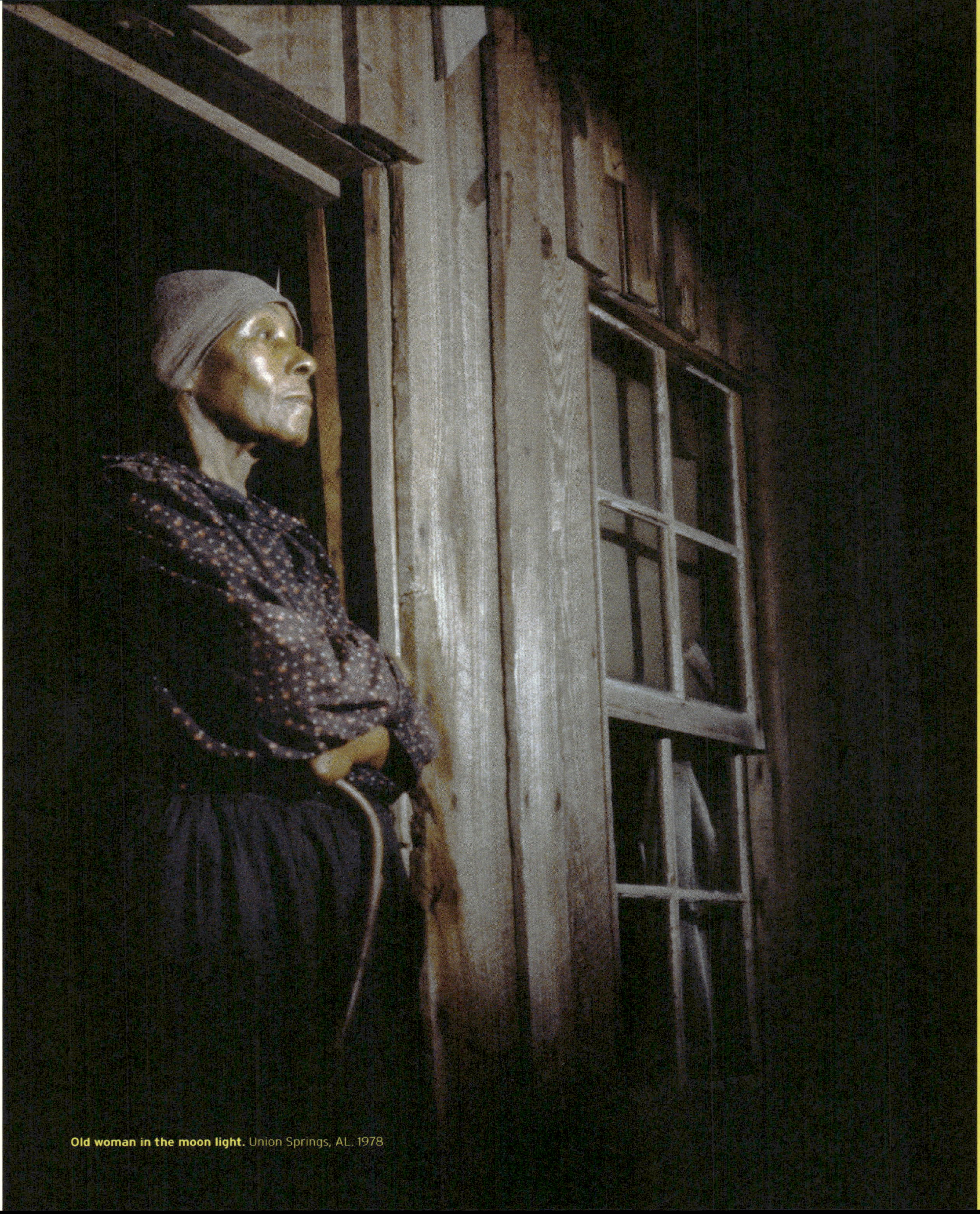

Old woman in the moon light. Union Springs, AL. 1978

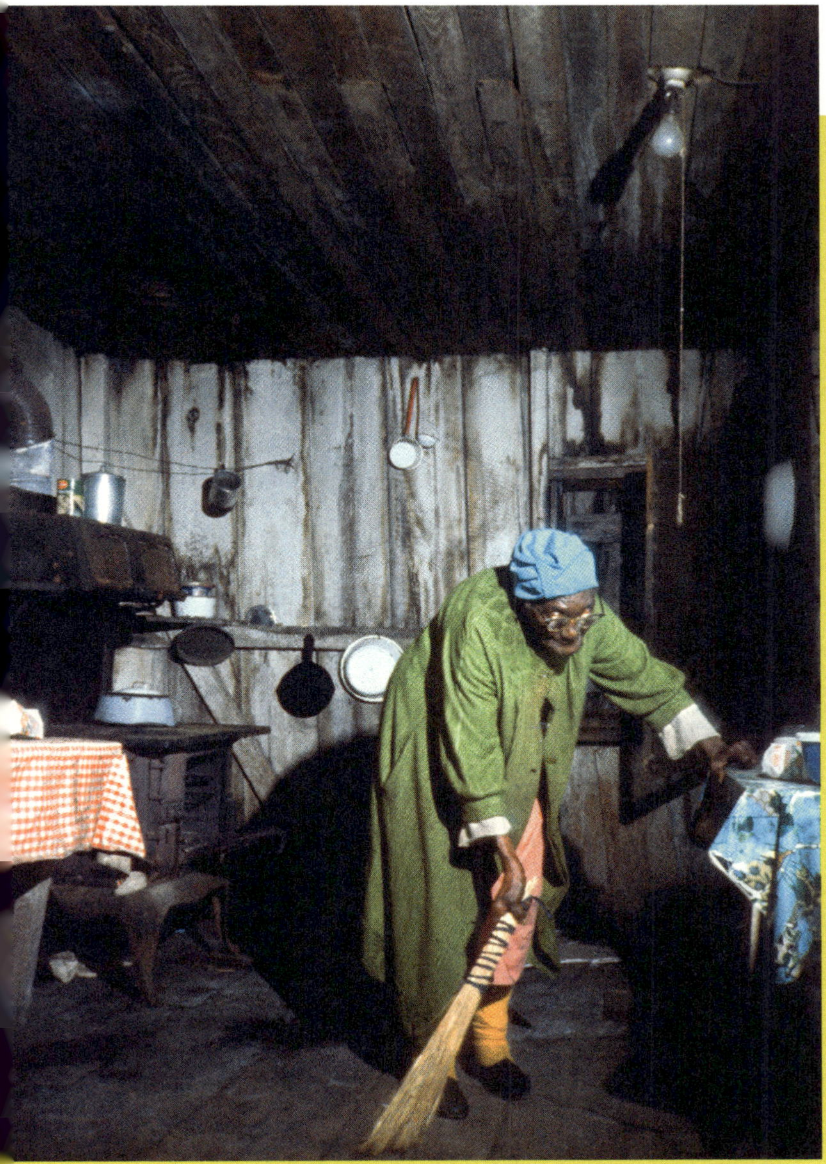

Anna King shortly before she died. Tuskegee, AL. 1975

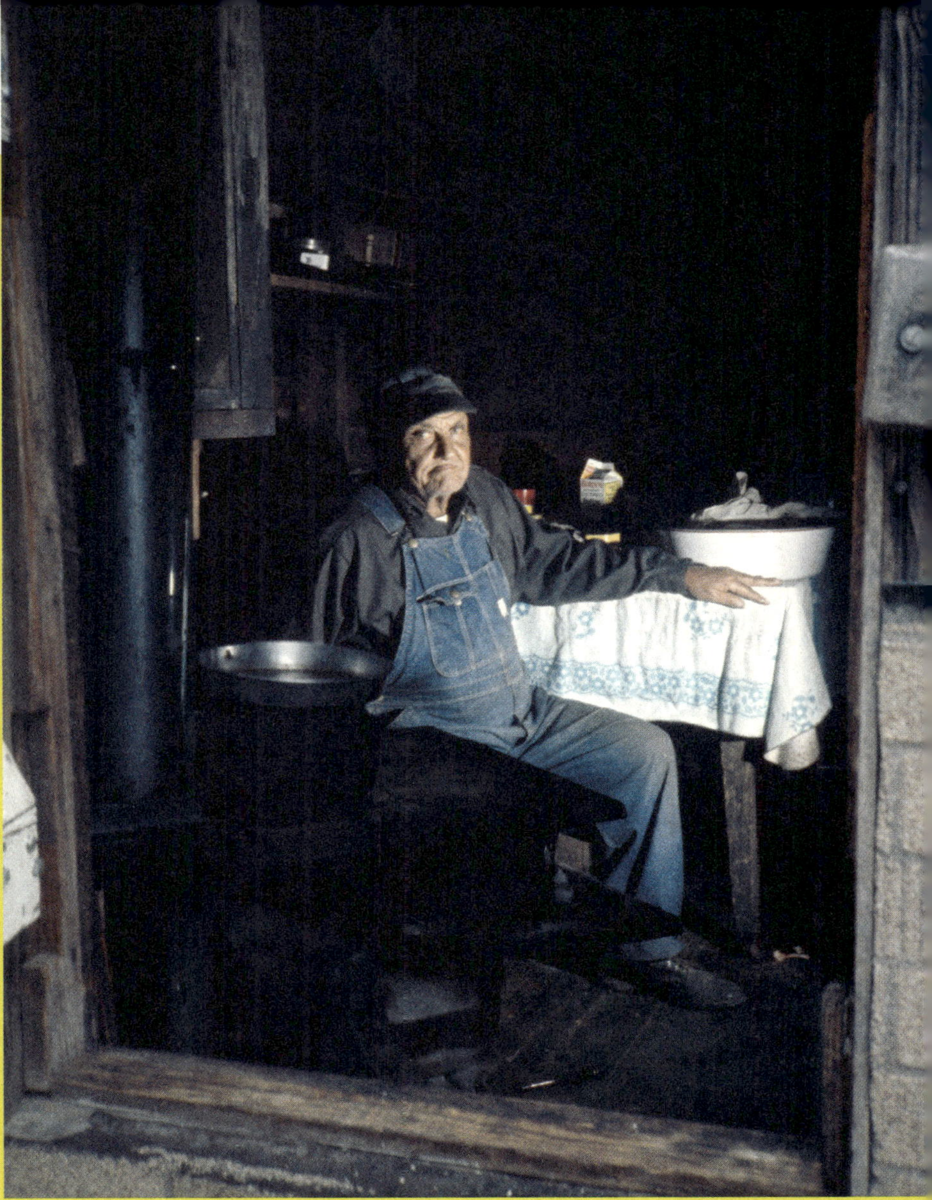

Sharecropper in his shack. Waynesboro, GA. 1974

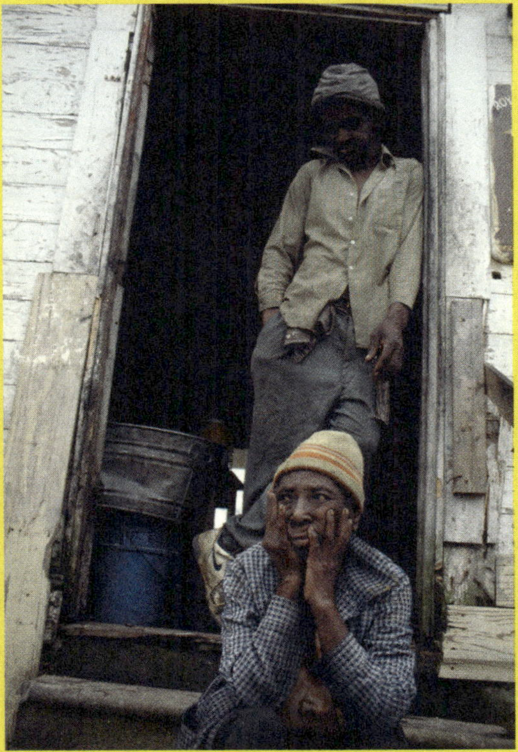

Ida and Joe in their shack.
Perote, AL. 1996

night

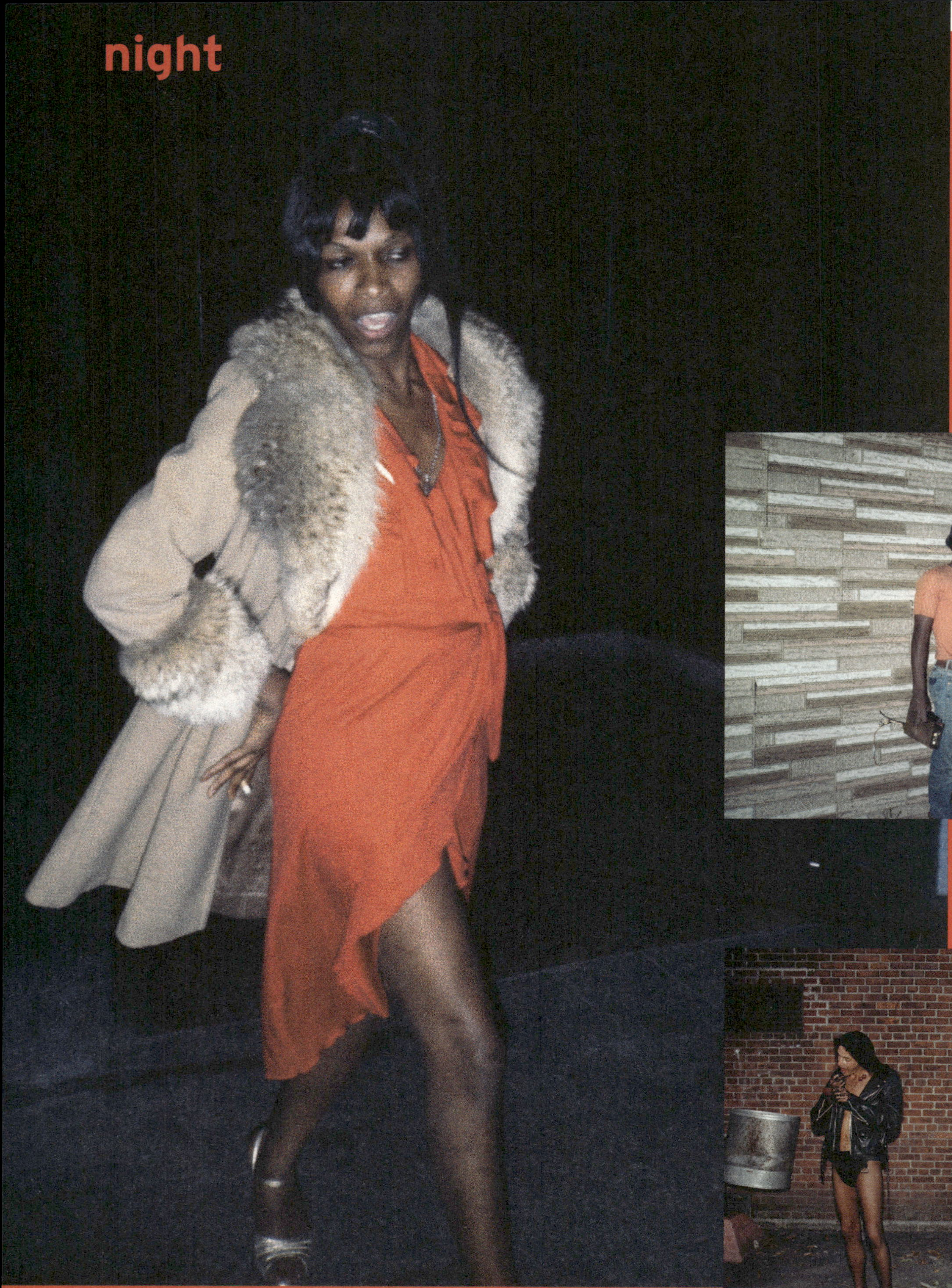

Looking for customers with my friend, the transvestite Tania. San Francisco, CA. 1975

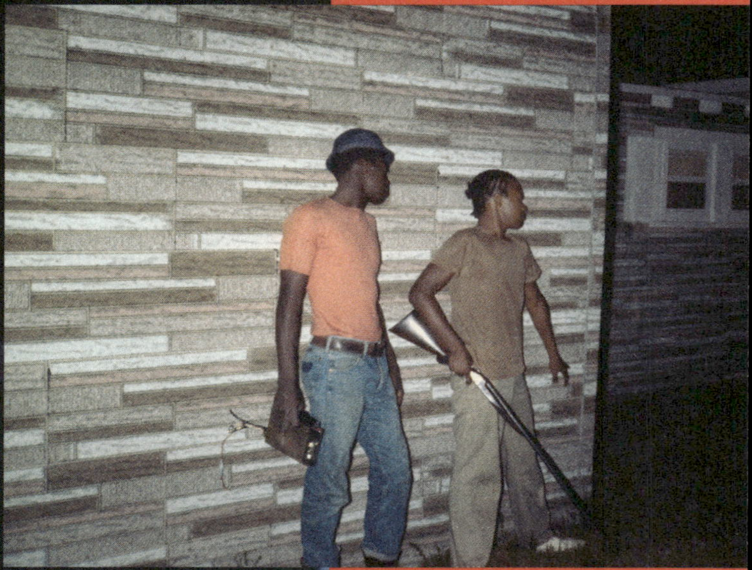

Willy Henry with another member of the street gang on the prowl on the night after he shot his own brother. Richmond, VA. 1974

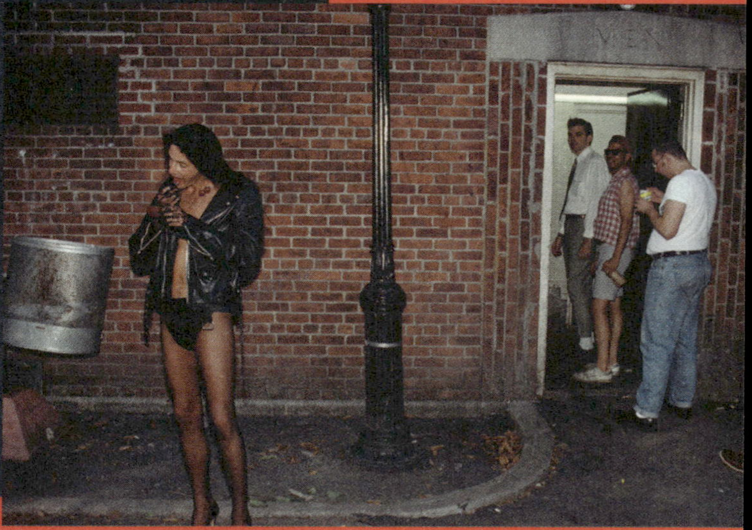

Transvestite in Tompkins Square Park. New York, NY. 1998

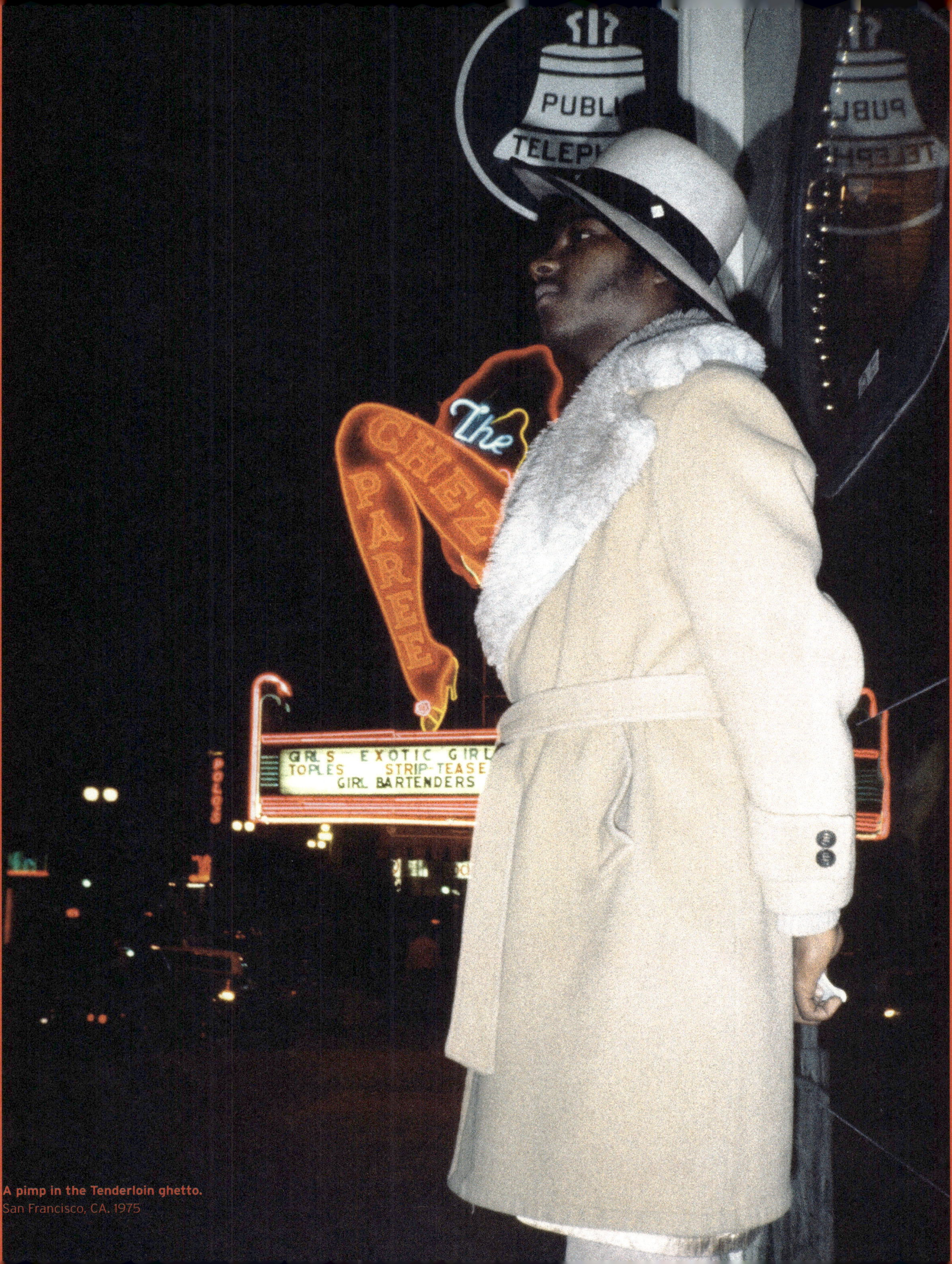

A pimp in the Tenderloin ghetto.
San Francisco, CA. 1975

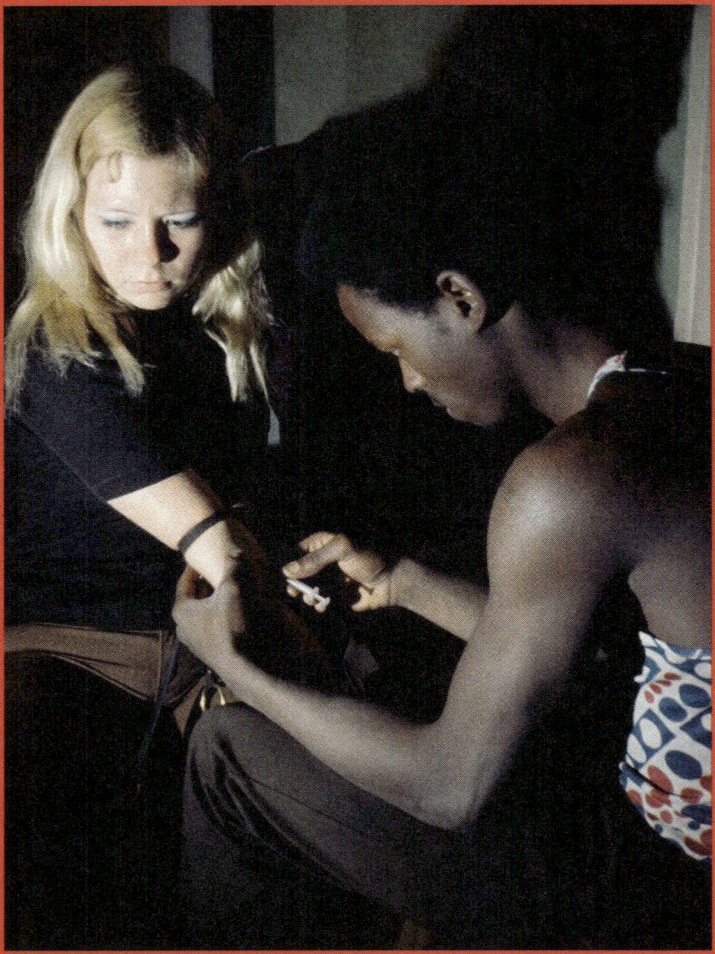

Don shoots up Aline before we share the matress for the night when I take photos of them screwing.
Jacksonville, FL. 1974

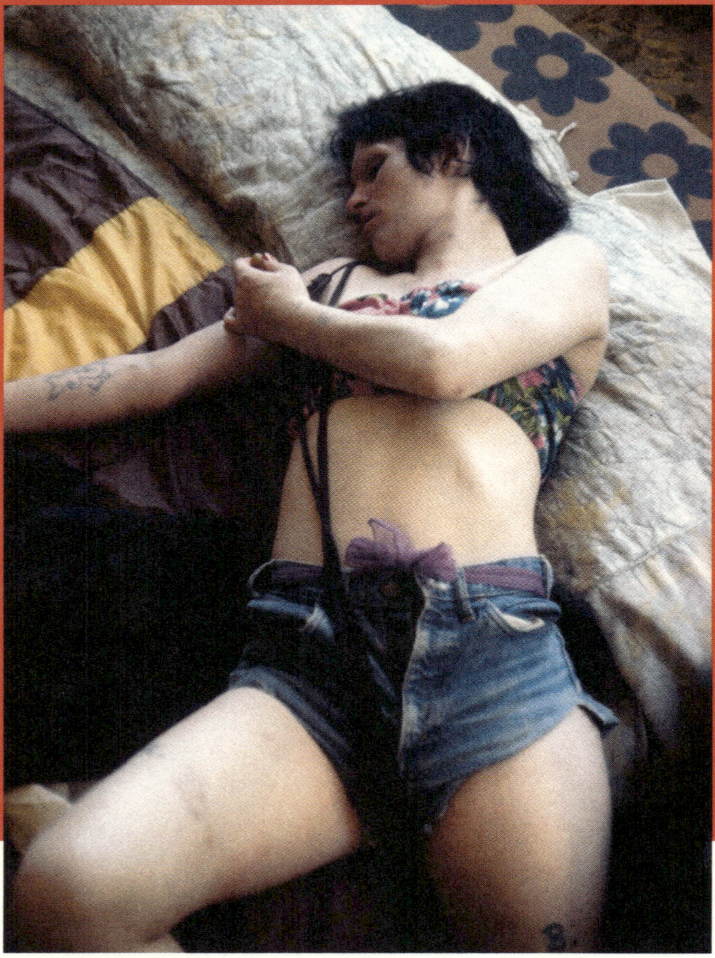

My transvestite friend, Carla, with whom I stayed in the Tenderloin ghetto was a heroin addict.
San Francisco, CA. 1975

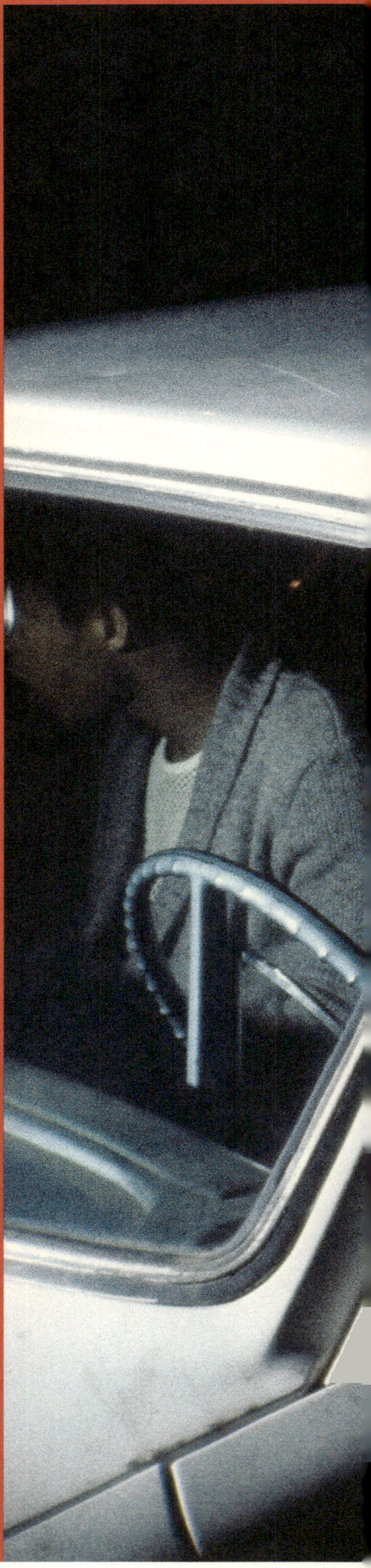

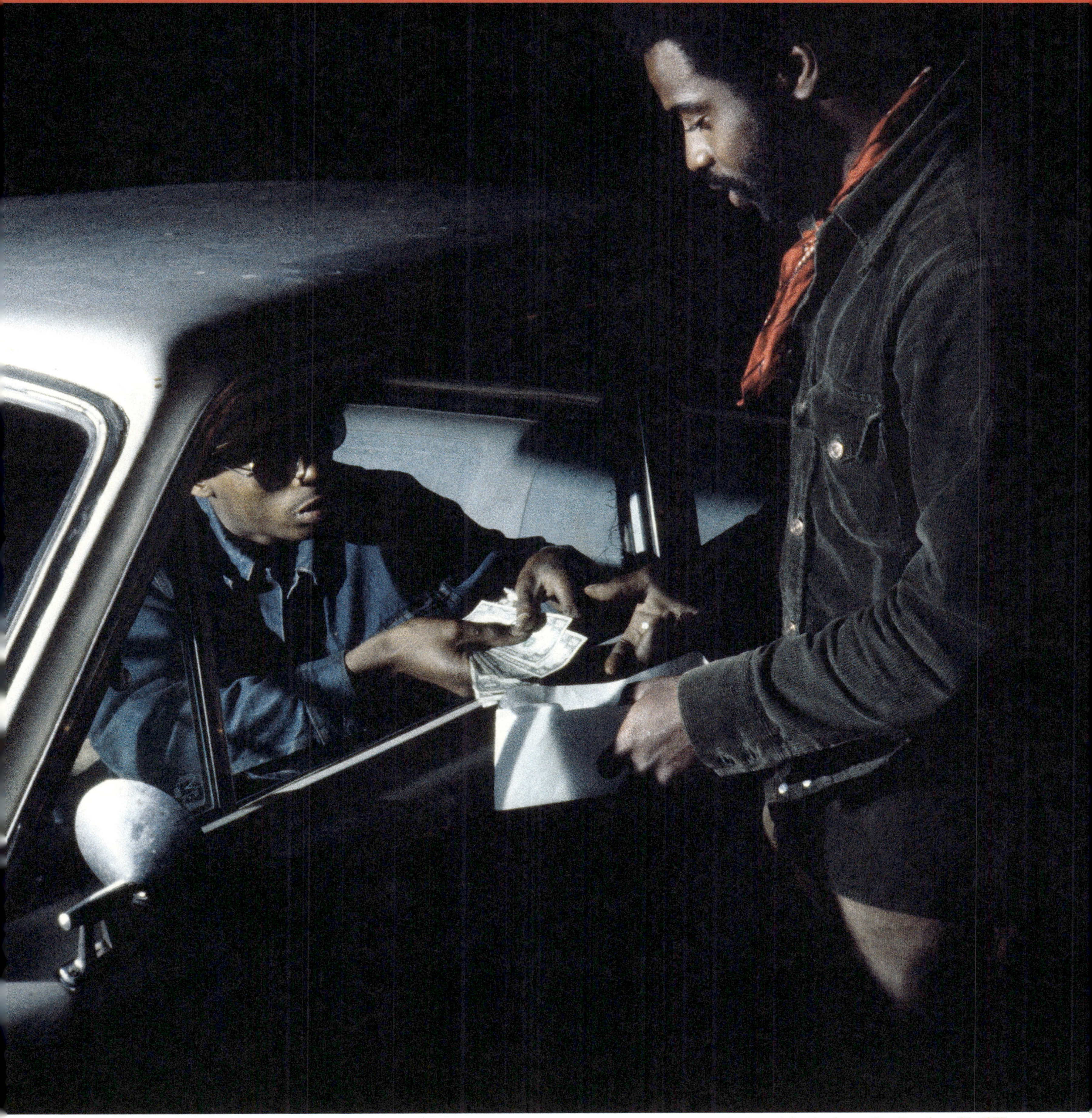

Pushers doing business. San Francisco, CA. 1975

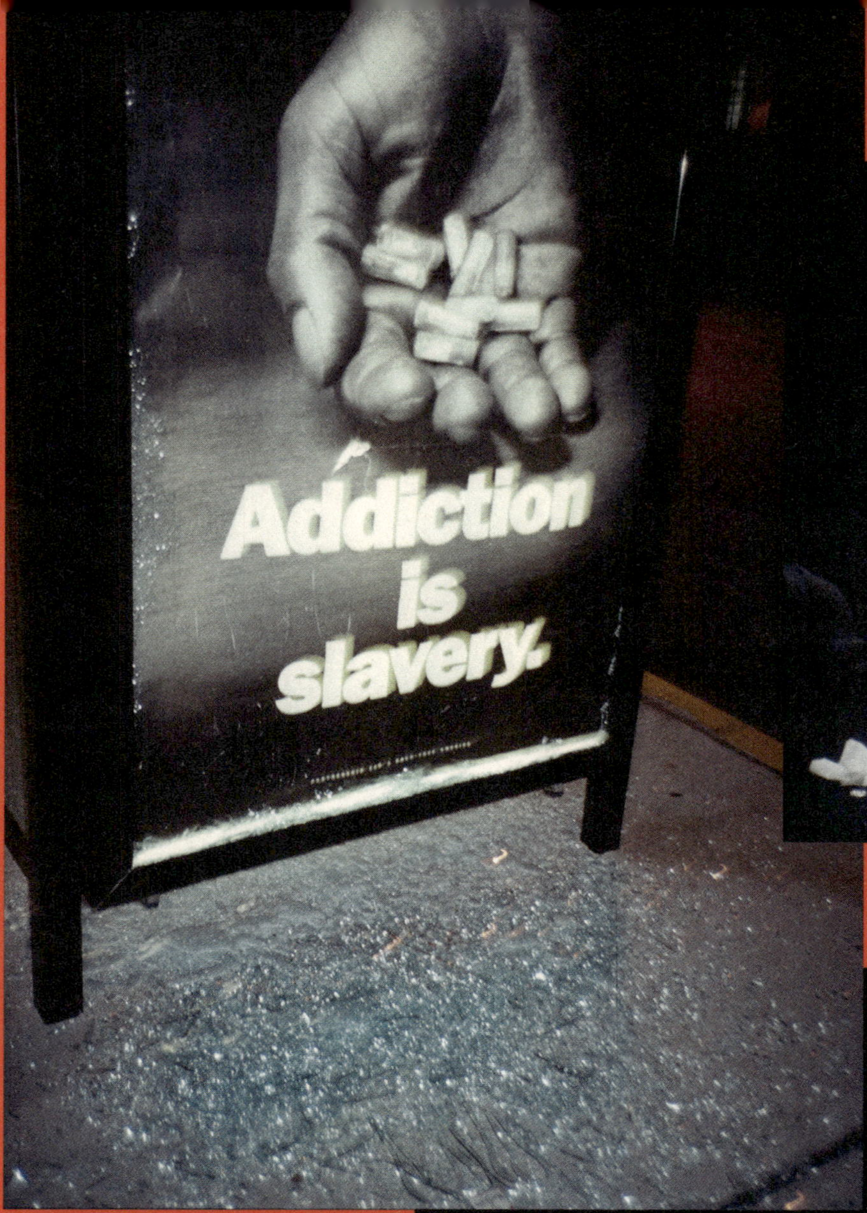

During the years at the hight of the crack epidemic I lost the greatest number of black friends. New York, NY. 1992

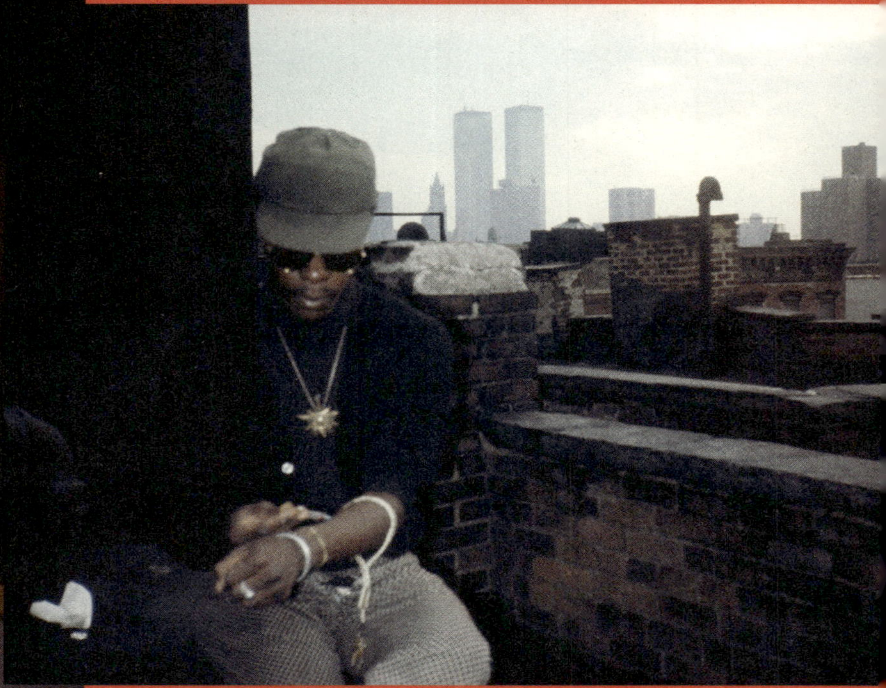

Drug addict and The World Trade Center. New York, NY. 1974

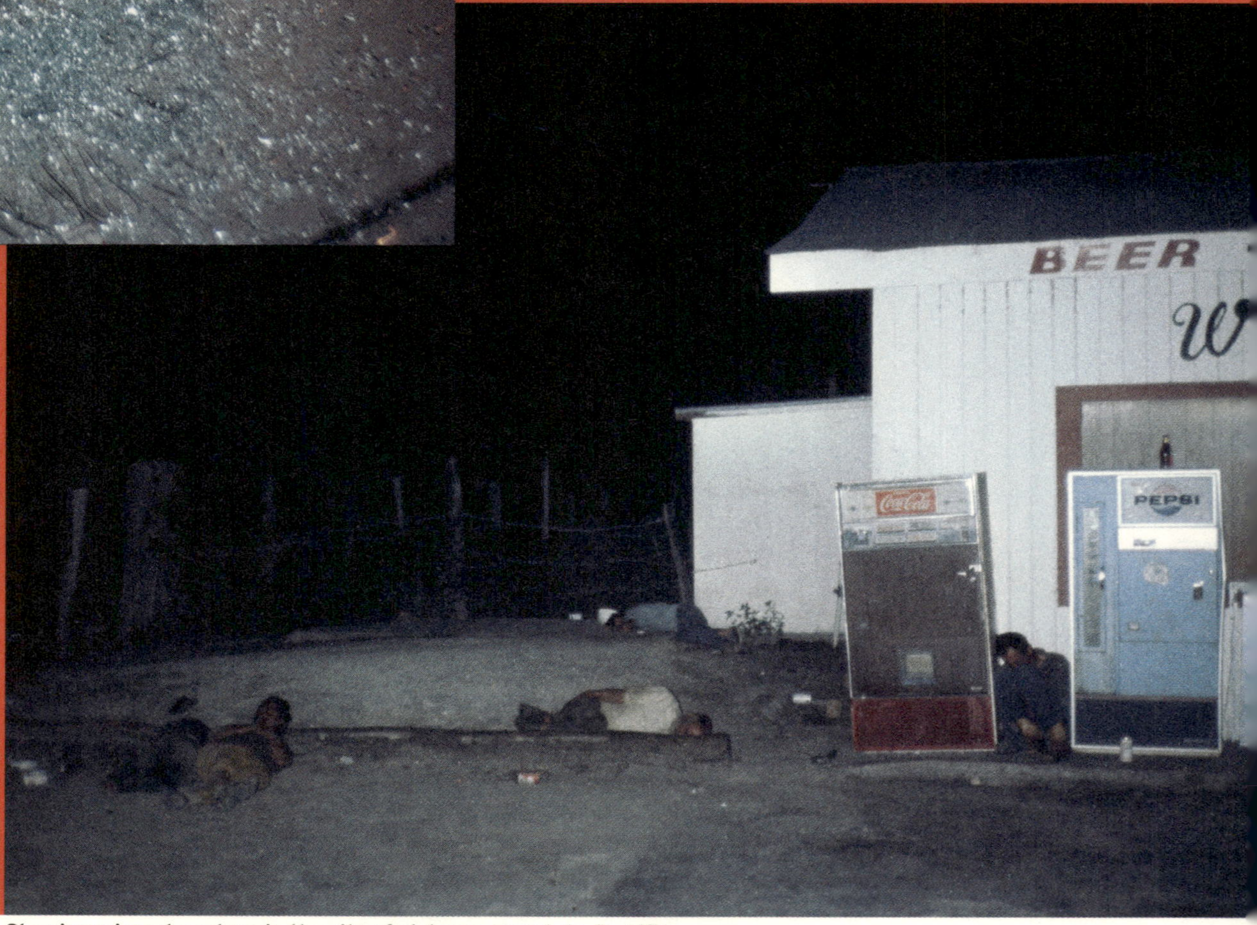

Sleeping migrant workers in the city of violence. Immokale, FL. 1974

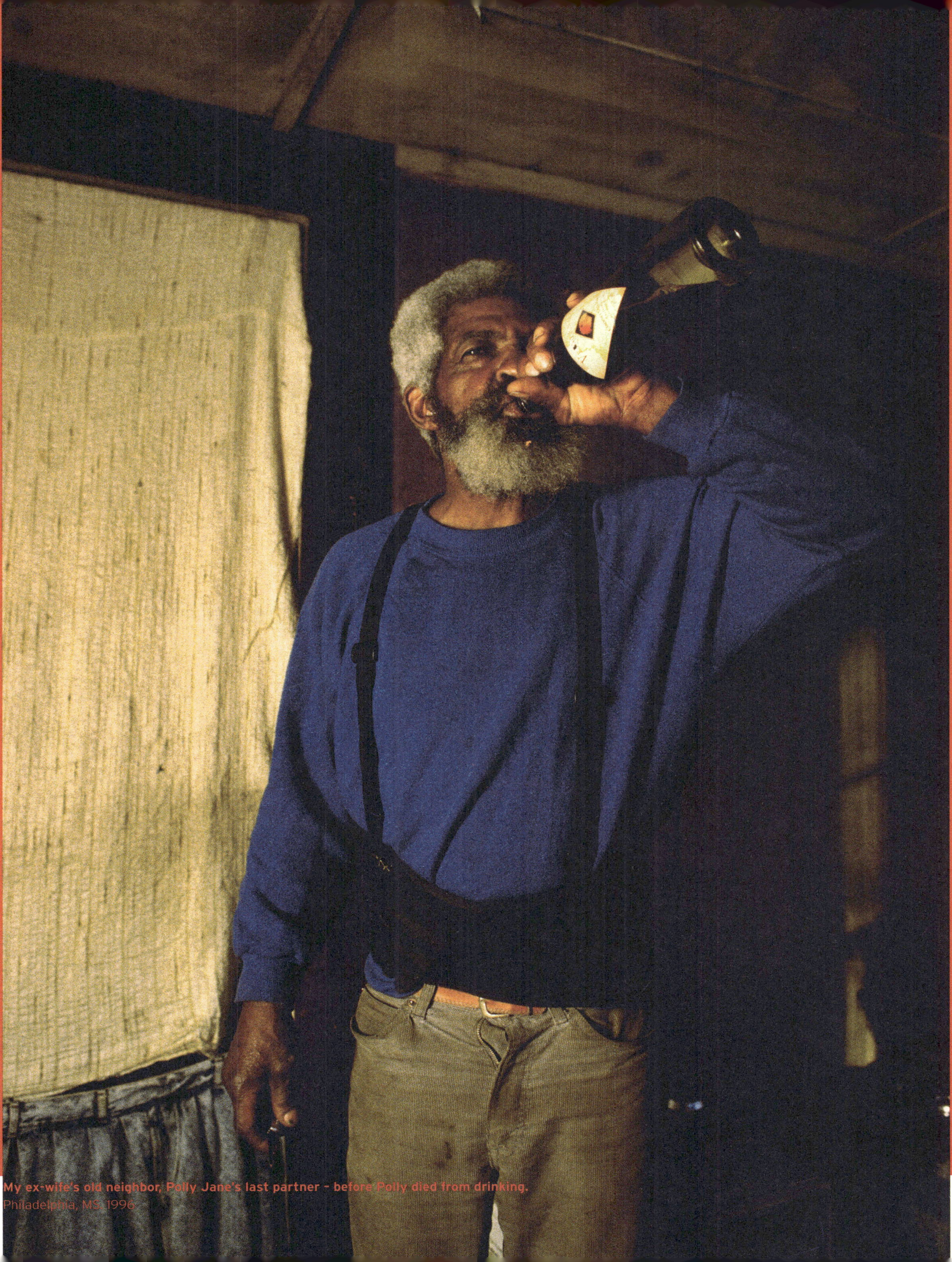

My ex-wife's old neighbor, Polly Jane's last partner - before Polly died from drinking.
Philadelphia, MS. 1996

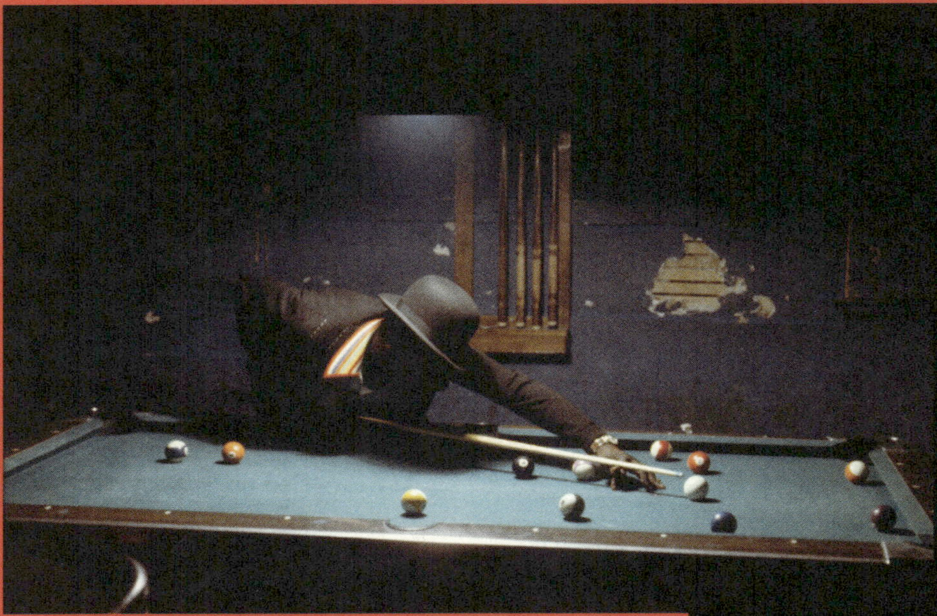

Pool player in the Fillmore ghetto. San Francisco, CA. 1975

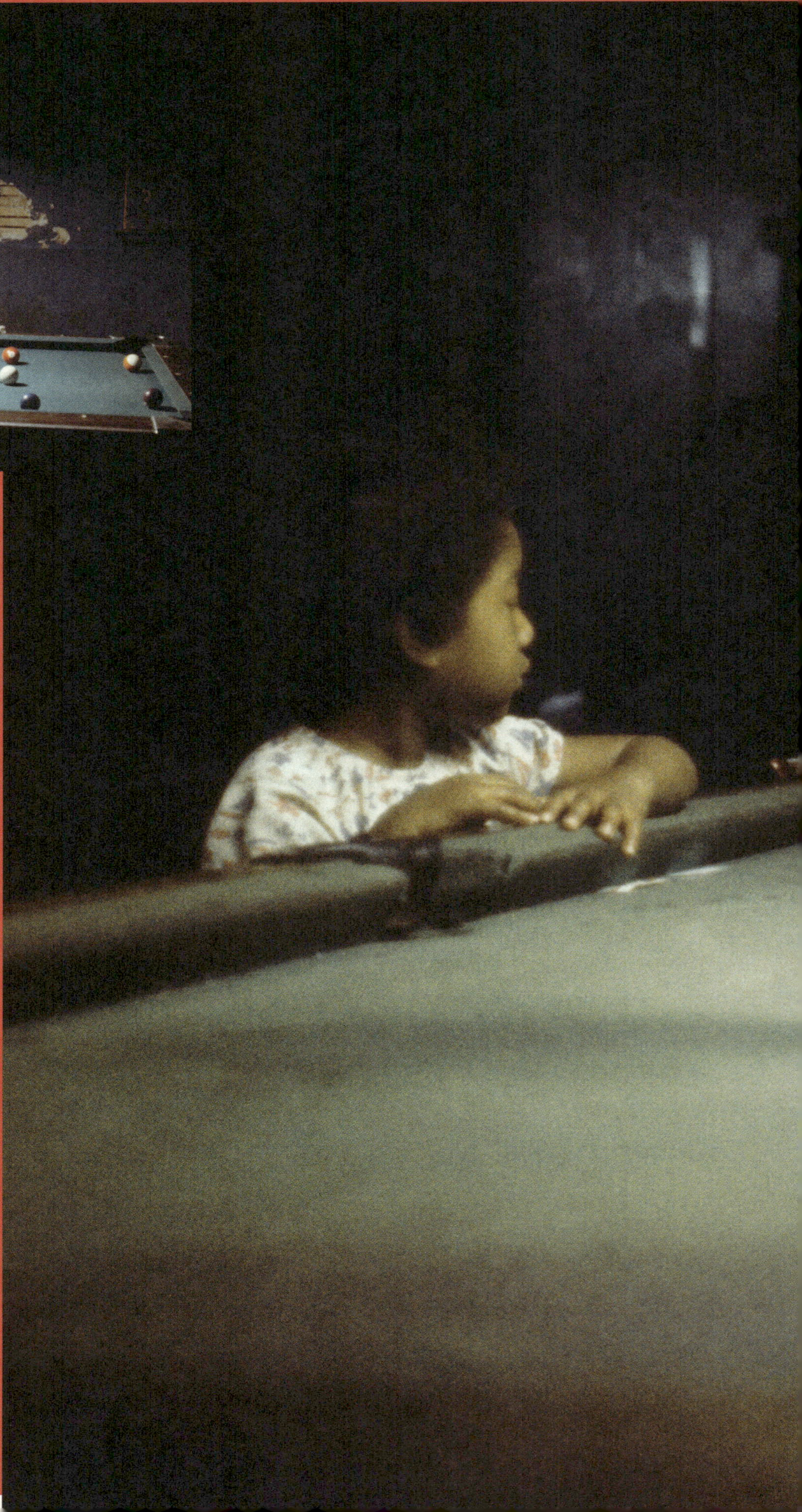

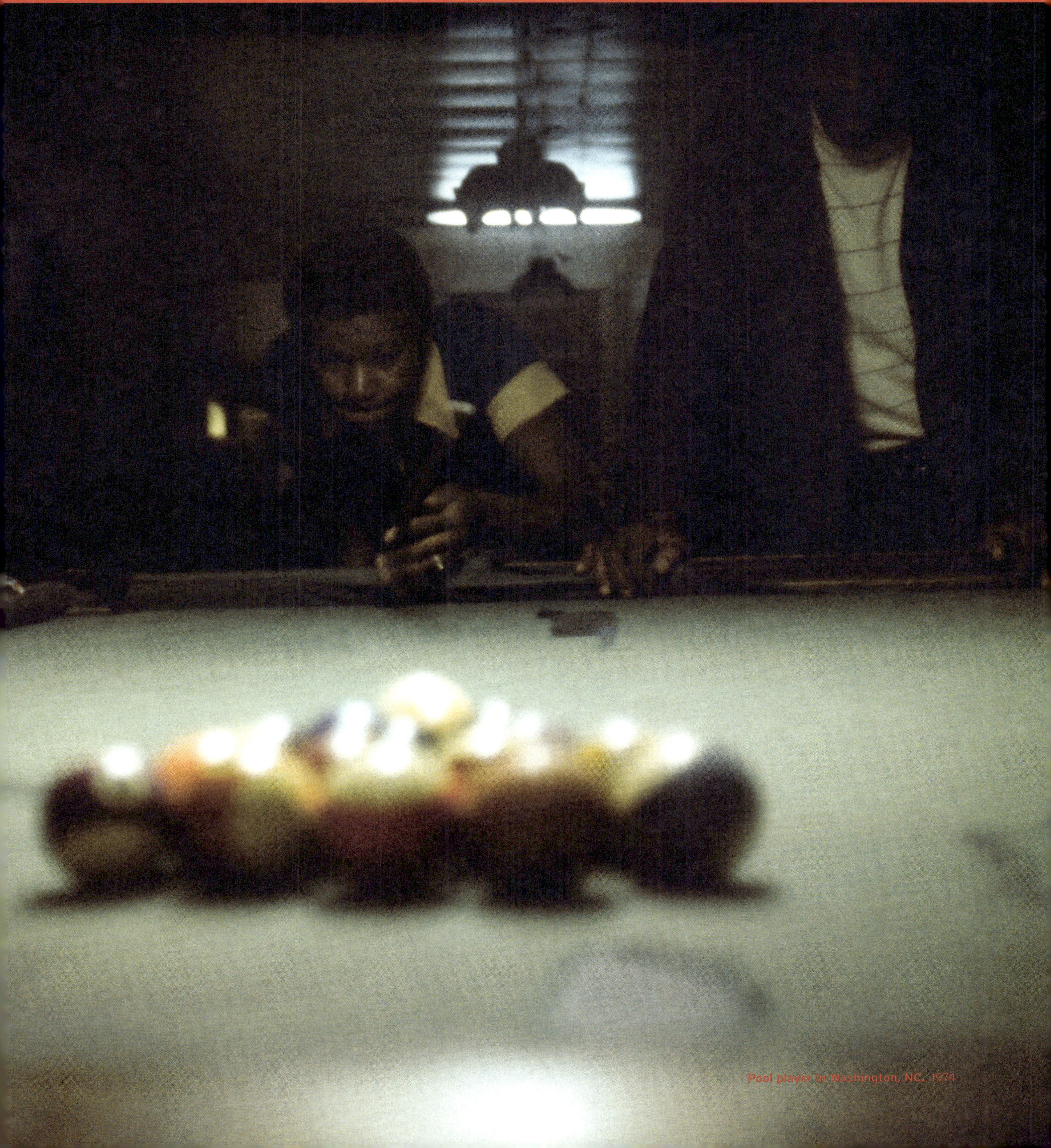

Pool player in Washington, NC., 1974

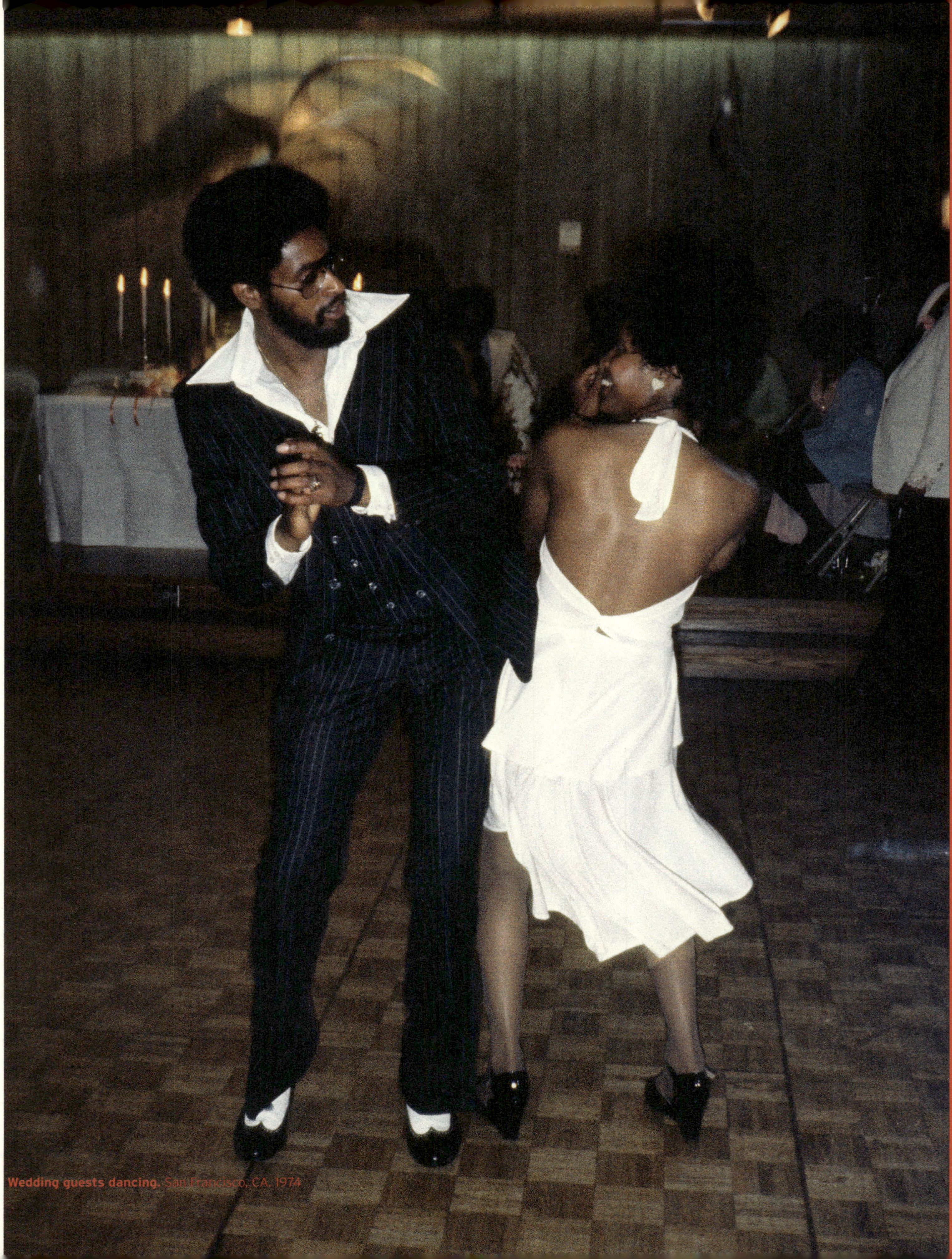

Wedding guests dancing. San Francisco, CA. 1974

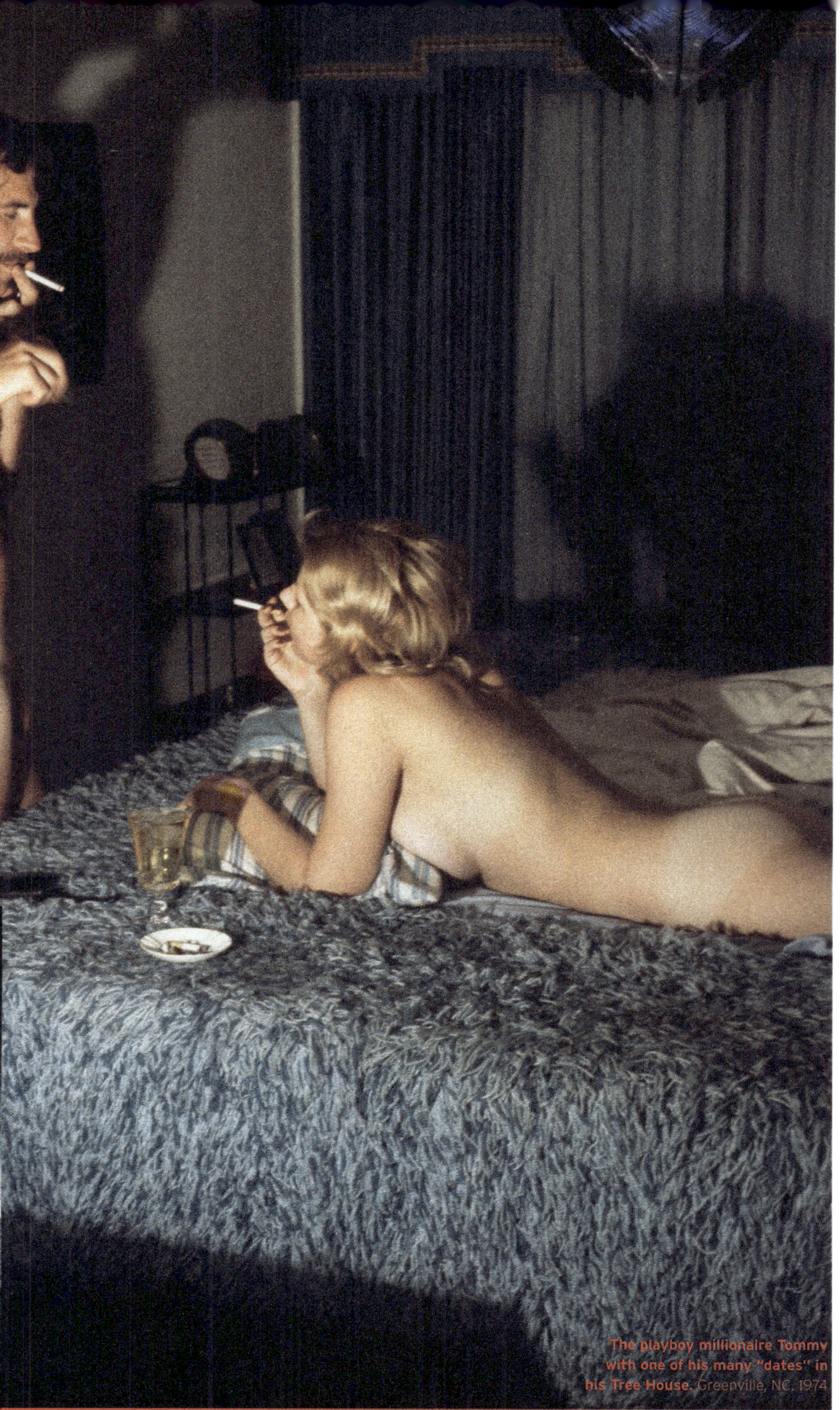

The playboy millionaire Tommy with one of his many "dates" in his Tree House. Greenville, NC. 1974

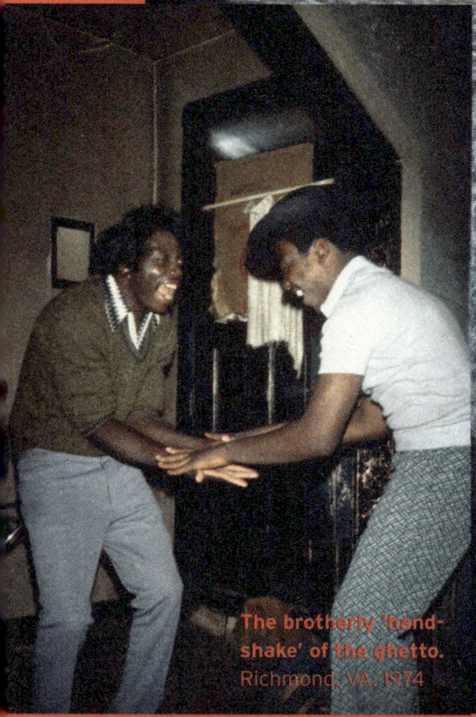

The brotherly 'hand-shake' of the ghetto. Richmond, VA. 1974

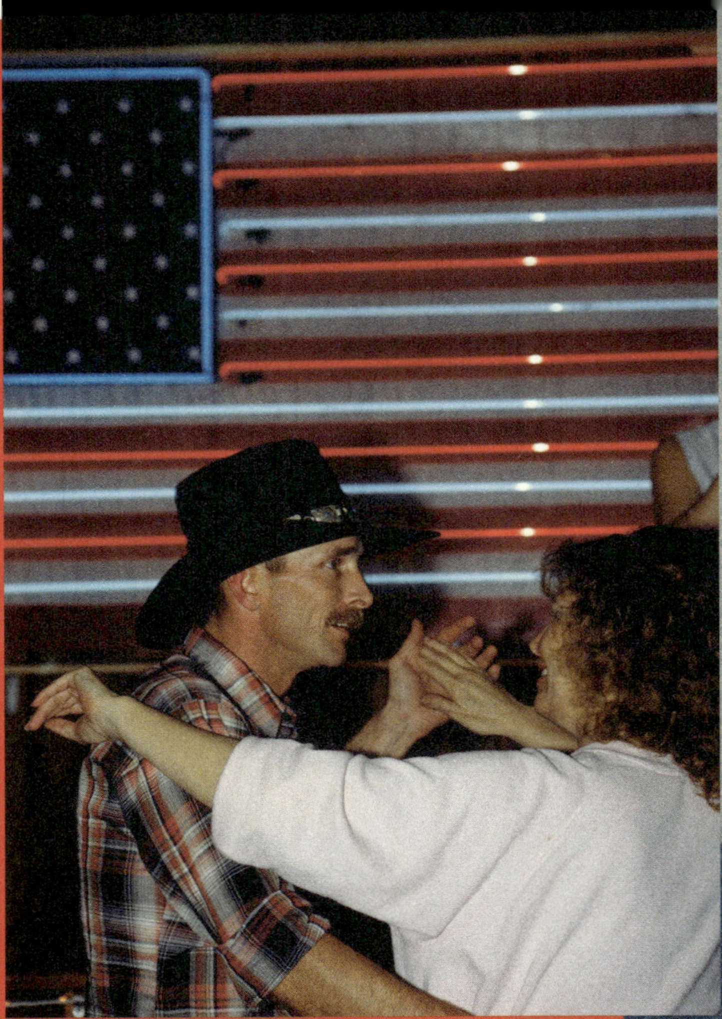

Dancing cowboys on Bourbon Street. New Orleans, LA. 1996

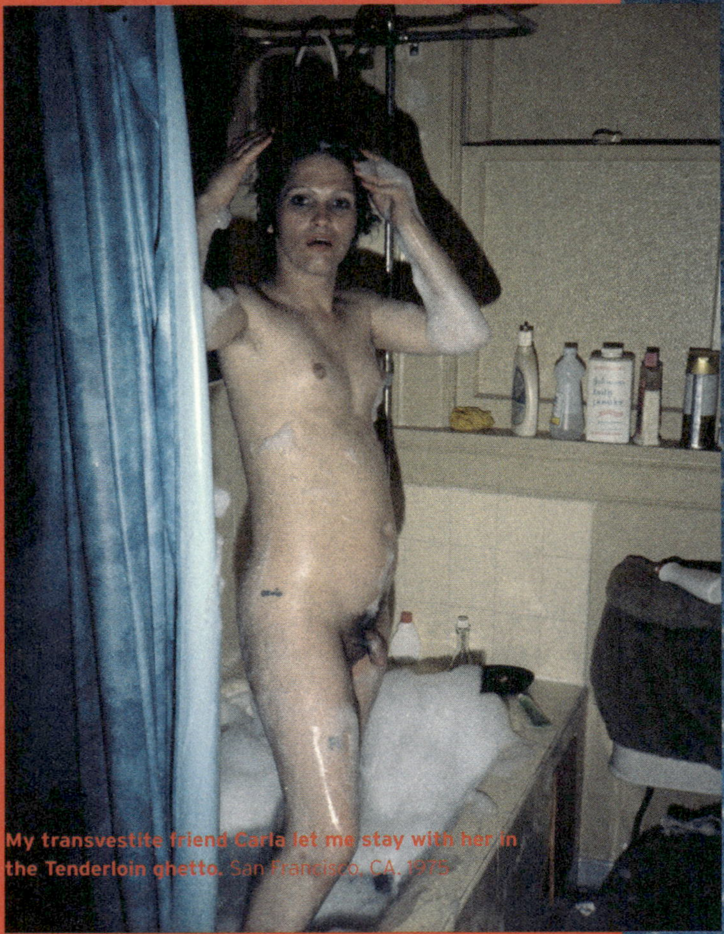

My transvestite friend Carla let me stay with her in the Tenderloin ghetto. San Francisco, CA. 1975

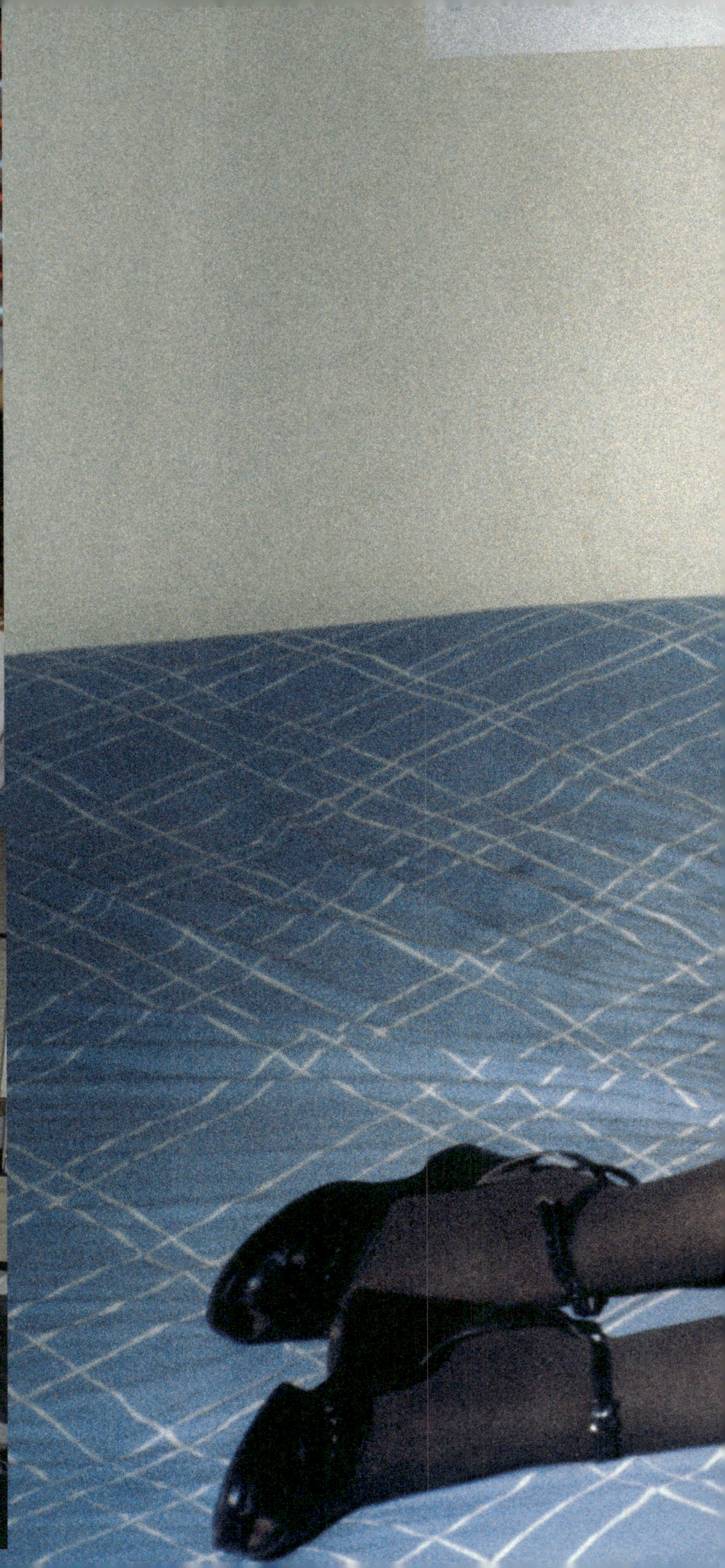

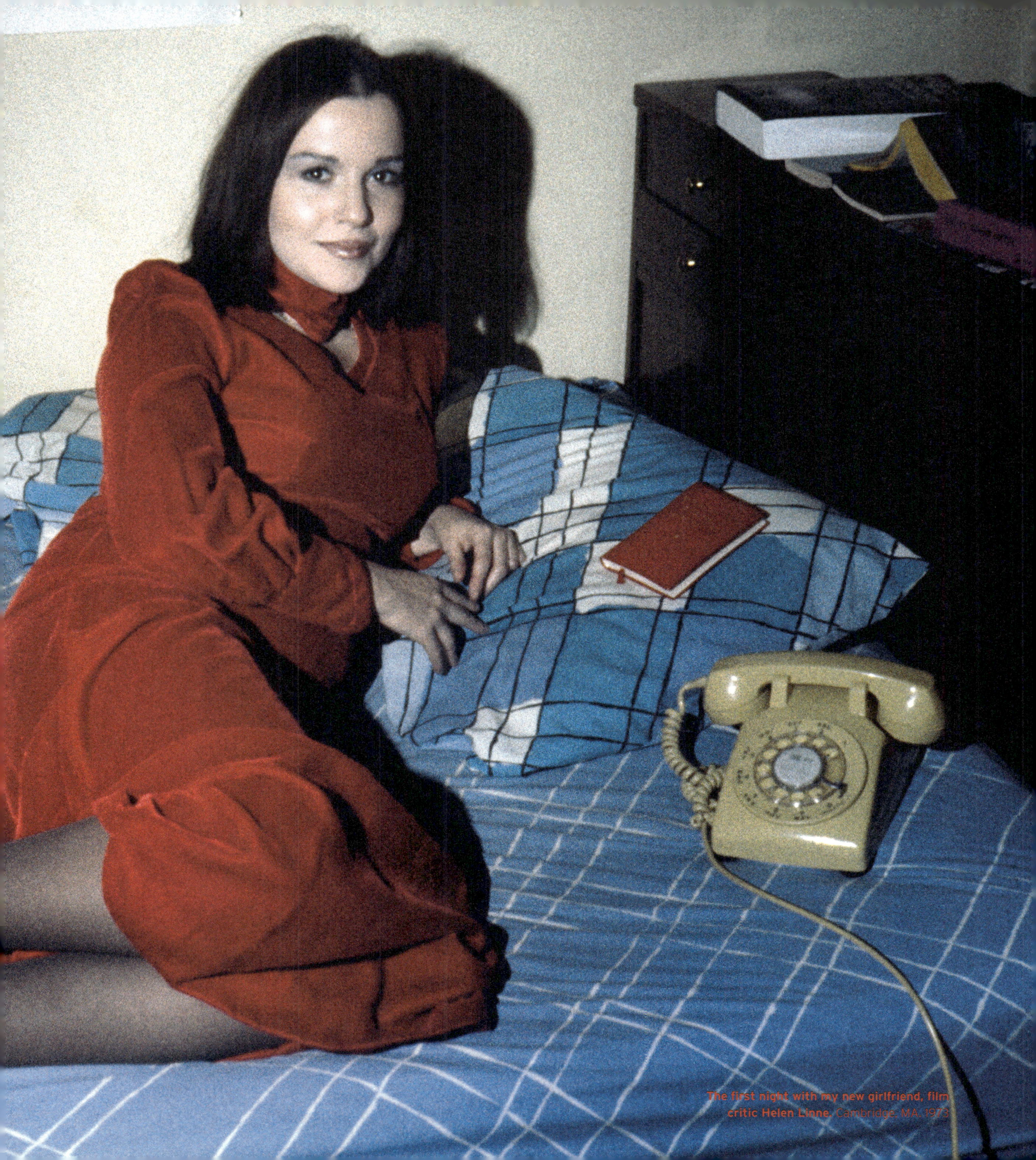

The first night with my new girlfriend, film critic Helen Linne. Cambridge, MA. 1973

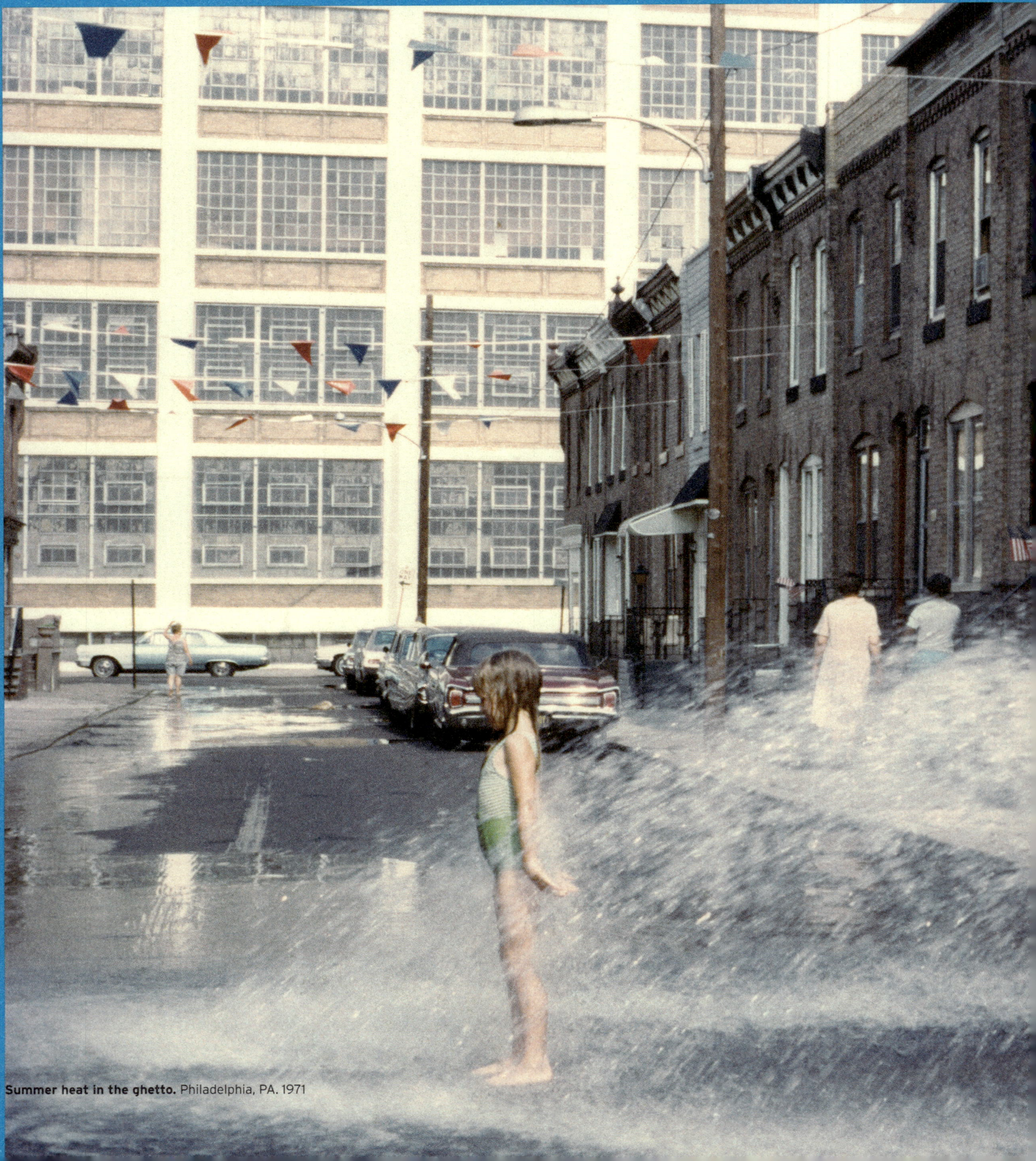

Summer heat in the ghetto. Philadelphia, PA. 1971

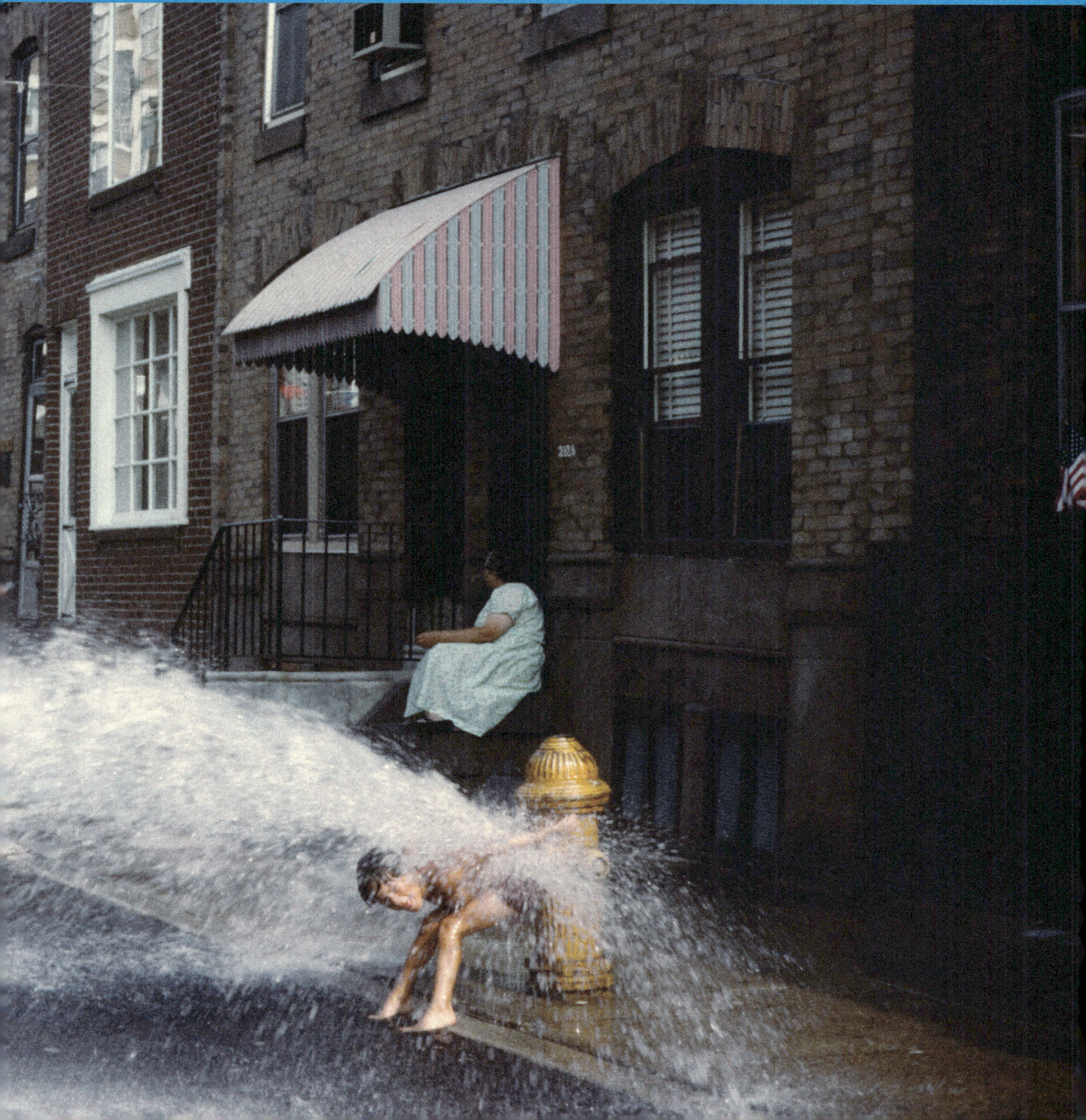

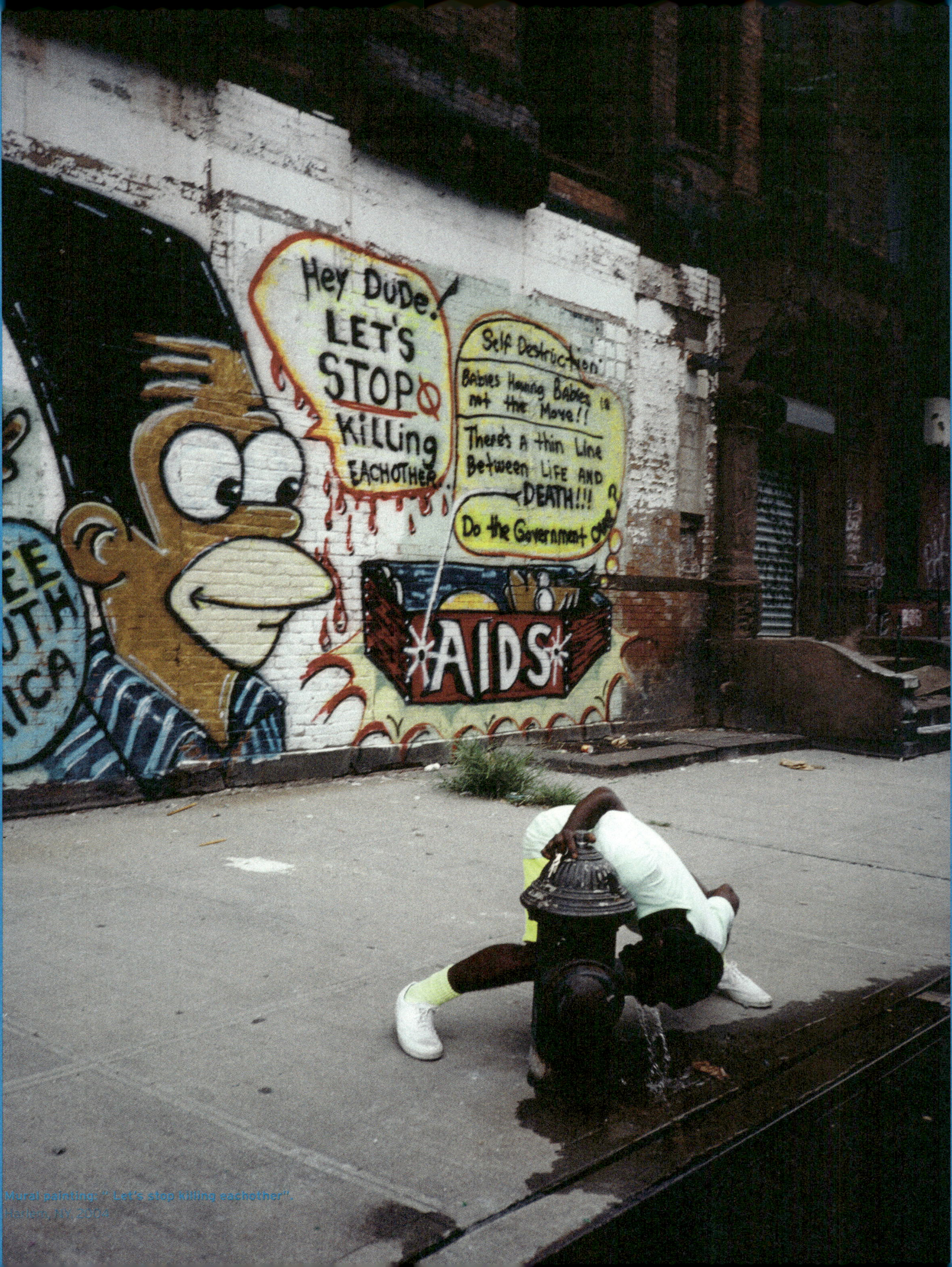

Mural painting: " Let's stop killing eachother".
Harlem, NY. 2004

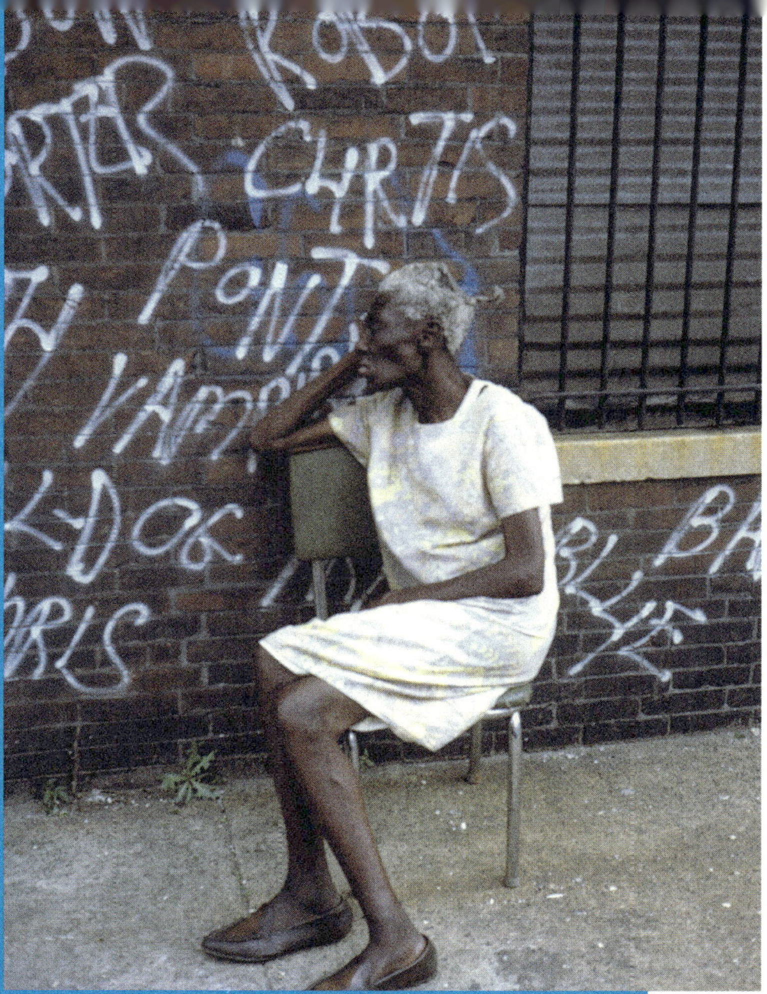

Depressed woman in the south ghetto. Philadelphia, PA. 1971

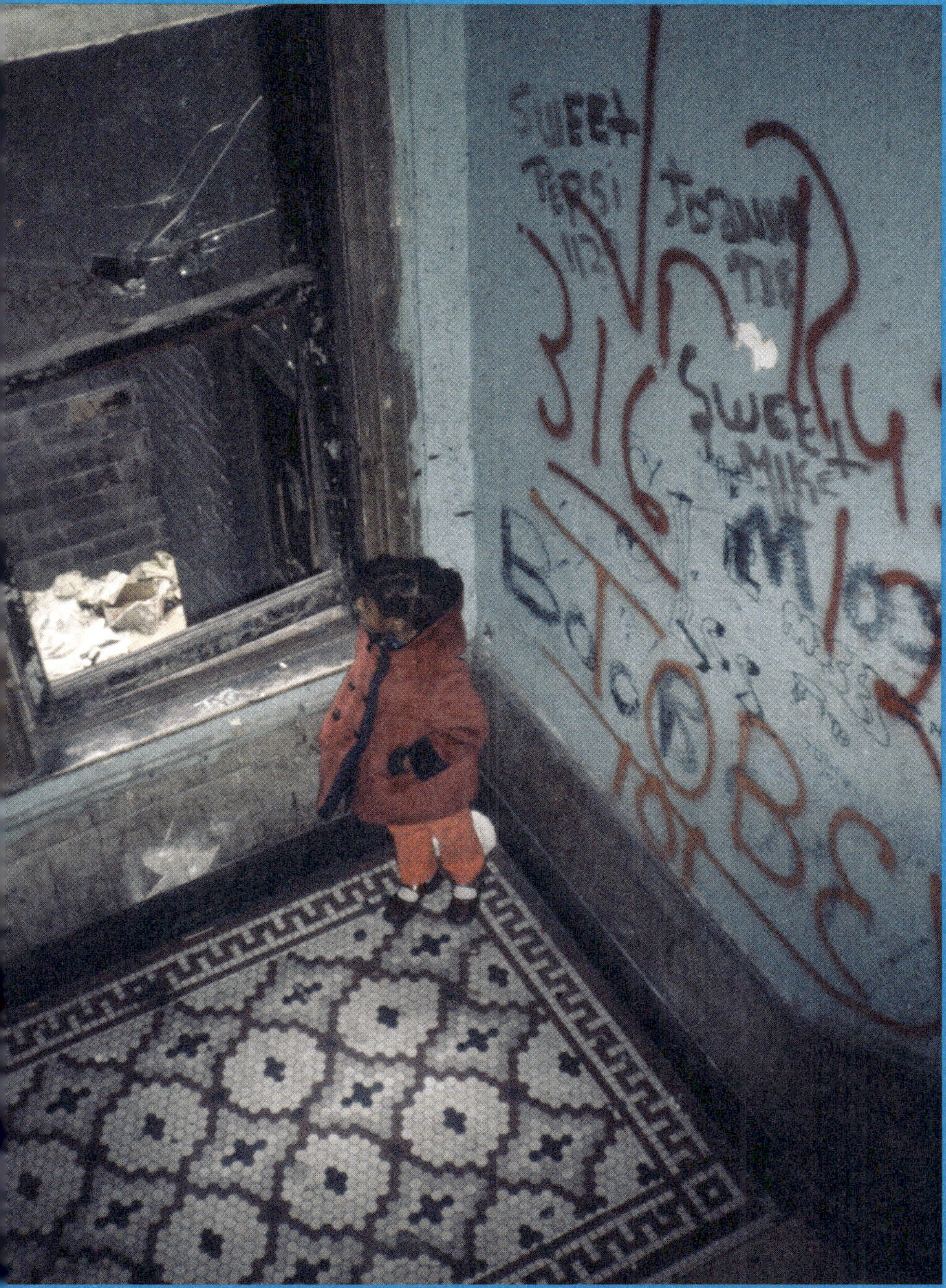

Girl in red in a hallway where a man was killed by the police the previous day. Bronx, NY. 1972

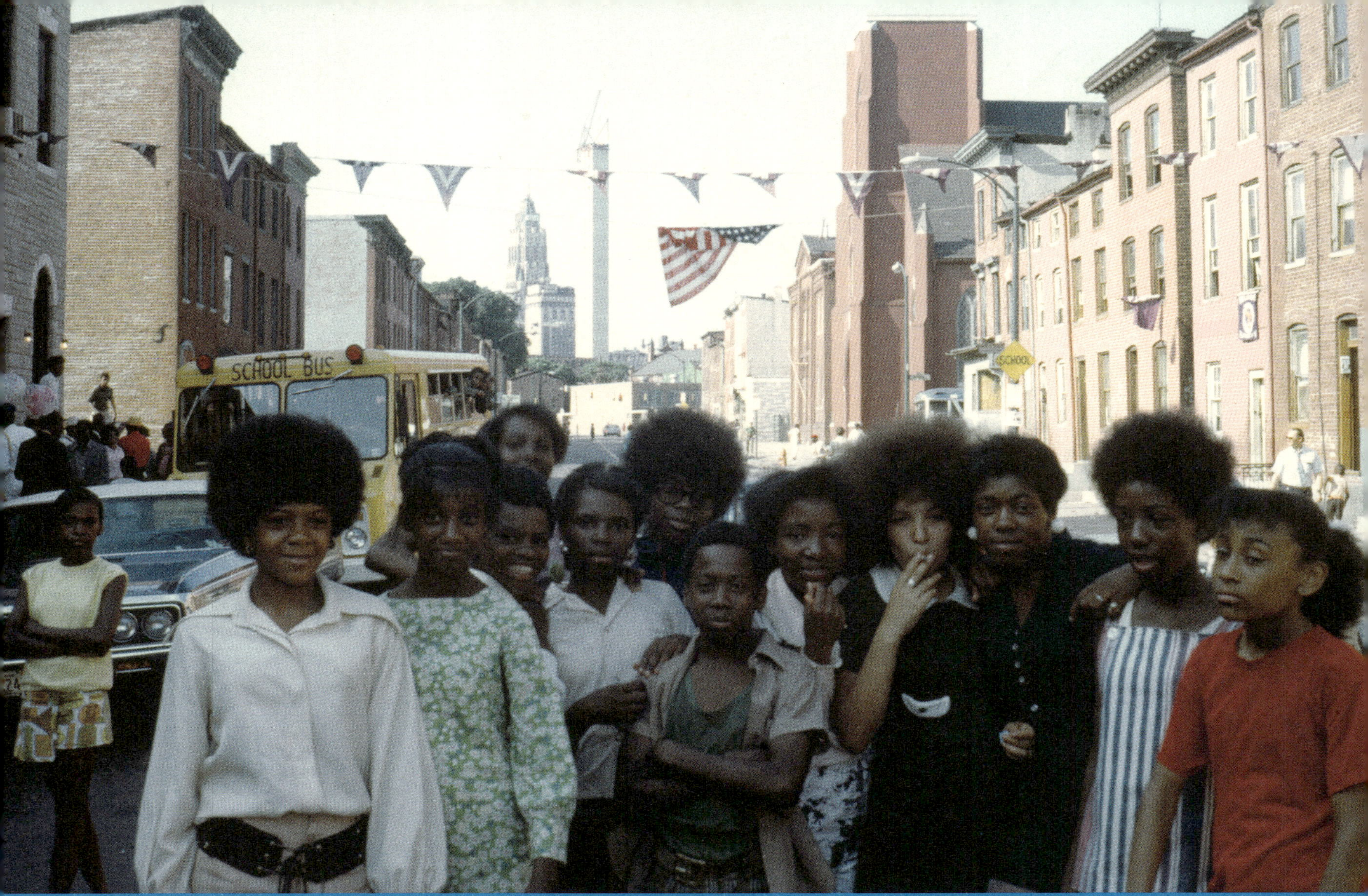

Young people in the ghetto. Baltimore, MD. 1971

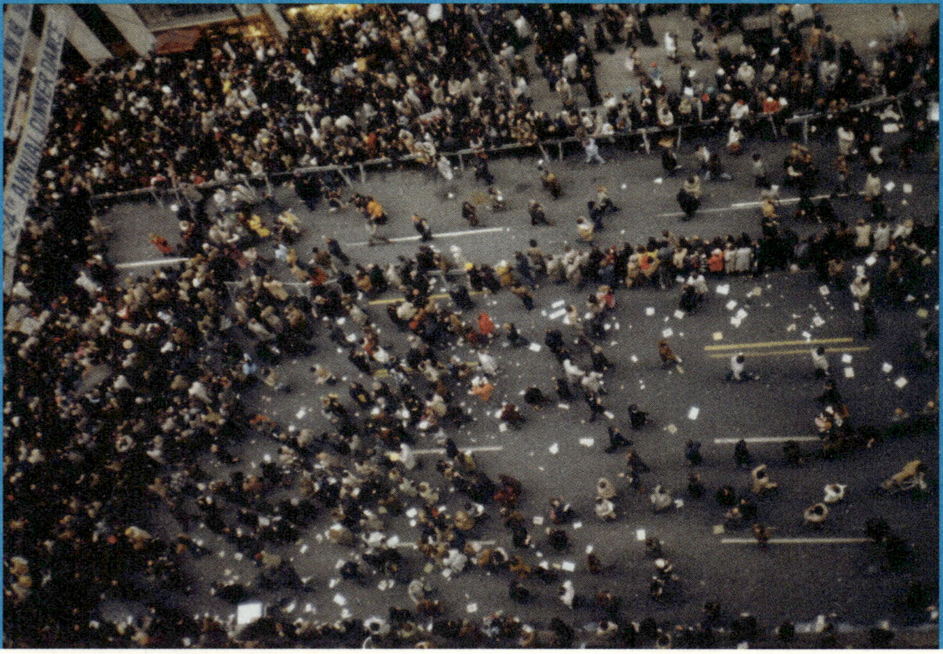

Tickertape parade on Broadway. New York, NY. 1973

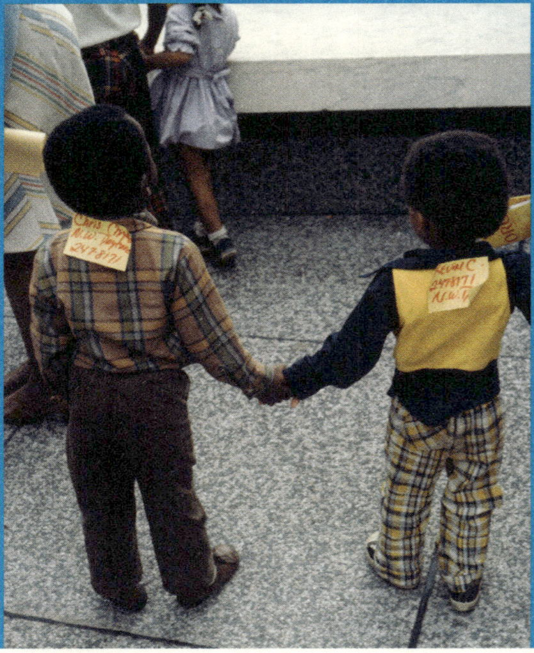

Children at the Town Hall. San Francisco, CA. 1975

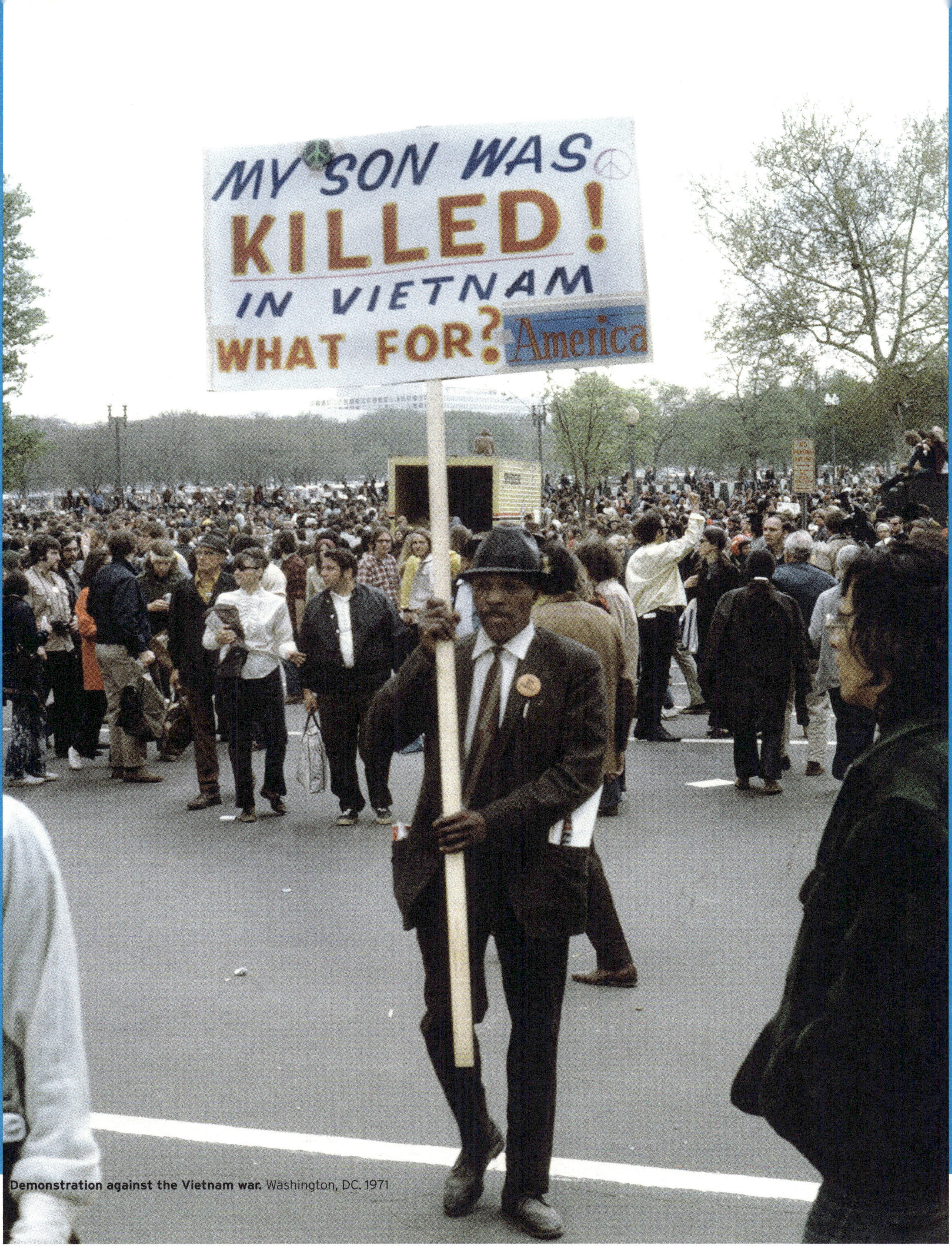

Demonstration against the Vietnam war. Washington, DC. 1971

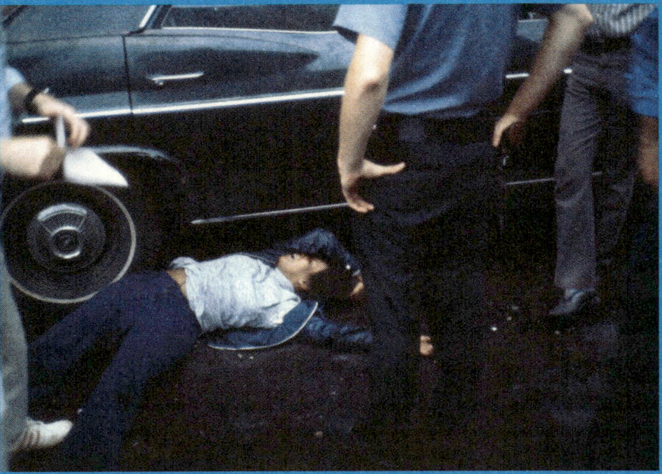

Woman shot outside my window. New York, NY. 1972

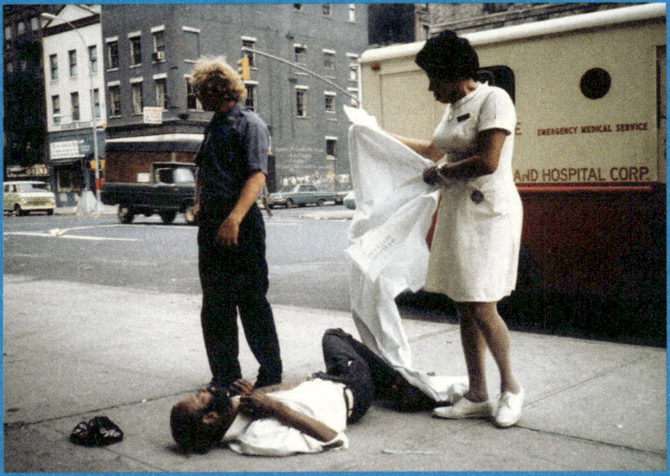

Dead man on 1st Ave. New York, NY. 1971

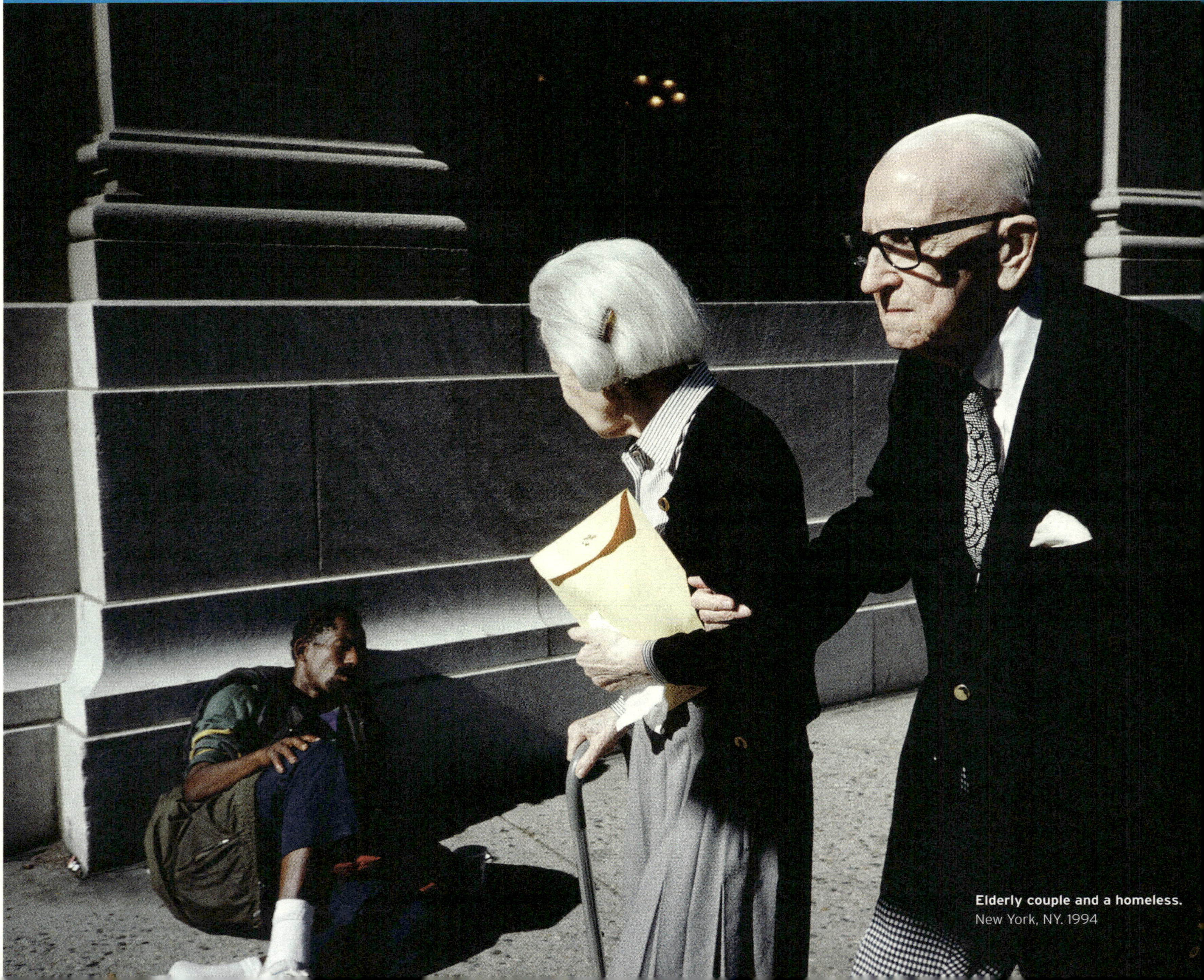

Elderly couple and a homeless. New York, NY. 1994

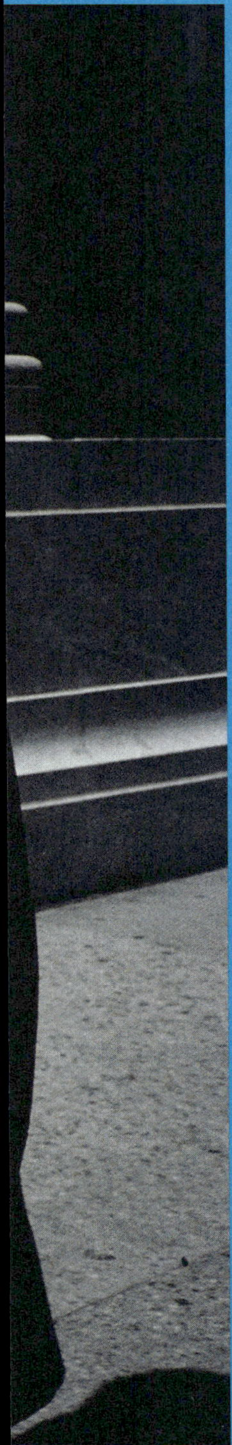

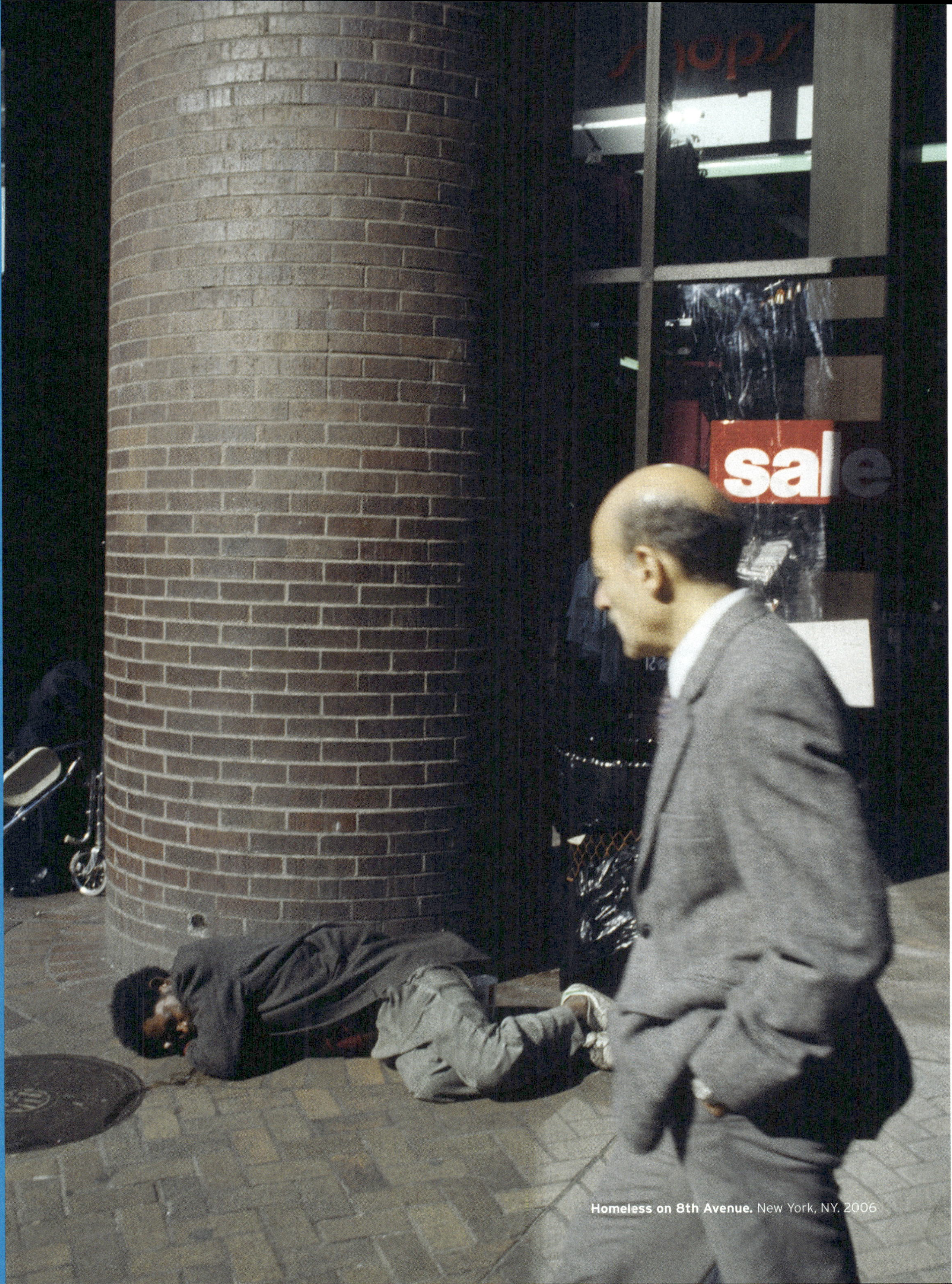

Homeless on 8th Avenue. New York, NY. 2006

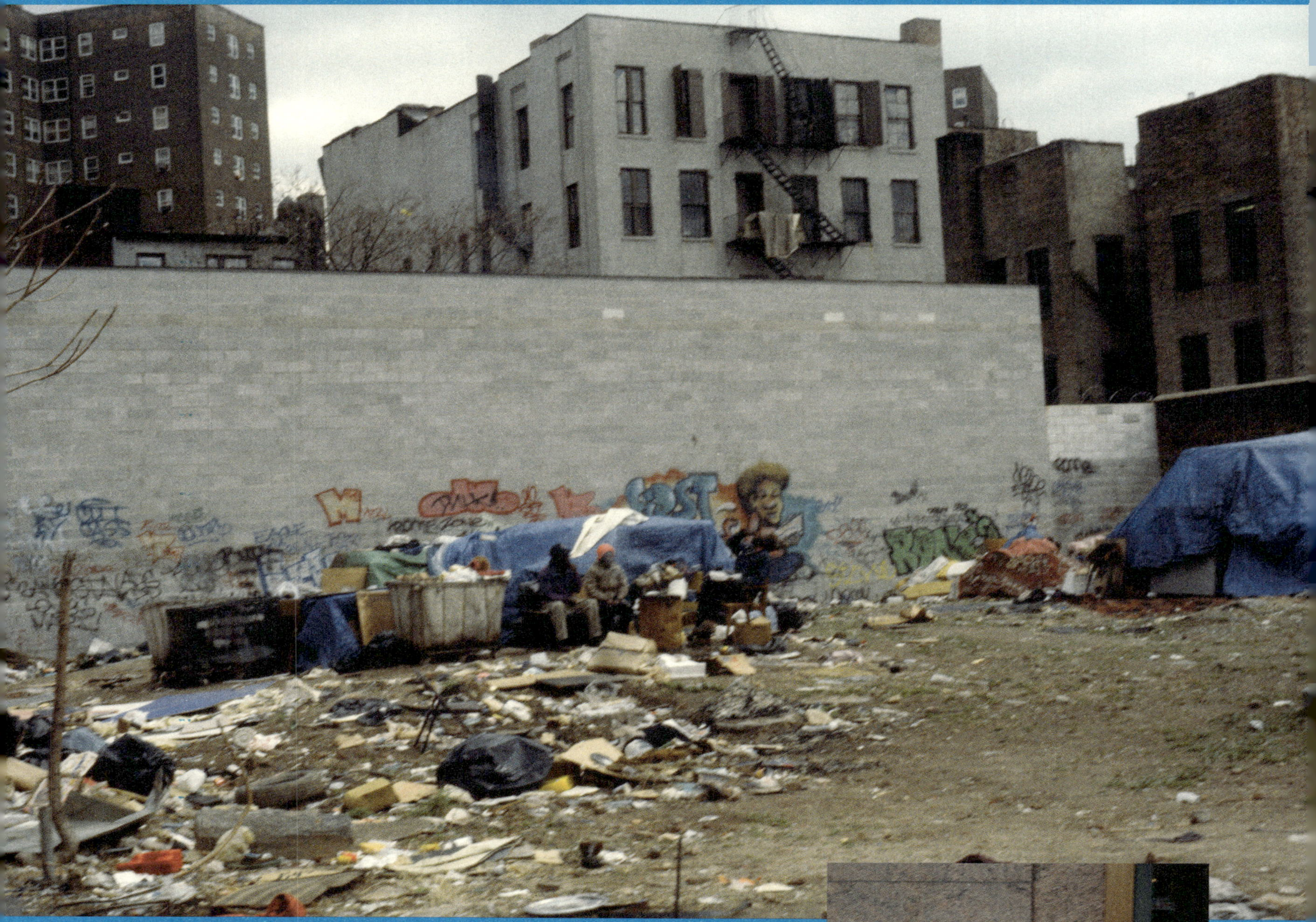

My homeless friend Ed's home before he was sentenced to life imprisonment.
New York, NY. 1989.

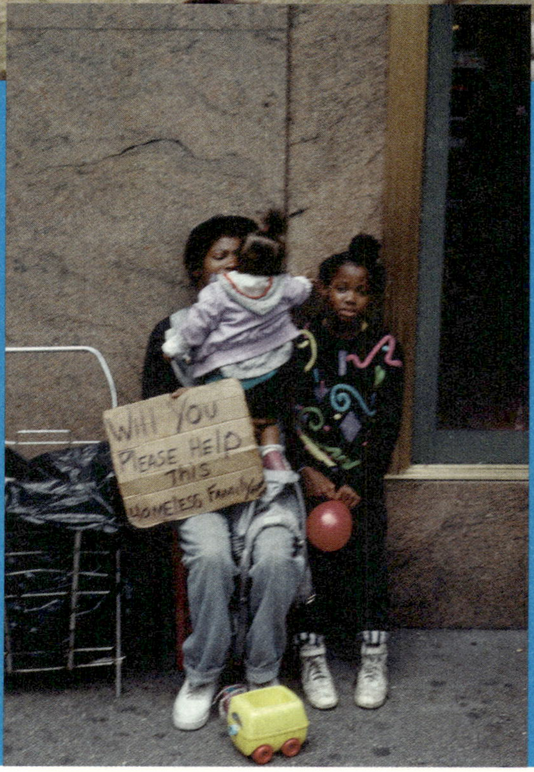

Homeless family begging.
New York, NY. 1992

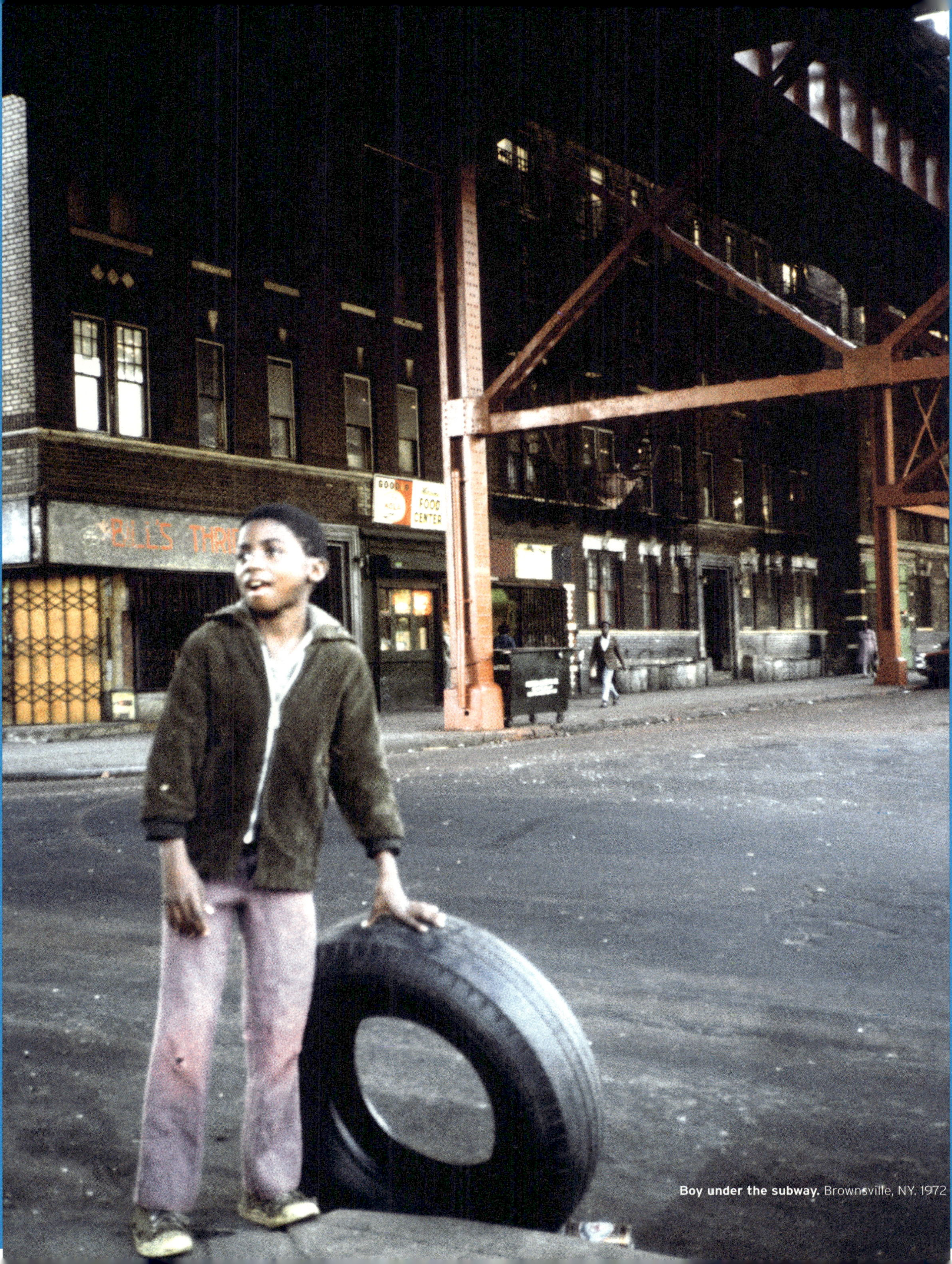

Boy under the subway. Brownsville, NY. 1972

A five hundred people long line for food during the present crisis. Harlem, NY. 2009

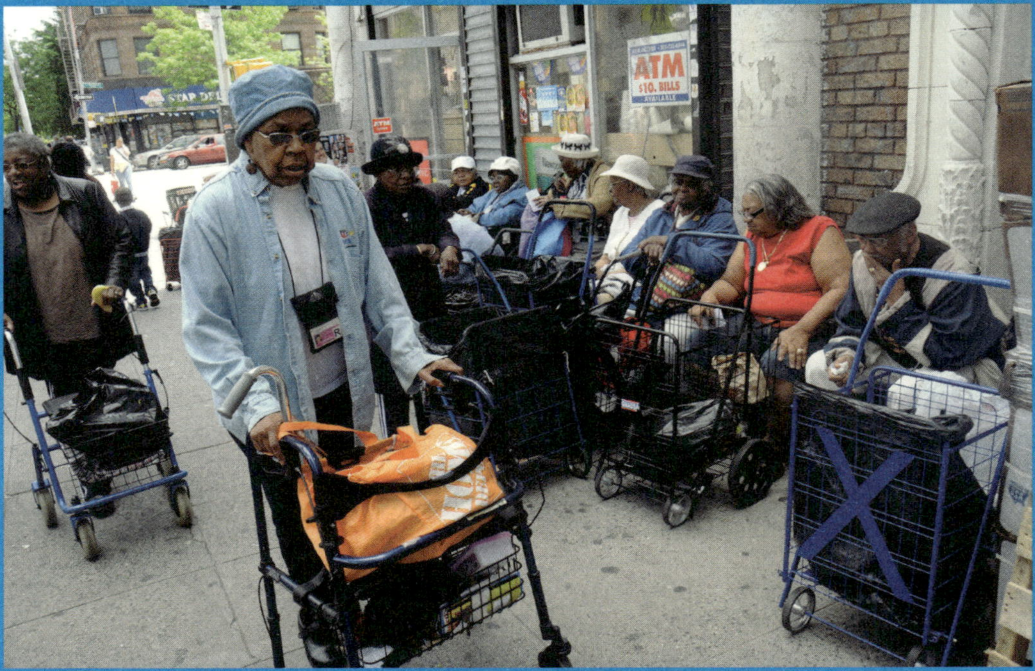

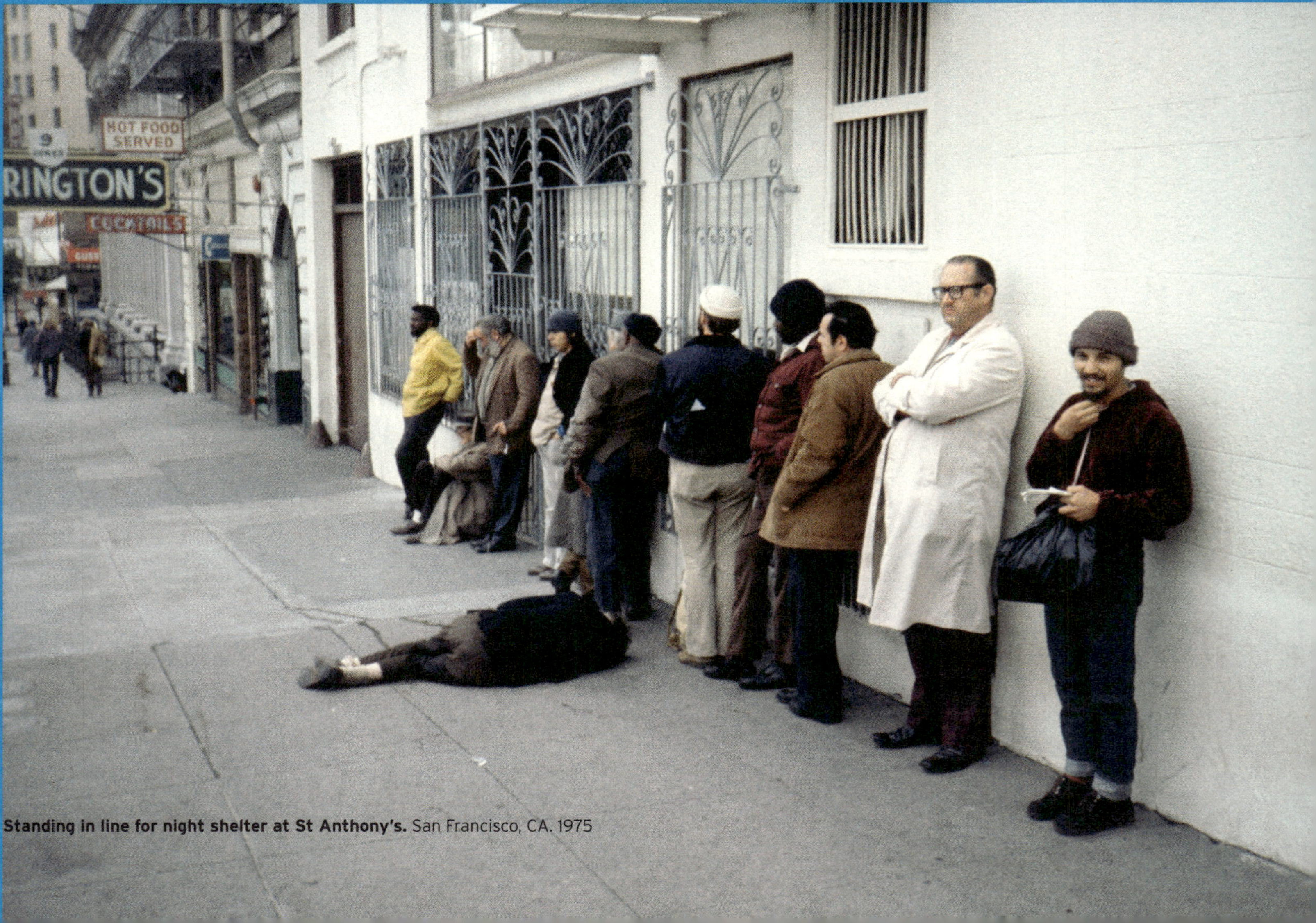

Standing in line for night shelter at St Anthony's. San Francisco, CA. 1975

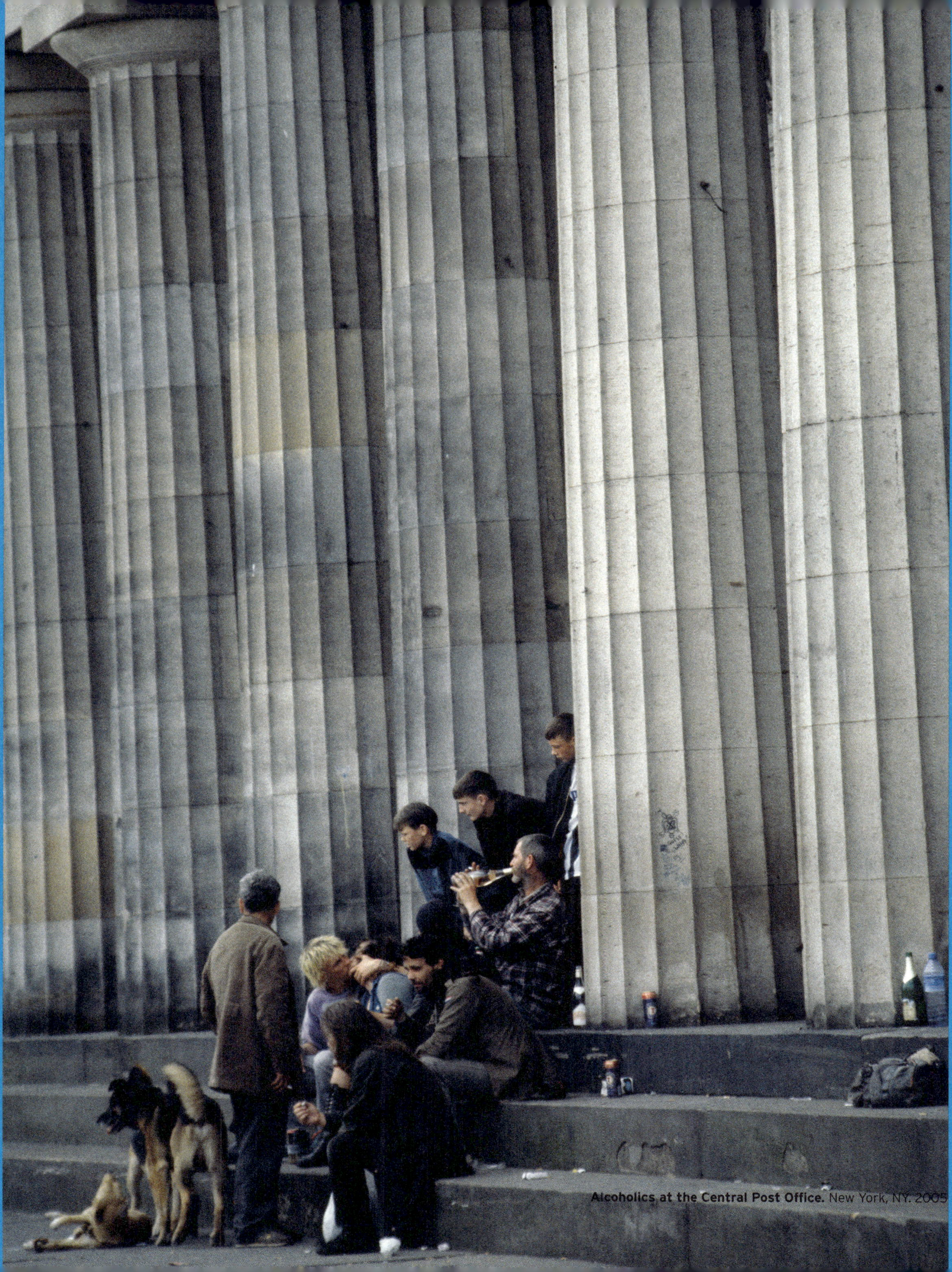

Alcoholics at the Central Post Office. New York, NY. 2005

Young criminals with their loot. Brownsville, NY. 1973

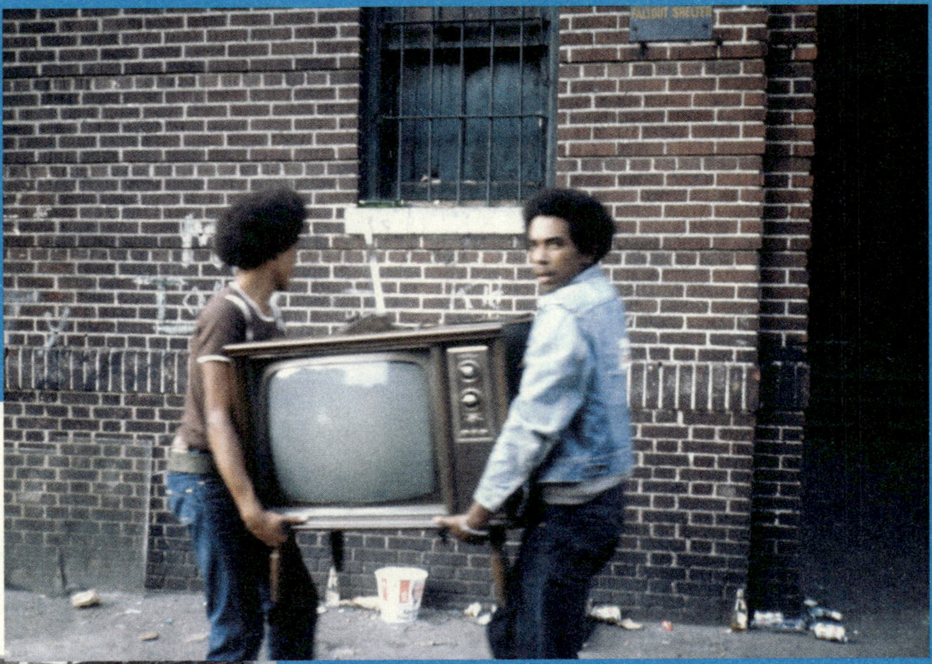

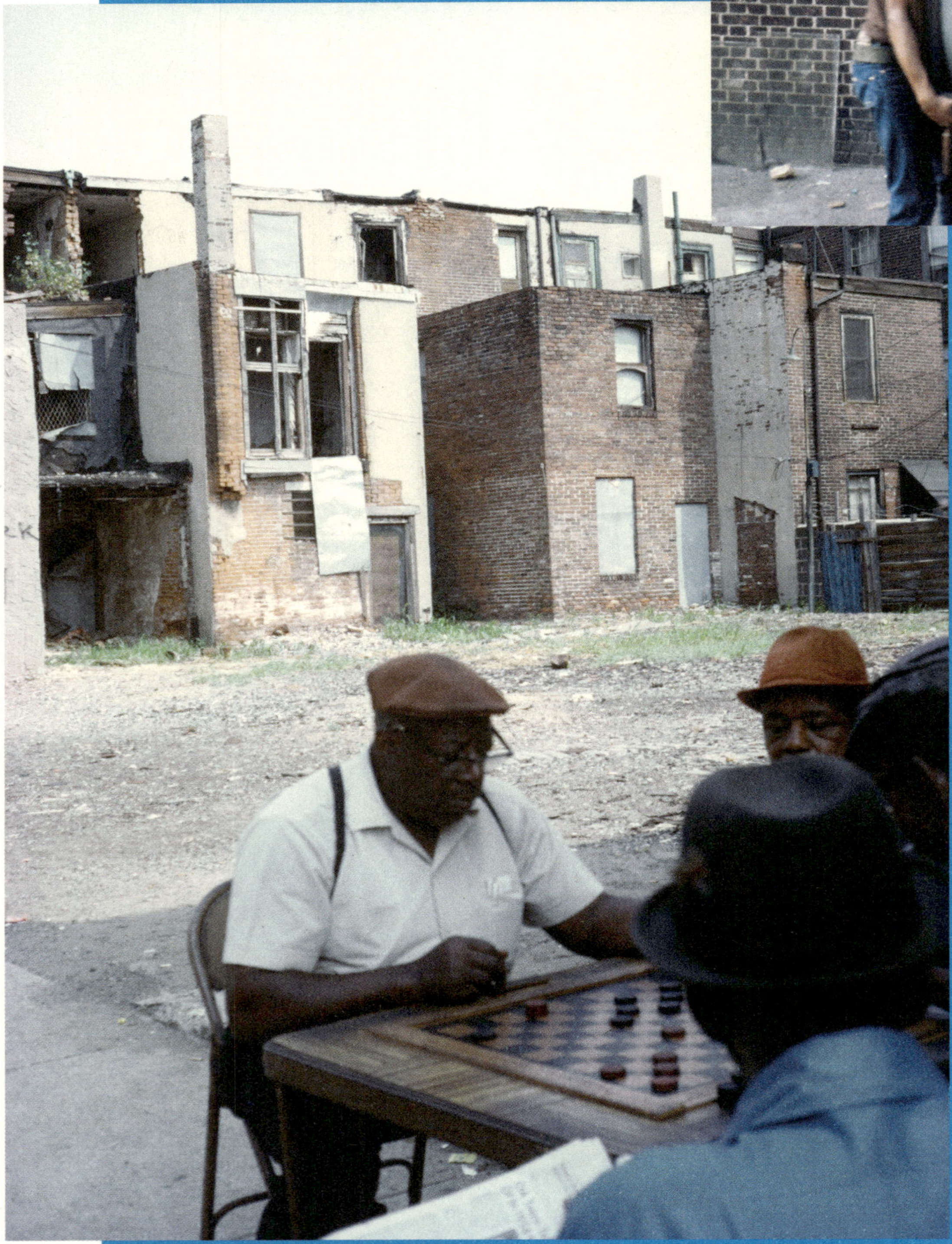

Board game players in the ghetto around Broadway. Baltimore, MD. 1971

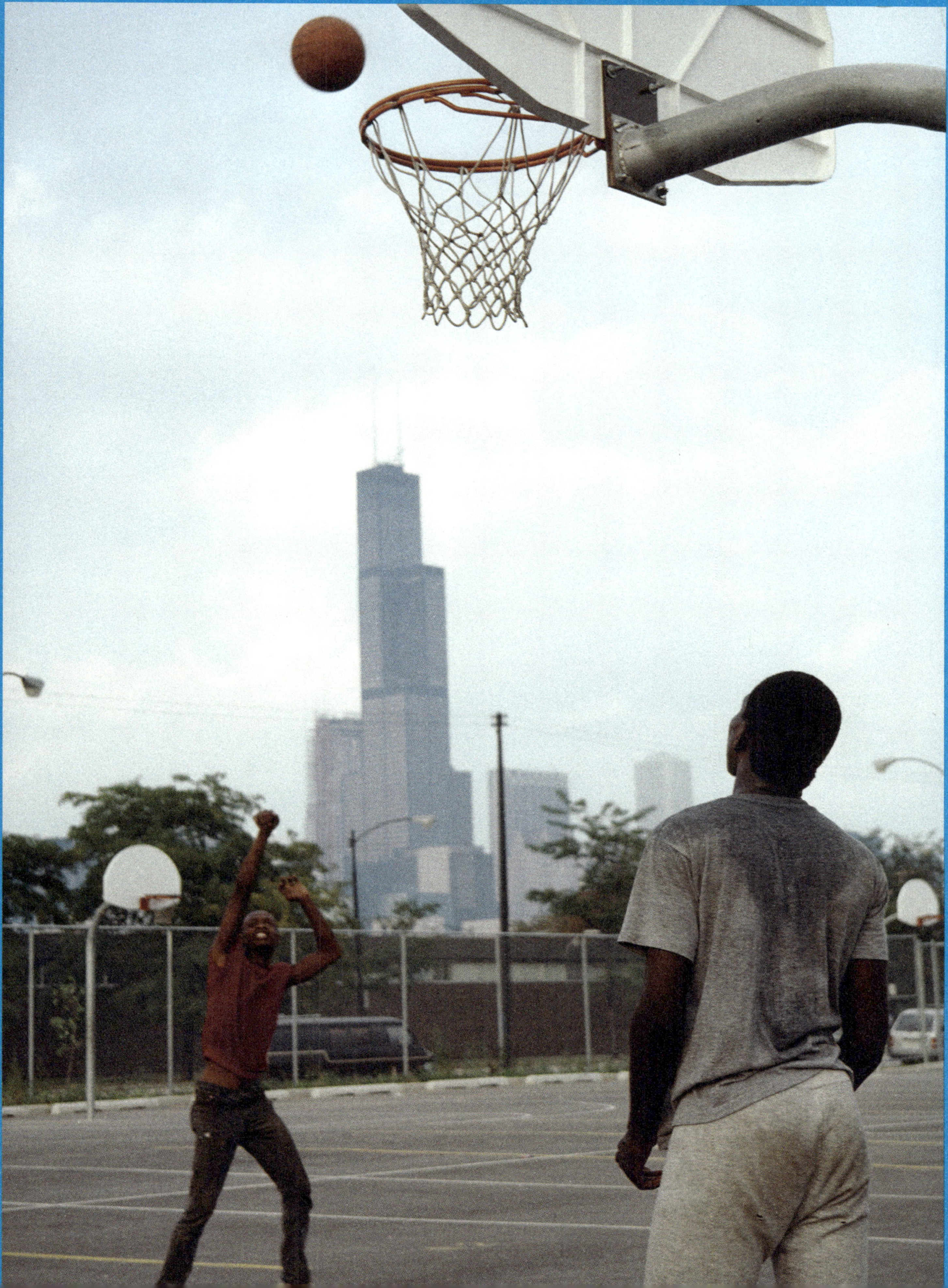

Basketball game. The south ghetto slum with the tallest building in the US, Sears Tower. Chicago, IL. 1988

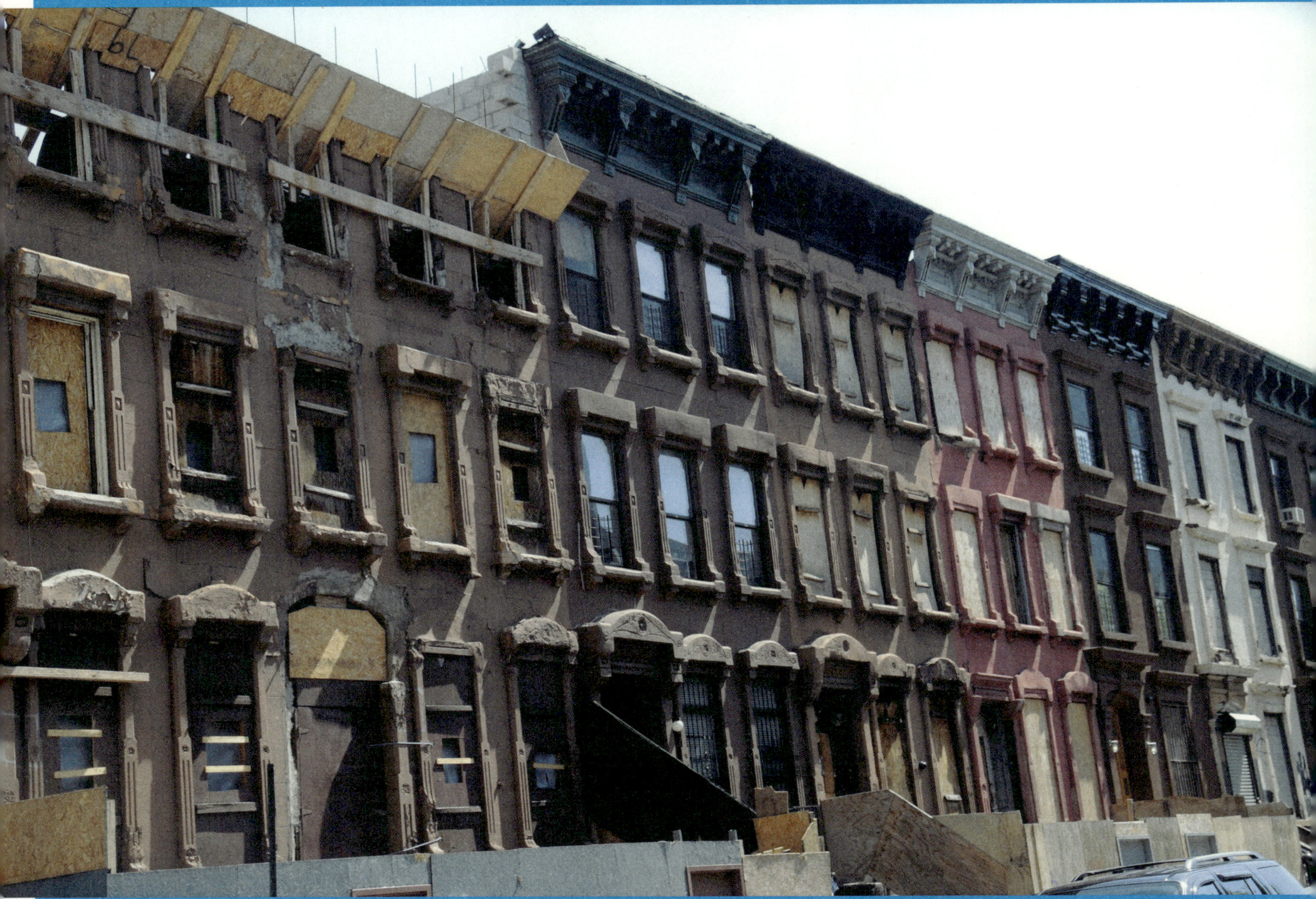

Renovation of Harlem after ex-president Clinton moved in; consequently the poor blacks had to move out. Harlem, NY. 2009

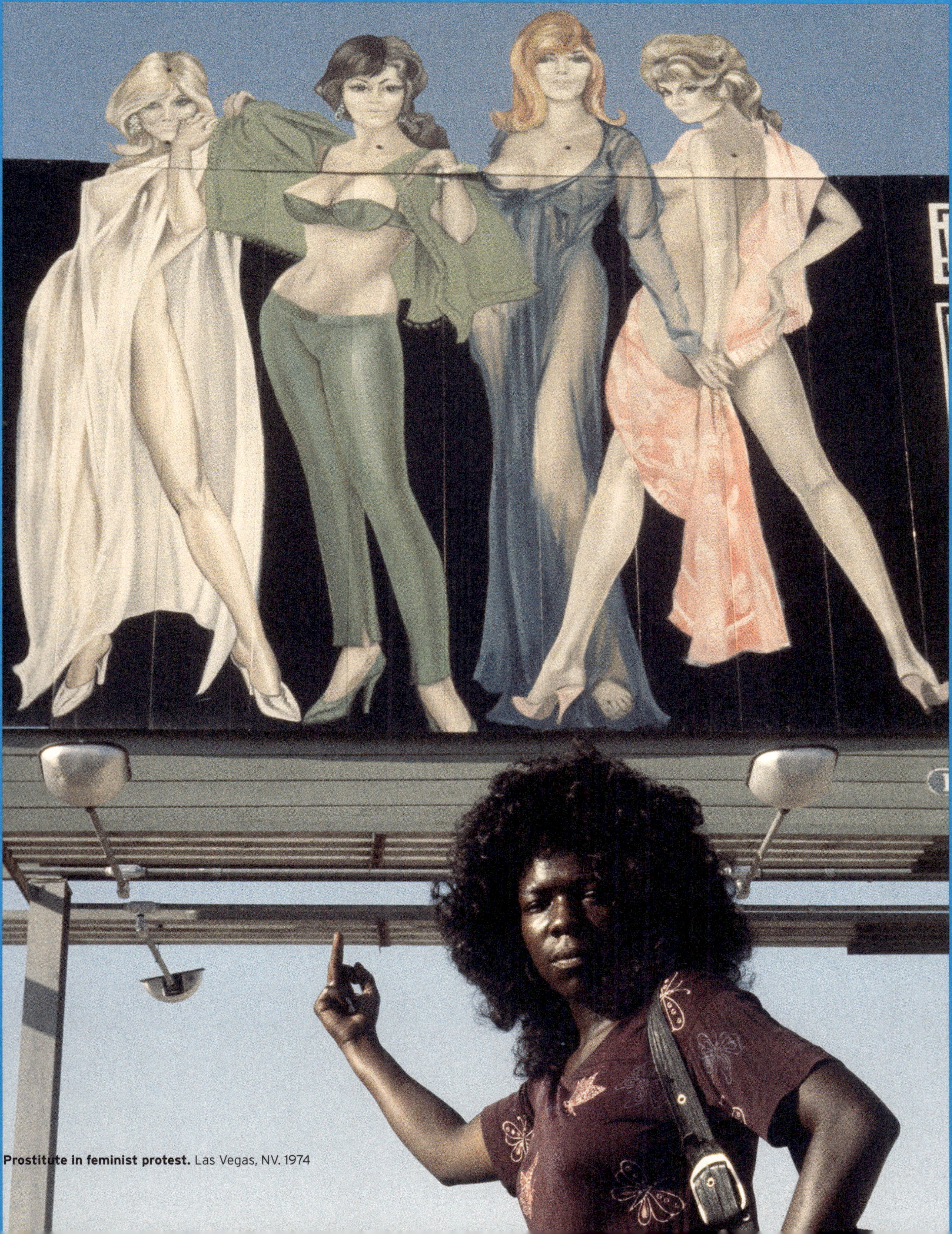

Prostitute in feminist protest. Las Vegas, NV. 1974

americans

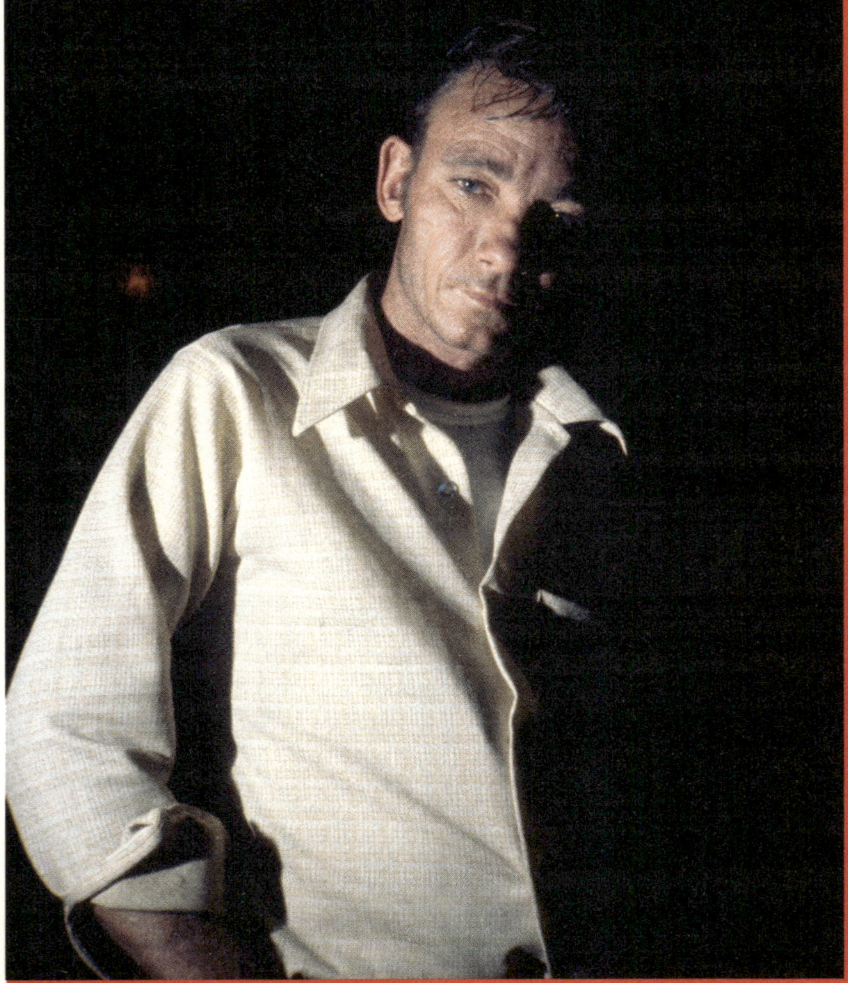

Redneck in a Mississippi bar. Union, MS. 1974

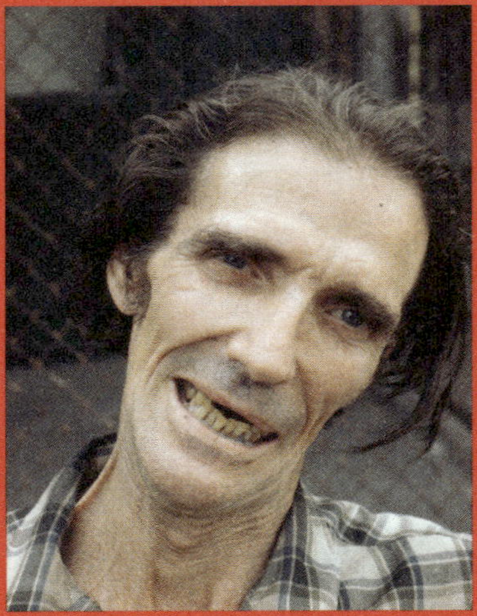

Poor white. Baltimore, MD. 1971

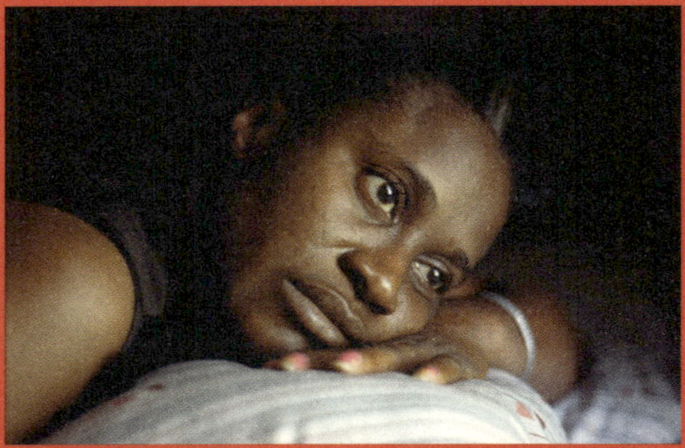

Crack addict who lived with her husband's ax murderer, and who eventually got killed herself. Union Springs, AL. 1989

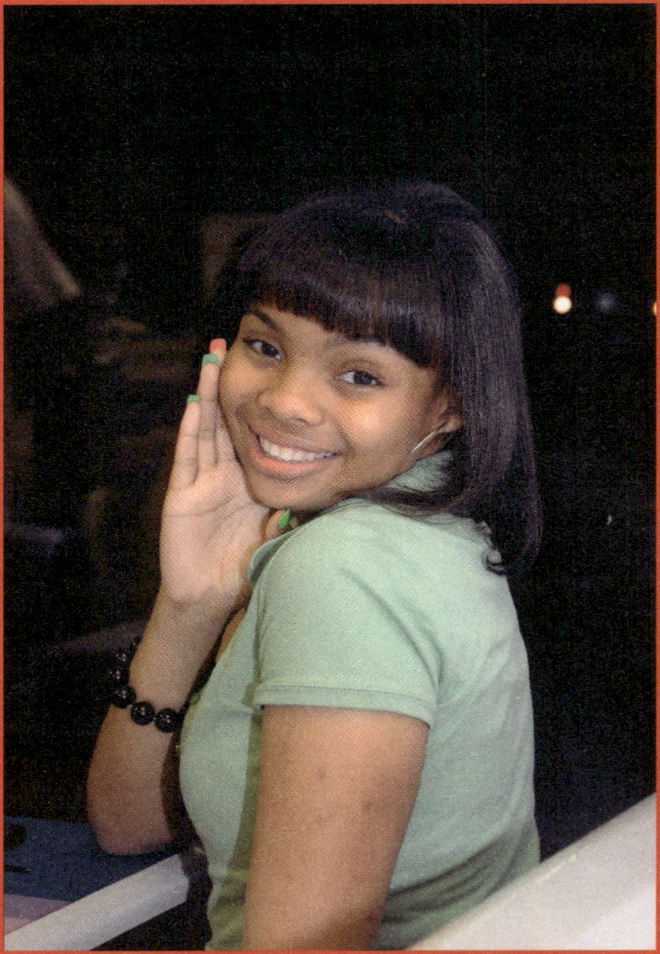

High school student at a Taco Bell restaurant. Natchez, MS. 2009

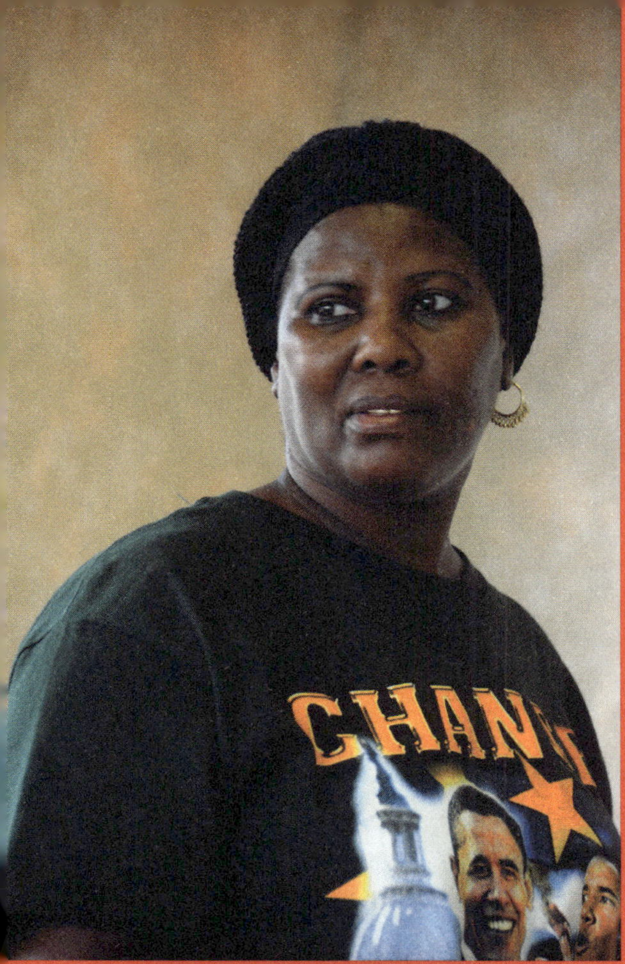

Poor migrant worker with Obama hopes. Bell Glade, FL. 2009

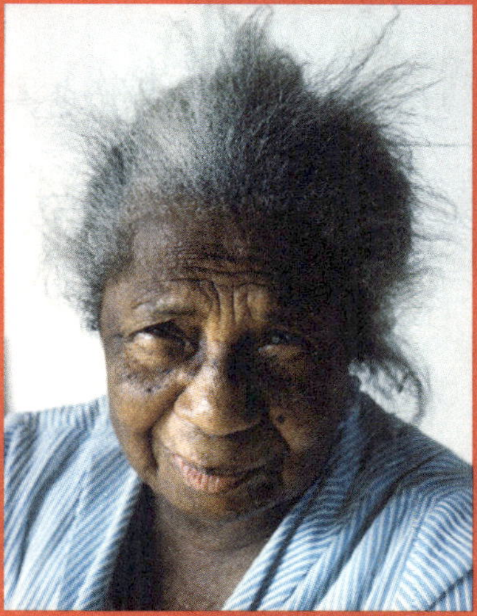

Old cotton picker. Bamberg, SC. 1973

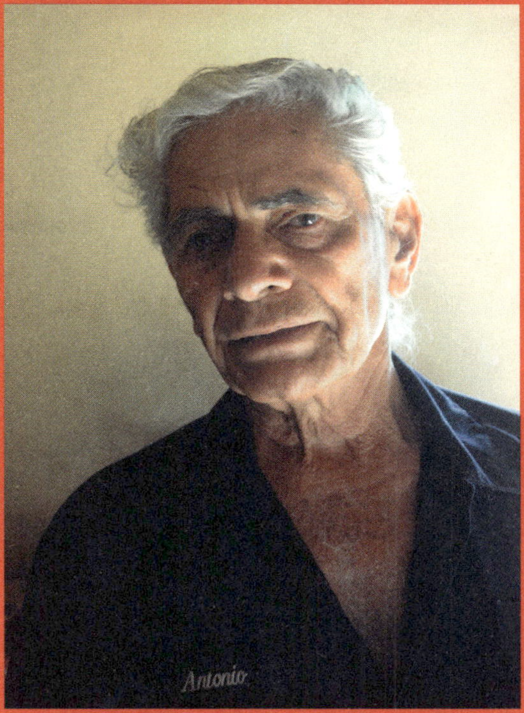

Mexican murderer in foot chains. Immokalee, FL. 2009

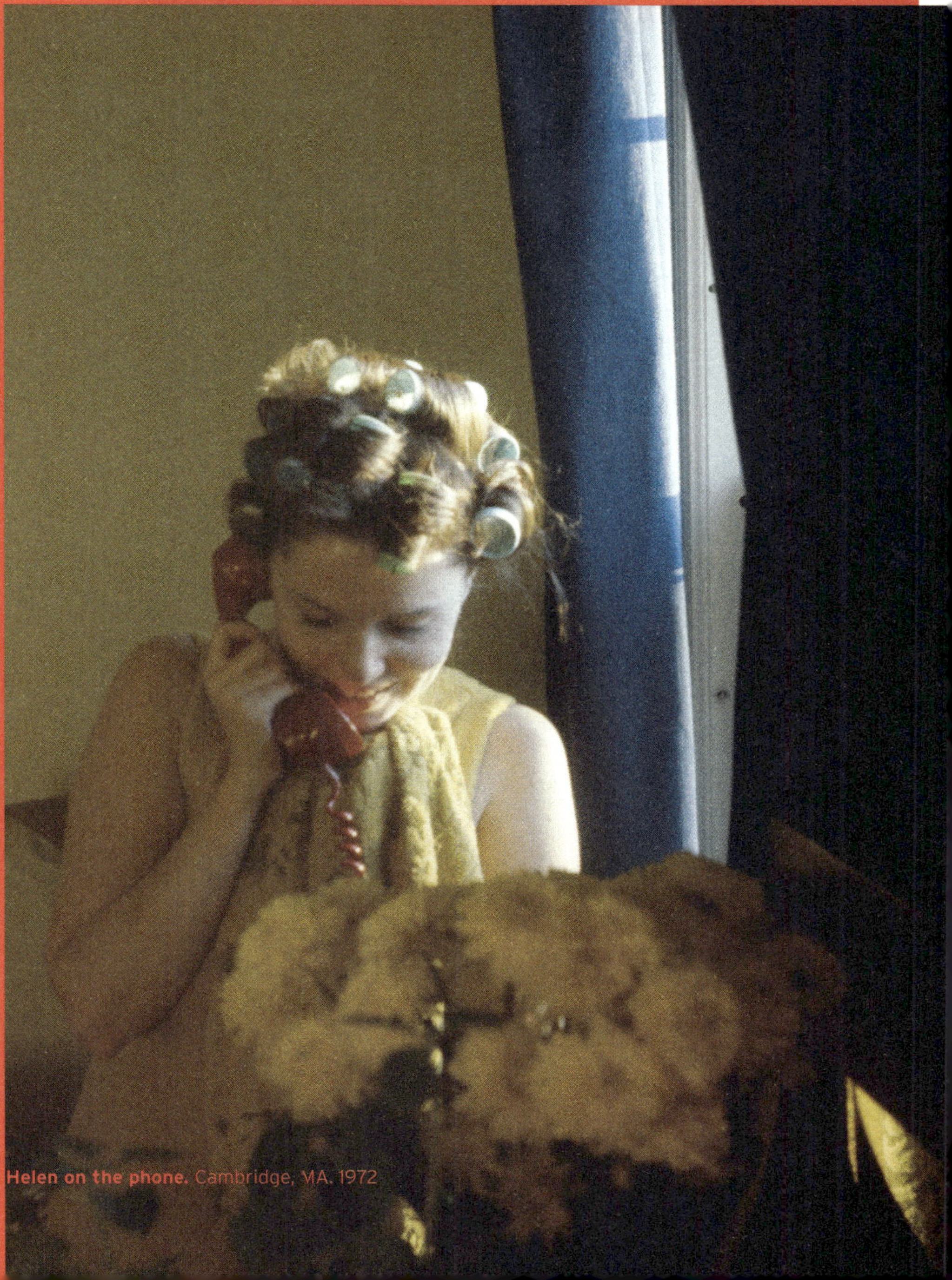

Helen on the phone. Cambridge, MA. 1972

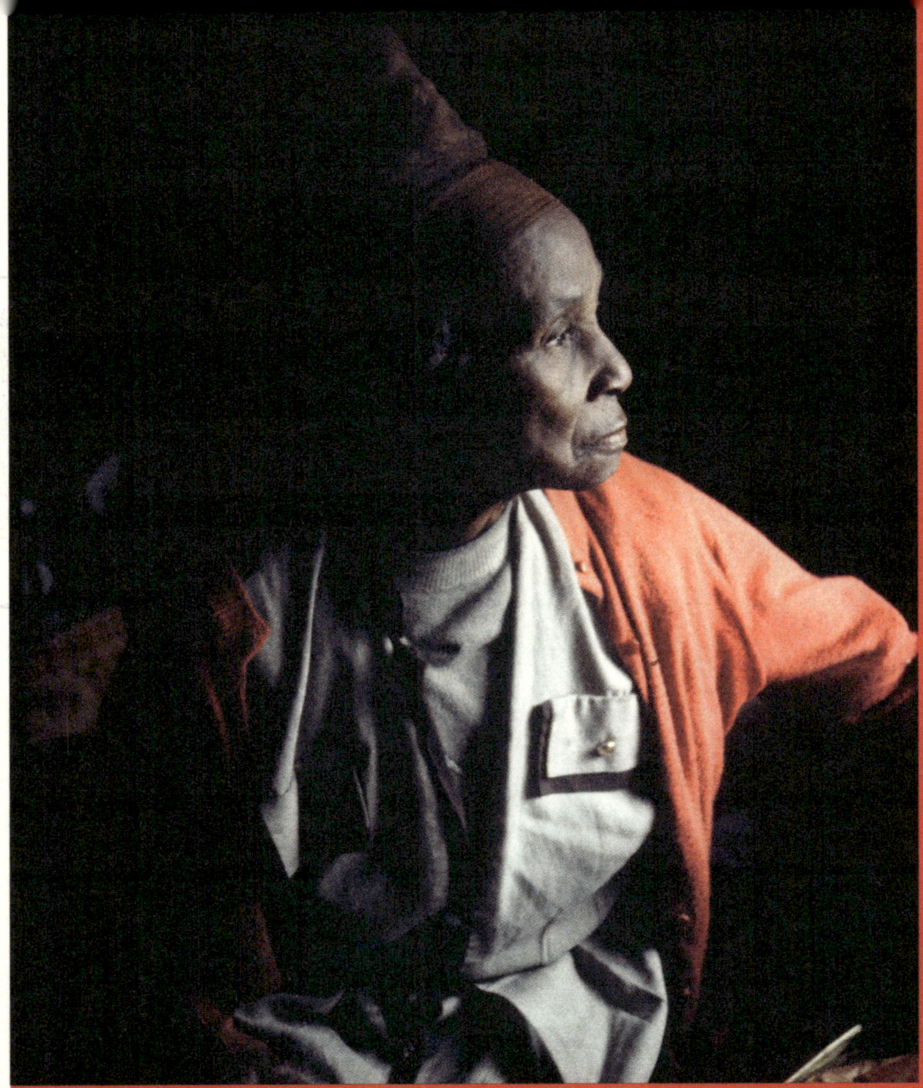

Old woman. Washington, NC. 1974

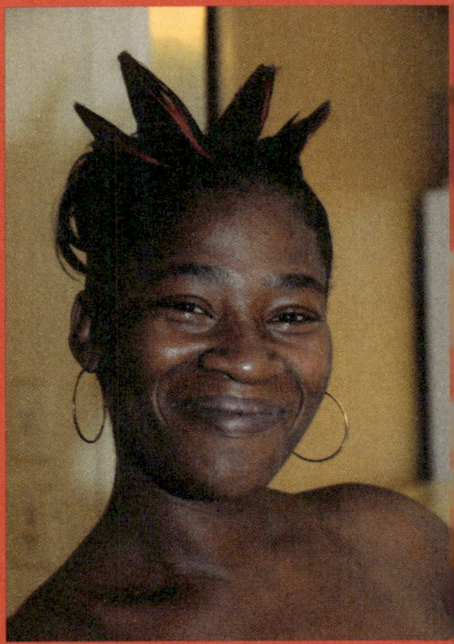

The niece of an ex-girlfriend. Gainesville, FL. 2009

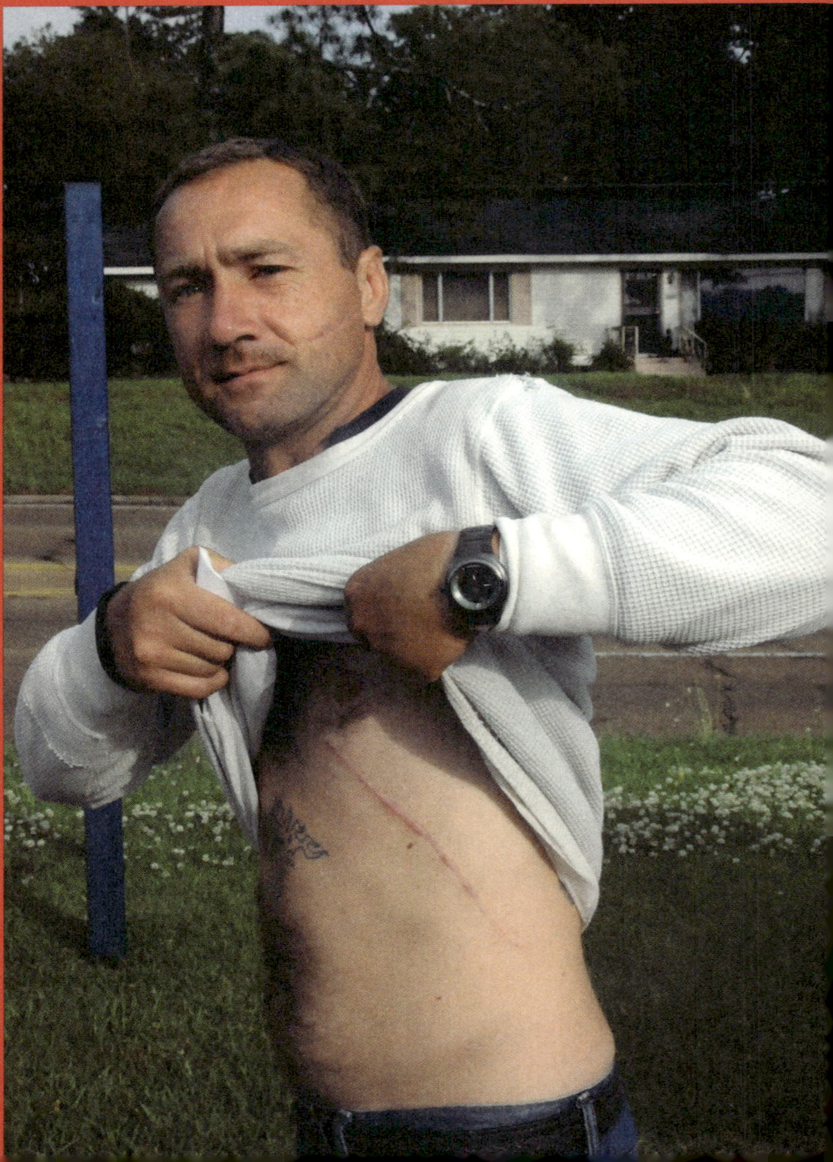

An unemployed hitchhiker I gave a ride, had just been attacked by blacks. Jackson, MS. 2009

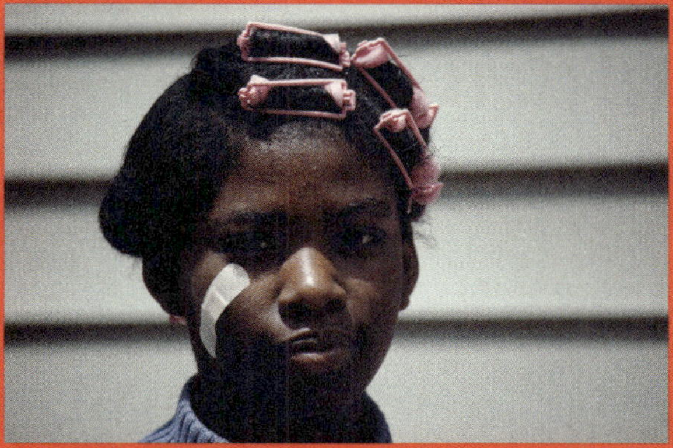

Young girl after a fight. Thompson, AL. 1995

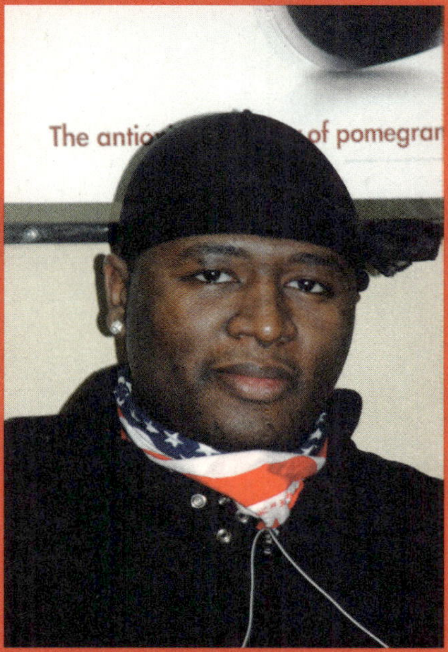

Young man in a Taco Bell restaurant.
Natchez, FL. 2009

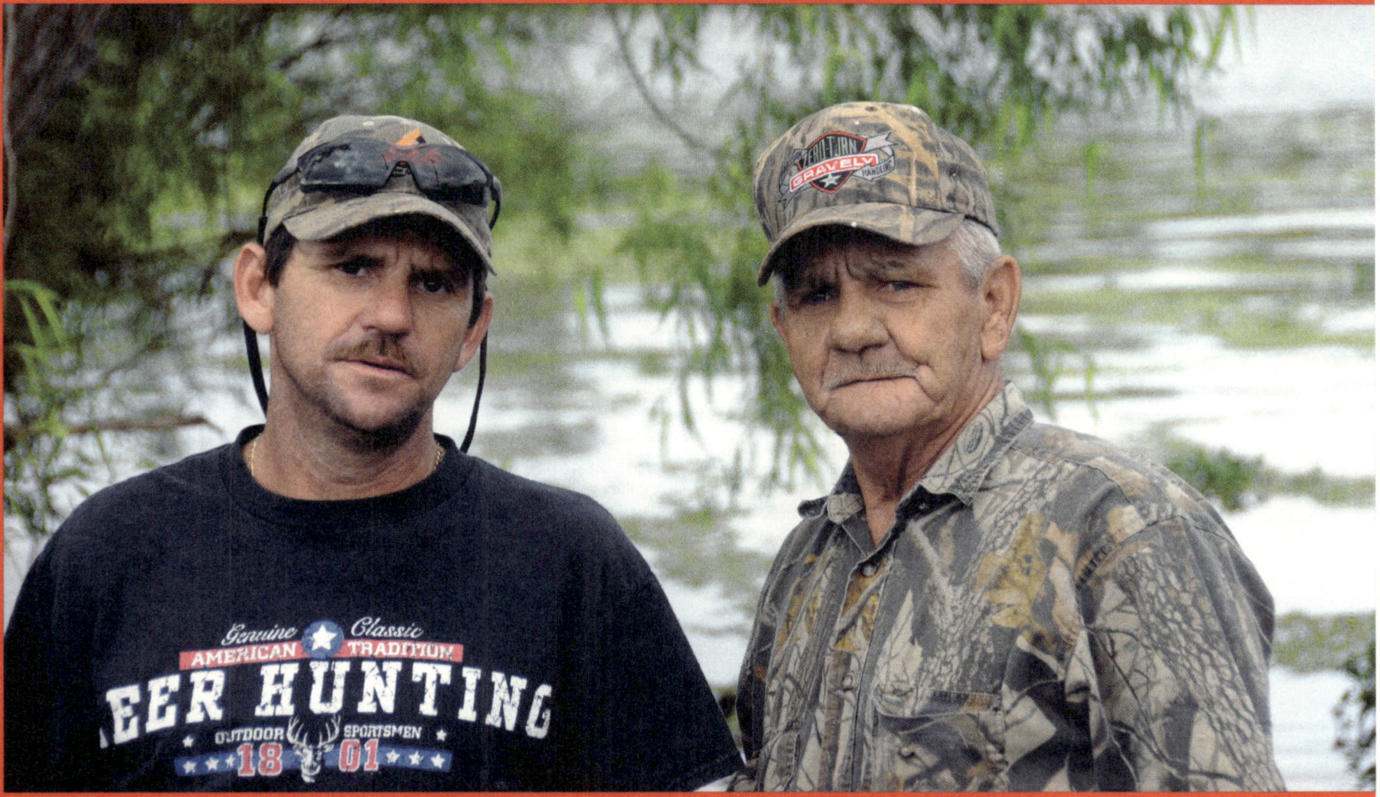

Two fishermen for crayfish in the swamps. Louisiana. 2009

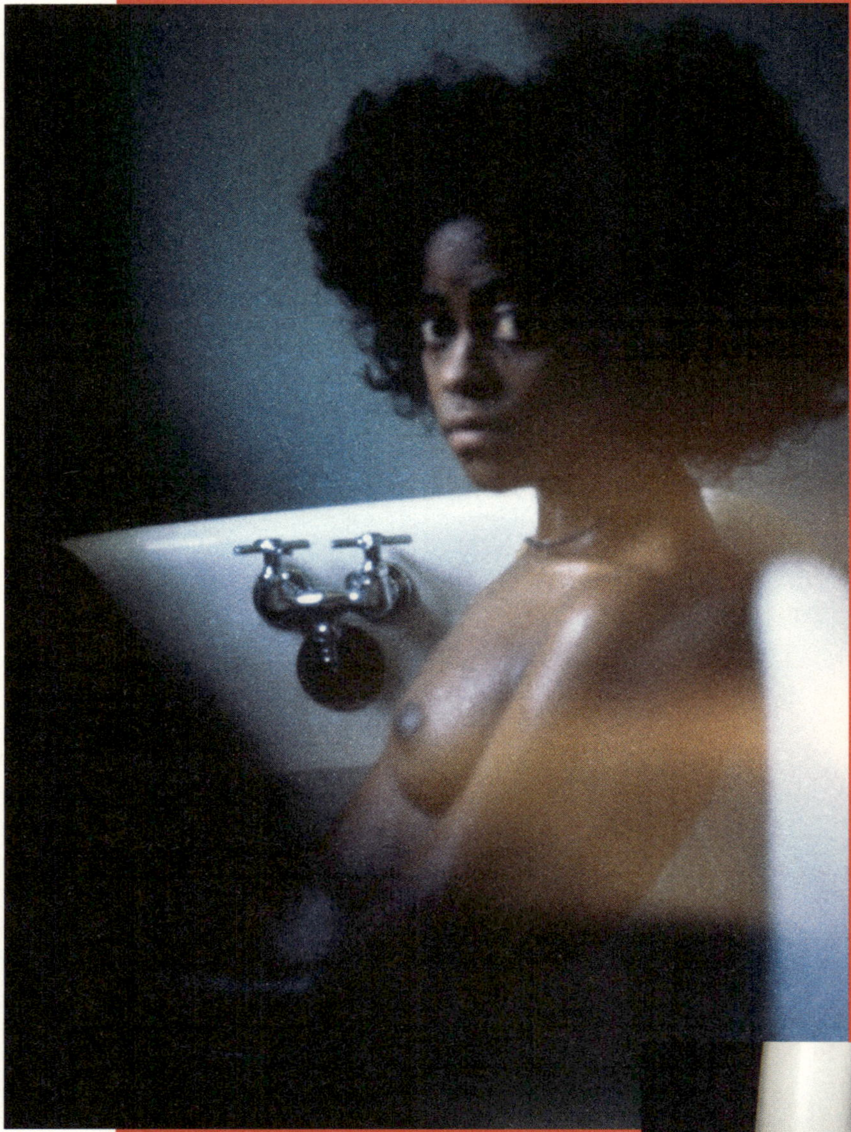

Leslie Manselles in the tub.
Hartford, CT. 1972

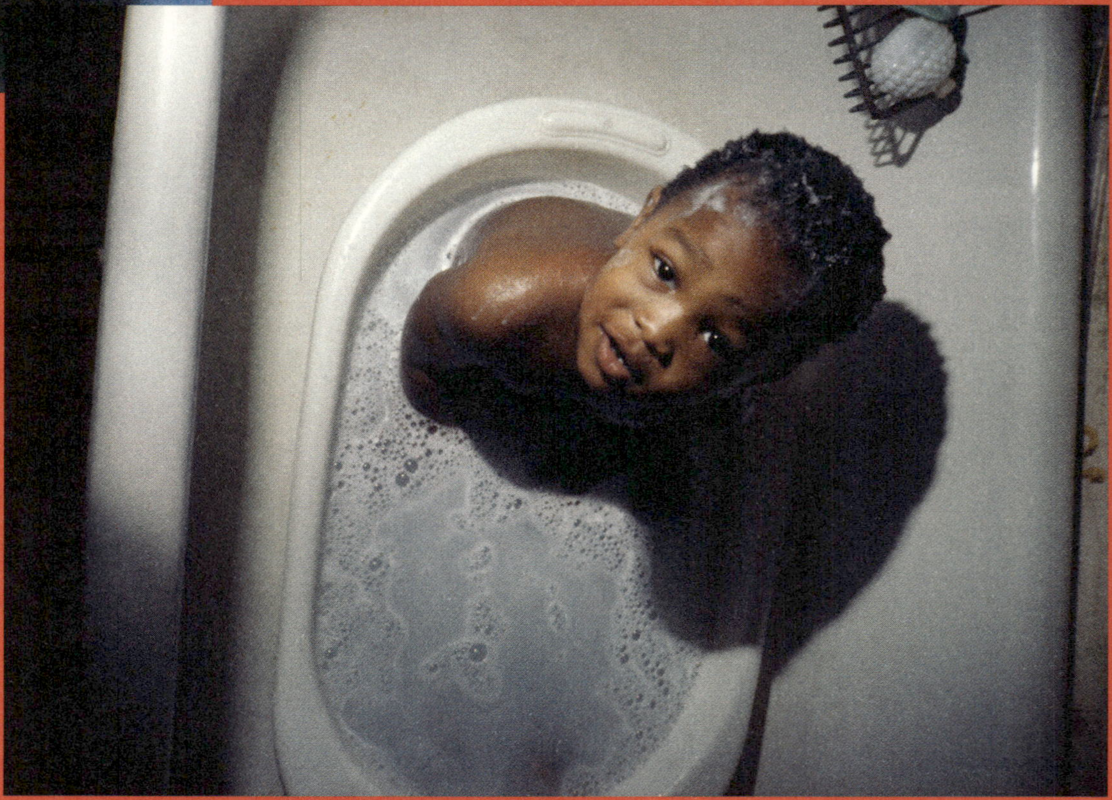

Michael, who is now unemployed and sick. Philadelphia, PA. 1972

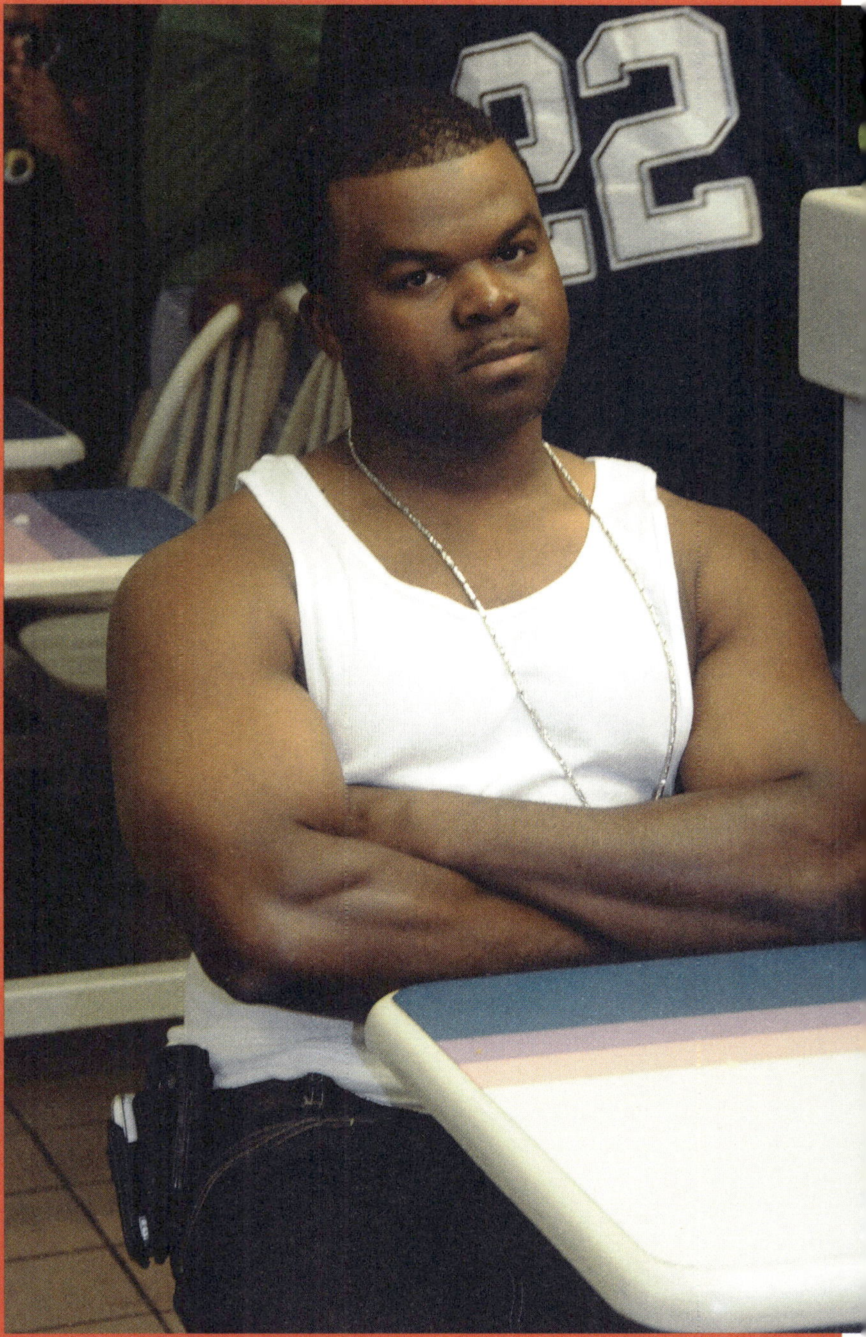

Young man. New York, NY. 2009

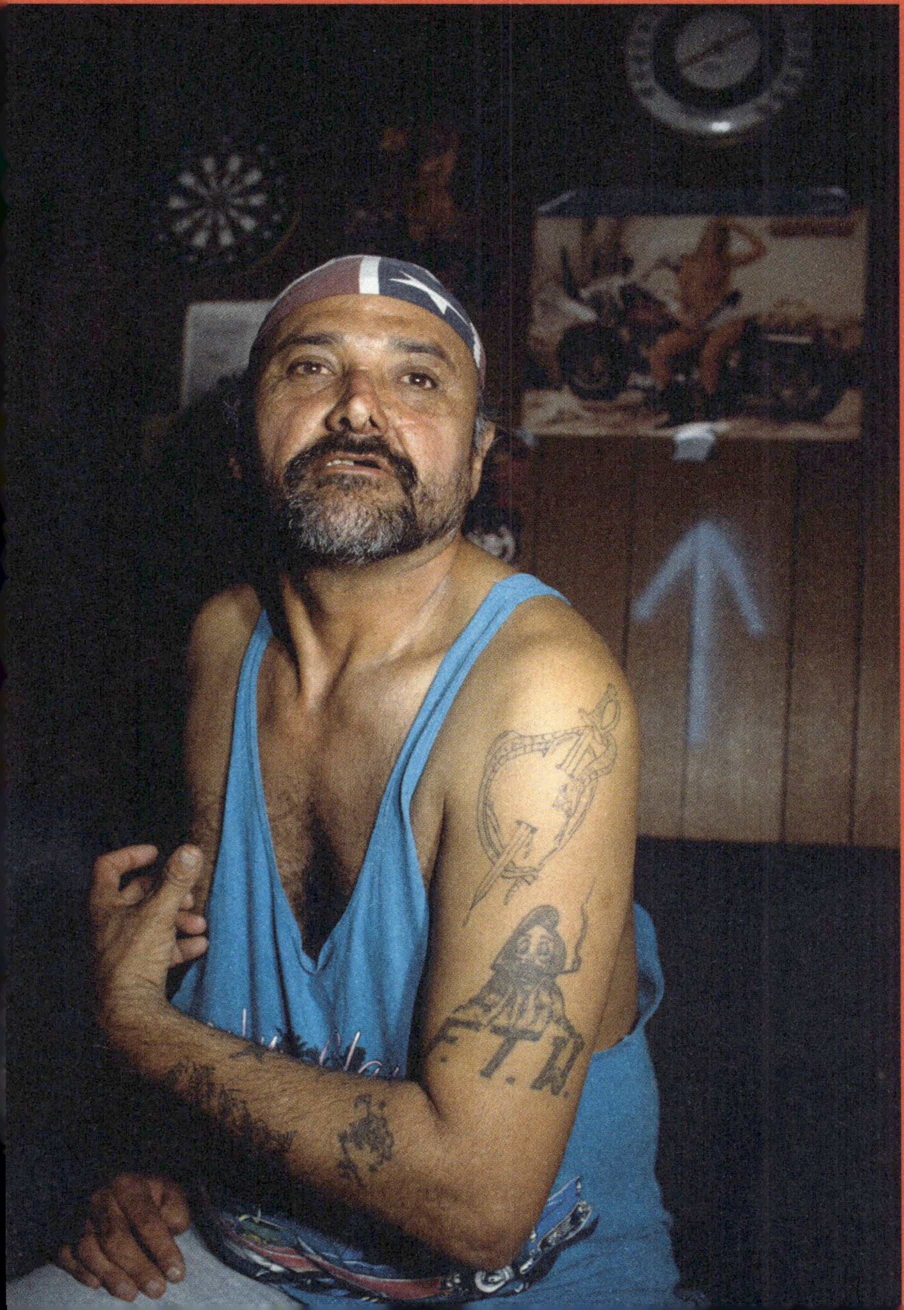

Drunk and violent bully in his shack.
Morgan City, LA. 1996

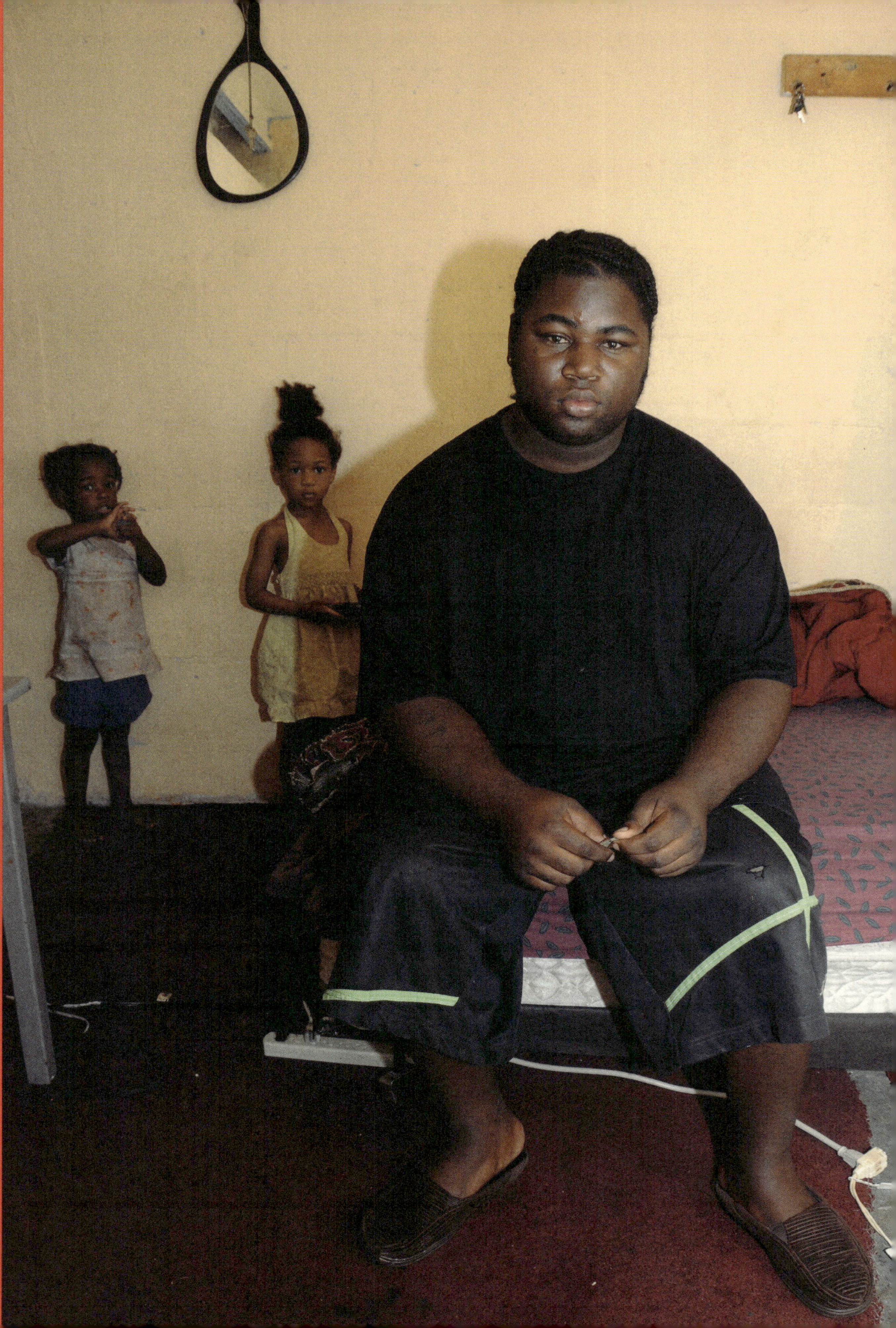

The sick migrant worker Sonny with his children.
Belle Glade, FL. 2009

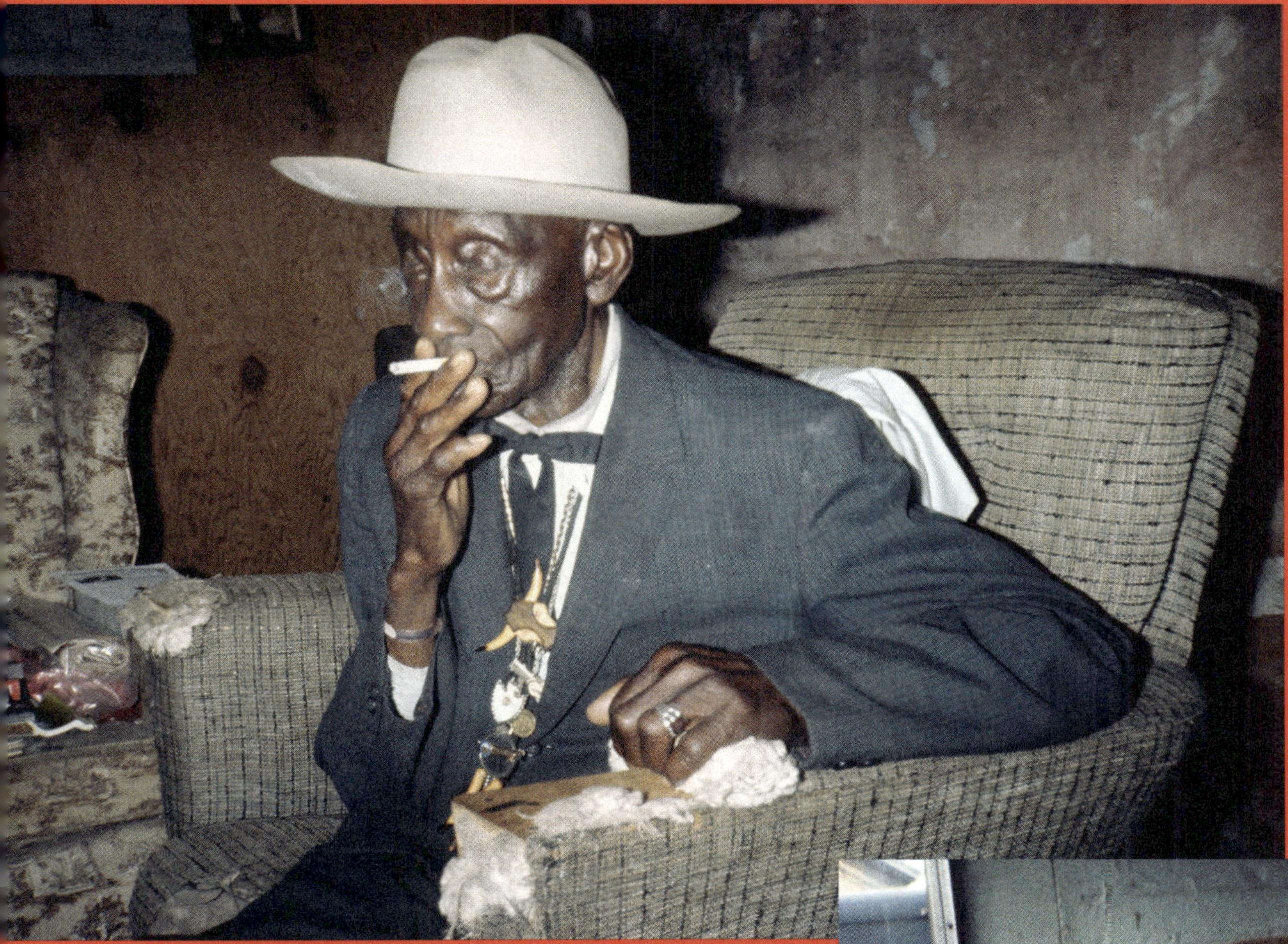

The 134-year-old Charles Smith was brought to USA as a slave.
Bartow, FL. 1974

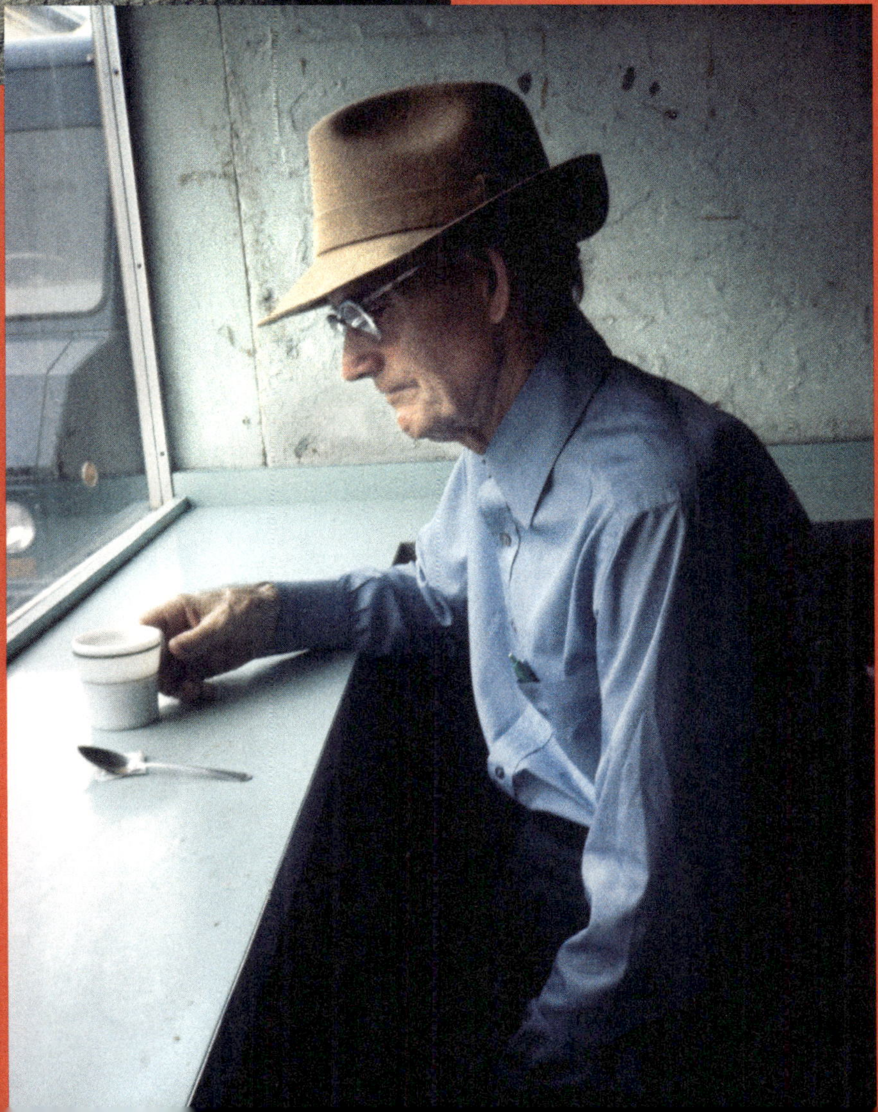

Poor white in a coffee shop.
Greenville, NC. 1974

sunsets

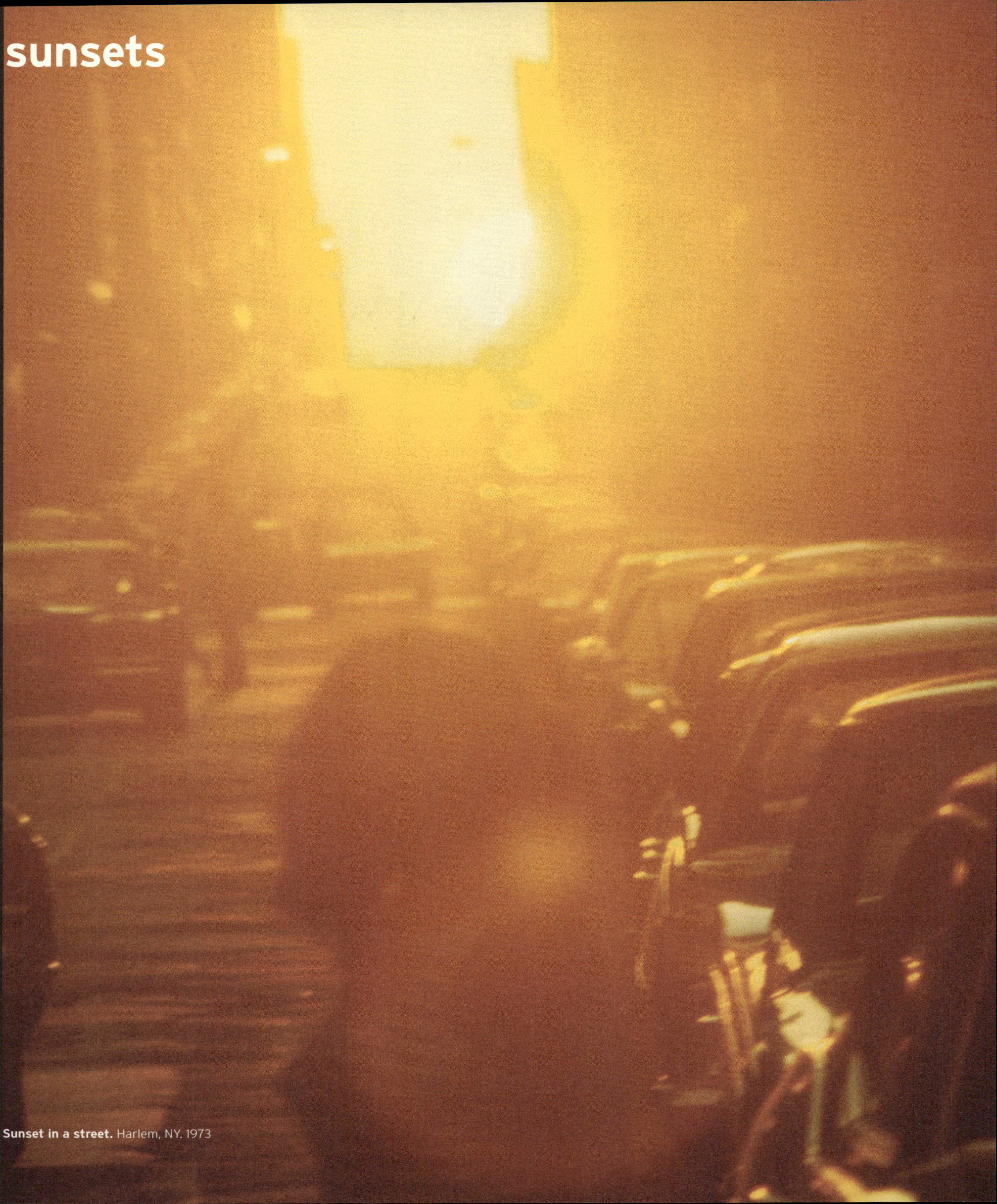

Sunset in a street. Harlem, NY. 1973

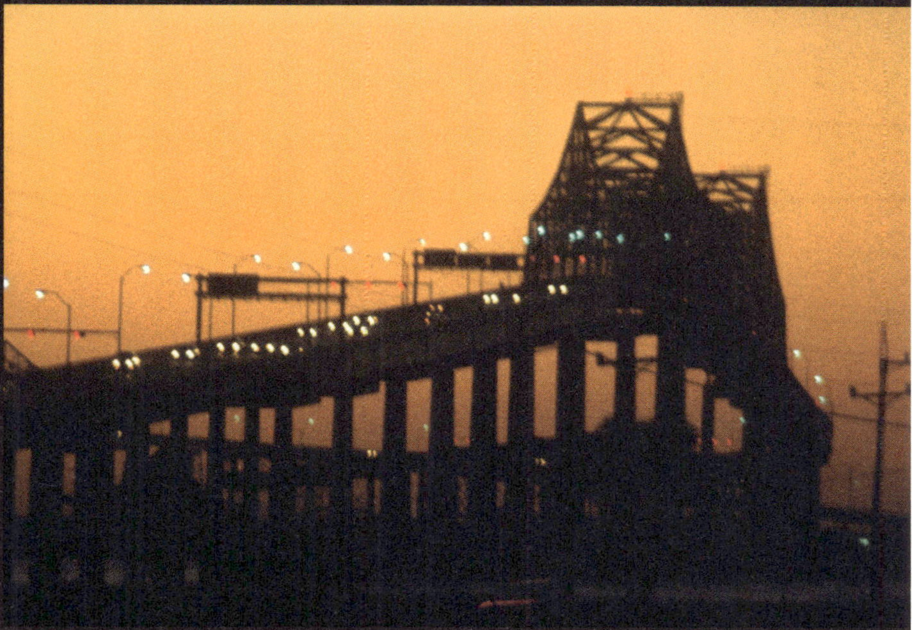

Sunset over a bridge. Charleston, SC. 1974

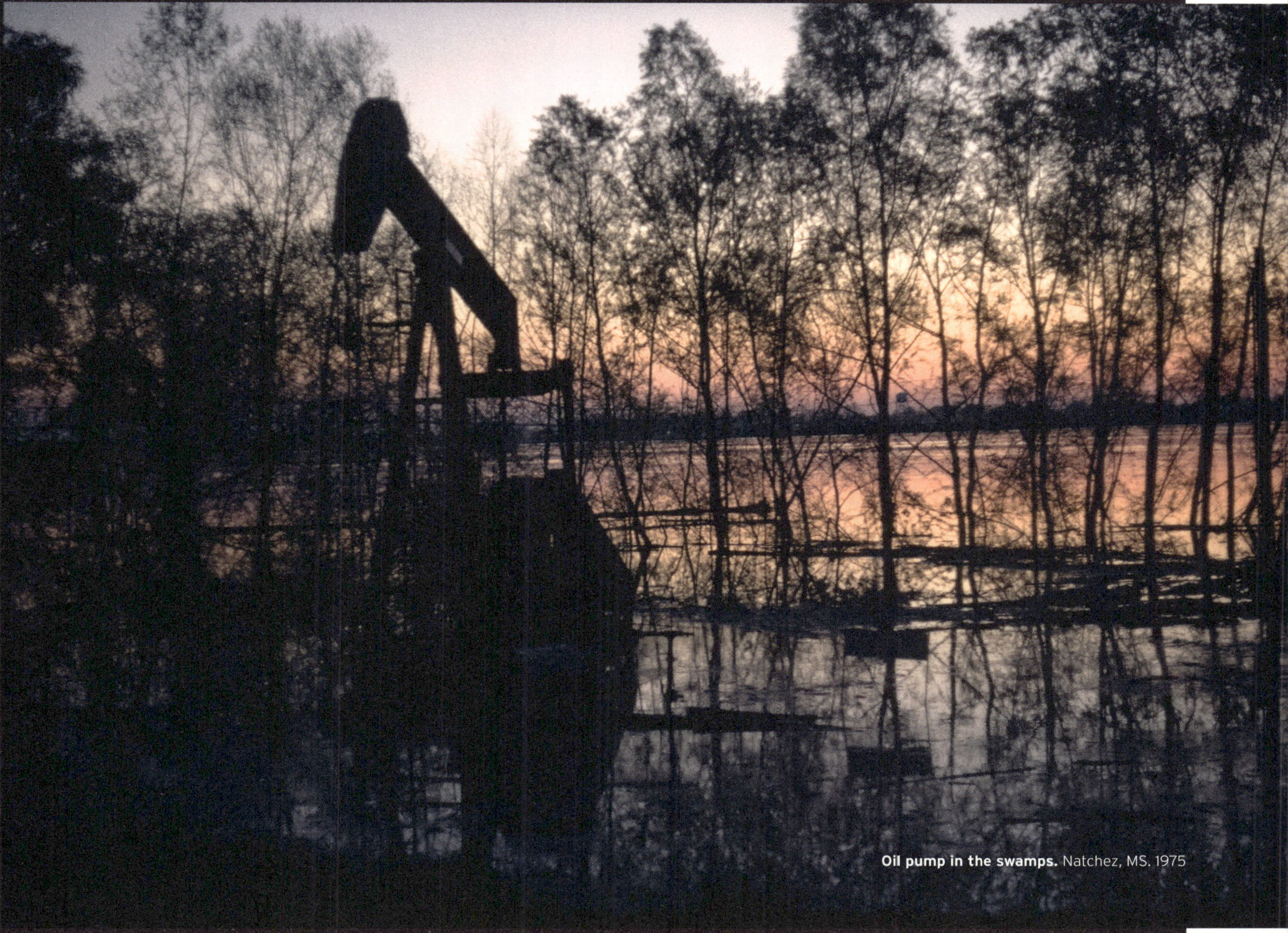

Oil pump in the swamps. Natchez, MS. 1975

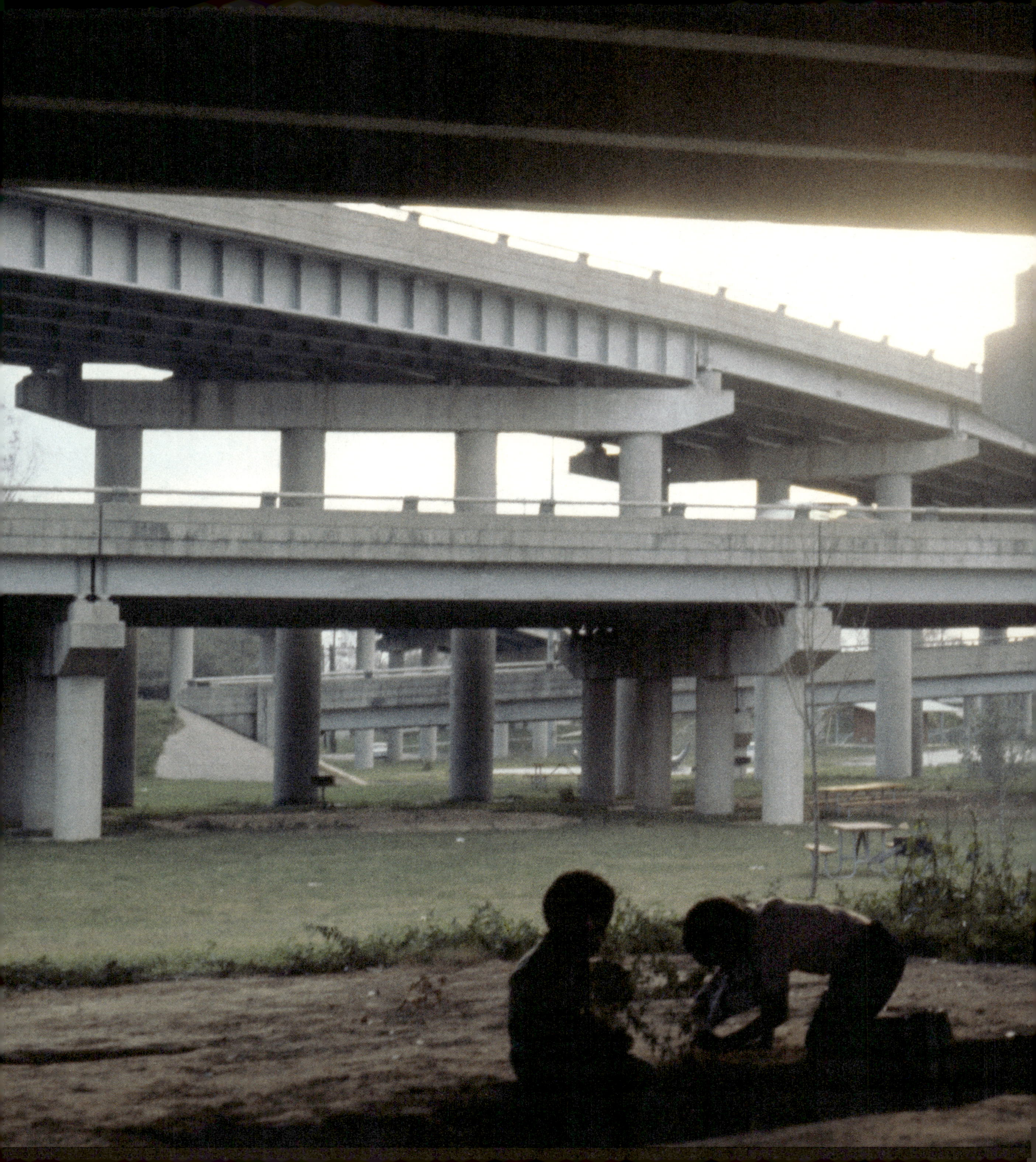

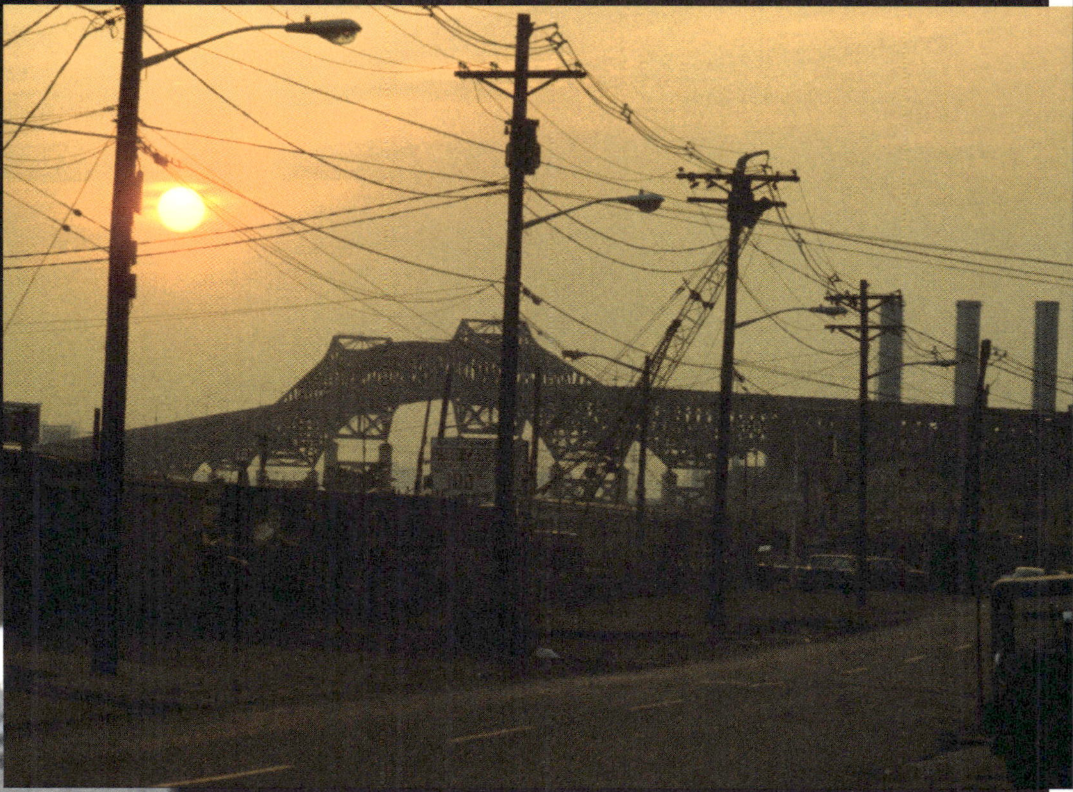

Sunset over a bridge. Charleston, SC. 1974

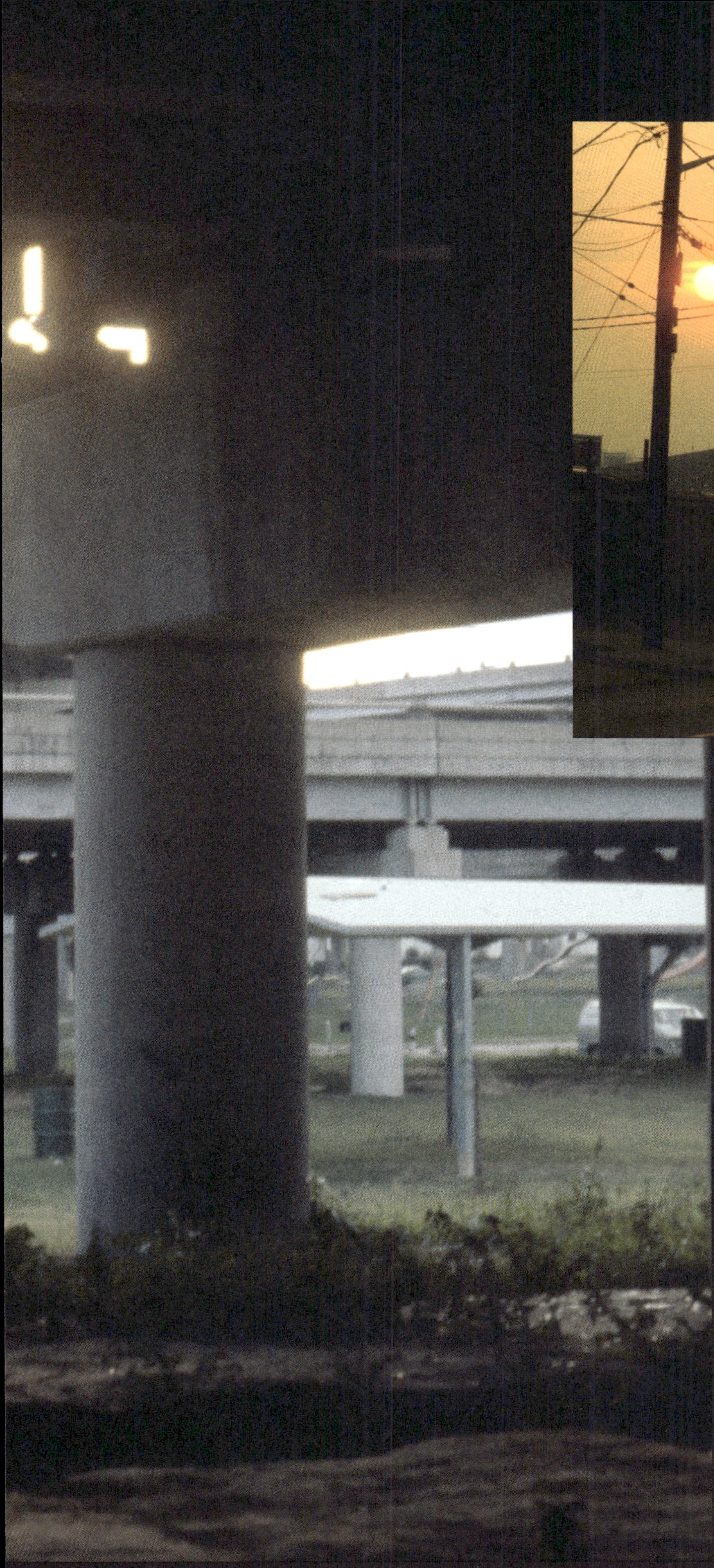

Ghetto children playing under the highways. New Orleans, LA. 1973

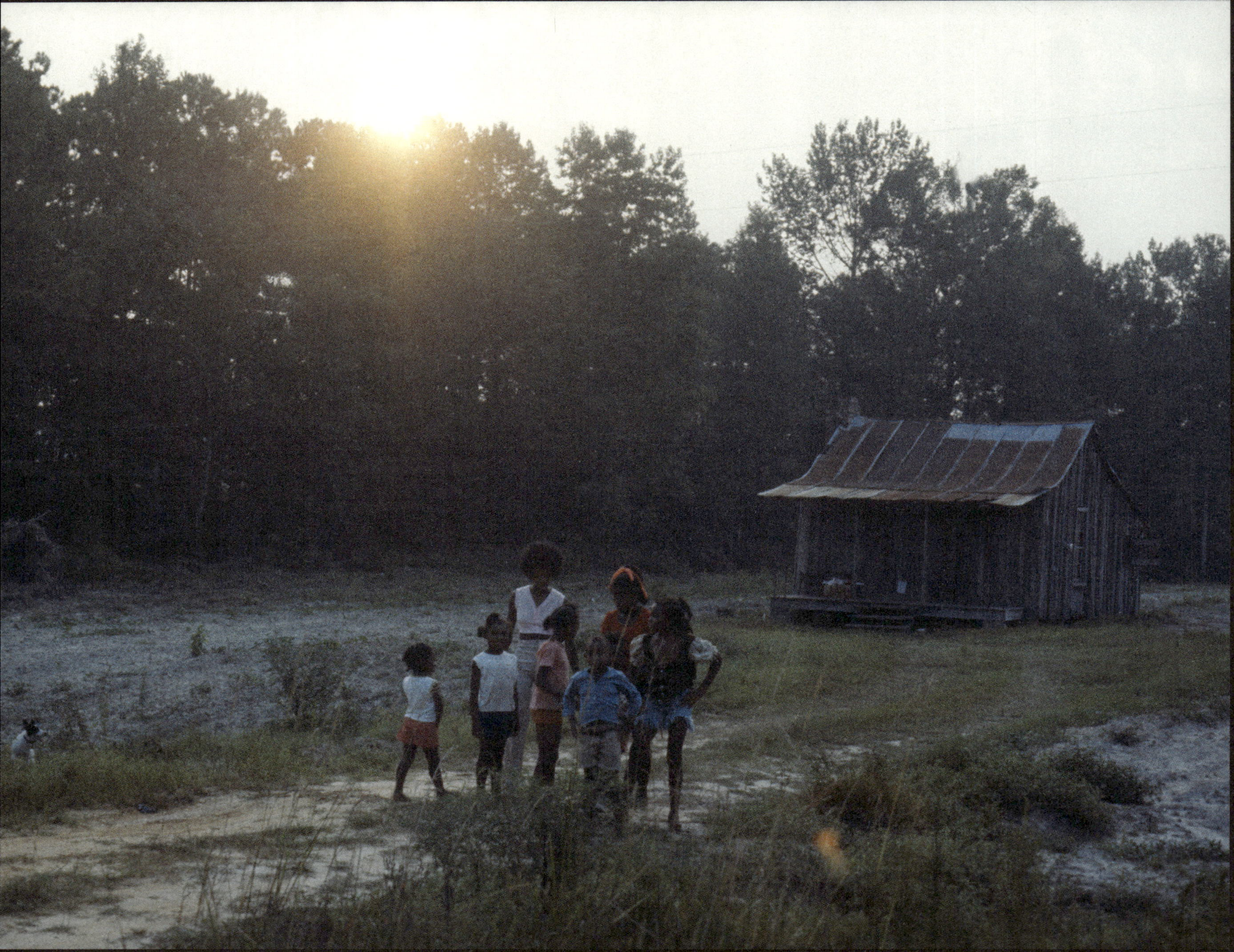

Children and shack in the sunset. Yazoo City, MS. 1974

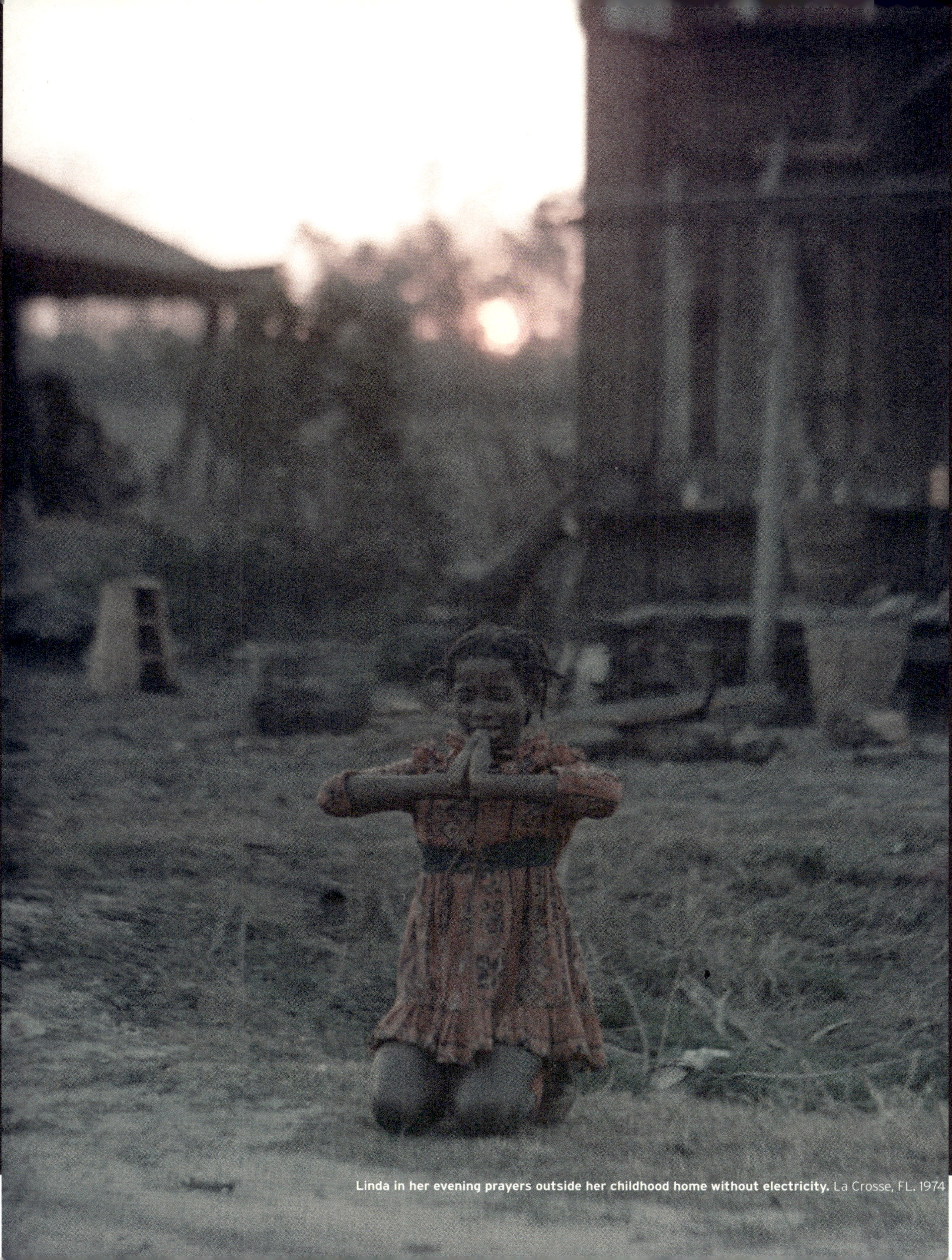

Linda in her evening prayers outside her childhood home without electricity. La Crosse, FL. 1974

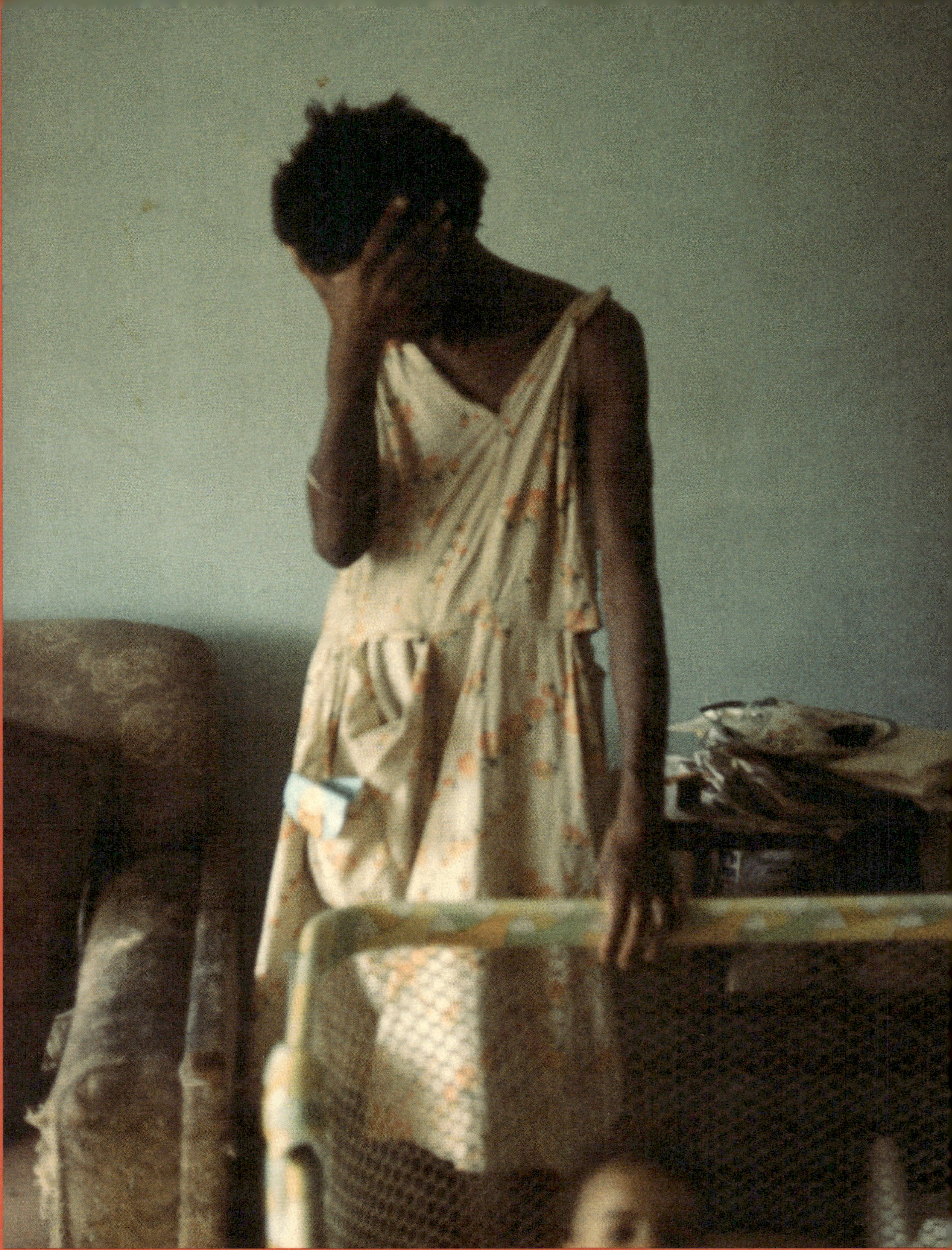

Nell in the projects. Jersey City, NJ. 1975

METTE MARCUS

the man who couldn't say no

an interview with JACOB HOLDT

The man who became synonymous with his slide-show and book "American Pictures" is presented at Louisiana; an updated look at Jacob Holdt's highly personal yet universal world – America portrayed with sensitivity and rare glimpses into places where only those who say yes can go. Louisiana curator Mette Marcus, the exhibition's organizer, spoke with the vagabond, artist and controversial public personality about his photographs and the fresh questions they continue to raise.

MM: Mounting a show of your photographs, it's hard to get around Jacob Holdt, the person, and the whole story of your background, your motivations and your American journey. The American Pictures project, already familiar to so many Danes, is such a landmark.

JH: When you tell me that you think a biography of some sort should be included in the show, that you want to give people insight into who I am as a person, we then need to consider what kind of biography we want to tell. I've spent so much time among black Americans and worked with the problems of black America that you might say I've ended up writing my own biography – for instance, in interviews – in terms of that. Then there was the recent movie Milk, about the gay American politician Harvey Milk, and *Jyllands-Posten* (the Danish daily – ed.) ran a debate that prompted me to sit down and write about my involvement with people in the gay movement. All of a sudden, I was able to see and define myself in an entirely different way. This is just to say that there are many ways of understanding a person. There are many angles on my life, too, but the focus was always on *that* (points to a copy of American Pictures). I'm even a bit surprised myself when I'm reminded that I'm other things besides what I'm best known for today. I have lots of pictures about other Americans than impoverished blacks.

MM: Your project was to fight inequality and racism in the U.S. and later use the pictures you took as a starting point for a general discussion about inequality. Why pick that and not another fight – after all, there were plenty to choose from back then, in the early 1970s?

JH: But, you've got a completely wrong impression of me as a person. I never picked anything myself. Nor am I now that Louisiana is picking me. I always just bent with the wind. I never really chose anything in the U.S. I was involved in a fight in Denmark. I was an anti-Vietnam war activist and hounded by the police. At one point, a American Vietnam deserter is staying in my back-alley apartment. He meets a Canadian girl and her parents are so happy about my taking care of her that they invite me to Canada. That's how it all began. I work for a year or so up in Canada and get involved in various liberation movements. I meet an Argentinian and we dream about going down and supporting Allende's revolution in Chile. It's always my goal to hitchhike down to Latin America, but the trip through the States becomes decisive. First, a black gay man rapes me in San Francisco and three days later three black men rob me at gunpoint. The anger and pain I encountered at both these events was a watershed. I was launched in two directions at once. Gay liberation was just starting up in San Francisco at the time. Meanwhile, there was black liberation. But again, this wasn't something I consciously decided to do. From the get-go, it was as if black people took me by the hand and led me into their world of pain. In retrospect, I can see it was incredibly exciting what was going on at the time, things like the Black Panthers. It was an exciting time. When the black political activist Angela Davis was jailed, I was staying with some of her friends. So I was suddenly caught up in something I hadn't chosen myself.

I was trying to hold on to my anti-war involvement, and when everyone was going to the big demonstration in Washington I got a ride – at the time, I was still too scared to hitchhike – all the way to Detroit, where I was invited to stay with some black men in the roughest part of town – including one who just befriended me on Facebook yesterday! He later fled to Europe. He was sick of teaching high school to kids who'd be polishing their guns in class. A week later, I went with them to Washington for the big anti-war demonstrations. I plan to go back to Detroit with them afterwards, but I keep getting drawn into one violent ghetto after another. Blacks are always drawing me into their world. So, I never picked them, they always picked me. Don't make me guilty of anything, please!

MM: Then you start taking photographs. Often of situations that would be impossible for an ordinary tourist in the States to experience. You typically stay with the people you photograph. This picture, for instance, shows a despondent-looking black woman and we just catch a glimpse of her baby in the playpen. It doesn't look like a happy situation. How did the picture come about?

JH: That's Nell Hall, and her grandchild

in the playpen. I met Nell's daughter Evelyn at a bar in New York – she was pregnant. It's interesting that you pull out this picture, because at the time I didn't know that I'd be doing something on oppression. I had an idea of showing black life more generally. I already had "black death" represented and at some point I get the desire to show 'black birth', as well. I had seen W. Eugene Smith's "Nurse Midwife" from the 1950s, of a midwife with women giving birth in shacks, and I thought I'd do something like that. Every time I met a black woman who would soon be giving birth, I asked for permission to photograph and waited up the last nights before they came to term to make sure I got everything – and at the last moment, they always decided to go to the hospital and have a C-section. So, one, I was denied that sort of shanty romanticism and, two, I was never allowed to go into the delivery room. Every time, I was denied a good birth picture.

MM: Why did you take this picture?
JH: Well, I could tell it was a disturbing image. At the time, I was obsessed with the image white people have of black people – the grinning character, the 'pleasing nigger', that black people have learned to play since slavery days. Pleasing the white man. I saw it when I worked with black people in the cotton fields. When the white boss came around it brought out the 'happy clown', one of the many stereotypes created by slavery. All of a sudden, some of them would start acting crazy. But what I saw when I lived with them was this unbelievable sadness and apathy. Case in point, when I lived with Nell and Evelyn – the first and second day, she sits there smiling and everyone's having fun. As a rule, I had to stay with people two or three days before reality crept in, before they were suitably relaxed around the photographer to allow me to interpret what I saw and see the deeper, underlying reality. Then you may ask, Is this the true, deeper reality? And yes, it is. Some things whites didn't see, don't see. They see it as something else. So it was important for me to sit and wait for those moments that, so to speak, showed the reality before the photographing stranger intruded. And that takes time. So, I went to a woman's home to take a birth picture and ended up taking a picture describing oppression. That, there, doesn't exist out in the street. You simply don't see it. But, again, I am drawn into it.

MM: So your intention actually was to take a positive picture, to capture a slice of life?
JH: Yes, you could say that. In this particular case. But then I am drawn into her reality. Today, that housing project is closed because of crime. Some of the few times I really had fear in me was when I walked out there.

MM: We can't tell that from your pictures, though. We don't feel a tinge of fear.
JH: If I'd really been scared, of course, I couldn't have taken these pictures. Then I would've stayed away from those neighborhoods. It was only when I learned to tackle racism – that is, the fear of other people – that I could even do *American Pictures*. The first two years I didn't dare go into Harlem at night. But, the moment I started thinking about black people in a positive way and have trust in them, that whole world opened up. Courage is about conquering your fear. People often ask me, "How did you get the guts to do it"? Well, I didn't have (that racist) fear anymore, so I didn't need as many guts as when I started out.

MM: In your book, there are two places where the film snaps, so to speak. One is where you describe the funeral of someone you don't know. You can't take any pictures, because you find it so awful. It would seem that, meeting people you don't know, the misery becomes too overwhelming for you to take pictures, while you don't have an issue about photographing the miserable situations of people you know? Does putting a camera in front of your eye act as a filter?
JH: I never thought about that. There is actually a situation where I tried to photograph a homeless man down on the Bowery in New York and he attacks me with a knife. I get this guilt and feel I need to make friends with him. I spend the whole night talking with him and eventually do make friends with him. So you have a point. In that case, I was photographing someone before I knew him. And I always thought that was exploitation, taking pictures of homeless people just lying in the street.

MM: Why is that?
JH: Well, I really felt that was taking advantage of people. On the other hand, if you do so based on a friendly relationship and people really *take part* in your pictures, that's legitimate. But the whole thing about going out and photographing some suffering people and then exhibiting their suffering – anybody can do that, but to me it's like cheating. I happened to do it that night with the homeless man, because I was with Marilyn and we were busy going somewhere, so I just took his picture without any kind of prior communication, because the situation was, I can use this picture. I really regretted it and felt guilty about it. It is clearly overstepping my boundaries to photograph someone before I have struck up a kind of friendship with him/her.

MM: The issue of exploitation, can't that be seen from the other side, as well? That you, a white man, capturing the suffering of black people, are still somehow using them?
JH: That's always an issue. I see the same thing in Denmark, too. If people who are ghettoized only meet contempt and rejection from the society, there's a reaction. They have no faith in the white man, and ever so often when a well-meaning blue-eyed man like me comes in, there's distrust. Some don't want to have anything to do with you at all, others can't do without an alliance with white people who open up to them. At the time I was traveling, a lot of black people adamantly did not want to have a white man staying in their house. That was the attitude of a huge number of people. The poorest blacks were afraid of whites in a differ-

ent way, of course. But the middle class, which was in a period of powerful political liberation, often wanted nothing to do with white people. I remember when I was picked up by black middle-class families and they sometimes got so offended at what they saw in my pictures that they ordered me out of the car, saying things like, "Is that how you see black people?" or, "That is an exploitation of our pain." This was expressed in all sorts of ways. So, I met resistance not only from white people – in some places I was a "nigger lover" and in a lot of places I couldn't even say what I was doing. In the South, especially, I could never tell whites what I was doing on the black side of town. It was an incredible balancing act. If I was staying with a white family and I came in at night and they asked me, "Well, what did you do today?" I'd say something like, "Just hanging around." And remember, I didn't always get support from black people, either. The whole thing about palling around with the enemy is symptomatic for all oppressed people. You are ostracized if you do. And the "white devil" comes in many disguises, including that of good intentions.

MM: Still, you seem to have been very conscious about what kind of pictures you were taking, wanting to use them for something special. You also seem to be very conscious of stereotypes and what pictures are capable of doing?
JH: I was conscious of oppression. Increasingly so. It has to do with how I interpret this world, the world of poor black Americans – how shall I go about showing the oppression I see. Take those pictures there, with the wallpaper peeling down the walls. Very few underclass blacks were living like that at the time, of course, but it shows the state of mind I sensed among them. So I used such pictures to show a general state. Most people, after all, are able to hold on to their pride and their dignity. They are able to paper their walls. But the deeper apathy you find in a broken person – that's what I wish to foster an understanding of. Being broken like that is expressed in many different ways, including escaping into drug abuse, or drug dealing and crime – as we see with immigrants in Denmark, gang wars, that kind of thing.
I have myself discriminated in my pictures. I think I more or less subconsciously chose the more attractive members of a family and chose to take pictures of them. I'm not crazy about group shots with 10 or 20 people at once. So I sit there waiting – when is a single person alone with his or her thoughts? Simply because I knew that white racism discriminates against certain aspects of black culture, I always had to speak to the deeper humanity in whites – in that sense, I had to be racist myself.

MM: So you used your own prejudices about what a white person would think was esthetic or visually acceptable?
JH: No. I think you have to say I used my knowledge. When I was on the road and I showed my pictures to white people, I saw how they reacted to a certain kind of picture. "Argh, how can you be with this filthy…." So, perhaps I tended to seek out situations that they couldn't argue against. I don't know if that's predicated on my own racism or the racism I saw in white people. I could never have interpreted that reality if I'd only been on the black side of society. Moving back and forth daily between whites and blacks, I had to translate in my own head how the other side would see my pictures.

MM: What do those pictures mean to you that aren't about people you're staying with but show police, landscapes, billboards, buildings?
JH: Generally, they have served as symbols for me, or as contrasts, to use as building blocks to construct a story.

MM: Do you, in fact, call yourself a photographer?
JH: It depends on the context I'm in. In literary circles, I call myself a pho-tographer. In photographic contexts I call myself a writer or, more neutrally, a vagabond. I called myself that for years, because that's what I felt I was. For years after I returned from the States, I wanted to get back on the road, but I was simply sidetracked by having one succes after another. I was never a photographer, but I've often been labeled one. I'm constantly referred to as "the photographer Jacob Holdt" and I don't really think that's what I predominantly am. I never went to shows of photography, I would never personally go to Louisiana to see a photography show. I've always said I wasn't a good photographer but a good vagabond. Good at getting into homes no one else could get into, but where anyone could have taken a good picture.

MM: For years, you wouldn't show your pictures independently of your own words, as in your slide-show or book. What made you change your mind?
JH: A good friend, who needed a show, asked me if I would select some of my pictures for him to hang, and so I forgot my old principles – because I wanted to help him out, but again also because of my thing about saying yes to things.

MM: You're okay with it now?
JH: Well, I've shown my pictures without my words in a few places now, including the Capitol in Washington, D.C. – where I invited poor people I knew over there to come. It's fun to bring together people in power and people from the underclass – robbers and bandits. I'm always afraid that my pictures will be misunderstood. Without my explanations, I'm afraid they will only reinforce the racism that already exists. There are so many high schools in the U.S. where I can't show my slides, because they're afraid that my pictures will reinforce their students' stereotypes about black people. Images of apathetic blacks tend to jog the stereotype of "the lazy nigger" in their minds.

MM: Is there something about the distance in time that makes it easier for you to exhibit your pictures from the 1970s today?
JH: Yes, it will be a bit easier for me to show them in the U.S.. Now that we have Obama maybe it will be easier for people to see the connection between now and the oppression back then.

MM: Some consider your project to be a religious project. I personally see it as more of a political project.
JH: So do I, though you can't slap a party label on it. It's interesting to me that people so often call me a leftist. You could say that I have a leftist approach to humanity, but I never voted for a left-wing party. I was always there in the middle where I could have a dialogue with the right and the left. Or bring out such a dialogue.

MM: Were you ever tempted to use the influence you have on so many people in terms of party politics?
JH: Several parties have actually headhunted me and I tend to say, "Sure, that would be fun." But thankfully, my family always put a stop on it, telling me it would ruin my message if I suddenly joined one or another party. That's not for me. I'm no good at that kind of thing.

MM: What does religion mean to you, in terms of your pictures?
JH: My father was a minister and I was always there in church listening, until I rebelled and only went every other Sunday. Christianity was always a part of my childhood. I probably rebelled more against the rhetoric around it than the inherent message of Christianity. It meant a lot to me, I think, to see the difference between the rhetoric in church and the real engagement in people. What I really respected about my father's work was his social work with people in the parish. I didn't think of him as a particularly religious person. What counted was his human engagement. My father talked with people who were going through hard times. On the road in the U.S. that was my experience, too – that people had a need to talk to me. Sometimes, I almost felt embarrassed to tell them I'd been traveling around the country for close to five years and mostly had a really good time. But I could justify having so much fun by at the same time having a kind of mission as an itinerant social worker.

I always loved the religious human being and it was great to live in a multicultural society like America. Then I could change faith by alternately living with Muslims, fundamentalist Christians or Buddhists. I think it's a beautiful thing to share people's faith and see how strongly faith lives in all people.

MM: But, why is that important? Is it because that's where hope is, or a faith in change?
JH: What I saw, I think, was a way for people to deal with their misfortune, faith as a refuge, an escape from the pain we people make for one another. Even within individual families, there's a need to escape or find a higher meaning. But I never made that escape. I never became religious myself.

MM: Let's look at some of your pictures again. There is very little confrontation or judgment in your pictures. Take this picture of a mass-murderer with his young daughter on his arm. Clearly, he doesn't treat her too well....
JH: Yes, people often ask me how I can just stand there and take pictures of the mother beating that girl. I just did. As I've said, it doesn't do any good to rebuke the mother by saying, "Don't whip your kids", because that only makes her feel worse about herself. On the contrary, it's about – by my presence, or anyone of us who has something to spare – helping them out of that kind of pain, so they feel better about themselves. I can't judge them.

MM: This guy looks like nothing special, apart from the fact that he owns a lot of guns and is proud of it. He doesn't look particularly aggressive or evil, in the posture you portray him in here.
JH: Well, I couldn't help but care about these people. They were so sweet, too – though I also have a picture of him gesturing with a knife to show how he murdered a black guy....

MM: Then there's a picture like this [of a half-nude black couple kissing in bed]. It's quite a relief to see a picture with some sensuality and love – at least that's what it looks like to me. Apparently, it was important for you to include this kind of picture, of people having sex or generally expressing love?
JH: Well, it's to show a broader range of human life. Plus, it was another aspect I experienced. After all, I had a lot of fun with these people, too. It's important to show that side of life, too – if I didn't show it, I'd be distorting the image. I think it's important to show that people can contain different aspects at once.

MM: This picture (Churchgoers after church service) is interesting because you are suddenly looking at things differently than you usually do when you photograph?
JH: Yes, here I'm being judgmental.

MM: How come?
JH: Well, I always have the contrast of white people enriching themselves and not caring about what goes on right around the corner from them. So, sure, there's some condemnation in that. Most white people see themselves as one big middle class and they're shocked at the contrasts I show. We're always reading about growing inequality in the United States, as the rich get richer and richer, but that's not how you experience society when you're inside of it. All you see, then, is working families all around. So, this is a very conscious attempt to *shake* people up to make them see the huge inequalities in the American society. As a Dane, coming from one of the world's most egalitarian societies, I didn't photograph the things that resembled my own society as much as the things that were completely different, the filthy rich and the filthy poor, which I'd never seen before. It was shocking to me. And I soon discovered how this was also a visually effective way to get my message out.

MM: Couldn't a case also be made to pity these ladies? After all, their situation is as historically determined as that of poor black people – or is it?
JH: That was actually a standing question for me, which I very clearly express in American Pictures – what is a person's responsibility in this? But in order to bring

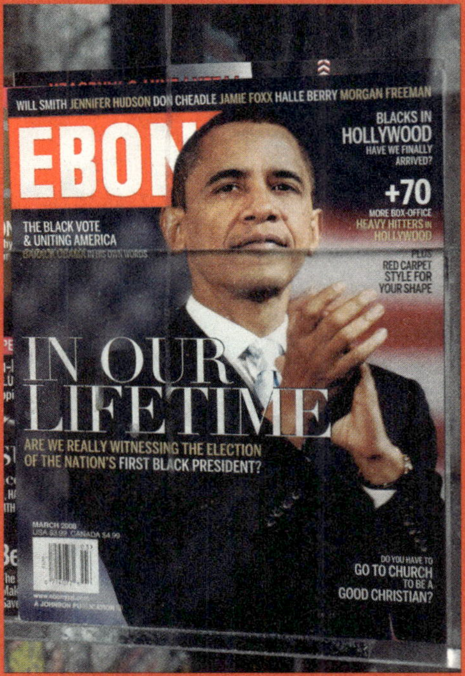

The weekly black magazine, Ebony, six months before the election of Obama. New York, NY. 2008

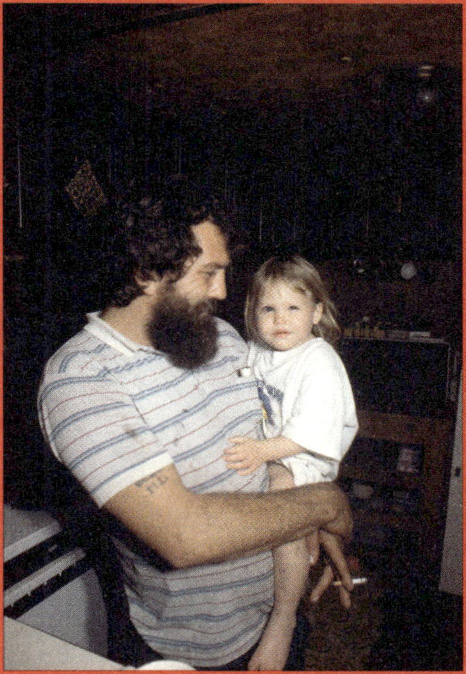

John with his daughter Gene. Mississippi. 1996

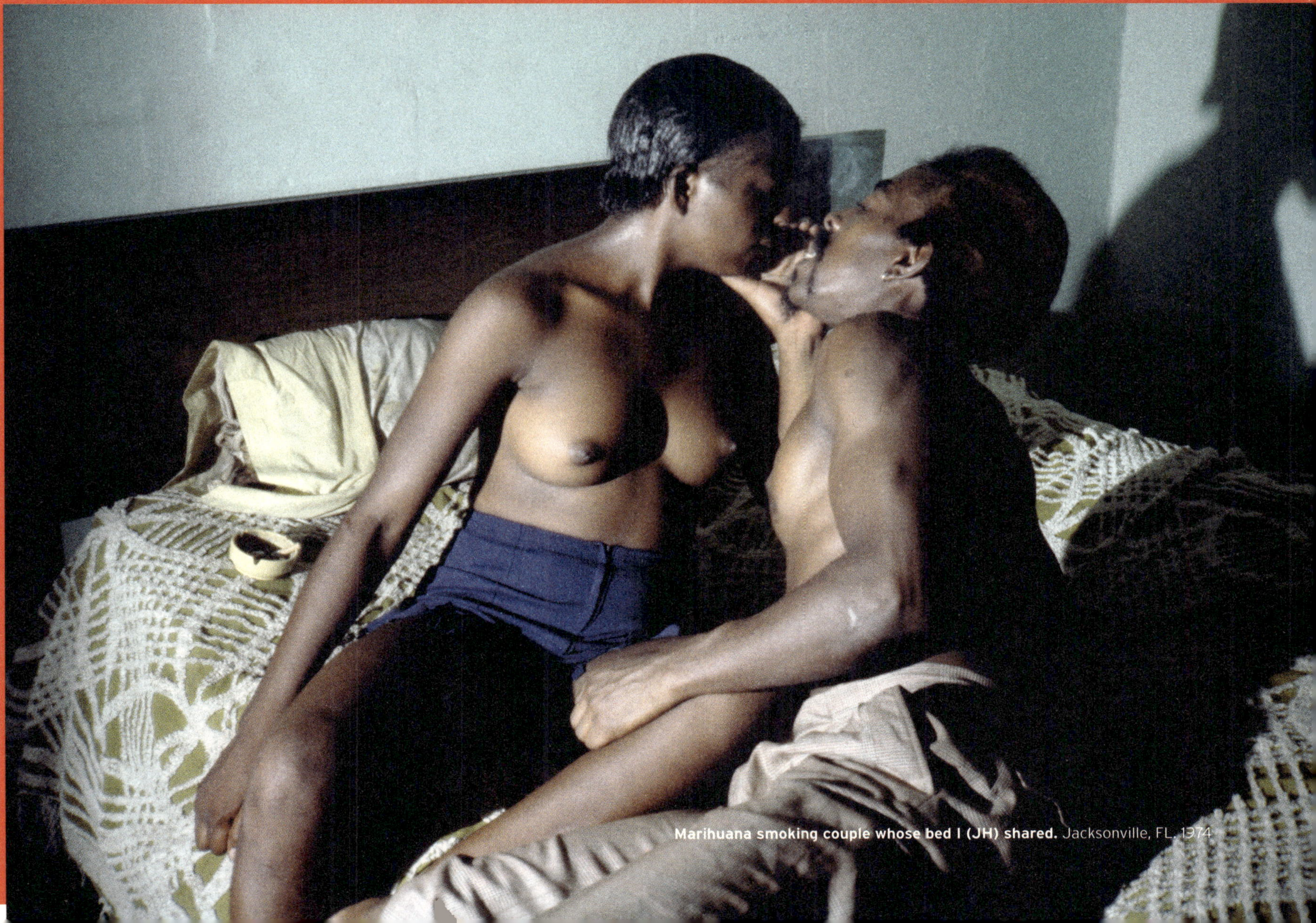

Marihuana smoking couple whose bed I (JH) shared. Jacksonville, FL. 1974

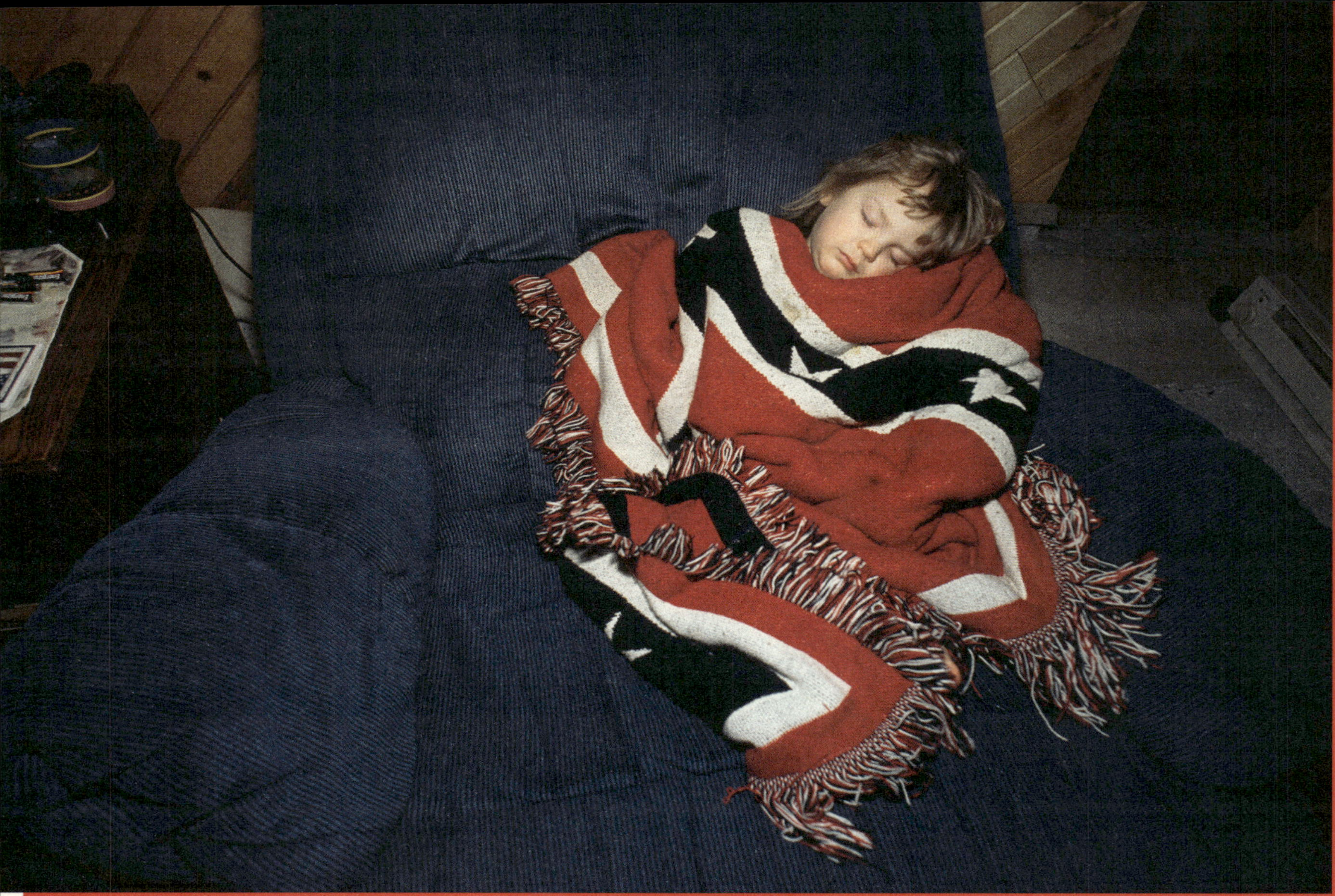

Wrapped with love in the empty symbol of hatred. Butler, IN. 2002

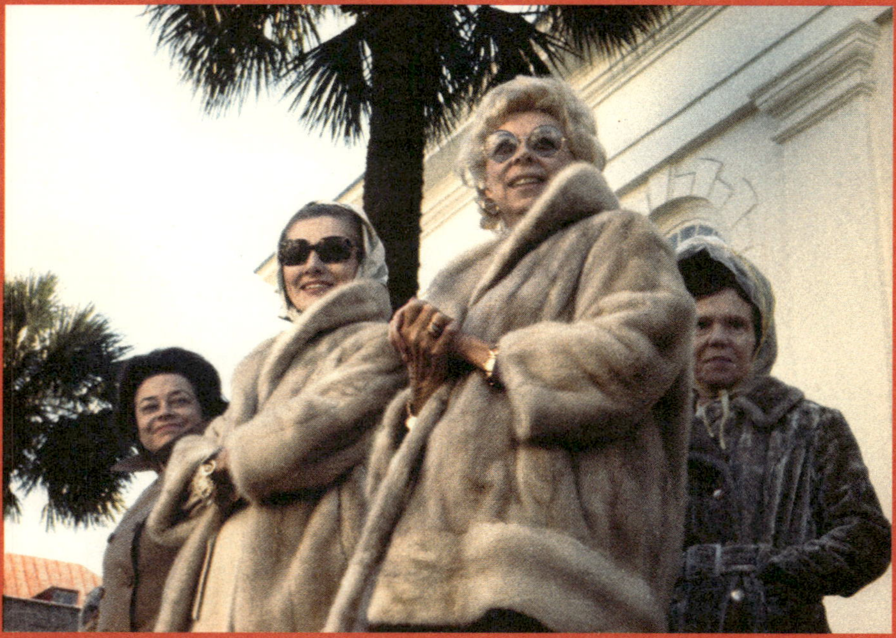

Churchgoers after church service. Charleston, SC. 1973

out different angles visually, I had to use condemning images.

MM: This is a very touching picture....
JH: Yes, the Klan leader's grandchild swaddled in the "flag of hate." The Confederate flag is used as a symbol of hate all over the world. But Catja, she doesn't become a hateful person. She is swaddled with love. Abused people become haters, if we have to use the word hate at all – I call it pain. Even though she has grown up among the Ku Klux Klan, she got an endless amount of love. Today, she is out of the KKK and is a well-adjusted big kid, because she got the love she needed. And that's really what this picture is about. The KKK may dress up in hateful symbols, but it isn't always about hate.

MM: A lot of your pictures make me think whether you asked people, "Hey, move over into the sunlight, please". Did you stage your pictures?
JH: No. I may at times have moved some things around, say, if there was a big garish plastic bowl in the middle of the floor that I thought would disturb the image, when I was shooting color slides. In that sense, sure, I cheated a little bit, but my goal was always to replicate the world the way it was. I was always working with 160 ASA film and didn't have an extra camera with high-speed film. So I needed some light and I typically put the flash behind a lamp and sometimes wrapped it in a piece of pink toilet paper to make it look like the light from an oil lamp in a home without electricity. I was always going around to stores asking for pink toilet paper, to get that reddish glow. It was the only way I could make those shots. Shooting with the flash alone flattens everything out, and the mood of the moment before the picture wouldn't come out at all. I was always trying to recreate that in different ways. After all, it was completely dark in a lot of these homes and I wouldn't have been able to get a picture without using a flash – I wouldn't have gotten any pictures at all.

MM: Are your pictures perceived differently in the U.S. and Europe?
JH: I've been subjected to an unbelievable amount of criticism in the U.S., especially from feminists who don't care for the nude pictures I took. They call them sexist. I took a lot of nude shots out of the slideshow when I first showed it in the States. Violence doesn't bother them – that's only what they expect from black people. In Denmark, it's the other way around: People are shocked by the pictures of violence. It was always the pictures of violence that shocked people, while no one ever commented on my nude shots. In the U.S., you can get arrested for breastfeeding your child in the street. There are a lot of toes you can step on in the U.S..

MM: People who visit Louisiana and see your pictures – what would you like them to think?
JH: I'd be happy, of course, if my message about oppression, etc., got through, but I don't expect it to. I'd be happy if you, as a curator, make me think about something that hadn't occurred to me before, if a new interpretation emerges. But I can't pass judgment anymore, I'm so used to being led around the ring....

MM: Did you ever feel like showing all the other pictures, all the ones that weren't included in American Pictures and show other sides of America?
JH: Well, as I told you earlier, it was always so that things that happened in my life only happened because someone came and asked me to do something. I've simply been busy saying yes to every offer I got. Now, Louisiana comes and asks me if I'd like to show some of my other pictures, too, and we'll end up doing something with them. My life was always like that.

Mette Marcus (b. 1971)
Is the curator of the exhibition *Faith, Hope & Love – Jacob Holdt's America*. Marcus trained as an art historian at the Courtauld Institute of Art, London, and the University of Copenhagen, and has been a curator at the Louisiana Museum of Modern Art since 2003.

excerpt from SUSAN SONTAG's

regarding the pain of others

To those who are sure that right is on one side, oppression and injustice on the other and that the fighting must go on, what matters is precisely who is killed and by whom. To an Israeli Jew, a photograph of a child torn apart in the attack on the Sbarro pizzeria in downtown Jerusalem is first of all a photograph of a Jewish child killed by a Palestinian suicide-bomber. To a Palestinian, a photograph of a child torn apart by a tank round in Gaza is first of all a photograph of a Palestinian child killed by Israeli ordnance. To the militant, identity is everything. And all photographs wait to be explained or falsified by their captions. During the fighting between Serbs and Croats at the beginning of the recent Balkan wars, the same photographs of children killed in the shelling of a village were passed around at both Serb and Croat propaganda briefings. Alter the caption, and the children's deaths could be used and reused.

*

In fact, there are many uses of the innumerable opportunities a modern life supplies for regarding - at a distance, through the medium of photography - other people's pain.

Photographs of an atrocity may give rise to opposing responses. A call for peace. A cry for revenge. Or simply the bemused awareness, continually restocked by photographic information, that terrible things happen. Who can forget the three color pictures by Tyler Hicks that *The New York Times* ran across the upper half of the first page of its daily section devoted to America's new war, 'A Nation Challenged', on November 13, 2001? The triptych depicted the fate of a wounded Taliban soldier in uniform who had been found in a ditch by Northern Alliance soldiers advancing toward Kabul. First panel being dragged on his back by two of his captors - one has grabbed an arm, the other a leg - along a rocky road. Second: panel (the camera is very near): surrounded, gazing up in terror as he is being pulled to his feet. Third panel at the moment of death, supine with arms outstretched and knees bent, naked and bloodied from the waist down, being finished off by the military mob that has gathered to butcher him. An ample reservoir of stoicism is needed to get through the great newspaper of record each morning, given the likelihood of seeing photographs that could make you cry. And the pity and disgust that pictures like Hicks's inspire should not distract you from asking what pictures whose cruelties whose deaths are *not* being shown.

*

Non-stop imagery (television, streaming video, movies) is our surround, but when it comes to remembering, the photograph has the deeper bite. Memory freeze-frames; its basic unit is the single image. In an era of information overload, the photograph provides a quick way of apprehending something and a compact form for memorizing it.

The photograph is like a quotation, or a maxim or proverb.

Each of us mentally stocks hundreds of photographs, subject to instant recall.

Cite the most famous photograph taken during Spanish Civil War, the Republican soldier 'shot' by Robed Capa's camera at the same moment he is hit by an enemy bullet, and virtually everyone who has heard of that war can summon to mind the grainy black-and-white image of a man in a white shirt with rolled-up sleeves collapsing backward on a hillock his right arm flung behind him as his rifle leaves his grip; about to fall, dead, onto his own shadow.

*

What does it mean to protest suffering as distinct from acknowledging it? The iconography of suffering has a long pedigree. The suffering most often deemed worthy of representation is those understood to be the product of wrath, divine or human. (Suffering from natural causes, such as illness or childbirth is scantily represented in the history of art; that caused by accident, virtually not at all - as if there were no such thing as suffering by inadvertence or misadventure.)

The statue group of the writhing Laocoön and his sons, the innumerable versions in painting and sculpture of the Passion of Christ, and the inexhaustible visual catalogue of the fiendish executions of the Christian martyrs - these are surely intended to move and excite, and to instruct and exemplify. The viewer may commiserate with the sufferer's pain - and, in the case of the Christian saints, feel admonished or inspired by model faith and fortitude - but these are destinies beyond deploring or contesting.

It seems that the appetite for pictures showing bodies in pain is as keen, almost, as the desire for ones that show bodies naked. For many centuries, in Christian art, depictions of hell offered both of these elemental satisfactions.

*

No moral charge attaches to the representation of these cruelties. Just the provocation: can you look at this? There is the satisfaction of being able to look at the image without flinching. There is the pleasure of flinching.

*

Transforming is what art does but photography that bears witness to the calamitous and the reprehensible is much criticized if it seems 'aesthetic'; that is, too much like art. The dual powers of photography - to generate documents and to create works of visual art - have produced some remarkable exaggerations about what photographers ought or ought not to do. Lately, the most common exaggeration is one that regards these powers as opposites. Photographs that depict suffering shouldn't be beautiful, as captions shouldn't moralize. In this view, a beautiful photograph drains attention from the sobering subject and turns it toward the medium itself, thereby compromising the picture's status as a document. The photograph gives mixed signals. Stop this, it urges. But it also exclaims, What a spectacle!

*

Photographs objectify: they turn an event or a person into something that can be possessed, and photographs are a species of alchemy, for all that they are prized as a transparent account of reality.

Often something looks, or is felt to look, 'better' in a photograph indeed, it is one of the functions of photography to improve the normal appearance of things. (Hence, one is always disappointed by a photograph that is not flattering.)

Beautifying is one classic operation of the camera, and it tends to bleach out a moral response to what is shown. Uglifying, showing something at its worst, is a more modern function: didactic, it invites an active response. For photographs to accuse, and possibly to alter conduct they must shock.

*

But do people want to be horrified? Probably not. Still, there are pictures whose power does not abate, in part because you cannot look at them often. Pictures of the ruin of faces that will always testify to a great iniquity survived, at that cost: the faces of horribly disfigured First World War veterans who survived the inferno of the trenches; the faces melted and thickened with scar tissue of survivors of the American atomic bombs dropped on Hiroshima and Nagasaki; the faces cleft by machete blows of Tutsi survivors of the genocidal rampage launched by the Hutus in Rwanda - is it correct to say that people get used to these?

Indeed, the very notion of atrocity, of war crime is associated with the expectation of photographic evidence. Such evidence is, usually, of something posthumous; the remains, as it were - the mounds of skulls in Pol Pot's Cambodia, the mass graves in Guatemala and El Salvador, Bosnia and Kosovo. And this posthumous reality is often the keenest of summations.

*

And photographs echo photographs: it was inevitable that the photographs of emaciated Bosnian prisoners at Omarska, the Serb death camp created in northern Bosnia in 1992 would recall the photographs taken in the Nazi death camps in 1945.

Photographs of atrocity illustrate as well as corroborate. Bypassing disputes about exactly how many were killed (numbers are often inflated at first), the photograph gives the indelible sample. The illustrative function of photographs leaves opinions, prejudices, fantasies, misinformation untouched. The information that many fewer Palestinians died in the assault on Jenin than had been claimed by Palestinian officials (as the Israelis had said all along) made much less impact than the photographs of the razed center of the refugee camp.

*

Photographs of the suffering and martyrdom of a people are more than reminders of death, of failure; of victimization. They invoke the miracle of survival. To aim at the perpetuation of memories means, inevitably, that one has undertaken the task of continually renewing, of creating, memories - aided, above all, by the impress of iconic photographs. People want to be able to visit - and refresh - their memories. Now many victim peoples want a memory museum, a temple that houses a comprehensive, chronologically organized, illustrated narrative of their sufferings.

*

Compassion is an unstable emotion. It needs to be translated into action, or it withers. The question is what to do with the feelings that have been aroused, the knowledge that has been communicated. If one feels that there is nothing 'we' can do - but who is that 'we'? - and nothing 'they' can do either - and who are 'they'? - then one starts to get bored, cynical, apathetic.

And it is not necessarily better to be moved. Sentimentality notoriously, is entirely compatible with a taste for brutality and worse. (Recall the canonical example of the Auschwitz commandant returning home in the evening, embracing his wife and children, and sitting at the piano to play some Schubert before dinner.) People don't become inured to what they are shown - if that's the right way to describe what happens - because of the *quantity* of images dumped on them. It is passivity that dulls feeling. The states described as apathy, moral or emotional anesthesia, are full of feelings; the feelings are rage and frustration. But if we consider what emotions would be desirable, it seems too simple to elect sympathy. The imaginary proximity to the suffering inflicted on others that is granted by images suggests a link between the faraway sufferers – seen close-up on the television screen – and the privileged viewer that is simply untrue, that is yet one more mystification of our real relations to power. So far as we feel sympathy, we feel we are not accomplices to what caused the suffering. Our sympathy proclaims our innocence as well as our impotence. To that extent, it can be (for all our good intentions) an impertinent – if not an inappropriate – response. To set aside the sympathy we extend to others beset by war and murderous politics for a reflection on how our privileges are located on the same map as their suffering and may – in ways we might prefer not to imagine – be linked to their suffering, as the wealth of some may imply the destitution of others, is a cask for which the painful stirring images supply only an initial spark.

*

Consider two widespread ideas – now fast approaching the stature of platitudes – on the impact of photography. Since I find these ideas formulated in my own essays on photography – the earliest of which was written thirty years ago – I feel an irresistible temptation to quarrel with them.

The first idea is that public attention is steered by the attentions of the media – which means, most decisively, images. When there are photographs, a war becomes 'real'.

Thus, the protest against the Vietnam Wear was mobilized by images. The feeling that something had to be done about the war in Bosnia was built from the attentions of journalists – 'the CNN effect', it was sometimes called – which brought images of Sarajevo under siege into hundreds of millions of living rooms night after night for more than three years. These examples illustrate the determining influence of photographs in shaping what catastrophes and crises we pay attention to, what we care about, and ultimately what evaluations are attached to these conflicts. The second idea – it might seem the converse of what's just been described – is that in a world saturated, no, hyper-saturated with images, those that should matter have a diminishing effect: We become callous. In the end, such images just make us a little less able to feel, to have our conscience pricked.

In the first of the six essays in *On Photography* (1977), I argued that while an event known through photographs certainly becomes more real than it would have been had one never seen the photographs, after repeated exposure it also becomes less real. As much as they create sympathy, I wrote, photographs shrivel sympathy. Is this true? I thought it was when I wrote it. I'm not so sure now. What is the evidence that photographs have a diminishing impact, that our culture of spectatorship neutralizes the moral force of photographs of atrocities?

*

Citizens of modernity, consumers of violence as spectacle, adepts of possibility without risk, are schooled to be cynical about the possibility of sincerity. Some people will do anything to keep themselves from being moved. How much easier, from one's chair, far from danger, to claim the position of superiority. In fact, deriding the efforts of those who have borne witness in war zones as 'war tourism' is such a recurrent judgment that it has spilled over into the discussion of war photography as a profession.

The feeling persists that the appetite for such images is a vulgar or low appetite: that it is commercial ghoulishness.

In Sarajevo in the years of the siege, it was not uncommon to hear, in the middle of a bombardment or a burst of sniper fire, a Sarajevan yelling at the photojournalists, who were easily recognizable by the equipment hanging round their necks, 'Are you waiting for a shell to go off so you can photograph some corpses? Sometimes they were, though less often than one might imagine, since the photographer on the street in the middle of a bombardment or a burst of sniper fire ran just as much risk of being killed as the civilians he or she was tracking.

*

In early 1994, the English photojournalist Paul Lowe, who had been living for more than a year in the besieged city, mounted an exhibit at a partly wrecked art gallery of the photographs he had been taking along with photographs he had taken a few years earlier in Somalia; the Sarajevans, though eager to see new pictures of the ongoing destruction of their city, were offended by the inclusion of the Somalia pictures, Lowe had thought the matter was a simple one. He was a professional photographer, and these were two bodies of work of which he was proud, For the Sarajevans, it was also simple. To set their sufferings alongside the sufferings of another people was to compare them (which hell was worse?), demoting Sarajevo's martyrdom to a mere instance. The atrocities taking place in Sarajevo have nothing to do with what happens in Africa they exclaimed. Undoubtedly there was a racist tinge to their indignation – Bosnians are Europeans, people in Sarajevo never tired of pointing our to their foreign friends – but they would have objected too if, instead, pictures of atrocities committed against civilians in Chechnya or in Kosovo, indeed in any other country, had been included in the show. It is intolerable to have one's own sufferings twinned with anybody else's.

*

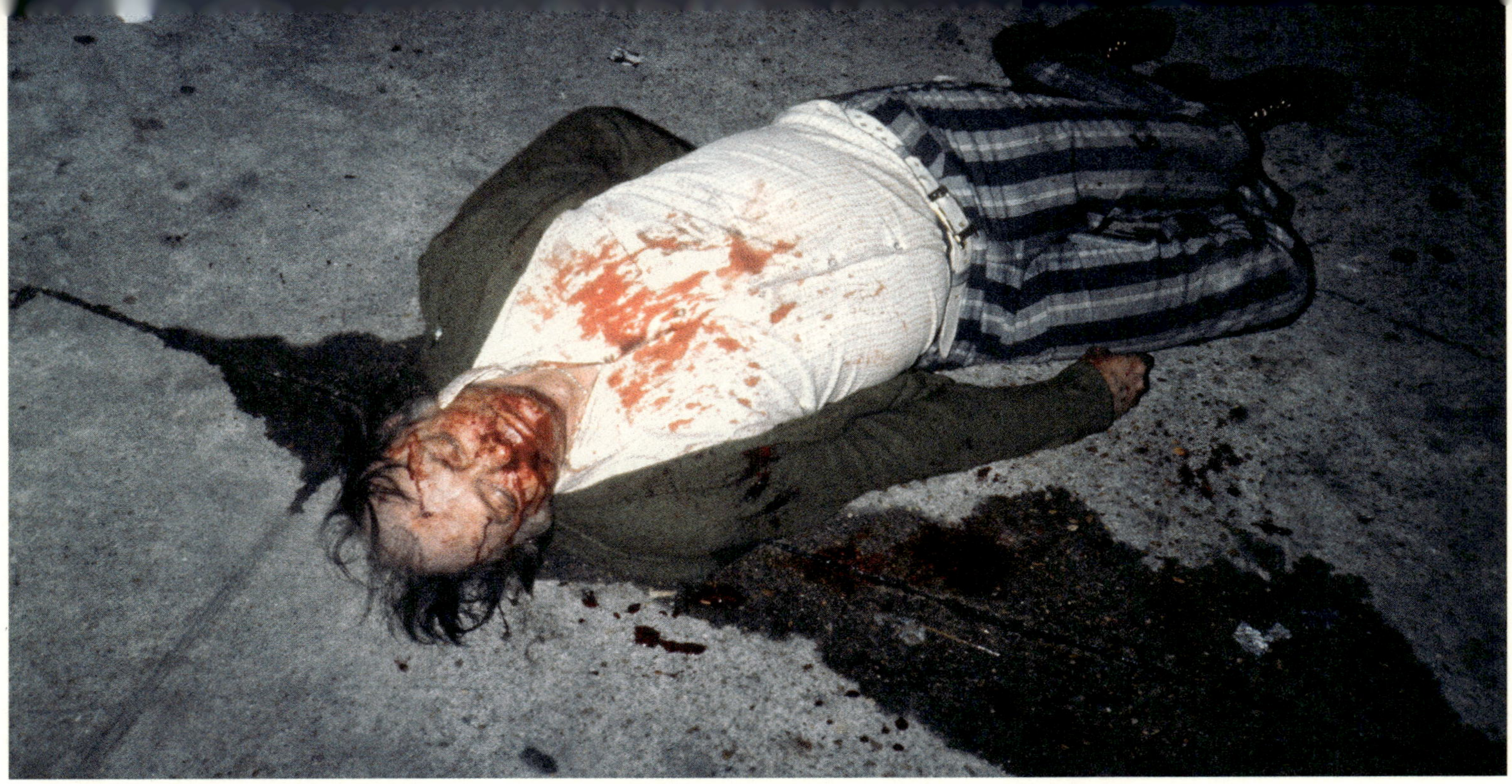

I (JH) was playing pool with Butch. When it was my turn, he stepped outside for a moment and murdered this man. New Orleans, LA. 1973

That news about war is now disseminated worldwide does not mean that the capacity to think about the suffering of people far away is significantly larger. In a modem life - a life in which there is a superfluity of things to which we are invited to pay attention - it seems normal to turn away from images that simply make us feel bad. Many more would be switching channels if the news media were to devote more time to the particulars of human suffering caused by war and other infamies. But it is probably not true that people are responding less.

That we are not totally transformed, that we can turn away, turn the page, switch the channel, does not impugn the ethical value of an assaults by images. It is not a defect that we are not seared, that we do not suffer *enough,* when we see these images. Neither is the photograph supposed to repair our ignorance about the history and causes of the suffering it picks out and frames. Such images cannot be more than an invitation to pay attention, to reflect, to learn, to examine the rationalizations for mass suffering offered by established powers. Who caused what the picture shows? Who is responsible? Is it excusable? Was it inevitable? Is there some state of affairs which we have accepted up to now that ought to be challenged? All this, with the understanding that moral indignation like compassion, cannot dictate a course of action.

The frustration of not being able to do anything about what the images show may be translated into an accusation of the indecency of regarding such images, or the indecencies of the way such images are disseminated - flanked, as they may well be, by advertising for emollients, pain relievers and SUVs. If we could do something about what the images show, we might not care as much about these issues.

*

Images have been reproached for being a way of watching suffering at a distance, as if there were some other way of watching. But watching up close - without the mediation of an image - is still just watching.

Some of the reproaches made against images of atrocity are not different from characterizations of sight itself. Sight is effortless; sight requires spatial distance: sight can be turned off (we have lids on our eyes, we do not have doors on our ears). The very qualities that made the ancient Greek philosophers consider sight the most excellent, the noblest of the senses are now associated with a deficit.

It is felt that there is something morally wrong with the abstract of reality offered by photography; that one has no right to experience the suffering of others at a distance, denuded of its raw power; that we pay too high a human (or moral) price for those hitherto admired qualities of vision - the standing back from the aggressiveness of the world which frees us for observation and for elective attention. But this is only to describe the function of the mind itself.

There's nothing wrong with standing back and thinking.

To paraphrase several sages: 'Nobody can think and hit someone at the same time.'

Susan Sontag (1933-2004)
American writer of fiction and non-fiction. A major participant in the critique of contemporary culture with several books and articles on for instance the metaphors of illness, photography, litterary theory and feminism. Her texts on photography – *On Photography* from 1977 in particular – have had a great impact on the way we view the medium today. The above extract from *Regarding the Pain of Others* has been drawn up especially for this catalogue and is published with the kind permission of Susan Sontag's heirs, litterary agent and publisher. Please also see the colophon of this book for further reference.

on the road

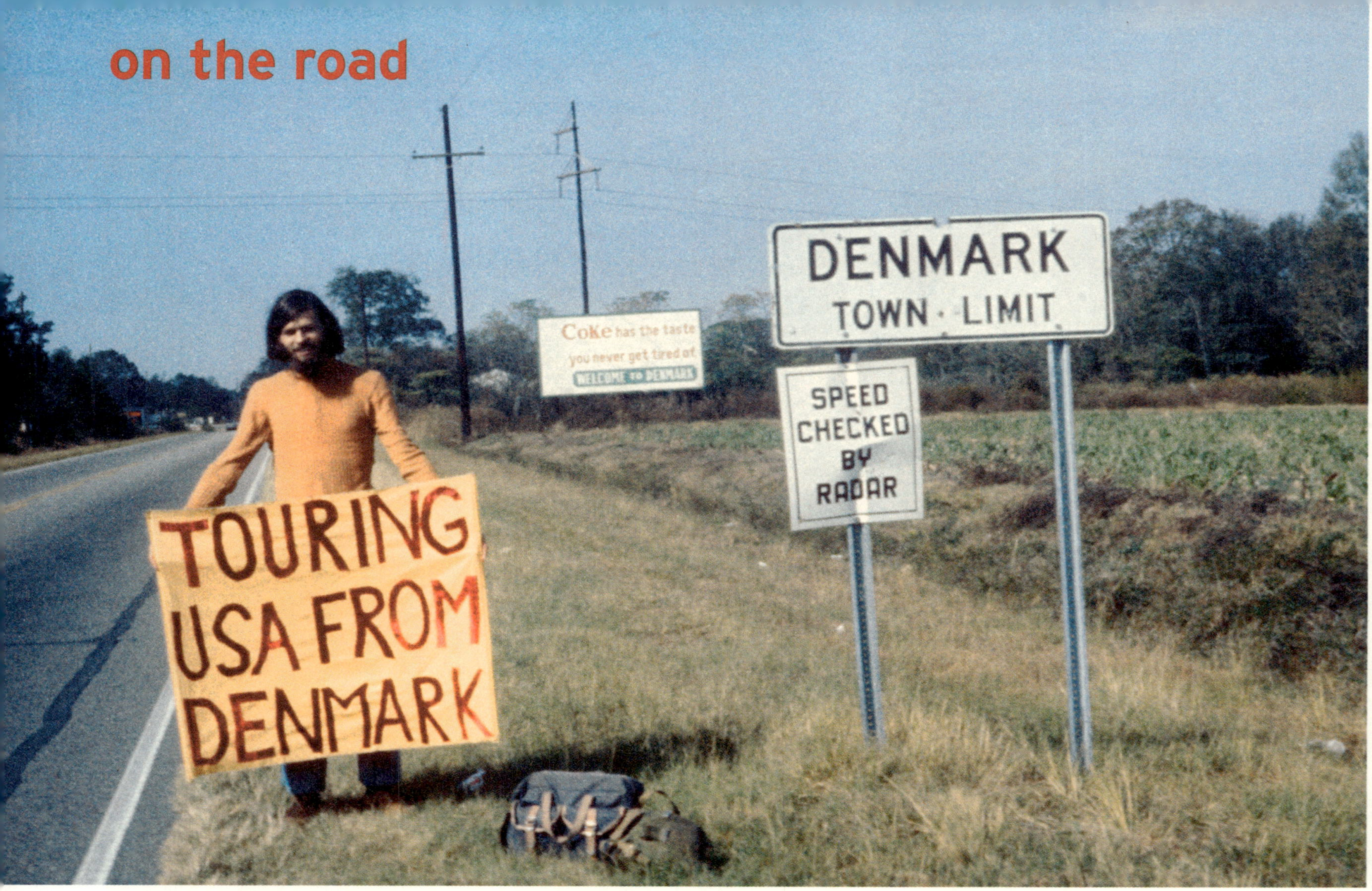

Jacob Holdt hitchhiking in South Carolina passing the town of Denmark. 1973

Jacob Holdt likes to refer to himself as a "vagabond". As a matter of fact, it is as a vagabond that he lived a significant part of his life after having emigrated first, in 1970, to Canada to work on a farm and shortly thereafter to the United States. In 1971, Holdt began to wander and hitchhike around the United States. The following year, he hitchhiked to Guatemala in order to support the guerilla struggle but realized that he could not support violence. In the years 1972-75, Holdt hitchhiked for more than 100,000 miles around the United States. During this period, he did not reside in any one place for more than a few weeks at a time; typically, he stayed only a few days.

I called myself Vagabond for years, because that's what I felt I was. For years after I returned from the States, I wanted to get back on the road, but I was simply *side-tracked* by having one hit after another.

In 1974, Holdt married a black American woman. They moved into a ghetto area and dwelled there in a condition of dire poverty, surrounded by criminality, to boot. After half a year, Holdt fled out on the highway, but in late 1975 he brought her with him to Denmark.

In Denmark, the success of the slide-show lecture *American Pictures*, served to send Holdt around to different places in Denmark and eventually to many other places in Europe - and later on, the United States. In 1981, Holdt resumed hitchhiking around the United States. This time, he set out from the San Francisco Film Festival and made the cross-country excursion to New York.

Afterward, in 1982, he hitchhiked 5,000 miles through Africa in order to find suitable aid projects for which funds he had earned on the sale of *American Pictures* could be offered. Later that same year, Holdt hitchhiked in excess of 10,000 miles through the American ghettos with his 2-year-old son. By experiencing the world in this way, his son would ostensibly not be negatively affected by the racism of the whites: this was Holdt's primary purpose in making this trip.

Some don't want to have anything to do with you at all, others can't do without an alliance with white people who open up to them. At the time I was traveling, a lot of black people adamantly did not want to have a white man staying in their house. That was the attitude of a huge number of people. The poorest blacks were afraid of whites in a different way, of course. But the middle class, which was in a period of powerful political liberation, often wanted nothing to do with white people.

In 1986, Holdt - together with his family, wife and kid - settled in Boston, largely to distribute the *American Pictures*. Since coming back from this sojourn, Holdt has been residing primarily in Denmark, although he does continue to travel all over the world.

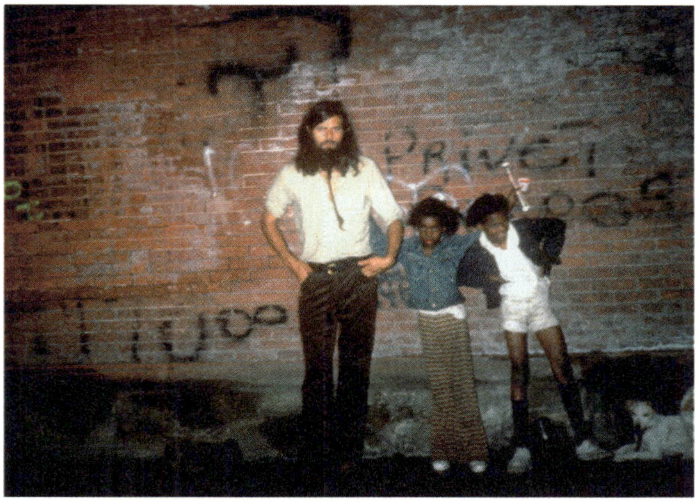

Jacob with kids in Harlem. Harlem, NY. 1972

What I really respected about my father's work was his social work with people in the parish. I didn't think of him as a particularly religious person. What counted was his human engagement. My father talked with people who were going through hard times. On the road in the U.S. that was my experience, too - that people had a need to talk to me.

Since the beginning of the 1980s, Holdt has been taking passengers along with him on his travels around the United States. The Danish poet, Pia Tafdrup, has accompanied him on several occasions. The Norwegian author, Eli Sæter, has also been with Holdt on a few of his American trips. Sæter's encounter with a few of the criminals that Jacob knows inspired her to write *En amerikareise*.

Still today, Holdt continues to take people along with him on his travels.

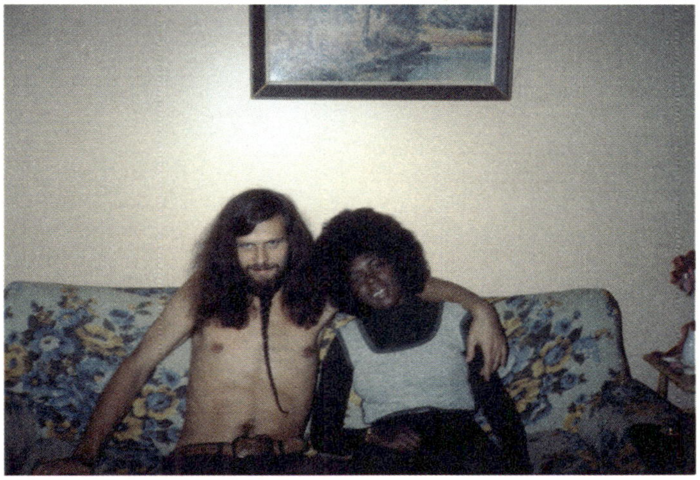

Jacob when he lived with the former heroin addict and prostitute Geegurtha after and before she went to prison again. Greensboro, NC. 1974

In 1994, Holdt flew to Haiti to photograph the American troops there, where he moved into the poorest and most violence-besieged slum areas, Cité Soleil.

From the outset of the 1990s, Holdt has worked as a photographer for the humanitarian organization, CARE. As part of this work, Holdt has traveled to Bolivia, Nepal, Thailand, Cambodia, Guatemala, Kosovo and Uganda.

However, the United States continues to attract Holdt's interest. He still goes on "American trips" every now and then - most recently, in the spring of 2009.

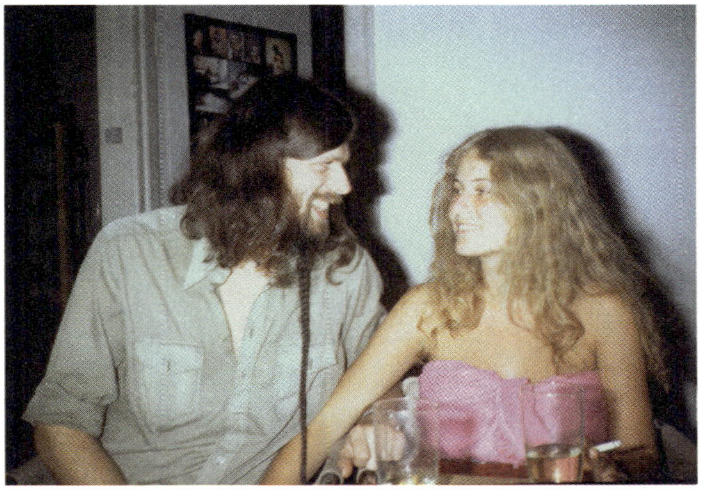

Jacob with his later wife, who at that time was a volunteer in the work collective American Pictures. Copenhagen. 1978

Holdt's activity as a photographer

In 1971, Holdt's parents sent him a camera as a birthday present: a Canon Dial. The unusual feature of this 35-millimeter camera is that it takes pictures in a half-frame format (18x24 mm negatives). Holdt has never received any form of instruction. All the technical know-how related to photography that he has acquired is self-taught.

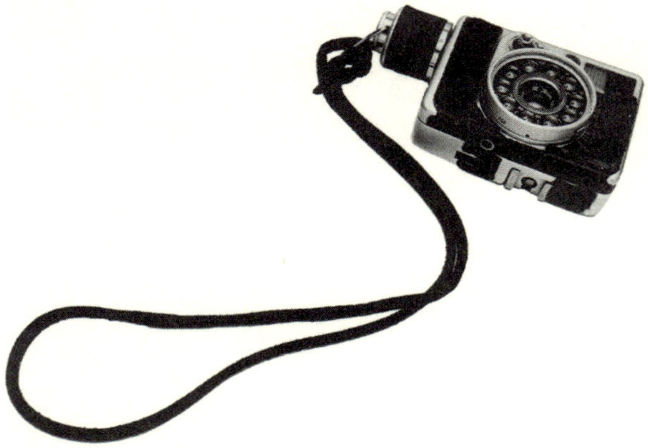

I was always working with 160 ASA film and didn't have an extra camera with high-speed film. So I needed some light and I typically put the flash behind a lamp and sometimes wrapped it in a piece of pink toilet paper to make it look like the light from an oil lamp in a home without electricity. I was always going around to stores asking for pink toilet paper, to get that reddish glow. It was the only way I could make those shots. Shooting with the flash alone flattens everything out, and the mood of the moment before the picture wouldn't come out at all. I was always trying to recreate that in different ways. After all, it was completely dark in a lot of these homes and I wouldn't have been able to get a picture without using a flash – I wouldn't have gott any pictures at all.

During the period 1972-75 Holdt spent a lot of time taking pictures: He shot approximately 15,000 photographs. Since that time, he has taken a great many pictures in America and in the rest of the world. During the years he spent as a 'vagabond' in the United States, Holdt sold his own blood twice every week in order to generate the money to pay for film and for developing his pictures.

I discriminated in my pictures. I think I more or less subconsciously chose the more attractive members of a family and chose to take pictures of them. I'm not crazy about group shots with 10 or 20 people at once. So, I sit there waiting – when is a single person alone with his or her thoughts? Simply because I knew that white racism discriminates against certain aspects of black culture, I always had to speak to the deeper humanity in whites – in that sense, I had to be racist myself.

Holdt has always been very concerned about getting to know the people whose pictures he is taking. Typically, he lives for some days with the people before he starts taking pictures of them.

As a rule, I had to stay with people two or three days before reality crept in, before they were suitably relaxed around the photographer to allow me to interpret what I saw and see the deeper, underlying reality. Then you may ask, is this the true, deeper reality? And yes, it is. Things whites didn't see, don't see. They see it as something else. So it was important for me to sit and wait for those moments that, so to speak, showed the reality before the strange photographer intruded. And that takes time.

From the beginning of the 1990s, Holdt started to work as a photographer for the humanitarian organization, CARE. As part of these efforts, he meets members of minority groups and oppressed or persecuted people in a number of countries all over the world: for example, in Kosovo, where he portrays the Albanians' homecoming to charred houses destroyed by fire and relatives whose corpses lay in mass graves.

I've always said I wasn't a good photographer but a good vagabond, good at getting into homes no one else could get into, but where anyone could have taken a good picture.

Holdt continues to take photographs wherever he is. Recently, in the spring of 2009, he traveled around the United States in order to visit old friends. While moving around, he also met people he had not met before, whose lots in life he managed to capture with the camera's lens. The result of these efforts now constitutes the latest update of Holdt's reservoir of American pictures.

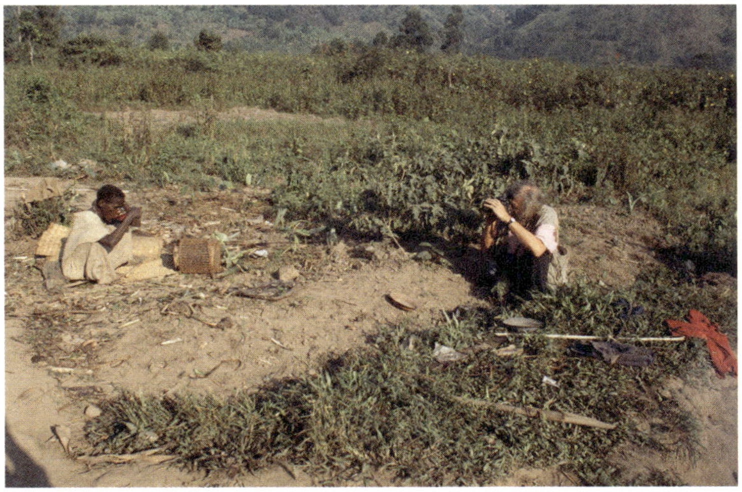

Jacob photographing a Batwa pigmy woman for CARE in the southern Uganda. 2006

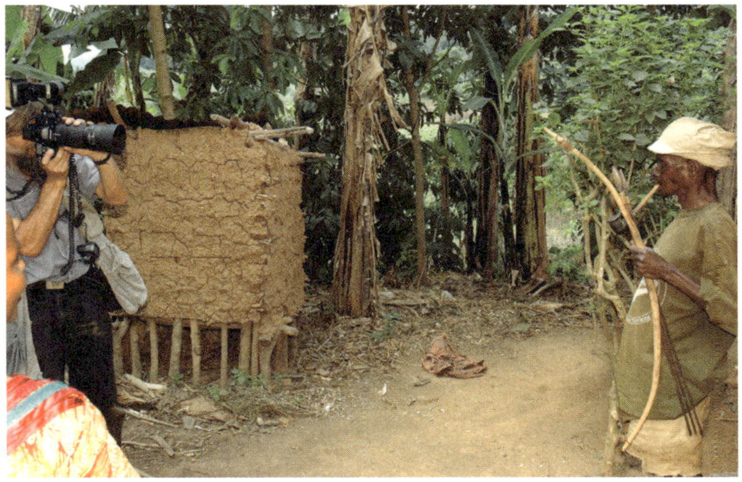

Jacob photographing a Batwa pigmy hunter for CARE in southern Uganda. Batwa, 2006

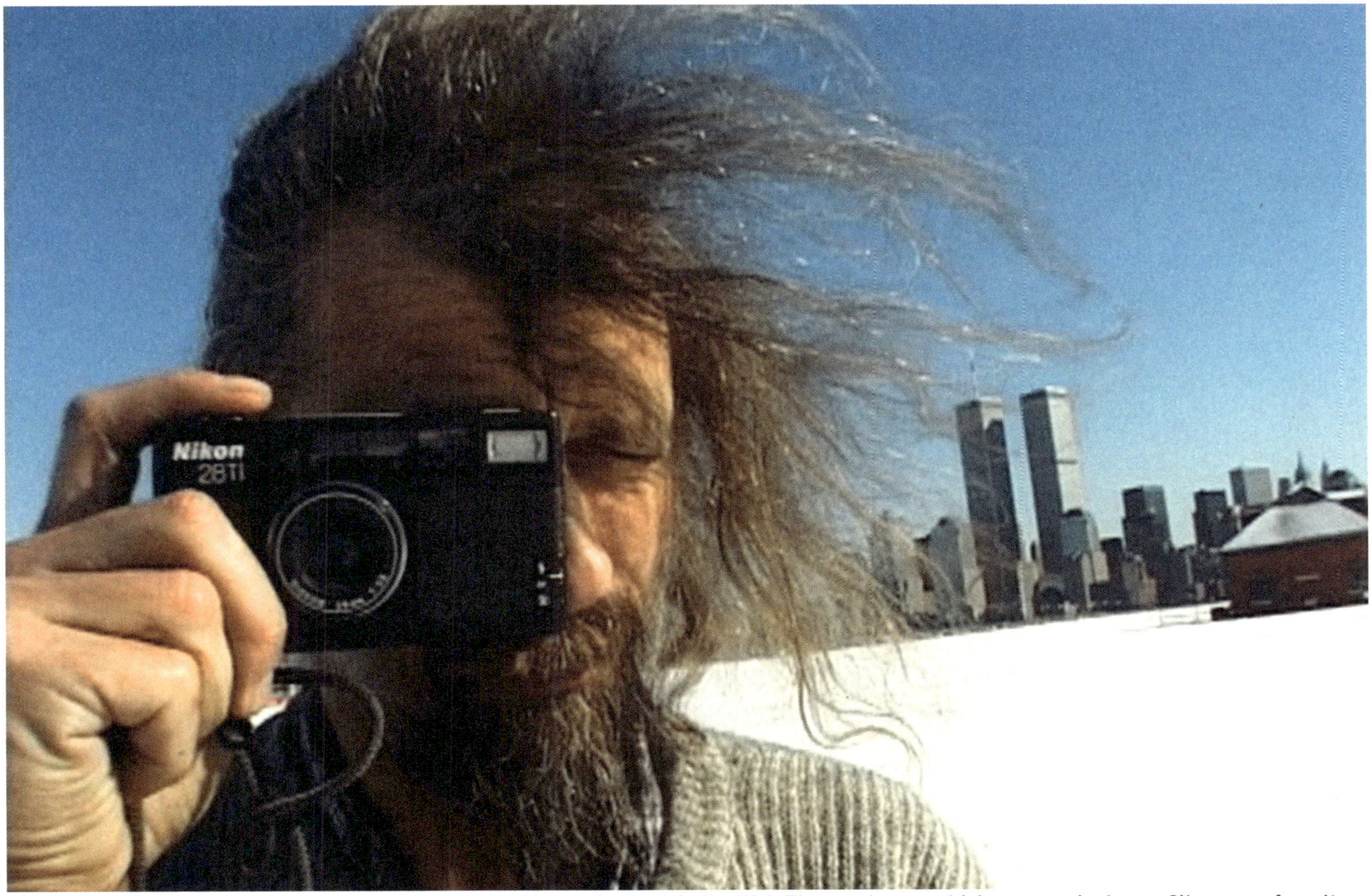

A Danish film crew came to the USA with Jacob to make the movie *Jacob in the USA*. They made some driving scenes in Jersey City across from the WTC. It was only a few months before 9/11.
Photo©Theis Mortensen, 2001

Holdt's political engagement

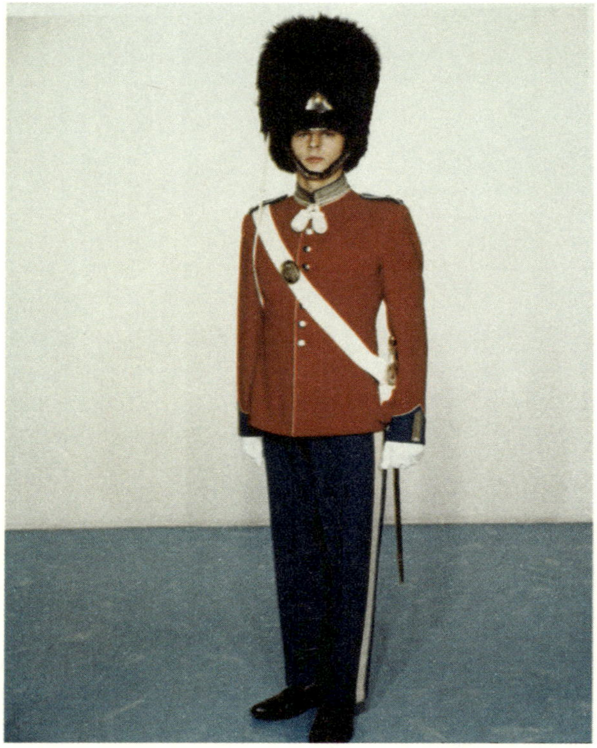

Jacob in the Royal Danish Palace Guard before he was kicked out for refusing to shoot and carry weapons. Copenhagen. 1967

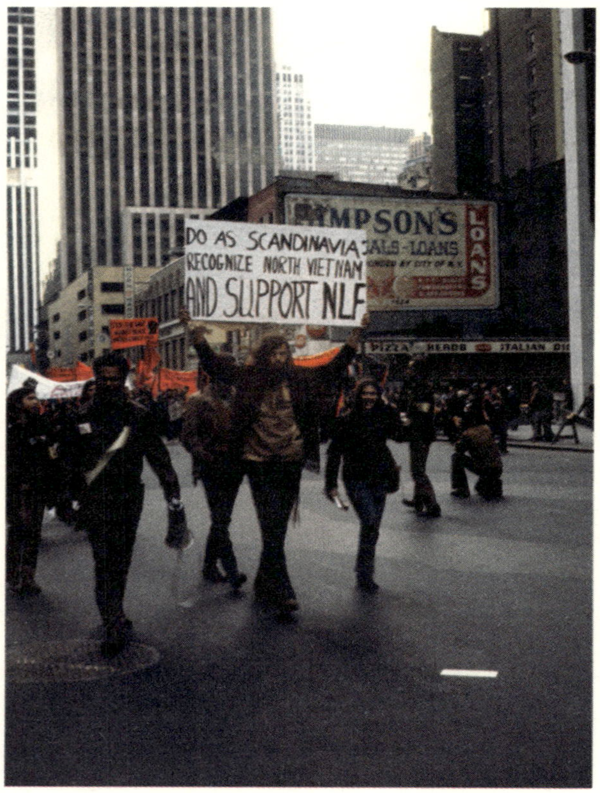

Jacob spent much of his first two years in the USA protesting against the Vietnam war. Here in one of the big demonstrations in New York. NY. 1972

Since the early days of his life, Holdt has continually engaged himself in the reality he was living in. In 1967, he was thrown out of The Royal Danish Palace Guard for refusing to shoot a gun. Two years later, at the age of 22, he painted Biblical quotes on the church where his father presided as a minister, in protest against the fact that money was being used on a church tower while millions of people were starving in Biafra. At the end of the 1960s Holdt was politically engaged in learning about problems in the Third World and was focused on questions surrounding the Vietnam War, motivated by a deep sense of commitment that carried him initially to Canada and then later to the United States.

Holdt took part in the anti-Vietnam war demonstrations in the United States and dedicated five years of his life to documenting the lives of some of the poorest black people in America. When he returned to Denmark, he made his slide-show lecture after which he was asked to make it into his Danish book *Amerikanske Billeder*, both of which offer an unequivocal and uncompromising statement about the social inequality between black and white people that prevailed in America at that time.

A consciousness about racial differences is a salient feature of Holdt's work. Among other things, he adamantly refused to allow a certain publishing house to publish his book in the United States because no black people were employed in the organization. Instead, he made his own efforts to set up a network among street people, homeles and criminals in the ghettoes, who then distributed and sold the book. However, Holdt's sense of engagement also touches upon many other aspects of the society where social inequities can be spotted.

I've spent so much time among black Americans and worked with the problems of black America that you might say I've ended up writing my own biography. .... Then there was the recent movie "Milk", about the gay American politician, Harvey Milk, and Jyllands-Posten (the Danish daily – ed.) ran a debate that prompted me to sit down and write about my involvement with people in the gay movement. All of a sudden, I was able to see and define myself in an entirely different way. .... I have lots of pictures about other Americans than impoverished blacks.

Holdt and ten co-workers started up the American Pictures Foundation for Humanitarian Aid to Africa, largely in order to provide support - channeled through the agency of Danida (the Danish International Development Agency) - to the ANC's anti-apartheid struggle. Later on, Holdt became involved in many other Africa-related projects: the purchase of farm machinery for Batsiranai, a cooperative farm in Zimbabwe; the erection of a school in Nyafaru, in Zimbabwe, for refugee children who had returned home after a period of exile; and the financing of a hospital in SWAPO's guerilla camp, Kwanzu Zul, in Angola. Also, in support of the ANC's efforts, Holdt actually smuggled secret documents from Harare to a resistance group in Botswana.

In 1984, the collective in Copenhagen was dissolved; for a number of years thereafter, the home on Købmagergade became an "open house" which was also used as a residence for some 40 to 60 Arab refugees.

Toward the end of the 1980s, Holdt developed a "racism workshop", which was presented in hundreds of American universities as a day long follow up to his slide lecture. These efforts continue to evolve and have resulted in a whole series of lectures and workshops that were offered publicly in the course of the 1990s, both in Denmark and internationally.

IBIS, a Danish NGO whose projects in Angola Holdt helped finance during apartheid, invited Holdt, in 2001, to document conditions after apartheid in Namibia and South Africa, where Holdt took part in the The World Conference against Racism (WCAR) organized by UNESCO, which was being held in Durban.

It's interesting to me that people so often call me a leftist. You could say that I have a leftist approach to humanity, but I never voted for a left-wing party. I was always there in the middle where I could have a dialogue with the right and the left - or bring out such a dialogue.

Holdt has also been working intensively to bring the machinations of the Ku Klux Klan into a more transparent view with respect to the general public's awareness. Among other activities, Holdt has taken one of the most rabid Ku Klux Klan leaders around with him to visit his black friends, in hopes of influencing the leader to leave the Klan.

Since 2002, Holdt has been focusing his efforts even more actively on the ongoing debate about integration in Denmark. He was chosen to sit on the advisory board of Critical Muslims and MixEurope. Today, he is widely respected as an active debater on public issues, who makes his opinions known through his often polemic contributions that appear in the daily press.

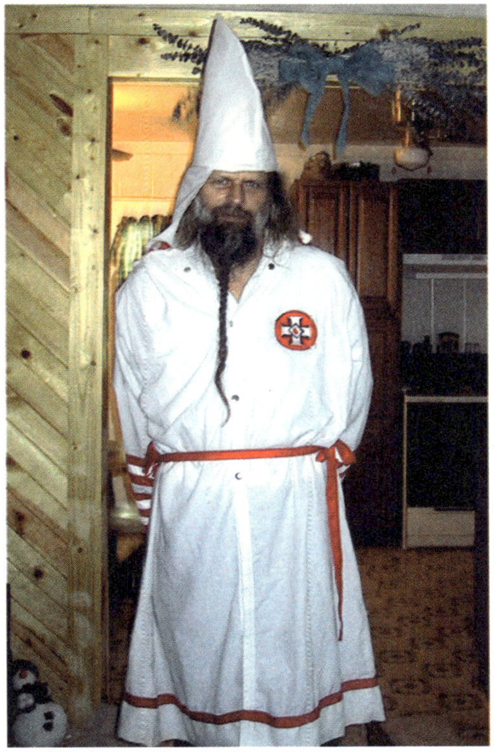

When Jacob became a "member" and even a webmaster for the Ku Klux Klan, the other klan folks amused themselves dressing up "our only anti-racist-member" in their clownish costumes. Butler, IN. 2002

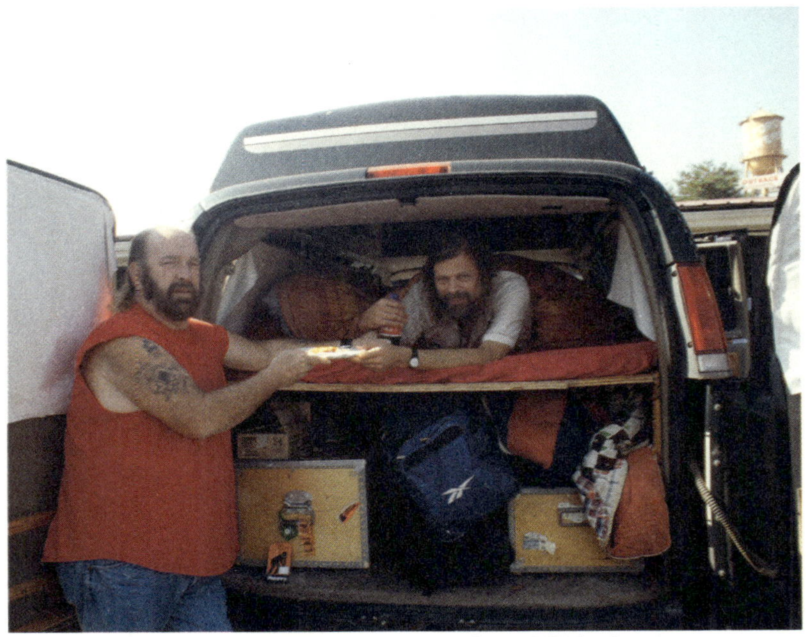

Jacob in the bed he has shared with everyone from KKK leaders to cosmetic millionaire queens. Anniston, AL. 2005

Holdt's role as a mediator

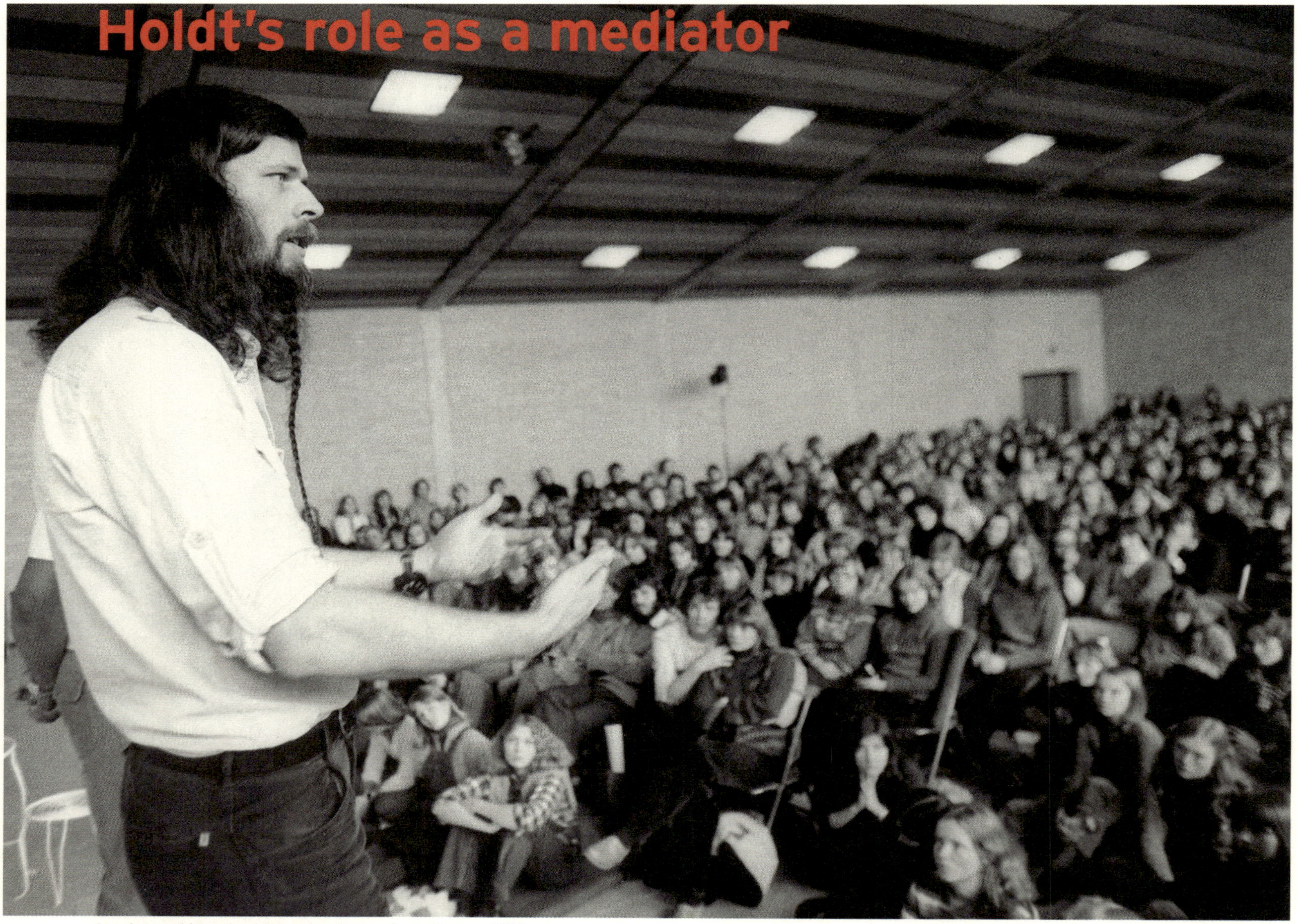

Jacob speaking at a high school near Copenhagen. 1977

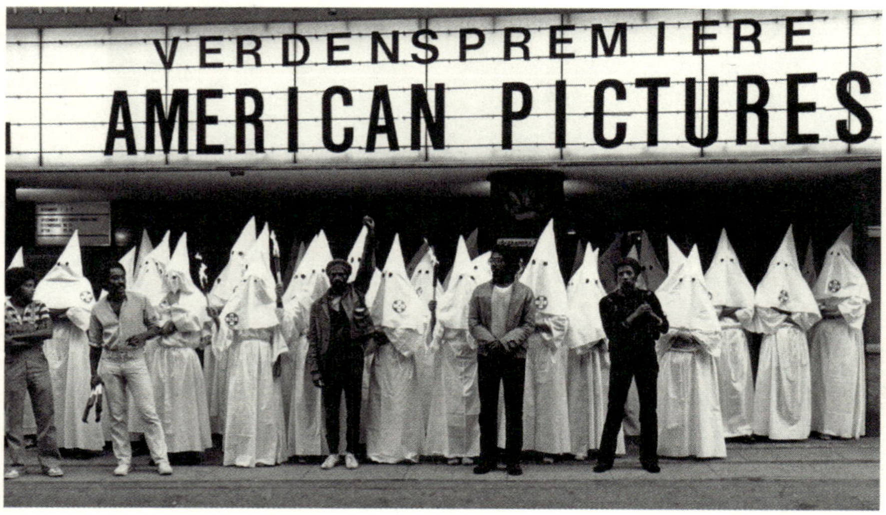

For the premiere of the movie version of *American Pictures* in 1982 Holdt's volunteers, dressed in home-made Klan robes, staged a protest demonstration against growing racism. 1982

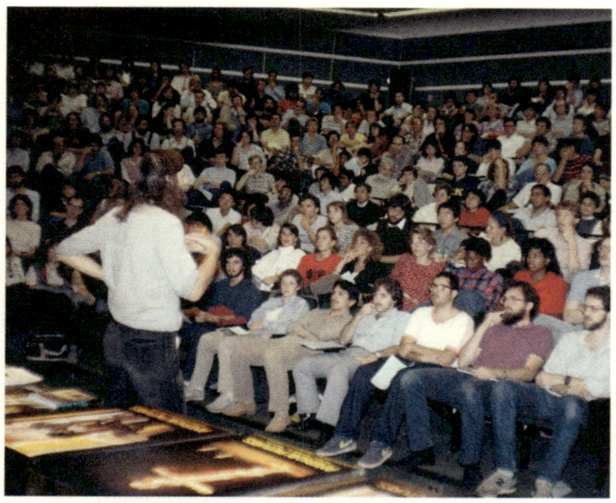

Jacob speaking at Tufts University. 1986

Jacob Holdt's role as a mediator and cultural commentator has been a central feature of his activity. In 1975, he started to write and photograph for The Black Panther Party newspaper and for the Danish daily newspaper *Kristeligt Dagblad*.

In 1976, Holdt created the first of his slide-show lectures, presenting a sequence of his pictures of America inside the rectory of the church where his father was a minister. Shortly thereafter, he began to receive invitations from all over Denmark to show his slide-show, which had come to be titled *American Pictures*. Husets Teater in Copenhagen, offered to host the show for a period of two months solid.

Later on the Danish daily newspaper *Information* published *American Pictures* as a book. It immediately became a best seller. The slide-show presentation also became a success and was shown in Denmark to some 2,000 people every single day. In 1977, Holdt opened his own theater on Købmagergade, one of the central pedestrian malls in Copenhagen, where *Amerikanske Billeder* began an unbroken 10-year run.

In 1978, the West German magazine *Der Spiegel* published the book as a serial feature. At the same time, the book became a best seller in West Germany. A feature-length movie version of the slide-show was also created, which was then presented at the Cannes Film Festival in 1981 and subsequently at film festivals in London, Berlin, Dublin, Moscow, South Africa, Los Angeles and San Francisco. The following year, Holdt and local volunteers opened a theatre in San Francisco for the steady presentation of Holdt's slide-show lecture.

From 1984, Holdt started to tour universities in the United States on a regular basis. In short order, he became one of the most widely employed lecturers in the history of American universities. At many of the most elite universities, viewing Holdt's slide-show presentation was made mandatory for all freshman students.

As a Dane, coming from one of the world's most egalitarian societies, I didn't photograph the things that resembled my own society as much as the things that were completely different, the filthy rich and the filthy poor, which I'd never seen before. It was shocking to me. And I soon discovered how this was also a visually effective way to get my message out.

At the close of the 1990s - and after more than 6,500 slide-show presentations, Holdt began to scale down his activity traveling around in the United States so that he could devote himself in an even more concentrated way to taking pictures of his friends in the ghettoes. Around this time, Holdt also resumed presenting the slide-show lecture in Denmark.

In 2002, Holdt started - in the United States - working with the Ku Klux Klan. He conducted a number of interviews with Klan members about the ill treatment they had suffered during their childhood, with an eye toward making an interactive DVD for teachers worldwide about racism and oppression. He is still trying to get funding for this project. However, a movie about Holdt and his involvement with the Ku Klux Klan has been produced.

Today, Jacob Holdt continues to present a great many talks and lectures to students, organizations and political forums. Not only is American Pictures continually being revised and updated but Jacob Holdt also offers an extensive group of other lectures and workshops dealing with the themes of racism and oppression.

These companioned with similar educational projects on his webside *www.american-pictures.com*

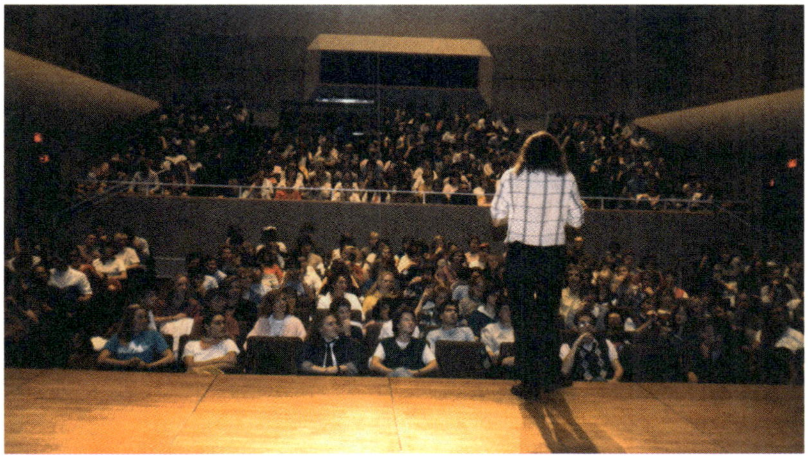

Jacob speaking at Hampden-Sydney College. Hampden-Sydney, VA. 1986

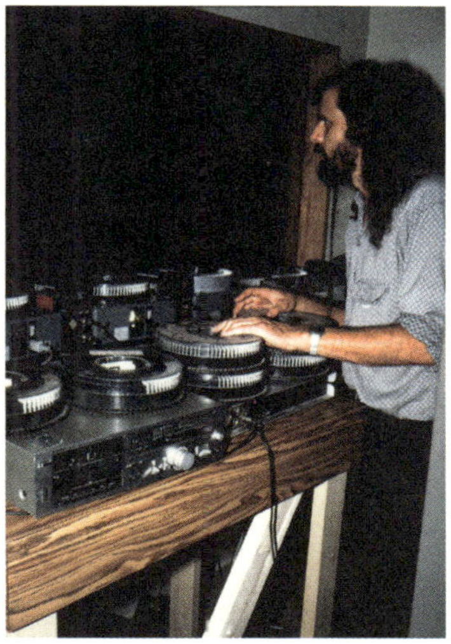

Jacob presenting his show at Williams College. Williamstown, MA. 1986

Faith, Hope & Love. Jacob Holdt's America
Edited by Michael Juul Holm and Mette Marcus
Desk editing by Agnete Braad

Translations from the Danish by Glen Garner and Dan Marmorstein
Extracts taken from REGARDING THE PAIN OF OTHERS

Published by arrangement with the Wylie Agency New York & London,
and Farrar, Straus & Giroux, New York.
Design by salomet grafik, Mette Salomonsen with
front cover tag by Marie d'Origny Lübecker and
a map of the USA by Gudrun Krabbe
Typeset in INTERSTATE and
printed by Rosendahls, Esbjerg on på Munken Print White 15
ISBN: 978-87-91607-67-7
Printed in Denmark 2009

This catalogue is published on the occasion of the exhibition
FAITH, HOPE & LOVE. JACOB HOLDT'S AMERICA
October 2, 2009 - February 7, 2010

Curator Mette Marcus
Curatorial Coordinator Eva Lund
Exhibition Architect Gudrun Krabbe

With support from

BIKUBENFONDEN

KNUD HØJGAARDS FOND

Technical support

COLORGRUPPEN A/S
FOSS FOTECH A/S
VINK A/S

DONG energy Sponsor for Louisiana Museum of Modern Art 2009

Realdania Sponsor of architectural exhibitions at Louisiana

Nykredit Sponsor of Louisiana Contemporary

C.L. DAVIDS FOND OG SAMLING Supports Louisiana Live